EARLY HIGH CHRISTOLOGY

EARLY HIGH CHRISTOLOGY

JOHN AMONG THE NEW TESTAMENT WRITERS

EDITED BY

CHRISTOPHER M. BLUMHOFER

DIANE G. CHEN

JOEL B. GREEN

FORTRESS PRESS

Minneapolis

EARLY HIGH CHRISTOLOGY
John among the New Testament Writers

29 28 27 26 25 24   1 2 3 4 5 6 7 8 9

Library of Congress Control Number: 2024933363

Cover design: Josh Eller

Print ISBN: 978-1-5064-9101-1
eBook ISBN: 978-1-5064-9102-8

CONTENTS

ABBREVIATIONS

General Abbreviations

AT	Author's translation
BCE	before the Common Era
bis	twice
c.	century
ca.	circa
CE	Common Era
cf.	*confer*, compare
ch(s).	chapter(s)
diss.	dissertation
ed(s).	editor(s), edited by, edition
e.g.	*exempli gratia*, for example
esp.	especially
et al.	*et alii*, and others
ET	English translation
etc.	*et cetera*, and so forth, and the rest
frag.	fragment
i.e.	*id est*, that is
km	kilometer(s)
mod.	modern
MR	map reference
ms(s).	manuscript(s)
n(n).	notes(s)
p(p).	page(s)
p.m.	*post meridiem*, afternoon
par(r).	parallel(s)
SBL	Society of Biblical Literature
trans.	translator, translated by
v(v).	verse(s)
vol(s).	volume(s)

Ancient Abbreviations

1 Clem.	1 Clement
1 En.	1 Enoch (Ethiopic Apocalypse)
1 Esd	1 Esdras
1 Macc	1 Maccabees
2 Bar.	2 Baruch (Syriac Apocalypse)
2 En.	2 Enoch (Slavonic Apocalypse)
2 Macc	2 Maccabees
3 Macc	3 Maccabees
Alexander Aphrodisiensis, *Probl.*	*Problemata*
Aristotle, *Eth. nic.*	*Ethica nicomachea*
Aristotle, *Hist. an.*	*Historia animalium*
Aristotle, *Poet.*	*Poetica*
Athanasius, *Ar.*	*Orationes tres adversus Arianos*
Athanasius, *Fug.*	*Apologia de fuga sua*
Athanasius, *Hom. Matt. 11:27*	*In illud Omnia mihi tradita sunt*
Barn.	Barnabas
Bel	Bel and the Dragon
Bonaventure, *Comm. In Ioh*	*Commentarius in Evangelium sancti Iohannis*
Cicero, *Off.*	*De officiis*
Clement of Alexandria, *Strom.*	*Stromateis*
Cod. Vitrinas	*Codex Vitrinas*
Cyprian, *Laps.*	*De lapsis*
Cyril of Alexandria, *Thes.*	*Thesaurus de sancta et consubstantiali trinitate*
Did.	Didache
Epictetus, *Diatr.*	*Diatribai*
Epiphanius, *Pan.*	*Panarion*
Eusebius, *Hist. eccl.*	*Historia ecclesiastica*
Gos. Pet.	Gospel of Peter
Gregory, *Or.*	*Orationes*
Herm.	Shepherd of Hermas
Herm. Vis.	Shepherd of Hermas, Vision(s)
Hippocrates, *Morb. Sacr.*	*De morbo sacro*
Ignatius, *Eph.*	*To the Ephesians*
Ignatius, *Magn.*	*To the Magnesians*
Ignatius, *Phld.*	*To the Philadelphians*

Ignatius, *Rom.*	*To the Romans*
Ignatius, *Smyrn.*	*To the Smyrnaeans*
Ignatius, *Trall.*	*To the Trallians*
Jerome, *Expl. Dan.*	*Explanatio in Danielem*
John Chrysostom, *Hom. Jo.*	*Homiliae in Joannem*
Jos. Asen.	Joseph and Aseneth
Josephus, *Ant.*	*Jewish Antiquities*
Josephus, *J.W.*	*Jewish War*
Jub.	Jubilees
Justin Martyr, *1 Apol.*	*Apologia i*
Justin Martyr, *Dial.*	*Dialogus cum Tryphone*
m.	Mishnah
Meg.	Megillah
MT	Masoretic Text
Num. Rab.	Numbers Rabbah
Origen, *Cels.*	*Contra Celsum*
Origen, *Comm. Jo.*	*Commentarii in evangelium Joannis*
Philo, *Prelim. Studies*	*On the Preliminary Studies*
Philo, *Abraham*	*On the Life of Abraham*
Philo, *Alleg. Interp.*	*Allegorical Interpretation*
Philo, *Creation*	*On the Creation of the World*
Philo, *Dreams*	*On Dreams*
Philo, *Embassy*	*On the Embassy to Gaius*
Philo, *Flight*	*On Flight and Finding*
Philo, *Migration*	*On the Migration of Abraham*
Philo, *Names*	*On the Change of Names*
Philo, *Posterity*	*On the Posterity of Cain*
Philo, *QG*	*Questions and Answers on Genesis*
Philo, *Sobriety*	*On Sobriety*
Philo, *Worse*	*That the Worse Attacks the Better*
Plato, *Phaed.*	*Phaedrus*
Plato, *Resp.*	*Respublica*
Plato, *Tim.*	*Timaeus*
Pol.	Polycarp
Pr. Man	Prayer of Manasseh
Pseudo-Apollodorus, *Lib.*	*Library*
Pss. Sol.	Psalms of Solomon
Sib. Or.	Sibylline Oracles
Sir	Sirach/Ecclesiasticus
Suetonius, *Aug.*	*Divus Augustus*
Suetonius, *Vesp.*	*Divus Vespasianus*

T. Iss.	Testament of Issachar
T. Jos.	Testament of Joseph
T. Jud.	Testament of Judah
T. Levi	Testament of Levi
Tacitus, *Hist.*	*Historiae*
Tertullian, *Marc.*	*Adversus Marcionem*
Tg. Jon.	Targum Jonathan
Tg. Ps.-J.	Targum Pseudo-Jonathan
Tg. Song	Targum Song of Songs
Tob	Tobit
Wis	Wisdom of Solomon

Modern Abbreviations

AASOR	*Annual of the American Schools of Oriental Research*
AB	Anchor Bible
ABD	*Anchor Bible Dictionary.* Edited by David Noel Freedman. 6 vols. New York: Doubleday, 1992
ABR	*Australian Biblical Review*
AcBib	Academic Biblica
ADPV	Abhandlungen des Deutschen Palästina-Vereins
AGJU	Arbeiten zur Geschichte des antiken Judentums und des Urchristentums
AJEC	Ancient Judaism and Early Christianity
AJSR	*Association for Jewish Studies Review*
AnBib	Analecta Biblica
ANRW	*Aufstieg und Niedergang der römischen Welt: Geschichte und Kultur Roms im Spiegel der neueren Forschung.* Part 2, *Principat.* Edited by Hildegard Temporini and Wolfgang Haase. Berlin: de Gruyter, 1972–
ANTC	Abingdon New Testament Commentaries
ArBib	The Aramaic Bible
AS	*Aramaic Studies*
AYB	Anchor Yale Bible
AYBRL	Anchor Yale Bible Reference Library
BAC	Biblioteca de autores cristianos
BAIAS	*Bulletin of the Anglo-Israel Archeological Society*
BBB	Bonner biblische Beiträge
BBR	*Bulletin for Biblical Research*

BCOTWP	Baker Commentary on the Old Testament Wisdom and Psalms
BETL	Bibliotecha Ephemeridum Theologicarum Lovaniensium
BHH	*Biblisch-historisches Handwörterbuch: Lande-skunde, Geschichte, Religion, Kultur.* Edited by Bo Reicke and Leonhard Rost. 4 vols. Göttingen: Vandenhoeck & Ruprecht, 1962–1966
Bib	*Biblica*
BibInt	*Biblical Interpretation*
BibInt	Biblical Interpretation Series
BMSEC	Baylor-Mohr Siebeck Studies in Early Christianity
BN	*Biblische Notizen*
Brit. Mus. Or. Add.	British Museum Oriental Additional
BSac	*Bibliotheca Sacra*
BSJS	Brill's Series in Jewish Studies
BSRel	Biblioteca di scienze religiose
BTB	*Biblical Theology Bulletin*
BThS	Biblisch-theologische Studien
BU	Biblische Untersuchungen
BZ	*Biblische Zeitschrift*
BZAW	Beihefte zur Zeitschrift für die alttestamentliche Wissenschaft
BZNW	Beihefte zur Zeitschrift für die neutestamentliche Wissenschaft
CBQ	*Catholic Biblical Quarterly*
ChB	The Church's Bible
ColT	*Collectanea Theologica*
CurBR	*Currents in Biblical Research*
CW	*Classical World*
DJG	*Dictionary of Jesus and the Gospels.* Edited by Joel B. Green, Jeannine K. Brown, and Nicholas Perrin. 2nd ed. Downers Grove, IL: InterVarsity Press, 2013
DLNT	*Dictionary of the Later New Testament and Its Developments.* Edited by Ralph P. Martin and Peter H. Davids. Downers Grove, IL: InterVarsity Press, 1997

DSD	*Dead Sea Discoveries*
DTT	*Dansk teologisk tidsskrift*
EBR	*Encyclopedia of the Bible and Its Reception.* Edited by Hans-Josef Klauck et al. Berlin: de Gruyter, 2009–
EC	*Early Christianity*
EJL	Early Judaism and Its Literature
EKK	Evangelisch-katholischer Kommentar
EncJud	*Encyclopedia Judaica.* Edited by Fred Skolnik and Michael Berenbaum. 2nd ed. 22 vols. Detroit: Macmillan, 2007
EvQ	*Evangelical Quarterly*
EWNT	*Exegetisches Wörterbuch zum Neuen Testament.* Edited by Horst Baltz and Gerhard Schneider. 2nd ed. 3 vols. Stuttgart: Kolhammer, 1992
ExpTim	*Expository Times*
FB	Forschung zur Bibel
FC	Fathers of the Church
FRLANT	Forschungen zur Religion und Literatur des Alten und Neuen Testaments
GCS	Die griechischen christlichen Schriftsteller der ersten [drei] Jahrhunderte
GSLNT	Geistliche Schriftlesung: Neuen Testament
HACL	History, Archaeology, and Culture of the Levant
HBibSt	Herders biblische Studien
HBT	*Horizons in Biblical Theology*
HNT	Handbuch zum Neuen Testament
HTCNT	Herder's Theological Commentary on the New Testament
HThKNT	Herders Theologischer Kommentar zum Neuen Testament
HTR	*Harvard Theological Review*
HUCA	*Hebrew Union College Annual*
HvTSt	Hervormde teologiese studies
IBC	Interpretation: A Bible Commentary for Teaching and Preaching
IBS	*Irish Biblical Studies*
ICC	International Critical Commentary
IDS	*In die Skriflig*
IEJ	*Israel Exploration Journal*
Int	*Interpretation*

ISFCJ	International Studies in Formative Christianity and Judaism
JBL	*Journal of Biblical Literature*
JCH	Jewish and Christian Heritage
JCPS	Jewish and Christian Perspectives Series
JHMTh	*Journal for the History of Modern Theology*
JJMJS	*Journal of the Jesus Movement in Its Jewish Setting*
JLT	*Journal of Literature and Theology*
JMS	Johannine Monograph Series
JPOS	*Journal of the Palestine Oriental Society*
JSJ	*Journal for the Study of Judaism in the Persian, Hellenistic, and Roman Periods*
JSJSup	Journal for the Study of Judaism Supplement Series
JSNT	*Journal for the Study of the New Testament*
JSNTSup	Journal for the Study of the New Testament Supplement Series
JSOTSup	Journal for the Study of the Old Testament Supplement Series
JSP	*Journal for the Study of the Pseudepigrapha*
JSPSup	Journal for the Study of the Pseudepigrapha Supplement Series
JSS	*Journal of Semitic Studies*
JTS	*Journal of Theological Studies*
KEK	Kritisch-exegetischer Kommentar über das Neue Testament (Meyer-Kommentar)
LBS	Linguistic Biblical Studies
LD	Lectio Divina
LNTS	The Library of New Testament Studies
LXX	Septuagint
ModTh	*Modern Theology*
NA[28]	*Novum Testamentum Graece*, Nestle-Aland, 28th ed.
NAB	New American Bible
NBL	*Neues Bibel-Lexikon.* Edited by Manfred Görg and Bernhard Lang. 3 vols. Zurich: Benziger, 1988–2001
NCB	New Century Bible
NCBC	New Cambridge Bible Commentary
NEB	New English Bible

Neot	*Neotestamentica*
NETS	*A New English Translation of the Septuagint.* Edited by Albert Pietersma and Benjamin G. Wright. New York: Oxford University Press, 2007
NICNT	New International Commentary on the New Testament
NIGTC	New International Greek Testament Commentary
NIV	New International Version
NovT	*Novum Testamentum*
NovTSup	Supplements to Novum Testamentum
NRSV	New Revised Standard Version
NT	New Testament
NTL	New Testament Library
NTS	*New Testament Studies*
NTT	New Testament Theology
NV	*Nova et Vetera*
OG	Old Greek
OT	Old Testament
ÖTK	Ökumenischer Taschenbuch-Kommentar
OTL	Old Testament Library
OTP	*Old Testament Pseudepigrapha.* Edited by James H. Charlesworth. 2 vols. New York: Doubleday, 1983, 1985
OWS	Oxford World's Classics
PaidCNT	Paideia Commentaries on the New Testament
PEQ	*Palestine Exploration Quarterly*
PG	Patrologia Graeca [=Patrologiae Cursus Completus: Series Graeca]. Edited by Jacques-Paul Migne. 162 vols. Paris, 1857–1886
PL	Patrologia Latina [= Patrologiae Cursus Completus: Series Latina]. Edited by Jacque-Paul Migne. 217 vols. Paris, 1844–1864
ProEccl	*Pro Ecclesia*
Qad	*Qadmoniot*
RB	*Revue biblique*
RBS	Resources for Biblical Study
RRJ	*Review of Rabbinic Judaism*
RevExp	*Review and Expositor*
RevQ	*Revue de Qumran*

RevScRel	*Revue des sciences religieuses*
RHR	*Revue de l'histoire des religions*
RNT	Regensburger Neues Testament
RSV	Revised Standard Version
SC	Sources chrétiennes
SJT	*Scottish Journal of Theology*
SLAG	Schriften der Luther-Agricola-Gesellschaft
SNTSMS	Society for New Testament Studies Monograph Series
SStL	Syriac Studies Library
StPatr	Studia Patristica
SymS	Symposium Series
SYNL	The New Synthese Historical Library
TBT	*The Bible Today*
THNTC	Two Horizons New Testament Commentary
TLG	*Thesaurus Linguae Graecae: Canon of Greek Authors and Works.* Edited by Luci Berkowitz and Karl A. Squitier. 3rd ed. New York: Oxford University Press, 1990
TvT	*Tijdschrift voor theologie*
TWNT	*Theologische Wörterbuch zum Neuen Testament.* Edited by Gerhard Kittel and Gerhard Friedrich. Stuttgart: Kohlhammer, 1932–1979
UNT	Untersuchungen zum Neuen Testament
VTSup	Supplements to Vetus Testamentum
WA	Weimarer Ausgabe
WBC	Word Biblical Commentary
WSA	The Works of Saint Augustine
WUNT	Wissenschaftliche Untersuchungen zum Neuen Testament
WW	*Word and World*
YFS	*Yale French Studies*
ZAC	*Zeitschrift für Antikes Christentum/Journal of Ancient Christianity*
ZDMG	*Zeitschrift der deutschen morgenländischen Gesellschaft*
ZNThG	*Zeitschrift für neuere Theologiegeschichte*
ZNW	*Zeitschrift für die neutestamentliche Wissenschaft und die Kunde der älteren Kirche*

CONTRIBUTORS

Richard Bauckham (PhD, University of Cambridge) is emeritus professor of New Testament studies, University of St. Andrews, Scotland, UK.

Markus Bockmuehl (PhD, University of Cambridge) is the Dean Ireland's Professor of the Exegesis of Holy Scripture in the University of Oxford, and a fellow of Keble College, UK.

Jeannine K. Brown (PhD, Luther Seminary) is David Price Professor of Biblical and Theological Foundations, Bethel Seminary, USA.

R. Alan Culpepper (PhD, Duke University) is dean and professor of New Testament emeritus, McAfee School of Theology, Mercer University, USA, and research fellow in the department of Old and New Testament, University of the Free State, South Africa.

David J. Downs (PhD, Princeton Theological Seminary) is Clarendon-Laing Professor of New Testament Studies at the University of Oxford and Laing Fellow of Theology and Religion at Keble College, UK.

Jörg Frey (Dr. theol. habil., University of Tübingen) is professor of New Testament at the University of Zurich, Switzerland, and research associate at the department of biblical studies of the University of the Free State, South Africa.

Tommy Givens (PhD, Duke University) is associate professor of New Testament studies, Fuller Theological Seminary, USA.

John Goldingay (PhD, University of Nottingham) is senior professor of Old Testament, Fuller Theological Seminary, USA.

Craig R. Koester (PhD, Union Theological Seminary in New York) is Asher O. and Carrie Nasby Professor of New Testament Emeritus, Luther Seminary, USA.

Jenelle Lemons (MDiv, Bethel Seminary) is adjunct instructor, Bethel Seminary, USA.

Alicia D. Myers (PhD, Baylor University) is associate professor of New Testament and Greek at Campbell University Divinity School, USA, and research fellow at the University of the Free State, South Africa.

Carey C. Newman (PhD, Baylor University) is executive editor, Fortress Press.

Michael Pasquarello III (PhD, University of North Carolina, Chapel Hill) is Beeson Professor of Methodist Divinity, Beeson Divinity School/Samford University, USA.

Wil Rogan (PhD, Fuller Theological Seminary) is assistant professor of biblical studies, Carey Theological College, Vancouver, BC.

Miroslav Volf (PhD, University of Tübingen) is Henry B. Wright Professor of Theology at Yale University Divinity School, USA, and Founding Director of the Yale Center for Faith & Culture.

Brittany E. Wilson (PhD, Princeton Theological Seminary) is associate professor of
    New Testament, Duke University Divinity School, USA.
Ruben Zimmermann (Dr. theol. Ruprecht-Karls-University of Heidelberg; habil.
    Ludwigs-Maximilians-University München) is professor for New Testament,
    Johannes Gutenberg-University of Mainz, Germany, and research associate at
    the department for Old and New Testament studies at the University of the Free
    State, Bloemfontein, South Africa.

MARIANNE MEYE THOMPSON

A Tribute in Three Parts

Christopher M. Blumhofer, Diane G. Chen, and Joel B. Green

Marianne Meye Thompson—gifted scholar and teacher, doctor of the church. Across her four-decade career, her teaching and publications have helped to shape countless lives and communities. On behalf of those lives and communities, the editors celebrate Marianne's service with personal words of tribute and appreciation.

The Mind of a Scholar and the Heart of a Pastor (Diane)

Having sat through 950 hours of Marianne's classes as her student and teaching assistant over a period of ten years at Fuller Seminary, I bore witness to this quintessential teacher, not to mention the coaching, challenge, and corrections I received during my doctoral studies. In formal and informal ways, Marianne piqued my curiosity about the ancient world of the NT, sharpened my attention to literary connections in the text, and, most importantly, encouraged me to nurture the life of the mind for the love of God and for service to the church.

Among the countless things I could rave about, concerning Marianne as professor and mentor, I would like to highlight three things. First is the way she could make a concept stick. To this day, when explaining the book of Revelation to students and church folks, I still use the images of a political cartoon, an impressionist painting, and a kaleidoscope that Marianne gave in NS501 New Testament II. On another occasion, much to the delight of her students (and perhaps to the chagrin of her colleagues), she treated her class to a tongue-in-cheek rendition of "Woes to the Fuller Faculty," set in the tone and language of Jesus's scathing invective against the scribes and the Pharisees in Matthew 23, which effectively showed the style of the text as reminiscent of the sweeping prophetic critiques found in the OT. Multiplying these creative approaches many times over in numerous NT courses over the years, one could imagine the number of ah-ha moments she generated for her students.

Second, Marianne was generous in sharing her gift and craft, allowing me to be more an apprentice than a hired hand. My role as her teaching assistant went far beyond grading boatloads of papers. She let me in on how she would plan courses, create syllabi, design assignments, set exam questions, and deal with students. At times she and I would disagree over what grade to assign to a particular paper. Typically, she would win and I would lose (read: defer). Through arguing grades with her, I learned to balance accountability with grace and separate nitpicking from critiquing. In class, from her color-coded handouts to her organized and animated delivery, I observed Marianne teach with the mind of a scholar and the heart of a pastor. As a faithful disciple of Jesus Christ, Marianne loved the church and did not shy away from its imperfections. She instilled in her students a deep respect for the biblical text by pursuing exegetical integrity and relevant hermeneutics. Watching her in action, not only did I learn how to teach, but why.

Third, as a dissertation supervisor Marianne set the bar high and left me with pointers and skills enough to last a lifetime. To get me through a writing block, she counseled, "Steer, don't stop." Slow progress was better than no progress. To train me to make a sound argument and own it with courage and integrity, she cautioned, "What others think about your work is none of your business." When my insecure tendency to impress led me to pad my footnotes with many tangential tidbits, to keep my writing focused, she wrote in the margins, "Cut, cut, cut. Less is more." To prevent me from being caught up in minutiae, but rather to put my thoughts on paper so I could see them, she said, "Dump and clean up later." While all these pointers were extremely helpful, the most important piece of advice came one time when I just could not bear to face another rewrite. She sent me an email with the subject line: "Write your passion." In there she wrote, "Yeah, you wrestle with exegesis, and sentences, and wording, and footnotes. But do you ever just close your eyes, put your fingers on the keyboard, and ask, 'What do I really think, deep down, whether I can prove it or not? Where is my passion, not for this dissertation, or even for this material, but for this reality?'" Her questions were both freeing and convicting, and they came just at the right time to give me enough of a jolt to press on toward the finishing line.

Marianne was a brilliant, engaging, articulate, committed, and wise teacher. Above all, she was faithful—first and foremost to the God who called her into this ministry and, emerging from that relationship, to every single student who had the privilege to come under her tutelage.

Giving Attention to the Text of Scripture (Chris)

Having first become familiar with Marianne Meye Thompson's scholarship while writing a dissertation of the Gospel of John at Duke University, it was a special privilege for me to join the faculty at Fuller Seminary and come to know Marianne as a colleague during the first years of my teaching. While we were on the same faculty, I experienced firsthand many of the virtues to which Marianne's friends and colleagues in this volume also attest. I came to appreciate Marianne's warm collegiality and friendship, which proved to be a regular source of encouragement and made her an easy conversation partner.

Marianne's willingness to attend my seminar on the Gospel of John during my first quarter in the classroom helped me to gain a seasoned and constructive perspective on my own teaching at an early stage. Her invitation to read and discuss recent John scholarship offered me the chance to engage cutting-edge scholarship with a scholar whose wisdom matches her breadth of knowledge. Her words of encouragement helped me navigate the stresses of the job candidacy process for a tenure-track position. As a developing teacher and scholar, I was, and remain, grateful for the lessons I have gleaned from Marianne's influence in my life. Of the many, I enumerate three.

The first advice about teaching the Bible that Marianne gave to me is to guide discussions of the Bible in the classroom and beyond with the right question, and for Marianne this consistently took the same form: "Where do you see that in the text?" Few questions can cut so effectively through interpretive claims that are either too abstract or simply wishful thinking than those that turn everyone's attention back to the biblical text. This good question is more than simply a tool for managing unwieldly discussions or overly enthusiastic proposals in exegesis courses. Presupposed by the invitation to test our ideas and proposals against the biblical text is the conviction that what we really need to learn and to know will be found as we give ourselves and our best thinking to a closer and more attentive study of the words of Scripture.

As a hallmark of Marianne's teaching and collegial conversation, this question also expresses a deeply rooted theological commitment: that Scripture is the gift of God that ultimately clarifies our understanding of both God and ourselves.[1] To turn to Scripture—and to develop the habit of continually returning to it—is to develop the practice of listening, attending, and submitting to the Word of God that is vital to both the Christian life and the life of the church. This is the gift Marianne offered to decades' worth of students at Fuller Seminary and to me as a junior colleague with this prompting to return to the text. It is no wonder that the habit of returning again and again to Scripture "with attention and love" proved able to sustain a career's worth of scholarship that was theologically significant to both the church and the academy.[2]

Second, and related, is the importance of tracing as closely as possible the language and the logic of a book or a passage. Nearly every page of Marianne's scholarship bears witness to this commitment. It shines, however, in her treatment of particularly complex or challenging texts. For example, the exegesis of John 8:31–47 in her commentary offers a case study in *thinking with* a particular text within its literary, narrative, and historical contexts.[3] In this instance, it is significant that a challenging scene in the text like Jesus's critique of "the Jews" (οἱ Ἰουδαῖοι) in John 8 is seen within the broader Johannine flow of thought and with close attention to the dynamics of the discourse (in this case, the audience Jesus addresses as those who "had believed in him" [8:31], and the activity [i.e., seeking to kill] that charges the encounter with hostility). The historical situation that gave rise to this discourse, and its enduring and often troubling history of reception, remain important areas of study and teaching and are rightly acknowledged. Yet the task of interpretation is not over until the discourse is set within its context, and this is what Marianne keeps before her readers. In this case, she draws our attention to the claim that structures John 8, and so much of the Gospel as well: Jesus is the Son of God, "the light who reveals God, the source of eternal life."[4] Close attention to John's unfolding narrative thus allows for biblical commentary that takes seriously the matters that the text takes seriously.[5]

Third, and again related to the virtue and practice of close attention to the biblical text, is Marianne's commitment to thinking theologically and pastorally with Scripture. To quote from one of her earlier works: "The challenge for the church is to cast its teaching in ways that are at once faithful to the message that has been handed on to it and that communicates to the cultures to which they minister. Such contextualization is always fraught with peril. But an unacceptable alternative is merely to repeat Christian jargon or the words of Scripture. Mere repetition, even of the Scriptures, does not guarantee understanding of or fidelity to them."[6]

There is a kind of biblicism that masquerades as fidelity, but it is in fact vulnerable to betraying its message. It repeats without understanding and therefore misspeaks. In classrooms and conversation, Marianne often issued the invitation to try to understand the meaning of a passage for us today with another of her characteristically simple but challenging questions: "So what do we do with this?" The conversations that followed on from this question consistently tacked between the situations of the church today and the specifics of Scripture and tradition. As we talked, our collective engagement with the Bible became the occasion for reflecting on how to be faithful today, and the distance between Scripture and the life setting of the church narrowed. In this way, the challenge of discerning the path of faithfulness occasioned a deeper engagement with Scripture. No conversation that I can remember ever ended with a simplistic or triumphant declaration, "Problem solved!" But they all ended having cultivated more wisdom and humility than we began with, and with those involved indebted to Marianne for leading us to that place.

Critical and Faith-ful Scholarship (Joel)

When I began serious biblical studies in the late 1970s, I found myself often enough in what seemed a foreign country—as though this academic realm had little space for faith and piety. At best, the ongoing significance of the biblical materials might be explored after the tough work of biblical criticism was completed, as an afterthought or postscript. Among the ways I found to put Humpty together again was a book written by the renowned NT scholar from Fuller Theological Seminary, George Eldon Ladd. This little book, *The New Testament and Criticism*,[7] demonstrated, first, that what was then known as *the higher criticism* need not be inimical to classical faith and, second, that the then-contemporary world of biblical scholarship itself provided exemplars of what Ladd might have called "evangelical biblical criticism." In retrospect, I have come to think that many of that older generation held biblical criticism and classical faith together through the vitality of their personal piety. The most recent holder of Fuller Seminary's George Eldon Ladd Chair in New Testament, Marianne Meye Thompson, took a different path, and, across her forty-year career, has shone the way for others as well.

For Marianne, serious biblical scholarship and classical Christian faith are not two things—the one over here and the other over there, awaiting a bridge to span the distance between them. This is not because she allows one to overwhelm the other, but because of the way she has learned to devote herself to the text of Scripture, and to model the same for others. Before I met her, I knew her already as someone who embodied what many might dismiss as an impossible experiment: a critical *and* faith-ful scholarship, centered and secure, not reactionary, and not driven by the promise of whatever is new that blows continuously like the desert winds through biblical studies. As she has heard me say, Marianne is what Fuller Seminary at its best has wanted to be. When I said yes to Fuller Seminary in 2007, it was in no small part to find myself walking the same halls as Marianne Meye Thompson.

By then, of course, our paths had crossed numerous times. We learned that we each had an Al(l)ison—theirs the Alison of the one *l*, ours of the two. We learned that we approached our NT classrooms similarly—with a foremost desire to get our students into the NT (its history, literature, language, and theology) rather than into the sometimes-peculiar waters of what scholars have said *about* the NT. (Our mantra: the text, the text, the text. . . .) And we learned that we could work together, having cowritten, with the late Paul Achtemeier, under Marianne's direction, a NT introduction.[8] Through that process, I learned of Marianne's genuine commitment to collaboration, a rare quality among scholars. I learned what it means to work with someone for whom a good result is more important than who gets credit or recognition for it. In fact, to this day we remain unsure who was the first writer and who was the second on one of the chapters in that introduction. (Perhaps an accomplished redaction critic will parse whose words are whose.) And from the way she approached our work on the introduction, I learned of her remarkable craft as a writer. (In fact, I continue to replay some of her axioms in my head: Don't bury the lead. Refer to the content of those texts, not to chapter and verse numbers. And so on.)

Apart from serving as the pastor of a local congregation, I do not know of a more (potentially) isolating profession than the professorate. Pulled in multiple, competing directions at once and with ever-increasing institutional expectations, avenues for partnership are scarce. If, as we are told, the average workweek for a full-time faculty person is pushing sixty hours, where does one find occasion or energy for comradery? Marianne made the impossible possible. As chair of our NT department or our Bible division, she promoted opportunities for allowing life to intrude into the profession, she took on unwanted tasks in order to ensure space for her new and younger colleagues to thrive, and she modelled a way of living into her vocation as a scholar-teacher that regarded the church and Christian mission as essential rather than impediments to flourishing. Marianne's contributions to scholarship are well known, as are her many engagements in scholarly collaboration, whether on Patmos or globetrotting for annual meetings of the Society of New Testament Studies or crossing the country for meetings of the Society of Biblical Literature or participating in NT and interdisciplinary gatherings around collaborative projects or flying here and there as an invited lecturer. I do not know whether other parts of her story are equally well-known, though—say, her habits of mentoring ordinands or weekly help with equine therapy, for example.

When one of my teaching assistants—the one to whom my dean referred as my über-TA—was nearing graduation, I jokingly commented about finding a way to delay the completion of her PhD program. I had similar thoughts as Marianne inched toward retirement. Who would take her mantle as advocate for the importance of the NT to the seminary and its curricula—and, indeed, for scholarly, faith-ful, text-focused engagement with the Bible? Who would take her place as exemplar and advocate for the integration of teaching and scholarship and faith and life in a world where higher education was increasingly loosed from its historical moorings? Who would take her place as one who cared for the development of younger colleagues and who took seriously the flourishing of everyone with whom she worked, colleagues and staff alike? Who would care enough, like she did, to ask hard questions, as she often did, about vocation and mission?

For me, the good news is that, for the last fifteen years or so of my faculty career, I was walking the same halls with Marianne—or a phone call, an email, or a text message away.

Celebrating Marianne

The gift of Marianne's words and deeds as a scholar and friend exceed what can be written here. The essays that follow aim to honor her example in, and her faithful commitment to, biblical scholarship that is literarily, historically, and theologically engaged, as well as scholarship that resources the church in its ongoing task of letting Scripture shape its life. Those familiar with the history of Johannine studies will note an allusion in this volume's subtitle to a work by Marianne's doctoral supervisor, D. Moody Smith, who in 1992 published a definitive study of the Fourth Gospel, *John among the Gospels: The Relationship in Twentieth-Century Research*.[9] Smith's book served as a definitive statement— though by no means the last one—on questions of John's literary dependence on the Synoptic Gospels. As it stands, when Marianne finished her PhD under Smith in 1985, the timing was right for the source- and form-critical questions of one period to begin to make room for a renewed engagement with theological questions and the theological interpretation of the NT. Having explored theological questions related to the significance of Jesus's humanity in her dissertation on John,[10] Marianne was well situated when the broader transition into specifically theological questions occurred in the field of NT studies.

As time passed, interest in John's theology continued to grow, and in the last generation—and largely spanning Marianne's career as a teacher—scholars advanced their understanding of the Christology of the NT. The presupposition of a past generation, especially that an early "low" Christology (e.g., Mark) later developed into a "high" Christology (John), has given way to much more nuanced understandings of how Jesus's identification with the God of Israel began in the earliest Christian communities and the texts that they read. The Gospel of John is not the end point on a trajectory. Rather, John's Christology expresses in a distinctive register a commitment to know the identity of Israel's God by coming to know Jesus the Messiah in his unique identity as God's Son.

In honor of Marianne, this volume gathers a fresh expression of studies on the Christology of John and on the relationship and interconnections that stand between John's theology and that of other NT texts and theological disciplines. In joy and gratitude for her friendship and scholarship, we honor Marianne Meye Thompson and her forty years spent studying and explaining the text and theology of the NT, and particularly the Gospel according to John.

Part One

John and His Christology

CHAPTER ONE

The Royal Man (John 4:46–54)

A Neglected Testimony for John's High Christology and Paradigm of Faith Development

Jörg Frey

THE STORY OF the royal man (βασιλικός)[1] and the healing of his son is one of the more neglected Johannine pericopes. This second miracle in Cana is less impressive than the first one, turning water into wine (John 2:1–11), and within the history of its interpretation, the Johannine passage has often stood in the shadow of its synoptic counterpart, Jesus's encounter with the centurion (Matt 8:5–13 // Luke 7:1–10). Artists usually present the centurion kneeling before Jesus,[2] while the encounter with the royal man is only rarely adopted in cycles of Jesus's miracles.[3] Among the series of Johannine miracle or "sign" narratives, this episode is probably the least spectacular. It lacks the deep symbolism of the wine miracle, and unlike the miracle stories in John 5, 6, 9, and 11, it is not accompanied by an interpretive discourse. Should the strange and contextually unconnected saying of Jesus in 4:48, "Unless you see signs and wonders, you will not believe," understood as a criticism of miracle-oriented faith, be the true "interpretation" of the narrative? Should this negative comment be the main point the evangelist wants to make, as Bultmann argued based on his assumptions about an underlying "Semeia Source"?[4]

Yet, this short narrative episode, presented by commentators often quite briefly,[5] has much more to say. It deserves a novel interpretation, in critical debate with recent and earlier interpretations, and in clearer view of the narrative's openness to interpretation. In the present context, I will focus on its neglected testimony for John's high Christology, on the character of the episode as an exemplary pattern of the development of faith, and as an invitation for readers to follow the example of the royal man.

The present contribution, dedicated to Marianne Meye Thompson, my dear colleague in the Colloquium Ioanneum, provides preliminary insights from the preparation of my commentary on John in the series Evangelisch-katholischer Kommentar (EKK), with consideration of its reception history.

Ambiguities and Questions

In a thought-provoking article, Tobias Nicklas presents the passage under the subtitle, "Abysses of a Story of Faith."[6] Apart from the important characterization of the episode as a "story of faith," he points to the ambiguities of the passage, suggesting a hermeneutical approach that considers the openness of the narrative. Exegetes should rather consider the text an "open work of art" (Eco).[7] Readers can adopt different perspectives at several points, and they are involved, guided through the text, and stimulated to gain new insights. Thus, we must look at those textual "abysses" or points of indeterminacy.

An initial ambiguity is caused by the preceding transitory section of 4:43–45, where the enigmatic v. 44 provides a notorious problem. Does the testimony of Jesus that "a prophet has no honor in his hometown (πατρίς)" point to his rejection in Nazareth (or Galilee) in agreement with the presentation of the saying in the Synoptics (Mark 6:4 and parallels)? Or can the saying have a completely different reference in the Johannine context where it seems to motivate Jesus's path from Judea and Samaria to Galilee (cf. John 4:1)? Can it point to Jesus's rejection in Jerusalem, such that the πατρίς referred to might not be Nazareth but Jerusalem, the place where the "house of his Father" (2:16) is located? How one answers this question is essential. If πατρίς refers to Nazareth and Galilee, the reception of Jesus in Galilee in v. 45 and the royal man's request in v. 47 are presented with a shadow of ambivalence or doubt. If it refers to Judea and Jerusalem, there is no need to search for a hidden fault in the attitude of the Galileans[8] or the royal man. In my view, this reading seems to fit better within the Johannine context. The alternative option is mostly caused by the harmonistic entry of synoptic data.

There is the general question of whether the Johannine scene should be read against the background of the synoptic parallels, and if so, whether the reader is intended to bring in missing information from there or rather take note of and consider the differences between the accounts. Should they conjecture on the basis of the synoptic parallels that the petitioner was a gentile? Does the βασιλικός, thus, stand for gentiles or rather for Jews, or is his ethnic background simply irrelevant here? Is the faith stated in v. 53 the faith of a Jew or that of a gentile, or just the faith of a "royal" follower of Jesus? And how does this connect with the symbolic geography of John 2–4? If the episode in Samaria already leads to faith among non-Judeans, with the textual climax of the universalistic christological predication "savior of the world" (4:42), do we have to assume that the way to Galilee continues this movement from the Jews to the wider non-Jewish world? Or is the return to Galilee also a return to that Jewish world depicted in the first Cana miracle?

A third puzzle is found in the saying in v. 48, which is unprompted and disconnected from the context. Jesus's rejection of the faith-filled request in v. 47 is difficult to understand. Is it a rebuke or rather a general statement? And who is addressed by the second person plural? Within the narrative, the man understands the answer to be a rejection of his request, so he asks repeatedly with greater intensity in v. 49. But why is he rebuked when he approaches Jesus with complete trust? Or is Jesus's statement primarily a reference to others—the Galileans, the Jews, or even the readers of the Gospel? The problematization of "signs and wonders" in v. 48 is especially surprising in face of the fact that a miraculous healing eventually takes place and that the father's request, which had first been rejected, is ultimately fulfilled. The stretched mode of the narration of the discovery of the miracle and its exact timing fits poorly with the idea that the miracle as such is inappropriate or that the request for such intervention is wrong.

This connects to the notorious question of the quality of the royal man's faith. How is his faith to be assessed in v. 47, in v. 50, and in v. 53? What does "believe" (πιστεύειν) imply here and in v. 48? When is the faith of the man "correct" and perfect—only in v. 53 or already in v. 50? What is missing before, in v. 47? And what kind of faith does the repeated mention of πιστεύειν and the whole dynamic of the narrative convey?

All these questions have been discussed extensively and controversially in the pericope's history of interpretation, from antiquity through the Middle Ages and the Reformation period to the present. The interpretations of the church fathers or the Reformers often widen our view of the text to ambiguities or to dimensions of meaning and a dynamic that are frequently overlooked in contemporary exegesis.

The Burden of Exegetical Traditions

In contrast to the majority of ancient and premodern interpreters who distinguished between the encounters of Jesus with the synoptic centurion and the Johannine royal man,[9] modern interpreters since D. F. Strauss and F. C. Baur consider the two pericopes to be variations of a single event with the result that the historical value of the narrative had to be determined by source criticism. While nineteenth century scholars were convinced that the evangelist could draw on the Synoptics,[10] scholarship in the twentieth century was mostly occupied by the search for John's sources, with the most widespread solution that John took the narrative from a miracle or "signs" source[11] that might have taken the material from Q or another earlier oral source.[12]

Bultmann, in his commentary, states the problems of this construction most honestly. There, he clearly sees v. 48 as disconnected from the narrative.[13] He assumes that the original narrative contained a dialogue between the man and Jesus (as does the synoptic parallel), which is now lost and, according to him, replaced by v. 48. "The evangelist has thus taken away from the story its original punch line in order to make it serviceable to the motif of 'the *pistis* and the *semeia*.'"[14] This means, however, that the shape and intention of the "original" story can no longer be reconstructed, nor can we obtain a full view of the changes made by the evangelist. Whereas the focus of the narrative seems to be at its end where the narration is conspicuously stretched, Bultmann claims that the climax of the text is now in v. 48,[15] and the main focus is the problem of the "naïve belief in miracles" the evangelist wanted to reject and correct as a misunderstanding of true faith.[16]

In this view, the evangelist was a dogmatic corrector, not a skilled narrator. He felt obliged to include the episode because it was part of the source he used, but he only includes it to criticize the miracle that is narrated. But if the denial of the value of this miracle was the primary focus of the episode, why did the evangelist include it at all? Could he not simply leave it aside or address the problem in a different form? Considering all we can see today about the evangelist's selectivity and narrative creativity, Bultmann's reconstruction and those of his successors raise more questions than their interpretations can solve.

In view of the Johannine text, it is also unclear which "naïve belief in miracles" is criticized. Is it the father's request, the attitude of the Galileans, or the synoptic tradition? The petition is earnest and filled with belief; it is by no means meant to be a precondition for further belief. There is also no request for a legitimizing sign, like the Jews' request in 2:18. It seems, rather, that Bultmann and his followers see a problem that is not present in the text itself but is brought into the text from their own dogmatic perspective. It is the modern apologetic interest in a faith without miracles that leads interpreters to distance the theologically advanced evangelist from the stories he narrates. The evangelist, thus, remains a theologically valid, canonical witness or even the ideal interpreter of faith, whereas his traditions (and also the assumed later redaction) can be considered naïve or theologically invalid. The entire construction of a semeia source (as its American version, the assumption of a "Gospel of Signs"[17]) ultimately serves the purpose of making the evangelist a biblical precursor of modern Protestantism, a theologian of the word who can reject as unnecessary all kinds of miracles that do not fit the modern scientific worldview and likewise any kind of sacraments.[18]

A second problem is closely connected. Twentieth century authors often construct a negative foil of the Jewish craze for miracles or search for spectacles,[19] which is then considered the main target of the evangelist's rebuke. The idea goes back to John Calvin who states that all Jews were all too crazy for miracles (*miraculorum nimis cupidi*), so dependent on miracles that they had no use for God's word (*pendebant a miraculis Iudaei ut verbo nihil residuum facerent*).[20] For the Jewish request for signs, Calvin refers to 1 Corinthians 1:22, but here and in later Protestant authors, the concrete example in mind may also have been a popular Catholic belief. In any case, the interpretation by Bauer, Bultmann, and others is based on a textually unfounded anti-Jewish (and possibly also anti-Catholic) stereotype.

In my view, a new interpretation of the royal man requires a fresh reading of the text as a whole, within its narrative structure, and unencumbered by the aforementioned exegetical and source-critical traditions. It is especially the perspectives of narrative analysis that can freshly reveal the inner dynamics of the episode and the characterization of the royal man.[21]

Some Narrative Observations

Within the present article, I cannot offer a full narrative analysis of the episode but only select aspects. The boundaries of the narrative are clear (vv. 46–54), with v. 54 offering a metatextual commentary that, among other elements, ties the passage back to the first Cana episode.[22] This results in a ring composition "from Cana to Cana"[23] that encompasses Jesus's act in the temple and his dialogues with Nicodemus and the Samaritan woman, establishing a spatial structure with symbolic overtones between Galilee, Judea, and Samaria.

The narrative in vv. 46–53 is brief, narrated in simple language with short, asyndetic phrases and dialogues in direct speech that create a vivid impression. As in 2:1–11, the manifestation of the miracle is narrated only indirectly, through its later discovery (vv. 51–53a). First, the healing is witnessed by the servants, who could not have known what Jesus said and are, thus, "unsuspicious witnesses," and the man has no choice but to listen to their testimony. Then, he learns about the time and recognizes the healing took place because of Jesus's spoken word. The man's response (v. 53b) is that he himself and, by extension, also his "household" "believe." The stretched narration of these events shows that the focus is on this story line and, ultimately, on the faith of the man and the implied insights one gains from it. This episode is a "story of faith."

The narrative is presented as clearly factual, not fictional or symbolic. The story is situated in real places, and it narrates real persons and a real physical healing. It is also quite clear that the faith established at the end is stimulated through the narrated experience of the healing of the son and the realization that this healing happened simultaneously with the word of Jesus, that is, through this word. Thus, the miracle has a positive function regarding the constitution or shaping of the man's faith.

Yet, the narration is also characterized by an ulterior dimension, which does not lift the factually narrated events into the realm of mere symbolism but brings them into the horizon of the whole way of Jesus to his cross and resurrection.[24] This is already suggested by the reference to the wine miracle (v. 46). Further indications are the leitmotif use of the words *die* (vv. 47, 49) and *live* (vv. 50, 51, 53),[25] the theme of *believing* (vv. 48, 50, 53), specifically *believing the λόγος* (v. 50), as well as *knowing* (v. 53), the phrase ἤμελλεν ἀποθνῄσκειν (v. 47), mention of the seventh hour (v. 52), and the characterization as a "sign" (v. 54; cf. 2:11). The narrative thus becomes an exemplary representation of Jesus's lifegiving activity through his word (see the threefold ὁ υἱός . . . ζῆ) and thus a "sign" of Jesus's entire saving activity culminating in the cross and resurrection.

The terminologically clustered talk of "life" (ζῆν, vv. 50, 51, 53), which is linked to "believe" (vv. 50, 53), picks up a line that extends from the prologue (1:4, 12) through the Johannine kerygma (3:16–17; cf. 3:36) and the water-of-life dialogue (4:14) and now culminates in 4:50. Life is promised in the word of Jesus (v. 50) and then recognized as coincident with his λόγος (v. 53). Thus, the exposition of Jesus's ministry offered in John 1–4 comes to a provisional conclusion with this episode that ultimately confirms that life is in the *logos*—not only the word of Jesus, but in himself.

An important narrative structure is connected with the difficult content of v. 48. As in John 2:1–11 and later in 11:1–44, a narrative sequence can be observed in which a person's request (v. 47) to Jesus is initially followed by a rejection (v. 48), but then by a fulfillment that far exceeds the original request (vv. 50–53). The repetition of this or a similar structure in several episodes of the Gospel suggests that a certain effect on the readership is intended by this narrative element. Therefore, the structure is to be interpreted in all its occurrences with regard to its didactic effect or intention,[26] rather than merely by redaction-critical dissociation. The question is: What does it teach about Jesus, his acting and his dignity, and what views or attitudes of the readers are negotiated or implicitly modified here? As a consequence, the rebuke in v. 48 is to be interpreted not primarily as a rebuke of the figure of the royal man, nor merely as a "dogmatic" rebuke of some Galileans or Jews, but rather as an enigmatic statement that inaugurates a process of reconsideration and learning among the readers.

The Royal Man as a Consistently Positive Figure and a Paradigm for Readers to Emulate

The central figure of the episode, apart from Jesus, is the nameless "royal" man[27] who appears only once in John, here in this episode. His prehistory and later life are of no interest. Only this encounter is important for the Gospel of John. He is, however, more than a "flat" character or mere cipher for a positive reaction to Jesus.[28] In these few verses, the royal man himself seems to undergo a process of deepening faith, and, because of this development, functions as a paradigm and example of faith for the readers of the Gospel while nevertheless being a figure open for readers to identify with.

The man is first introduced by mention of his professional position, as a βασιλικός, a servant of a "king"—probably Herod Antipas—who himself owns a house and servants. He belongs, therefore, clearly to the upper class in Galilee. As a person linked with the rulers, he might not be a sympathetic character at the outset. Yet, he is a father who travels to see Jesus—indeed, who presses Jesus with his request—doing everything in his power for his son, so readers quickly see his humanity and are able to sympathize with him. When later his servants go to meet him with good tidings, and in the end the people of his house believe together with him, he is finally depicted as social and accessible.

What is striking, however, is the unspecific term ἄνθρωπος used as a reference to him in the middle of the story (v. 50). It helps to present the figure in an open manner, as a human who hears and believes, an exemplary figure who invites readers to identify with him and act like him, namely, by believing in Jesus's word.[29] In contrast with his synoptic counterpart, the pagan centurion, the royal man's ethno-religious identity remains open. Readers may or may not fill in the blanks from the parallels. Prior to all ethnic evaluations, they themselves, according to his example, believe Jesus and his word.

Most strikingly, the protagonist of this episode does not become a victim of misunderstanding or "irony" at any point in the episode.[30] He appears even more clearly positive than the Samaritan woman. He is the only figure in the Johannine sign narratives who believes before seeing the sign (v. 50). Throughout the episode, he acts correctly toward the increase of his knowledge (the *anagnorisis*).[31] His deeper insight is gained by remembering the hour Jesus spoke to him and by drawing the appropriate conclusion from that sign, that is, by acknowledging Jesus's authority and dignity. In this respect, he is a person who sees the sign and proceeds from the sign to the truth signified. He is one who comes to true faith.

The Faith of the Royal Man—Its Time and Its Quality

From here, we can again discuss the nature and development of the royal man's faith. Within the episode, "believe" (πιστεύειν) is mentioned three times: first in the saying of Jesus (v. 48), then twice with respect to the man's act of believing (vv. 50, 53). The mention of belief in v. 48 helps frame the man's initial request for the healing of his son in v. 47 as an act of implicit faith. What is the quality of his faith at different points of the story? What does it imply, and when is it "perfect"? Is there really a "correct" and an "incorrect" faith? Are readers actually intended to assess the man's faith, or should they simply follow his example? Here, we can see that exegetical discussions from antiquity until the present have been overshadowed by dogmatic issues beyond the text.

In v. 47, there is no mention of faith. Yet the fact that the father goes on a lengthy journey to ask Jesus for help demonstrates a high degree of trust in Jesus's abilities and willingness to help. He has probably heard about Jesus's deeds and trustingly asks him to come. Such confidence in Jesus's healing power is found frequently in the Synoptics, not least in the words of the centurion whose faith is explicitly praised by Jesus (Matt 8:10, 13; Luke 7:9).[32] Admittedly, a reader versed in Johannine theology can already see that such a faith is insufficient. The man views Jesus as a healer who must come locally close to heal, possibly in the style of the prophets Elijah and Elisha, but not yet the creator whose word gives life, physical and eternal.[33] Nevertheless, it would be inappropriate to call such faith "incorrect"; rather, it is an initial faith, open to further experience and capable of development. The request for healing is not a precondition for faith. Conversely, trusting faith precedes the hoped-for healing. And in no way does the man want to make Jesus's acceptability dependent on such a "sign" or miracle. The man had the testimony of others, and he trustfully approached Jesus, asking for help. This is true faith, and without such initial faith, he would not have come to see Jesus.[34]

Based on v. 48, it is understandable that interpreters conjecture something must have been wrong with the man's faith. Other interpreters think the rebuke must at least include other characters implied within the narrative, if not primarily aimed at them. Still others suggest that the rebuke was a didactic move by Jesus, aimed at the growth of the man's faith.[35] The problematization of miracle-oriented faith is, of course, noticed by most interpreters, but the idea is that Jesus warns believers against waiting for miracles,[36] or teaches readers to believe the mere word (cf. v. 50). Not before the rise of the worldview of modernity have miracles been so fundamentally criticized.

When, in v. 49, the father does not allow himself to be shaken off and continues to plead fervently, he demonstrates a sign of persistent trust, of a faith that has proven itself in the face of challenge. Such persistence reminds the reader of Jesus's mother in 2:5, or the Syrophoenician woman in Mark 7:24–30. Of course, the royal man still asks Jesus to come to the place where his son is about to die. He has not changed his hopes. Nevertheless, the intensification of his request reveals his persistent trust. Some interpreters speculate that such persistent faith makes the father worthy of being heard,[37] yet John Cassian stresses, instead, that here, as elsewhere, salvation is not granted according to the strength of one's faith. Instead, God acts with overflowing grace beyond the limits of human unbelief.[38]

Most disputed is v. 50, where Jesus finally responds to the request, but not as the father expected. As in 2:1–11, Jesus acts on his own accord and not according to the request of others. He grants the supplicant not his presence with the sick person, not a sign or manifestation of the requested healing, but only his word. The phrase πορεύου, ὁ υἱός σου ζῇ ("Go, your son is alive!") forms "the climax of the narrative."[39] It is a response that both dismisses the supplicant and ends the encounter.

The weight of this phrase, repeated twice in vv. 51 and 53, cannot be underestimated. It adopts exactly the phrase Elijah says to the widow in Sarepta when he gives back to her the son raised from the dead: "Behold (βλέπε), your son lives." But the difference must be noted. There the widow can hold in her arms the proof of Elijah's powerful prayer, the manifestation of the miracle, and so recognize that he is the man of God and speaks a word of truth (1 Kgs 17:24 LXX). Here the father cannot recognize anything at first and can only believe that Jesus's words are not empty. Moreover, while Elijah prays to God for the life of the widow's son, the Johannine Jesus does not pray, but states, or even commands by his own authority (cf. also John 11:43).

Most important, therefore, is the correct translation of ὁ υἱός σου ζῇ as "your son *lives*." The future rendering, "your son *will* live,"[40] misses the point that Jesus is here proclaiming a present truth, indeed in a performative word "creating" life. Against the background of the motif of death already mentioned in vv. 47 and 49, the ζῇ is to be read not merely as an expression of physical recovery, but also as an allusion to the "eternal" life given in faith: The healing (from near death to recovery) is already here a sign of passing from death to life, as it happens when a person hears Jesus's word in faith (5:24). And, ultimately, not only is the father's son healed, but also the father is brought to life in faith.

Of course, the man could have heard Jesus's words as a rejection and banal consolation, even as an insult to him, an upper-class official whose invitation was rejected. Jesus will not come to his home to see the sick child. He could have left in disappointment or anger. Yet, the opposite is the case. The man hears the word of Jesus and "believes," or, with the aorist, he "came to believe." Whatever trust was there before, actual faith in Jesus and his word begins here, without any visible sign of confirmation. Jesus speaks the word, "Your son lives," and the father believes it. No further inquiry is narrated, but simply obedience. As Jesus said πορεύου ("go!"), "he went" (καὶ ἐπορεύετο). He does not bother Jesus further but goes on his long journey home, without seeing the fulfillment of his request.

Of course, the man's faith in v. 50 is still directed to the fact that his son will be healed, even if Jesus does not come to the home of the sick person, but only speaks his word. Only in v. 53 does the father's faith gain additional knowledge about the authority and identity of Jesus and, thus, a new shape. Nevertheless, one should not tear apart these two stages of the father's journey of faith and reject the first as incorrect or superficial. Unlike many other interpreters, Martin Luther praises the faith of the father when he believes at the word of Jesus: "Here, he is born again."[41] For Luther, such faith is the proper miracle, when someone believes the word having "seen and felt nothing at all." "Such Christians are a pure miracle."[42]

A brief look at the synoptic parallel may be appropriate here. The faith mentioned in v. 50 corresponds exactly to the faith expressed there by the centurion: "But speak only one word, and my servant will be healed" (Matt 8:8; Luke 7:7). It is precisely such a word that Jesus speaks here in the Johannine episode.

The centurion's word that shows his laudable faith is translated into a narrative. Now such a commendable faith is painted before the eyes of the readers in the figure of the royal man and his experience.[43]

Yet, the climax of the episode is in vv. 51–53, where the miracle is discovered in retrospect, and the faithful father comes to a decisive insight and to a more insightful faith. What the father believed upon hearing Jesus's word, without seeing, is now confirmed as real. The healing has happened, even without the physical presence of Jesus. This could be the end of the episode.

But since John is concerned with more than mere belief in the healing power of Jesus, another plot line is added. The man inquires of his servants the time when his son's condition improved, and they answer, "Yesterday, about the seventh hour," i.e., shortly after noon, before 1:00 p.m. Now the father "recognizes" the temporal coincidence. The healing of his son took place at exactly the time Jesus spoke his word. This makes it even clearer that the healing, indeed the "life," was brought about by Jesus's spoken word, "Your son lives." This means that Jesus's word not only promises but directly creates what it says, the healing, or rather, life. In Jesus dwells the power of the creator to give life (cf. 5:26). This motif of life—both physical life in health and "eternal" life in faith—is unmistakably emphasized by the second repetition of Jesus's word from v. 50.

It would be inappropriate to interpret the question about the time in v. 52 as a suspicious demand for "verification." There are clear theological reasons for inserting this narrative element. The temporal coincidence is to be emphasized so that not only the father but even more so the readers can draw their conclusions from it.

There is, however, an enigmatic element: the mention of the seventh hour. Like other temporal notes in John (cf. 3:2; 4:6),[44] this element might not be inserted for purely historical purposes. Yet there is no other mention of a seventh hour that could help interpret the information. There is, however, the mention of the sixth hour, not only in Jesus's encounter with the Samaritan woman (4:6), but also as the hour of Jesus's condemnation for crucifixion (19:14), which must have happened immediately thereafter, in the seventh hour. Should, then, the mention of the seventh hour be a hint that Jesus's life-giving word is connected with his crucifixion, indeed is grounded in the salvific event of his "exaltation" on the cross? After all, the threefold mention of the "hour" makes readers pay attention to such textual relations, especially since in the first Cana episode Jesus's "hour" (2:4) already posed a riddle that is ultimately resolved only in relation to his death and the crucifixion scene. The readers are at least invited to discover such connections.

Now, the father's belief is no longer only faith in the possibility of healing, but belief in the one who himself has the power to give physical and "eternal" life, who gives this gift through his word. It is faith in Jesus, the life-giver, who is God (1:18).[45]

As confirmation of the truth and fertility of his faith, the royal man—like his "predecessor," the Samaritan woman (4:39–42)—is also depicted as a "missionary" through whom others come to faith. "His household," i.e., his wife, children, possibly other relatives, and his servants are included not only in the "discovery" of the miracle but also in the faith in Jesus. For the first and only time in John, a whole (extended) family comes to faith. The servants who "confirmed" the initial faith of the man now take part in his faith. They have not met Jesus personally and have not heard his word directly, yet precisely in this manner they are in the same situation as the readers of the Gospel, who cannot see Jesus physically but only believe through the testimony of others or the testimony of the book and its "written signs" (20:30). With this narrative element, the royal man—who first trusted due to the testimony of others—and his "house" are prefigurations of later readers of the Gospel, and of the only way they can come to faith: through the testimony of others, i.e., the "signs" of the book.

The High Christology of John 4:51–53 in Its Johannine Context

With its climax in vv. 51–53, the faith story of the royal man is a clear testimony of John's high Christology. Jesus is depicted not merely as a miracle worker or prophetic intercessor in the style of Elijah, but precisely as the one whose word has the power to create, to bring the dead to life, and to convey not only physical but even more so eternal life. The christological predications of the prologue are clearly adopted here. In Jesus and his word, or, rather, in him as the Logos, is life (1:4; cf. 5:26), and as he was involved in the creation (1:3), so he does the proper works of God when healing the sick (5:17) and raising the dead (11:1–44). As he demonstrated his authority over water and wine in 2:1–11, he now shows that the power of life is in his word. Yet, these insights can only be articulated when the episode is not torn apart into source material and the evangelist's correction. When read in the framework of the whole Johannine work, even verses that were often attributed to an earlier source support the christological testimony of the final text.

John's high Christology is not merely conveyed by christological titles, such as God, the Son, Son of Man, or *Kyrios*, and by the famous *Ego-eimi*-sayings, with and without metaphorical predications.[46] It is also conveyed by narrative episodes such as the wine miracle (2:1–11), where Jesus acts not only as the eschatological Messiah but also as the divine creator, or the healing of the man born blind (9:1–41), where the healed man in the end prostrates himself before the

Son of Man (9:38) who makes the blind see and blinds those who claim to see (9:39–41). His divine, life-giving power is most prominently demonstrated in the Lazarus episode in which the narrative figures of Mary and Martha again represent a "lower" christological view, and the readers are again taught through the device of request—rebuke—response[47] to perceive the divine dignity of Jesus who can even raise those already in decay.

Yet, John's high Christology is presented in an incarnational context. Jesus is not a "divine man," hovering over the earth, but shares completely the circumstances of human life,[48] as his thirst in Samaria (4:6) but also his experience of rejection in his πατρίς (4:44) demonstrate. After all, he voluntarily suffers the dishonorable death on the cross, which only faith can recognize as victory over the world (16:33).[49] And even his word about the "signs and wonders" implies a kind of lament about human unbelief or desperation. Jesus's dignity is visible only to the eyes of faith, and such faith is, according to John, not accessible to humans as they are, but only through an opening of the eyes, a miracle.

Accordingly, in our passage, the miracle of the healing of the son, is not performed before the eyes of the father or of the Gospel readers. Its discovery is only narrated in retrospect. This corresponds to the strategy of indirect revelation, which characterizes most of the Johannine sign narratives. What does this mean for Jesus's miraculous deeds? They are not at all irrelevant, for indeed as an initial stimulus for attention, as "signs" that point to a deeper dimension, and with regard to the disclosure of a deeper knowledge of faith, their relevance cannot be underestimated. But their meaning is subtle and complex. Faith does not simply follow a miracle, and of course a miracle is not a condition for faith. Ultimately, the man's faith is confirmed by the news of the healing that occurred, but not in the sense that faith "merited" or even "achieved" this fulfillment. For if the fulfillment was already present in Jesus's creative word, this word, and thus the divine work, preceded the faith established in v. 50. Thus, faith is grounded in Jesus's word, not in the miracle experienced. And, finally, it is not the healing as such, but the healing effected at a certain point in time, and thus through Jesus's word, that is the sign that leads the man to the realization of Jesus's authority and brings him to a deepened, discerning faith.

Thus, the episode in its literary design presupposes the cognitive process of the post-Easter period, the development of faith and in particular the development of a Christology that is attributed to the activity of the post-Easter Spirit (14:25–26; 16:13–15).[50] The readers of the Gospel can no longer directly perceive Jesus's deeds. They can only see the signs in retrospect, through the text, and they nevertheless are supposed to believe. The actual sign for them is not the acts of the earthly Jesus, but the literary text,[51] skillfully designed to disclose his dignity and to convey insights that were inaccessible to the contemporaries of the earthly

Jesus (cf. 2:21; 12:16) but are now considered the knowledge of true belief in Jesus, the Jewish Messiah, Savior of the world, and even "God."

The Episode as an Example of the Development of Faith in Post-Easter Times

The reading presented here has shown that the royal man is a completely positive, even exemplary figure. No shadow of doubt need fall on the image of his faith. He does not fall prey to any misunderstanding and gradually comes to a faith that is fully on the level of the knowledge of faith the Gospel of John wants to convey. In the end, like the Samaritan woman, he stands as an example and mediator of faith. He is a sympathetic figure and a role model, open for the readers to identify with. The faith inspired by the episode is a discerning faith that draws the right conclusion from the signs offered to it; it is the personal faith in Jesus as the creative giver of physical and eternal life, as God.

Not coincidentally, this faith also comes about only on the basis of the testimony of witnesses. It thus corresponds to the paradigm of faith transmission already present literarily in John 1:35–51 and 4:39–42 (cf. also John 20). The initial trust of the royal official in Jesus appears to be motivated by the reports of witnesses to his deeds (v. 45). Furthermore, it is only the testimony of the servants (v. 52) that informs the man about the healing of his son and thus the hearing of his request, and only the information about the time of the healing lets him recognize the sign's meaning. Only through the right conclusion from the sign—through connection of the experience of the fulfillment of his request, the word of the witnesses, and the remembered word of Jesus—does he come to believe in Jesus's divine dignity and power. Thus, the present narrative proves to be an exemplary "story of faith" for post-Easter readers. It presents the dynamics of the emergence of faith as a multistage process, to which both the word of Jesus and the experience of the protagonist contribute.

This dynamic of faith was noticed by many interpreters. Among the most precious interpretations are the numerous sermons of Martin Luther on this Johannine passage. He broadly elaborates on this in an early sermon from 1516:[52] "Three degrees of faith are described to us, namely, faith that is still in its infancy, that is on the increase, and that is perfect." The first is awakened by works of God, "of a general or special kind," "but one must not stop there." "To increase in faith, that is when . . . one believes the mere word without asking for a work." Perfect faith also no longer asks for instructive words, but "gives itself . . . away completely."[53] In a later sermon, Luther distinguishes between saving faith and faith that has proven itself in temptation and on the cross: "If anyone has even the smallest drop or spark of the love and grace, he will be saved. But Scripture teaches that one must increase and continue."[54] "So God does with all whom

He strengthens in faith. He brings him to another and higher degree or level, so that he becomes strong and now believes in a different way than before."[55]

The royal man is presented as a paradigm of such a development of faith. He shows a personal change in his faithful attitude that clearly leads to the final stage: personal faith in Jesus, the divine life-giver. The episode of the royal man is therefore an often neglected and unrecognized testimony to the high Christology that pervades the entire Gospel of John from the prologue to Thomas's climactic confession (20:28). The episode is a paradigm for the period of the post-Easter community. Jesus gives life *in absentia* through the pure word, and whoever recognizes the signs and hears his word comes to belief and has "eternal" life in him.

Jesus the Temple in John 10

A Contribution to the Narrative Christology of the Fourth Gospel

Ruben Zimmermann

THE TEMPLE MOTIF runs through the Fourth Gospel like a red thread and is not limited to the two Greek terms τὸ ἱερόν and ὁ ναός.[1] Statements about the sacrificial cult, temple festivals, or high priests, as well as certain functions such as atonement, the presence of God with his people, or the δόξα (glory, כָּבוֹד) of God also belong to the semantic domain of temple and temple cult. In the narrative design of the story about Jesus, it is noticeable that the Fourth Evangelist, deviating from the Synoptics, places the cleansing of the temple at the beginning of the narrative (John 2:13–22). In a direct comment to the readers in 2:21, the author links the temple to a christological statement: "But he spoke of the temple of his body."

It is therefore not surprising that the temple Christology of the Fourth Gospel has repeatedly been the subject of NT research.[2] However, John 10 is rarely, if ever, considered in these works.[3] Omitting John 10 from the discussion of the temple motif is largely due to methodological approaches and forms of christological expressions. For a long time, NT research on Christology focused on so-called christological titles such as Messiah, Son of Man, or *Kyrios*, such that hardly any attention was given to other forms of christological expression. Literary research on John, however, has recognized that the titles are also nothing more than cold, lexicalized metaphors. Furthermore, the evangelist of the Fourth Gospel wanted to make the classical titles transparent again with respect to their figurative content by means of the narrative. For example, the evangelist presents the *Kyrios* as the master of the house (John 13), who despite his superior status, takes on the task of a slave by washing his disciples' feet. Additionally, Jesus is not simply called the Messiah, but is actually anointed with oil (John 12). In part, even a kind of narrative role reversal is staged, in which Jesus takes on the task of the bridegroom, shepherd, or gardener of paradise and is linked precisely in this way with traditional metaphors for God. In this way, a transfer of well-known religious statements about God or the cult to Jesus takes place.[4]

I am grateful to Jacob Cerone for proofreading this article.

If one asks about the medial shaping of christological statements, one must therefore by no means remain limited to titles or confessional formulas. More recently, NT research has also shown in various places that metaphors and narratives in particular have an essential share in the formation of christological confessions. One can rightly speak of a "metaphorical Christology" or "narrative Christology."[5]

In the following article, I would like to continue on this path and examine the temple Christology of the Fourth Gospel in terms of its metaphors and narratives, focusing on chapter 10, which is often overlooked in this context.[6]

The Temple in the Narrative of John 10

Chapter 10 of John's Gospel is performed as a speech and a dialogue.[7] However, these speech-acts are also integrated into a narrative context, with a narrative setting created in a discreet way. As I have described in detail elsewhere,[8] I see chapter 10 as a literary unit. The reasoning behind this view is briefly summarized here, as it forms the premise for the following thesis.

The Literary Unit of John 9:39–10:42

Strictly speaking, Jesus's speech does not begin in John 10:1, but already in 9:41. However, this verse is a response to the Pharisees' question in 9:40, which is motivated by Jesus's speaking in 9:39. Therefore, the literary unit must begin with 9:39. Frequently, interpreters assume a sharp caesura between 10:21 and 10:22. However, Klaus Scholtissek and others have pointed out the structural parallelism of the two discourses with four parts:[9]

A.　John 9:39–10:21: First Discourse (Good Shepherd Discourse)
　　1.　Part (9:39–10:6)
　　　　Introduction:　　　　question of the Pharisees (9:39–41)
　　　　Jesus's speech:　　　Amen-saying (10:1a)
　　　　　　　　　　　　　　parable of the shepherd (10:1b–5)
　　　　audience's reaction:　negative effect (10:6): lack of
　　　　　　　　　　　　　　understanding
　　2.　Part (10:7–21)
　　　　Introduction:　　　　(10:7a)
　　　　Jesus's speech:　　　Amen-saying (10:7b)
　　　　　　　　　　　　　　10:7–16 "I am" sayings (door, shepherd)
　　　　　　　　　　　　　　10:17–18 christological conclusion
　　　　audience's reaction:　dividing effect (10:19–21)
　　　　　　　　　　　　　　1. reaction: demonization of Jesus (10:20)
　　　　　　　　　　　　　　2. reaction: reference to Jesus's sign (10:21)

    B. John 10:22–42: Second Discourse (Conflict over Jesus's Claims)
        3. Part (10:22–31)

Introduction:	indications of place and time (10:22–23)
	quest for the Christ of the Jews (10:24)
Jesus's speech:	10:25–30: aims at unity with the Father
audience's reaction:	negative effect (10:31): attempted stoning

        4. Part (10:32–42)

Introduction:	question of Jesus (10:32)
	accusation of blasphemy (10:33)
Jesus's speech:	10:34–38: aims at reciprocal immanence with the Father
audience's reaction:	dividing effect (10:39–42)
	1. reaction: attempt to seize Jesus (10:39)
	2. reaction: faith of the "many" (10:40–42)

The Good Shepherd discourse (10:1–21) and the conflict over Jesus's claims (10:22–42) each have a double structure composed of two parts. Each of the four parts concludes with a note about the effect of Jesus's speech (reaction), first with a brief report of a negative reaction, then with a more detailed report of division. All in all, there is an escalation that leads from incomprehension (vv. 6, 20) to the intention to kill (vv. 31, 39) or from doubt (v. 21) to faith (v. 42). With regard to the introductions of each part, we also observe an intensification from the question of blindness and sin to the question of παρρησία and blasphemy, i.e., the highest form of sin. *Stylistically,* too, a strict division into figurative pastoral speech and christological revelatory speech—as is often assumed in interpretations—cannot be proven in the text. The shepherd imagery is developed in the first part of the discourse; nevertheless, it remains in the second section of ch. 10 (vv. 26–29). This assignment is underlined by a series of *motif* and *keyword links*: an unmistakable reference back to the first section appears in vv. 26–29, in which the shepherd metaphor is taken up with identical formulations as in 10:1–18.[10] With the striking verb "to rob" (ἁρπάζω), vv. 28c and 29b create a reference back to v. 12, where there is discussion of the wolf robbing sheep from the shepherd (ὁ λύκος ἁρπάζει). Additionally, the evangelist stresses the idea of mutual "knowing" or "recognizing" (γινώσκειν) in both parts (vv. 14b, 15a–27, 38).

    How precisely the author formulates and plays with the different connotations of language in order to create interconnections is further illustrated by the following two examples. In 10:11–18, the phrase "to lay down one's life" (τὴν ψυχὴν τίθημι) is used several times (vv. 11b, 15c, 17b, 18b), emphasizing that Jesus lays down his life voluntarily. While no one can take Jesus's life away (v. 18a), the Jews, conversely, must acknowledge Jesus's sovereignty over their lives (v. 24c). To make these power relations unmistakably clear, the evangelist ironically uses the same formulation familiar from v. 18a (αἴρω τὴν ψυχήν). Similarly, the author juxtaposes the sheep's inability to escape from the *hand* (ἐκ τῆς χειρός) of the Son (v. 28c) and the Father (v. 29b) with Jesus's escape from the *hand of* the Jews (ἐκ τῆς χειρός, v. 39).

Another reference is made by the resumption of the signal word καλός, which was used in the first part to qualify the behavior of the "good shepherd" in contrast to that of the hired servant (vv. 11ab, 14a). In vv. 32–33 the term refers to the good works (ἔργα καλά) of Jesus.

Similar deliberate *links between the figurative level and the narrative level* may be seen in the use of ἀνοίγω (v. 3: doorman opens; v. 21: Jesus opens his eyes) and ἀκούω (10:3b, 8b, 16d, 27: hearing the shepherd; 9:40a; 10:20c: hearing Jesus). Likewise, the author associates Jesus's (final) departure in 10:39 with the departure of the sheep and their shepherd in 10:3b. The motif of "coming" runs throughout the chapter. In 9:39 there is talk of Jesus's "coming into the world" (εἰς τὸν κόσμον τοῦτον ἦλθον), which is taken up inclusively in 10:36 as "sending into the world" (ὁ πατὴρ . . . ἀπέστειλεν εἰς τὸν κόσμον). The "coming in" is also the central distinguishing criterion between shepherds and robbers (vv. 1, 2, 9, 10). Furthermore, Ezekiel 34 and 37:15–28, i.e., central texts of OT shepherd metaphors, which are reference texts of John 10:1–21,[11] were among the compulsory readings of the temple Dedication Festival.[12] Because of the latent discussion with the temple or the temple cult, as well as the metaphorical code that the body of Jesus can be identified with the (new) temple (2:19–22), readers cannot limit the details about Jesus's location in 10:22 too quickly to mere geographical coincidence.[13] In John 10, Jesus's conflict with the Jews, which has been building since John 7, comes to a preliminary climax.[14]

The Narrative Setting (Space and Time) in John 10

The *place of the event* on the narrative level is the temple or the temple forecourt. According to 8:59, Jesus leaves the temple and meets the man born blind, who is sitting in front of the temple gate[15] or on the temple forecourt, as is usual for beggars (9:8). This location is decisive for the entire discussion about the healing of the blind and is also valid for the first and second portions of the Good Shepherd discourse. During the speech (first discourse), Jesus and his interlocutors are *in front of* the temple or at the temple gate. John 10:23, however, mentions a new setting. Jesus is now *within* the temple. Strictly speaking, he is walking around in the hall of Solomon (10:23: καὶ περιεπάτει ὁ Ἰησοῦς ἐν τῷ ἱερῷ ἐν τῇ στοᾷ τοῦ Σολομῶνος). Solomon's portico (ἡ στοὰ τοῦ Σολομῶνος) is considered the oldest part of the Herodian temple,[16] because it was considered to be a remnant of the first, Solomonic temple.[17] Solomon was not only the first builder of the temple, but, according to 1 Kings 8, he was the first to dedicate the temple. Since the narrative is set during the Feast of the Consecration of the temple (see below), mentioning Solomon could also be in line with the evangelist's efforts to exaggerate the events in order to elevate Jesus with respect to central OT figures. While the Feast of the Consecration of the temple recalls the consecration of the Second Temple, the fact that the speech occurs within Solomon's hall means that the narrative casts it within the horizon of the first, original temple. According to Acts, Solomon's portico apparently also played a central role in the constitution of the first Jerusalem congregation of Christ followers. This part of the temple was where the apostles gathered and proclaimed Jesus to the people in Acts 3:11 and 5:12.[18]

In the Gospel of John, Jesus leaves this place only when his opponents attempt to seize him because of what he has said. The evangelist emphasizes this "exodus" in a striking way: (1) he reports on the change of location twice (John 10:39: ἐξῆλθεν; 10:40: καὶ ἀπῆλθεν), and (2) he provides geographical details that alert readers to the vast spatial distance between Solomon's portico and the subsequent events. Jesus leaves not only the temple, but also Jerusalem and goes to the other side of the Jordan, to the place where John had baptized before (10:40). Jesus now remains in that place (καὶ ἔμεινεν ἐκεῖ, v. 40). Finally, the evangelist further emphasizes that it is only there (ἐκεῖ, v. 42), beyond the Jordan, that many come to faith.

Jesus's first two speeches are thus situated *in front of the temple* (9:39–10:21), whereas his third and fourth speeches are located *in the temple* (10:22). After his exodus from Jerusalem, Jesus remains in a place *without a temple* where many come to believe (10:40–42), thus returning to his starting point (1:28).[19]

At the center of the entire passage is not only a place, but also one or two *temporal references*. Jesus teaches in the temple in Jerusalem at the time of ἐγκαίνια, here probably to be read as a *terminus technicus* for the *Feast of the Dedication of the temple* (Hanukkah),[20] and in *winter* (χειμὼν ἦν, 10:22–23). Two possible dates fit this description. The Festival of Hanukkah[21] commemorates the rededication of the temple after its desecration under Antiochus IV Epiphanes (175–164 BCE). According to 1 Maccabees 4:52, this historical event is dated to the 25th of Kislev, i.e., the second half of December in 164 BCE,[22] so the indication of the season is accurate. In the course of his efforts at Hellenization, the Syrian ruler Antiochus IV[23] had a second altar placed on top of the great altar of burnt offering in the Jerusalem temple on the 25th of Kislev, 167 BCE. This event is called the "abomination of desolation" (βδέλυγμα ἐρημώσεως) in 1 Maccabees 1:54. It is unclear whether this altar has the "meaning of a sacred stone,"[24] or possibly bore a pictorial representation. In any case, the temple was desecrated by its presence. After the "Torah faithful" freed themselves from foreign, Syrian rule by means of the so-called Maccabean Revolt under Judas Maccabeus, the temple was cleansed and rededicated (1 Macc 4:36–61; 2 Macc 10:1–6).

A number of motifs and even linguistic parallels lead to the assumption that John 10 deliberately refers to the reports about the Feast of the Dedication of the temple in the Maccabean books and thereby contrasts Antiochus IV and Jesus, or the Jews around Judas Maccabeus and Jesus's interlocutors.[25] Thus, the Jews' accusation of blasphemy (John 10:33) could allude to the "self-deification" of Antiochus IV, who had given himself the epithet ἐπιφανής (God who appeared) (1 Macc 1:10).[26] Like the shepherd in John 10:16, Antiochus IV's political goal was the unification of the people (1 Macc 1:41).[27] The blasphemer Antiochus IV finally meets his death by falling stones (2 Macc 1:1–13); similarly, the Jewish interlocutors wish to stone Jesus (John 10:31).[28] But whereas according to 1 Maccabees the temple is (re)consecrated or "sanctified" (1 Macc 4:48: καὶ τὰς αὐλὰς ἡγίασαν),[29] according to John 10:36 Jesus is "sanctified" (ὃν ὁ πατὴρ ἡγίασεν).[30] Additional details increase the plausibility of the reference: 1 Maccabees 4:38 mentions the "court" (αὐλή) and "doors" (θύραι).[31] In 1 Maccabees, there is also mention of keeping the desecrated stones of the altar safe (1 Macc 4:43, 46, cf. 4:47) in a suitable place within the temple "until a prophet would come and rule over them" (v. 47: μέχρι τοῦ παραγενηθῆναι προφήτην τοῦ ἀποκριθῆναι περὶ αὐτῶν). The fact that Jesus's Jewish interlocutors attempted to stone him in John 10:31 could thus also be formulated—as some exegetes argue—as a contrast to 1 Maccabees 4:46–48, because the stones that would have served for the erection and *dedication* of the new altar in the old temple are taken up in service of the *desecration* of the "new temple."[32]

A comparable purification or rededication is further reported in 2 Chronicles 29–31, where Hezekiah's reform of the cult, only hinted at in 2 Kings 18:1–6, is described in detail. Some details of this consecration are to be mentioned in the horizon of the Gospel of John. According to 2 Chronicles, Hezekiah first orders the doors at the house of the Lord to be opened (2 Chr 29:3: ἀνέῳξεν τὰς θύρας οἴκου κυρίου). According to 2 Chronicles 29:7, these are the "doors of the temple court,"[33] which the predecessors (fathers) had closed. Furthermore, Hezekiah orders the people to "throw out" everything unclean from the temple (2 Chr 29:5, 16: ἐκβάλλω).[34] The goal of this action is the "sanctification" or rededication of the temple (2 Chr 29:5, 17: ἁγνίζω).[35]

By way of summary, the accusation of blasphemy, the mention of sanctification, the door, the courtyard, and stones, and perhaps even the question about a/the messiah reveal connections between the events described in John 10 and the dedication of the temple as well as its theological significance (for instance in 1–2 Maccabees). Therefore, one may postulate that the mention of "Hanukkah" in

John 10:22 is of greater significance than offering a merely novelistic temporal reference.[36] Above all, the traditional connection between temple consecration and cleansing needs to be examined more closely in light of a possible link between the so-called Temple Cleansing in 2:13–25 and the mention of the Hanukkah festival in 10:22–39.

Characters and Plot in John 10

The "Pharisees" (9:39, 40; [10:6]), the "Jews" (10:19, 24, 31, 33, [39]), and "Jesus" (9:39, 41; 10:6, 7, 23, 25, 32, 34, [39, 40]) are mentioned as characters acting and speaking in 9:39–10:42. Furthermore, the "many" (πολλοί, 10:20, 41, 42) and the "others" (ἄλλοι, 10:21) still appear. In 10:21, the evangelist mentions the "blind" (τυφλοί), thereby establishing a connection with the introduction to the pericope (9:39–41) as well as to the entirety of John 9. The antagonists of Jesus are already introduced in John 9 (Pharisees in 9:13, 15, 16; the Jews in 9:18, 22).

The details of the action are sparse, but for that very reason their meaning is all the more important. Verbs of speech clearly dominate the narrative sections, with Jesus's speech in 9:39 at first seeming like a general proclamation, while dialogic narrative references predominate in what follows (λέγω, ἀποκρίνομαί; 9:40, 41; 10:1, 6, 24, 25, 32, 33, 34, 39). The responses to speech sections one and two are framed like comments from the narrator in that they indicate the attitude "toward these words" (διὰ τοὺς λόγους τούτους, 10:19; cf. 10:6). The responses to parts of speech sections three and four also have the same intention, but they indicate an intensification in that they now describe real actions: The Jews, according to 10:31, pick up stones (βαστάζω λίθους) to stone Jesus (cf. 8:59),[37] and want to "seize" him (10:39: πιάζω). In contrast, the "many" come to Jesus and believe in him (10:41–42).

If we disregard the introductions to the speech, the author is obviously interested in foregrounding references to the place of the event in the narrative portions of the pericope. While the dialogue takes place in the temple forecourt without further commentary (9:39–41; 10:19–21), after 10:23 Jesus walks around in the temple (περιπατέω) surrounded by Jews (κυκλόω, 10:24). After the last part of the speech, the evangelist emphasizes Jesus's change of location (ἐξέρχομαι, ἀπέρχομαι, 10:39, 40) and the fact that many followed him (10:41) by mentioning them twice. Jesus stays at his new destination, and those who followed him come to faith there (ἐκεῖ).

In summary, the narrative frame of John 10 describes a *change of location* from the temple forecourt or temple to John's place of baptism, whereby the two settings are contrasted with regard to the recognition of Jesus. While at and in the temple, there is a clear rejection of Jesus, to the point that his opponents attempt to stone him; at the place of baptism many come to believe. The fact that the evangelist highlights the behavior of the "many" (10:20–42) underscores the importance of this motif of contrast.

The Narrative Temple Christology

Interaction between the Narrative and the Metaphor in John 10

Since the horizon of the temple is now torn open on the narrative level of John 10, I would like to ask to what extent individual terms and motifs in the pastoral speech refer beyond the pastoral milieu to the temple or cult.

The term αὐλή (John 10:1, 16), which is not frequently used within the context of shepherding, is a *terminus technicus* for the temple forecourt. In the majority of the evidence within the LXX, αὐλή denotes either the tabernacle forecourt or the temple forecourt, which in the Herodian temple is also called "the forecourt of the gentiles."[38] The terms θύρα and θυρωρός, which are difficult to place within the semantic structure of the pastoral milieu, also point to the temple environment.[39] Above all, the reference to the "door of the αὐλή" (10:1b, 2a) recalls the frequently mentioned doors or gates to the forecourt of the tabernacle or temple.[40] Furthermore, the verb ἀναβαίνω (10:1c) is not used often to describe the act of thieving,[41] but is a term classically used for pilgrimages and is used frequently in the Gospel of John for pilgrimage to Jerusalem for feasts.[42]

Against this background, the "sheep" in John 10 can be seen in a new light. When sheep are mentioned in the temple area or more precisely in the forecourt of the temple, these animals are being kept ready as sacrifices. If the mention of sheep as sacrificial animals activates among the readers the associative sphere of the cult, the handling of these sheep is to be particularly appreciated. The thief's behavior is depicted concretely in 10:9. He comes "to rob, to sacrifice, and to kill" (ἵνα κλέψῃ καὶ θύσῃ ἀπολέσῃ). Against the background of the cult, no special Johannine meaning needs to be constructed for the second term θύω.[43] Instead, "the proper and quite predominant meaning"[44] of "to sacrifice" can apply to 10:9 as well. The author here deliberately uses the cultic term to allude to the sacrifice of animals performed by those who have made the pilgrimage to Jerusalem for the feast (10:1: ἀναβαίνω). The good shepherd, however, leads the doomed sheep out of the outer court (10:3–4) and saves their lives (10:10).

Finally, the term ἁγιάζω (10:36), in the LXX as a rendering of the Hebrew קדשׁ, has an almost exclusively cultic meaning.[45] Instead of sanctifying the temple, as would be expected at the Feast of the Dedication of the temple, we read that Jesus himself was sanctified by the Father (10:36: ὃν ὁ πατὴρ ἡγίασεν καὶ ἀπέστειλεν εἰς τὸν κόσμον).[46] The theological profundity of this statement is revealed above all when one includes the broader horizon of the Gospel, which will be accomplished in the following.

John 10 in the Horizon of the Gospel's
Use of the Temple Metaphor

John 10 is closely woven into the overall narrative structure of the Gospel. On the one hand, this can be seen in the use of key terms that also play a major role in other parts of the Gospel or are striking because of their rarity.[47] On the other hand, it is also evident in the interconnection with other scenes on the narrative level, whereby the temple motif in particular will be brought into focus here.

From the very beginning, Jesus's public speaking and activity in the Gospel of John is repeatedly and deliberately localized in and around the temple (cf. 2:13–25; 5:1–18; 7; cf. 18:20). Frequently, this involves reports of disputes (especially between the Jews and Jesus) that show that ultimately it is not about the temple as a building, but about the "central religious symbol that holds the presence of God."[48] In my opinion, the narrative details of John 10 can also be placed in the series of temple disputes. Jesus's first and last appearance in the temple can be related to each other like an *inclusio*. During his first journey to Jerusalem, Jesus appears in the temple (2:13–25), and 10:22–24 reports Jesus's last appearance in the temple area, which ends with his exodus from the temple and the city (10:39–42). In 10:39, Jesus returns to his starting point (1:28).

In the following, this thesis of a direct relationship between the first and last temple scenes will be supported by linguistic and theological observations. The Synoptics report the scene known as the "cleansing of the temple" (John 2:13–25) within the context of the passion narrative (Mark 11:15–19 par.),[49] whereas John places it deliberately at the beginning of Jesus's public ministry and links it with the question of authority (cf. Mark 11:27–33 par.), as well as Jesus's statement about the future destruction of the temple during his trial (Mark 14:58 par.).[50]

While the synoptic narrative of the temple expulsion (Mark 11:15–19 par.) speaks only of moneychangers and those who were selling doves, John mentions repeatedly that Jesus drove out the sheep and cattle (τά τε πρόβατα καὶ τοὺς βόας, John 2:15).[51] This mention of the sheep is more than just a novelistic detail. Since it is hardly plausible historically that sheep and cattle were sold in the porticoes of the Herodian temple,[52] one must suspect that a theological meaning lies behind this addition, one that is probably related to the function of the animals mentioned within the temple cult. "Thus, with the description of the expulsion also of the large cattle the sacrificial cult is cut to the quick, since it became impossible without suitable sacrificial matter."[53]

The driving out of all sheep is encountered with the same terminology in 10:4a:

[14]καὶ εὗρεν ἐν τῷ ἱερῷ τοὺς πωλοῦντας βόας καὶ πρόβατα καὶ περιστερὰς καὶ τοὺς κερματιστὰς καθημένους, [15]καὶ ποιήσας φραγέλλιον ἐκ σχοινίων

πάντας ἐξέβαλεν ἐκ τοῦ ἱεροῦ τά τε πρόβατα καὶ τοὺς βόας, καὶ τῶν κολλυβιστῶν ἐξέχεεν τὸ κέρμα καὶ τὰς τραπέζας ἀνέτρεψεν

[14]And he found sitting in the temple the sellers of oxen, and sheep, and doves, and the changers. [15]And he made a scourge of cords, and drove them all out of the temple, even the sheep and the oxen: and the coins of the changers he poured out, and the tables he overturned. (2:14–15)

(τὰ πρόβατα) ὅταν τὰ ἴδια πάντα ἐκβάλῃ, ἔμπροσθεν αὐτῶν πορεύεται

When he has driven out all his own *sheep*, he goes before them. (10:4ab)

The forcible driving out of the sheep in John 10 is an unusual formulation for the driving out of livestock[54] and represents a rather disturbing duplication of the aforementioned leading out (ἐξάγει αὐτά, 10:3d). Furthermore, it creates dissonance with the image of the loving shepherd who leads by voice and on the basis of an intimate relationship. However, the mention of the driving out of the sheep from the temple gains a specific meaning if one recognizes in it a deliberate connection back to the temple cleansing scene in 2:14–15.

Against the context of the temple cleansing, Jesus leading out the sheep from the temple is enriched with symbolic profundity. The shepherd comes, drives out the sheep, and saves them from being offered as sacrifices (cf. 10:9–10). The thieves, for their part, put them to death as sacrifices (θύω, v. 10). The shepherd's commitment to protecting his sheep goes so far that he gives his own life. Within the broader context of the Gospel of John, one could even say that Jesus is himself sacrificed like a sheep (1:29, 35; 19:14).[55]

The movement mentioned on the level of the shepherd metaphor (the shepherd comes in, and the sheep go out of the courtyard) is also reflected narratively. Jesus goes from the temple forecourt (9:39–10:21) to the inside of the temple, where he is surrounded by the Jews (κυκλόω, 10:24), before he finally goes out of the temple,[56] and many—analogous to the sheep—follow him to the other place.

Furthermore, the discussion following Jesus's temple cleansing in 2:18–22 is revealing. Within the context, the Fourth Evangelist incorporates the Jesus logion from the synoptic tradition about tearing down and rebuilding of the temple (Mark 14:58 par.).[57] According to Mark, this "Tempellogion" is an accusation of false witnesses in the trial against Jesus. The majority of exegetes recognize it to be an authentic word of Jesus.[58] Through the contrast emphasized in Mark 14:58 between the "temple made with hands" (χειροποίητος) and the "temple not made with hands" (ἀχειροποίητος) erected by Jesus, Jesus's word stands in a widely attested Jewish interpretive tradition of Exodus 15:17b, which praises God as the sole builder of the eschatological temple.[59] When Jesus names himself as the builder of this temple, he proves himself "in all clarity as the personal representative of God's Zion reign, or as the Son . . . acting on behalf of the one God."[60] For Jostein Ådna, this logion "represents an outstanding expression of Jesus' messianic mission."[61]

In John 2:18–22, the Tempellogion appears in the context of a so-called Johannine misunderstanding. The introductory question asking for a σημεῖον, the literary-hermeneutical device of the misunderstanding,[62] as well as the concluding reader's comment with a post-Easter retrospective, indicate the importance the evangelist attaches to these verses. It functions like a hermeneutical key. What was conceptually contrasted in Mark 14:58 (χειροποίητος, ἀχειροποίητος) is scenically depicted in John. The temple built in forty-six years[63] is a "temple made with hands." Jesus, however, builds another, eschatological temple. While the evangelist leaves the resolution of many misunderstandings in the Gospel of John entirely to the reader, he obviously feels compelled to intervene and to clarify here. In the postscript of John 2:21–22, the evangelist identifies the temple promised by Jesus with the body of the risen Christ. Jesus is not only the builder of the new temple as in the synoptic tradition, but his own body is itself now identified with the temple (ναὸς τοῦ σώματος). Only after Easter are the readers of this Gospel able to understand the meaning of this metaphor. The resurrected Jesus himself is the new temple.[64]

If this clear metaphorical code is already set forth in the first temple scene within the Gospel, we can assume that John wants to provide his readers with a key to understanding additional temple metaphors within the Gospel.[65]

With the narratively staged temple image, the evangelist presents a metaphor of Christ in John 10 that proves to be the core of a network of metaphors running through the entire Gospel: "The revelation of Christ in the Gospel of John redefines the place of God's presence (cf. 1:1–18, 51; 2:18–20; 14:6, etc.) and God's worship (cf. 4:21–24) in critical distinction. . . . Jesus himself is *in persona* the 'new temple,' the place of the experience of God and of the true worship of God."[66] The next section will consider this christological dimension of the temple metaphor, with special attention to John 10.

The Function of Temple Christology in John

The narrative temple metaphor in John 10 can be placed in the series of temple scenes within the Gospel (2:13–25; 5:1–18; 7; etc.), and it brings the controversy at and around the temple to a preliminary conclusion and climax. The setting of Jesus's speeches in front of and in the temple shows once more that John consciously ties his theology to Jewish traditions. The temple is not generally devalued, but quite consciously introduced as the "house of the Father" (2:16). Only through Jesus's person, however, does the temple become what it is actually supposed to be, namely, the place of God's presence, of atonement, the source of living water, etc.[67] Through Jesus's presence, the temple is constituted anew as a place of God's presence.

This Johannine "temple Christology" must not be equated with a general critique of the cult, which resulted in the demand for the abolition of the temple, but it stands in a series of the evangelist's christological efforts to surpass and fulfill Jewish cult traditions and especially feasts.[68]

The evangelist's mention of the feast of Hanukkah (10:22) calls to mind the dedication of the Second Temple, but as Jesus walks around Solomon's portico (10:23), the evangelist ties the scene back to Solomon's First Temple as well. The historical consecrations of the temple, whether by Solomon (1 Kgs 8) or in the Hanukkah festival under Judas Maccabeus (1 Macc 4:52), are now contrasted with Jesus's sanctification by God himself (John 10:36, cf. 6:69; 17:9). The proclaimed proximity of Jesus to God is therefore—in contrast to Antiochus IV—not blasphemy, as Jesus's opponents think. God's glory no longer dwells (only) in the Jerusalem temple but has become visible in Christ as the "new temple" (2:21; cf. also 1:14). With this, John's "temple Christology," which was already laid out in other temple scenes, reaches its climax. God himself inaugurates the new temple.[69] God's presence is no longer bound to a certain place of worship (cf. 4:21), but to a certain person. In contrast to a general or even anti-Judaistic critique of the Jewish cult, John's emphasis in his temple theology is christological.[70] The temple as a place of God's presence is brought to its fulfillment by Jesus Christ.[71]

John's temple theology has unavoidable tendencies to devalue the Jerusalem temple. This is clear enough already in Jesus's act of "cleansing of the temple" (2:13–21), which not only has a reformational quality, but "already carries the germ of the end"[72] within itself. In that John reveals the temple "as ναός τοῦ σώματος Ἰησοῦ, as the body of the Risen One (2:21–22), the final exodus of God's presence and, thus, the loss of meaning, even to the point of the temple's nullity, is recognizable at an early stage."[73] That for the evangelist also the cult of sacrifice is specifically in view is already recognizable by his explicit mention of the sacrificial animals in the cleansing scene. Jesus casts the oxen and the sheep out of the temple (2:15), a formulation that the evangelist takes up again in 10:4a when the sheep are cast out of the courtyard. For the sheep, however, this is not an act of violence but a salvific act (10:9). By being driven out, they are ultimately saved from certain sacrificial death and are instead led to true life (10:10, 28). Jesus gives life to the sheep by paradoxically laying down his own life (10:11–18). Within the horizon of the entire Gospel, the reader is reminded of the lamb metaphor introduced already at Jesus's first appearance (1:29, 36[74]), which was used in particular as an interpretive key to Jesus's death.[75] While Jesus drives the sacrificial animals out of the (temple) courtyard (2:15; 10:4), he himself is led into the courtyard (cf. 18:15: εἰς τὴν αὐλήν) and finally slaughtered like the (Passover) lamb (19:14, 36).

Another implicit criticism of the sacrificial cult could be read out of John 10 regarding the exclusionary effect of the cult. Apparently there were circles that denied the blind access to the temple (2 Sam 5:8; 11Q19 XLV, 12–13[76]), which becomes especially significant when understanding John 10 against the background of the healing of the blind in John 9.[77] Even more significant might be the exodus from the temple or from the "court (of the gentiles)" in view of the fact that gentiles were not permitted to participate in the temple cult and certainly not allowed to enter the interior of the temple.[78] Jesus's exodus from the temple in John 10 therefore has primarily no (new, e.g., against Jews) exclusionary intention, but wishes to have an integrative effect, be it for the blind or for the sheep who are not of this court (10:16: ἃ οὐκ ἔστιν ἐκ τῆς αὐλῆς ταύτης). The flock is gathered in the risen Christ, who is the *one* shepherd and the new temple. The Christ-temple (2:21) permits no exclusion. With this in mind, the words about the door gain new meaning. The door of Christ not only leads out of the Jerusalem temple (10:7c), but also into salvation (10:9). Thereby the reader is already directed to a later I-am-word in which Jesus claims to be the only way to the Father (14:6). To reach God, therefore, no sacrificial cult is necessary, not even the Jerusalem temple. Christ himself is the new temple; according to John 10 he has been consecrated; he is the door to God that opens the way to heaven (1:51; cf. Gen 28:17).[79] Faithful discipleship and belonging to Jesus lead to salvation. The narrative conclusion of John 10 perhaps invites us to go a step further. By leaving the temple and going beyond the Jordan to an earlier place of baptism (John 10:40; cf. 1:28), Jesus is able to bring many to faith (10:42).

Conclusion

The narrative setting of John 10 (temple, temple dedication, exodus), its embedding in the overall narrative framework of the Gospel, and the semantic development of some motifs and terms on the figurative level (αὐλή, vv. 1, 16; ἐκβάλλω, v. 4; θύω, v. 9) allow the conclusion that the metaphorical code from the first temple scene (i.e., Jesus's body as the temple in 2:21) is taken up here in the last temple scene. Just as motifs of cleansing and sanctification are already traditionally two interrelated aspects of the temple dedication (e.g., 2 Chr 29–31; 1 Macc 4), so also it is natural that they would be present within the Gospel of John. John 2:13–25 and John 10 thus form an *inclusio* in which the evangelist connects the "cleansing of the temple" in John 2 with the consecration or sanctification of Jesus in John 10 (10:36) as the "new temple," thus surpassing the ἐγκαίνια (Hanukkah).[80] By means of the narrative, the readers encounter a depiction of Christ as the "new temple." According to John, Jesus himself is the place of God's presence, surpassing the Jerusalem temple and fulfilling its function (e.g., access to God in the sacrificial cult) christologically.

CHAPTER THREE

Christ Stopped at Ephraim (John 11:54)

Markus Bockmuehl

CHRIST STOPPED AT Eboli: *Cristo si è fermato a Eboli*. Set in Mussolini's Italy, Carlo Levi's (1902–1975) landmark memoir, like Francesco Rosi's 1979 movie of the same title, chronicles the internal exile of this anti-fascist, urbane Jewish doctor and artist from Turin. In 1935, he spent a year among remote, bone-crushingly poor and culturally desolate southern villages of what is now the province of Basilicata. So poor and so desolate, indeed, that it seemed even the coming of Christ had passed them by. History itself never traveled beyond the provincial town of Eboli—into a land where, "as is the way with symbols," Christ's sojourn and absence are above all literal.[1] And yet, amidst the grim struggles of peasants abandoned by the bourgeoisie and a pathetically ineffectual church, Levi himself ends up bridging this gulf as a physician to the poor—his existentialist humanism almost hinting at traces of a substitute messianic presence.[2]

Christ also stopped for a time at Ephraim, almost certainly as a matter of historical fact: "Therefore Jesus no longer moved about publicly among the people of Judea. Instead he withdrew to a region near the wilderness, to a village called Ephraim, where he stayed with his disciples."[3] Similarities between these two temporary sojourns are evocative, even if in some ways antithetical: Carlo Levi's stay turns on the idea of Christ himself having forsaken the hinterland, while in the latter Christ visits it, Levi-like, for refuge—and, as we shall see, according to later legend, even for a permanent miracle.

In John's Gospel, Christ pauses for a period of refuge at a time of acute danger to his life. Following turbulent events after raising Lazarus at Bethany, Jesus quits the immediate neighborhood of Jerusalem to draw breath, away from any limelight, in the obscure "city" (πόλις) of Ephraim.[4]

This is a move that echoes previous escapes to mountains, the Jordan valley, and elsewhere.[5] Jesus, the evangelist tells us, "remained" (ἔμεινεν) or, as many early manuscripts have it, "spent time" (διέτριβεν) at Ephraim with the disciples.[6] He stayed for an unspecified period of possibly several months,[7] before returning once more to Bethany in time for his final Passover (12:1).

But why this place and what transpires there during this time of internal exile? John discloses nothing—except that the place is selected because Jesus's life is in danger and he can no longer circulate openly in public (11:53–54). Jesus retreats into messianic secrecy and safety.

The following argument examines the meaning of John 11:54 first in relation to a little-noted change in William Wrede's view of the "Messianic Secret" in Mark and John and of the historical possibility of messianic consciousness in the life of Jesus. Turning from there to christological secrecy in John's Gospel more generally, we finally consider geographic, archaeological, religious, and reception-historical dimensions of the withdrawal to Ephraim, before suggesting conclusions for its interpretation.

Re-Wreding the Messianic Secret?

In the present century, Johannine critics have been affirming the Fourth Evangelist's close knowledge of Mark with increasing confidence for almost as long as their predecessors once denied it with equally poised certainty among the assured results of scholarship.[8] One possible correlation concerns the scholarly trope known as the "Messianic Secret," which has its epicenter in the Gospel of Mark. From the start, Mark's demons repeatedly recognize Jesus as Messiah, but he warns them to remain silent about him[9] and similarly prohibits publicity around his healing miracles.[10] Even the disciples are included in such instructions to silence about his identity.[11] This is perhaps in part because, unlike the demons, they are cast as roundly uncomprehending, despite benefiting from Jesus's private instruction on matters like the kingdom parables, the transfiguration, or the coming messianic birth pangs.[12]

Generations of students have rightly imbibed these facts as crucial to Mark's Gospel. More specifically, they have been taught to associate the study of this "Messianic Secret" explicitly with William Wrede's (1859–1906) work of that title from 1901.[13] Jesus himself, Wrede explains there, expressed no messianic aspirations during his lifetime. It was a claim his followers first applied to the risen Jesus, and only then gradually transferred back to his earthly life in their narratives about him. Jesus's messianic identity was never more than "proleptic."[14]

Textbooks have long since declared Wrede's book comprehensively mistaken or at least in need of substantial correction and greater nuance. At the same time, his definitive views on the subject are still widely thought to be those of his 1901 book, whose influence in Anglophone scholarship was greatly prolonged by the seventy-year delay of its English translation. Standard treatments in English continue to assume as unproblematic that Wrede's Jesus never claimed messianic identity or secrecy during his lifetime and did not "become" Messiah until after the resurrection: "Only in the later tradition, according to Wrede, did the idea arise that Jesus was Messiah during his lifetime. In Wrede's opinion, the tradition could not have developed in this way if Jesus had actually claimed to be the Messiah."[15]

Such textbook assurances notwithstanding, it has been known for over two decades that Wrede's famous book did *not* in fact represent his last thought on the subject. He fully appreciated that his 1901 viewpoint would be regarded as "radical."[16] And yet, by the time he wrote to his former teacher and benefactor Adolf von Harnack on January 2, 1905, he had changed his mind about the likelihood that Jesus had a messianic self-consciousness: "I am more inclined than before to believe that Jesus regarded himself as chosen to be the Messiah."[17] To be sure, he continued to regard Mark as a creative redactor rather than a historically reliable source. He still doubted that Jesus could have been regarded as "Son of God" even on Harnack's historically evaporated understanding[18] and denied that Paul was in any meaningful sense Jesus's interpreter or "continuer" (*Fortsetzer*).[19] Nevertheless, Wrede now considered it historically likely that Jesus did after all harbor a messianic claim or aspiration. But in that case, might this carry pragmatic and equally historical repercussions for the concern about secrecy? Rather than being reduced to a literary and apologetic counsel of convenience, the Messianic Secret lays claim to the realm of historic plausibility in the life of Jesus himself.

John's Messiah in Secret

What does all this entail for John's Gospel? Like Mark (1:1, 11), John makes the messianic identity of Jesus clear from the very first chapter—and he famously associates that identity throughout with strikingly exalted christological claims. What sense might it make, therefore, to speak of a Messianic Secret in John? Wrede himself, for one, thought that the Messianic Secret also had a Johannine dimension. Although he accepted no substantive links to Markan or Synoptic themes, his programmatic volume regards both Gospels as distant from "the real life of Jesus," and he compared John's treatment to what one might see in applying a large magnifying glass to Mark's composition.[20] (Significantly for our purposes, he included no comment on John 11:54.[21]) Others have since explored aspects of a possible Johannine Secret more fully, some finding in it unambiguous proof of dependence on Mark,[22] or a clear reader-response driven case that the real "truth" and message is not just the Son so much as the medium—the Fourth Gospel—itself.[23]

Purely at the textual level, there is plenty of Johannine emphasis on the hiddenness of Jesus. The world did not perceive him and his own did not accept him (1:10–11). The Messiah is present but unknown, so that the Baptist's mission is to allow him to be revealed to Israel (1:26, 29, 31). Even as Word made flesh (1:14), he evidently still chooses to reveal his glory only at particular signal moments (2:11; cf. 17:24): his revelatory miracle at Cana remains discreet for the benefit apparently only of his disciples (2:11). Jesus then visits Jerusalem for the Passover and performs signs, but without "entrusting himself" to the people (2:24). The fact that Nicodemus comes by night (3:2) evidently suits both parties. It seems this "teacher in Israel" is not himself a disciple; that question resurfaces later in the Gospel with Joseph of Arimathea, who is one only in secret (κεκρυμμένος, 19:38).

Jesus's recurrent avoidance of public prominence has the effect of keeping important aspects of his true identity hidden from the comprehension even of the disciples, as also in Mark. Though they may have "seen his glory" and "believed" in him at Cana, they never seem to understand the source of his true nourishment (4:32–33), his heavenly destination, or his way to the Father (14:4–8).

Famously, after feeding the five thousand, Jesus "again" flees alone to a mountain explicitly to avoid a messianic acclamation by force (6:15).[24] Ancient scribes appreciated the dramatic nature of the narrative. Codex Sinaiticus adds that this was not an excursion but an escape (φεύγει not ἀνεχώρησεν), while Codex Bezae draws intertextually on Mark 6:46 to suggest its purpose was for prayer (κἀκεῖ προσηύχετο). Surprisingly, but perhaps for reasons to which we return below, the need for such evasive isolation is short-lived: John's Jesus shuns the limelight only until the morning (τῇ ἐπαύριον, John 6:22).

Themes of both secrecy and disclosure intensify considerably in chapter 7. Having at first rebuffed his brothers' encouragement to reveal himself publicly at the Festival of Sukkot (7:2–9), Jesus nevertheless travels to Jerusalem "secretly" or perhaps "as if in secret" ([ὡς] ἐν κρυπτῷ, 7:10).[25] For the first half of the festival, he is nowhere to be seen (7:14), but after that he emerges to speak confidently in public (παρρησίᾳ), thereby provoking the question of his messianic identity (7:25–31). The crowds briefly muse about what an improbably Galilean messiah could possibly mean by "going away"—perhaps to the Greek-speaking diaspora (7:35; cf. 12:20) where they cannot find him (7:25–42; cf. 8:21–22)? All in all, it does seem that for all his proclamation and striking self-identifications, John's Messiah at the same time remains hidden in several epistemologically decisive respects. It is not that he is actively trying to conceal his identity, as in Mark; but finding him is decidedly a matter of divine gift rather than of human quest or resolve: "This is why I said to you that no one is able to come to me unless it has been given to them from the Father" (6:65; cf. 8:19). John, much like Mark and Matthew, goes on to appeal to Isaiah in attributing the people's incomprehension to the fact that God has actively blinded them.[26]

Part of what is hidden and incomprehensible about the Johannine Messiah is evidently his preexistence. At no point throughout the Gospel do his own people—from the disciples to "the Jews"—receive him as the coeternal Word (1:10–11). They cannot recognize or accept that it was he whom Abraham rejoiced to see at Mamre (8:53, 56–58) and whom Isaiah saw in the temple (12:41). His identity as Messiah is concealed from them. In relation to the Pharisees, this is either because he does not observe the Sabbath according to their halakic prescription (9:16; cf. 5:16, 18; 7:22–23), or because he appears to them a sinner (9:24–32), or else demon-possessed and mad (10:20–21). The key question of whether or how this obscure and controversial Jesus could possibly be the Messiah is not only implicit throughout the text but also repeatedly made explicit, by no means always in a hostile fashion.[27]

It is shortly before the beginning of the passion narrative, following the raising of Lazarus at Bethany and the decision of the Sanhedrin (11:45–50), that Jesus retreats to Ephraim (11:54)—the episode that will occupy us more fully below. Even after returning from there, further open controversy resumes about a Messiah who "must be lifted up" (12:34; cf. 3:14; 8:28)—and once again this leads Jesus to disappear into hiding (12:36).

This hiddenness of the Messiah is repeatedly questioned in the Gospel, and not only by his brothers. Even among the Twelve, Judas "not Iscariot" (possibly Thaddeus?[28]) evidently finds the ministry's seeming hide-and-seek reluctance a little trying, not to say Pythonesque: "Why do you intend to show yourself to us and not to the world?" (14:22).

And yet, this is only ever one pole of a key Johannine dialectic. Jesus in fact repeatedly alternates between concealment and public confession. The Fourth Gospel tracks a parallel but contrary narrative of disclosure in which Jesus, having previously acted in secret (ἐν κρυπτῷ, 7:4, 26; cf. 11:54) or spoken "in figures" (ἐν παροιμίαις, 16:25, 29; cf. 10:24; 11:14), will now or soon speak plainly and openly (παρρησίᾳ, 16:25, 29; cf. 7:4, 26; 18:20). Indeed, for our purposes it seems particularly important to note the frequency with which John's story closely sequences secrecy and withdrawal, with Jesus appearing decisively in public to declare or manifest the glory of God. Chapters 6 and 7, 11 and 12 are among the more obvious examples, but there are others. Secrecy and withdrawal do not compromise but accentuate and reinforce the public claims of divine sonship.

Marianne Meye Thompson rightly draws attention to the ambivalent narrative contours of this "Hidden Messiah" dynamic: "John contrasts speaking 'openly' (or with *parrēsia*) and speaking figuratively (10:24; 11:14; . . . 16:25, 29), characterizes Jesus as speaking publicly and openly (7:26; 18:20), and indicates that at times Jesus was not able to work publicly (11:54) or that people were unable to speak publicly about him (7:4, 13) or were fearful of doing so. When Jesus does not work or speak with *parrēsia*, publicly or openly, he is waiting for 'his hour' to arrive or refusing to seek his own honor."[29] At the same time, the Gospel never compromises Jesus's claim to have spoken his message openly and for all to hear: "Jesus' claim to have spoken openly, in the synagogue and temple, and to have said nothing 'in secret' does not include his lengthy final discourse to his disciples. But his claims about his own mission from God and his call to believe have been laid out repeatedly in public discourse; these are indeed the substance of the written Gospel."[30]

All in all, then, the Fourth Evangelist clearly unfolds his own version of a Messianic Secret—even if here it is more about his divine sonship. To be sure, John's secret is never exactly Delphic in its opacity; nor does his Jesus ever emulate Epicurus's counsel to "live obscurely" (λάθε βιώσας[31]). Unlike in Mark, one gets no sense of deliberate obscurity over his teaching. As Morna Hooker suggests, the difference is that in John, "The glory has been revealed, but men have been blind. . . . The veil in John is on the human side."[32] That veil covers even the disciples. The only exceptions are John the Baptist and the Samaritan woman's converted compatriots (e.g., 1:33; 4:39–42).[33] John's Jesus imposes no secrecy on his messianic identity; instead, the focus is on the inability to comprehend who he is as Son of Man and Son of God. And yet, in this way, and for different reasons, both Mark and John come to share the motif of christological hiddenness.

At the same time, for John and perhaps also for Mark, there is an almost gnomic, prudential sense that silence and concealment allow a potential Messiah to bide his time and choose his moment without his agenda being hijacked or alienated. Notwithstanding some continued scholarly posturing by Wrede's heirs and successors,[34] it is this vocational purpose that links messianic hiddenness at the literary and theological level quite plausibly to its social and political context in the lifetime of Jesus, as we now know Wrede himself came to see late in life. In fact, it reflects key aspects of Jewish messianic expectation from antiquity to the present day.[35]

Ephraim

The Ephraim episode certainly feeds into such a narrative of epistemic concealment and disclosure, representing a culminating episode of messianic secrecy on the threshold of the passion week and Jesus's final Passover visit to Jerusalem. But does this geographic location signify anything more than a symbolic cipher or punctuation in the narrative?

Even its location remains sufficiently shadowy to prevent any uncontested archaeological or topographical identification. Josephus has Vespasian's troops sweep it up in the spring of 69 CE, seemingly on an afternoon's stroll through the pleasant Judean hill country from Caesarea on their way to Jerusalem— and shortly before Vespasian's elevation to higher duties in Rome. The legion marches south through the toparchies of Gophna and Acrabattene, installing garrisons along the way in the apparently adjacent "small cities" of Bethel (?) and Ephraim, Βήθηγά τε καὶ Ἐφραὶμ πολίχνια (*J.W.* 4.551).[36] A few months later, interestingly, that region's temperate climate and secure environment would encourage Titus to have Jewish aristocratic refugees from the siege of the capital withdraw (ἀνεχώρουν, cf. John 11:54) from Jerusalem to the small city (πολίχνιον) of Gophna in order to wait out the end of the war in complete safety (μετὰ πάσης ἀσφαλείας, *J.W.* 6.115–116).

Josephus thus locates Ephraim a little under twenty kilometers from Jerusalem's Damascus Gate as the crow flies, but its precise coordinates remain disputed. There is a good *prima facie* case to associate it with the "district (nome) of Aphairema," which both 1 Maccabees and Josephus describe as having been transferred from Samaria to the territory of Judea by Demetrius II Nicator (145–141 BCE).[37] That episode plausibly accounts for a measure of ambiguity in the sources between "Aphairema" the district and Ephraim the city, on the border of the biblical territory of Benjamin.[38]

More promisingly, perhaps, Eusebius's *Onomasticon* (ca. 320) identifies Ephraim as a "village" rather than a city in his day (νῦν ἐστι κώμη), but nevertheless as the largest village near the northern administrative border of the district of Roman Aelia (i.e., Jerusalem). He links it to Ephron (Josh 15:9) or Aphra (Josh 18:23), five Roman "milestones" due east of Bethel and twenty north of Jerusalem.[39] Epiphanius (ca. 315–403) is in broad agreement with this topography, although evidently dependent on Eusebius and perhaps characteristically a little more opaque. He identifies Haphra (Ophra?) in Benjamin or Ephraim "five miles East of Bethel" as a "large village" and former city. It is for Epiphanius the place to which Jesus flees in both John 6:15 and 11:54, and he goes on to report that when Jesus withdrew to "the city of Ephraim" in 11:54, he performed the miracle of permanently expelling all snakes and reptiles from the territory of the town.[40] The sixth-century Madaba Map, likewise, implies a compatible geolocation of Ephraim northeast of Bethel (Luz) and Rimmon.[41]

On the strength of this collective evidence, even if to date for no compelling archaeological reasons, most modern scholars have confidently identified Ephraim/Aphra with modern et-Taybeh الطيبة, one of the Holy Land's last remaining Christian villages,[42] nineteen kilometers north of Jerusalem and seven kilometers northeast of Beitin (ancient Bethel).[43] Although fuller excavations have yet to be carried out, extant remains include a large Byzantine church of Saint George, plausibly suggesting a pilgrimage site.[44] The possibly gradual change of name from ʿAphra to et-Taybeh ("good" or "kind") could be a medieval Islamic development intended to avoid associations of ʿAphra with Arabic *ʿafrit* (عفريت "demon")—a euphemistic substitute that is also historically attested for at least one of the several other Middle Eastern villages called ʿAphra or et-Taybeh.[45]

This identification has much to be said for it and has at times approached the status of a consensus, although there have always been dissenting voices. Among the most influential of the latter has long been that of W. F. Albright, who favored Khirbet Samiyeh/Khirbet Marjameh, located five kilometers northeast of Taybeh at ʿAin Samiyeh.[46] Its topography, archaeology, and greater distance from Bethel make it a less likely candidate.

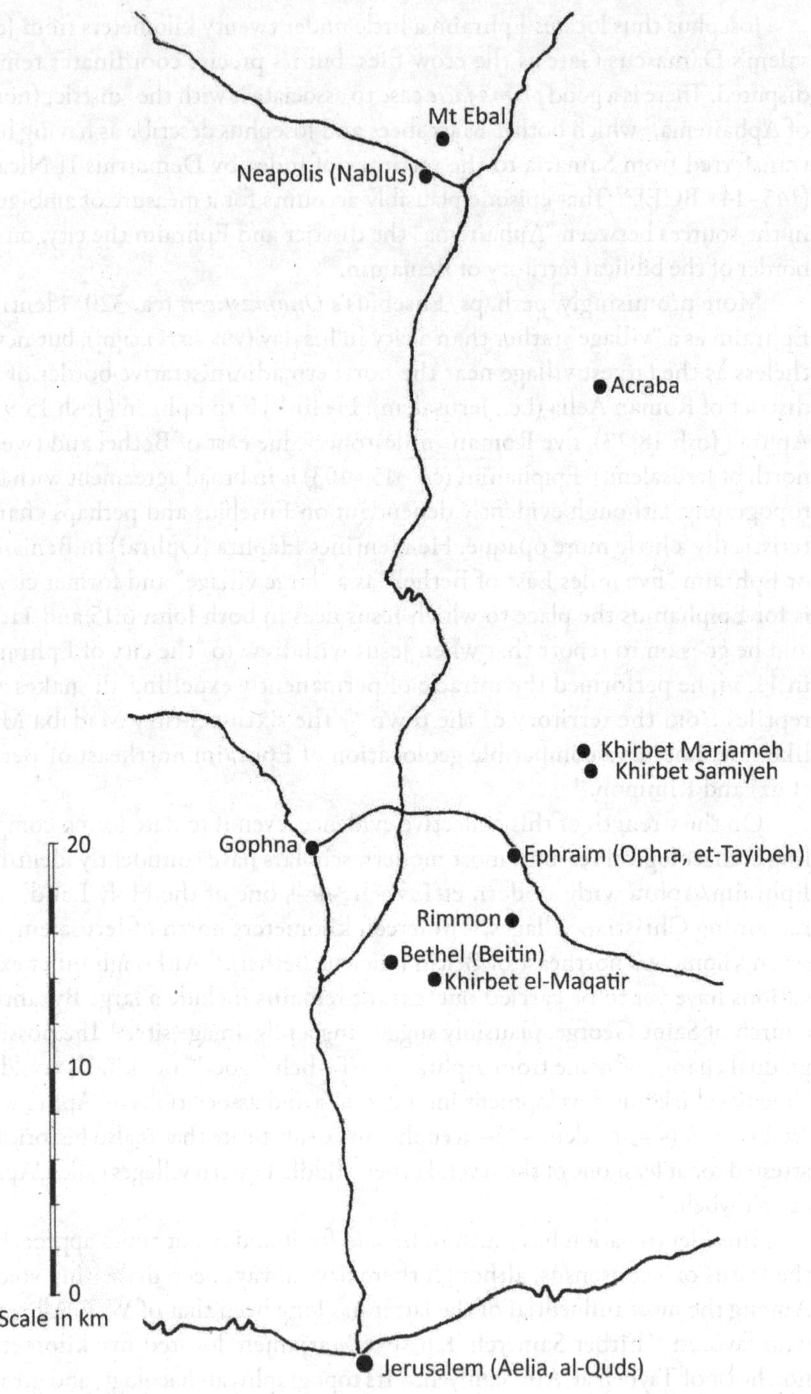

Central Palestine in the First Century: Some Key Ancient and Contemporary Place Names.

Others have in recent years advocated for Khirbet el-Maqatir (خربة المقاطير), an interesting fortified site adjacent to the modern Highway 60 from Ramallah to Nablus in the western outskirts of the town of Deir Dibwan and opposite the Israeli "outpost" of Giv'at Asaf, one-and-a-half kilometers southeast of Beitin and 15 km north of Jerusalem, and thus also in the neighborhood identified by Josephus and others.[47] It appears to be the only walled settlement in the vicinity, which might make it eligible as a "city."

El-Maqatir goes back to the Bronze Age, but was abandoned during the exile and only rebuilt by the Hasmoneans around 100 BCE, with subsequent restorations following earthquakes in 64 and 31 BCE.[48] The Roman-era defensive settlement benefited from strong fortifications, including a surprisingly large tower,[49] walls, and an elaborate system of subterranean passages, caves, and cisterns.[50] Underground caves yielded the remains of seven women and a boy who had hidden there but were killed by the Romans in the year 69,[51] which is also the latest date of the otherwise well-attested coins from the First Revolt.[52] Coinage from Tyre, from the Emperor Trajan and from Year 3 of the Bar Kokhba revolt (i.e., 134–135) might imply the site's temporary revival and reengagement in the Jewish national cause. During the Byzantine period, the site was home to a monastery.[53] Excavators also turned up three *miqva'ot* (ritual immersion baths) in a small area along with unusually high proportions of late Second Temple stoneware,[54] suggesting a notable degree of Jewish observance.[55]

The evidence continues to favor et-Taybeh. El-Maqatir's proximity and location southeast rather than northeast of Bethel contradict the evidence of Eusebius, Epiphanius, and the Madaba Map. Its archaeological footprint might seem to question even the diminutive πολίχνιον for what would have to be an almost implausibly "small city"—particularly given Josephus's deliberate objection in the same context to minor villages *falsely* considered small cities (ψευδοπολίχνιον, *J.W.* 4.552: Caphethra). Unlike Taybeh with its view of the Jordan valley, el-Maqatir is also not self-evidently "near the wilderness" (John 11:54) or a significant point of reference for Vespasian's main conquests en route to Jerusalem.

Origen and the Rabbis on the Meaning of Ephraim

Early readers did not always know what to make of John 11:54, although along with similar passages, it was repeatedly cited to justify both flight from persecution and desert monasticism as something the Lord himself "both taught and practiced."[56]

Origen's commentary on John may here serve to illustrate the preferred patristic approach of characterizing Christ's withdrawal as exemplary: this is what Jesus meant by saying, "If they persecute you in one city, flee to another" (Matt 10:23).[57] By this teaching, Origen insists, the Word wants to prevent us from rushing hastily and irrationally into martyrdom.[58] Cyril of Alexandria follows this reading: in John 11:54, Jesus teaches us "to yield before the fever pitch of those who are angry and not to thrust ourselves into danger, not even when it is for the sake of the truth. . . . When we are overtaken by dangers, we should stand firm, but when they are coming, we should step out of the way because of the uncertainty of the outcome."[59]

Interestingly for our purposes, Origen then explicitly compares this retreat to Ephraim with the Messianic Secret in Matthew. Although he gives no impression of close geographic knowledge, he insists that "this is like what is written in Matthew"[60] about the Messiah's withdrawal from Judea to begin his ministry in the Galilean territory of Naphtali and Zebulon (4:12–13). Origen similarly draws a link with Jesus's retreat to the garden in the Kidron valley that ends in his arrest—a point he finds himself defending elsewhere against the charge of Celsus's Jew that Jesus was caught "while trying to hide and escape most disgracefully."[61] In more problematically anagogical terms, Origen insists that Christ no longer walks openly among the Jews "because the Word of God is not among the Jews."[62] Similar replacement rhetoric leads Origen to explain that the word "Ephraim" etymologically denotes the "fruitfulness" of the gentiles as the younger brother. In his homilies on Joshua, Jeremiah and the Psalms, Origen concedes that Ephraim repented from great sin in failing to cast out the Canaanites from their midst and in dividing the kingdom so that Samaria became emblematic for all schism and heresy.[63] But just as Manasseh is passed over and left behind in Ephraim's favor (Gen 48:13–20), so now the latter's fruitful harvest has been gathered and continues in place of the forgotten elder people. Jesus "remains" with his people in Ephraim, i.e., fruitfulness, to the present day.[64]

Writing a little over a century later, St. Ephrem the Syrian further develops the unexpected blessing of Ephraim in two hymns about the city that bears his name in John 11:54. Jacob figuratively crossed his arms to favor the younger brother Ephraim over the older Manasseh (Gen 48:13–14). So also the Messiah embraced the mystery of the cross when he fled Judea's hostile leaders to shelter first as an infant in Egypt (where Ephraim was born of a pagan mother) and then before his final Passover in the supposedly non-Jewish (!) city of Ephraim. Ephrem finally declares that city's numerical value by *gematria* to equal the sum of "cross" and "crucified."[65]

Rabbinic literature might have been expected to contribute geographic or sociocultural insight on its own, but it appears surprisingly silent about the city of Ephraim.[66]

That said, one other intriguing, admittedly tangential and non-geographic, connection does merit acknowledgement, even if it has little or no direct bearing on John 11:54. The rabbis do link the Messiah to the name Ephraim. He himself is repeatedly known as Ephraim or Messiah ben Ephraim, or Messiah ben Joseph, who is put to death before the coming of Messiah ben David (e.g., b. Sukkah 52a–b, citing Zech 2:3 and 12:10; cf. y. Sukkah 5:2, 23b),[67] perhaps in battle against God's enemies.[68] The Messiahs of David and Ephraim will collaborate like Moses and Aaron in achieving Israel's redemption.[69] More controversially, some have thought Messiah ben Ephraim's suffering or death to carry an atoning function, possibly even in pre-Christian texts.[70] Joseph Heinemann and others suggested a much-debated, specifically second century connection between the suffering and dying Messiah ben Ephraim and the defeat of Bar Kokhba.[71] And particularly in the ninth-century homiletical midrash Pesiqta Rabbati, some scholars have in recent years suspected a distinct influence of Christian messianism. In a view with some surprising similarities to that of Ephrem, the homilist here engages a Messiah whose name is Ephraim, who stands in a special relationship to God, is the son of Joseph, humbly ministers to the meek and calls disciples, is despised and suffers on Israel's behalf, returns from heaven as judge, and promises salvation and the resurrection of the dead.[72]

Concluding Observations

In John 11:54, Jesus withdraws from threats and conflict in Jerusalem to the quietness and security of Ephraim. John's Jesus, like Mark's, operates in a narrative involving both hiddenness and (continual or eventual) public disclosure around his true identity—a christological or messianic "secret." Far from merely "schematic," as Bultmann thought,[73] John 11:54 develops a theme distinctively located in the life of Jesus, and which both evangelists develop for specific literary and theological aims—Mark focusing on the Messiah, John on the preexistent Son of God. Just as William Wrede, the Messianic Secret's archevangelist, eventually came to accept that messianic consciousness and its corollaries have their place in the life of Jesus of Nazareth, so we have inquired here into the historical locus of John 11:54.

Regardless of whether the small "city" of Ephraim should be located at modern Taybeh, it served Jesus's purpose in providing a refuge among friends at a modest but safe distance from Jerusalem, perhaps in a markedly observant Jewish context and free from threats of Roman and high priestly harassment or arrest. As throughout the Fourth Gospel, Jesus's retreat from controversy or hostility is temporary and deliberate, facilitating reflection, prayer, and renewal for the task he has come to fulfill.[74] Early Christian readers saw this retreat from conflict and persecution as literally exemplary as well as symbolic, and popular legend came to associate his salvific presence in Ephraim with the miraculous expulsion of serpents from its territory. The nearby wilderness beckoned, but Jerusalem's Mount of Olives remained constantly visible on the distant horizon, both physically and metaphorically—and, thereby, the vocation of his coming "hour" (12:23). This is why Christ stopped at Ephraim.

CHAPTER FOUR

How Yahweh Finds Embodiment in John's Jesus

John Goldingay

THE *LOGOS* WAS there at the beginning, at creation, and before creation (John 1:1). If you were philosophically knowledgeable and you heard John refer to the *logos*, you might take him to be speaking of a rational principle immanent in the world. John's subsequent references to God's *logos* or Jesus's *logos*, however, would rather suggest that you should think of the prophetic word of God or of Jesus's message,[1] and if you had read Acts, you might think of the message, the *logos*, about Jesus. One way or another, though, this is a *logos* that goes back to the beginning, and it is then a *logos* that "became flesh" and was "full of grace and truth" (1:14). Thus "the law was given through Moses—grace and truth came about through Jesus Messiah" (1:17).[2]

That statement should seem one of the more eyebrow-raising ones in this eyebrow-raising Gospel. It would surely be a statement to make its Jewish or God-fearing listeners think, because if they have been listening to the Torah, the Prophets, and the Writings over the years, they will know that grace and truth were characteristics that Yahweh claimed in speaking to Moses at Sinai, and that the rest of these Scriptures incorporate multiple reaffirmations of that description. At Sinai, Yahweh describes himself more completely as "God compassionate and gracious, long-tempered and big in commitment and truth" (Exod 34:6). There would be nothing to raise Moses's eyebrows in that statement because it describes the way Yahweh has been behaving towards the Israelites in Exodus 32–33.

Although the Scriptures do many times take up those words in Yahweh's self-revelation in Exodus 34:6 (e.g., Neh 9:17; Pss 86:15; 103:8; 145:8; Joel 2:13; Jonah 4:2), they much more often take up an equivalent to John's more succinct phrase "grace and truth." The equivalent Hebrew phrase, *ḥesed wā'ĕmet*, often features in English translations as "steadfast love and faithfulness" (e.g., Gen 24:27; 32:10[11]; 2 Sam 2:6; 15:20; 1 Kgs 3:6; Pss 25:10; 40:10–11[11–12]; 57:3, 10[4, 11]; 61:7[8]; 86:15; 89:14[15]; 115:1; 138:2). "Faithfulness" translates *'ĕmet*, which denotes truth in the sense of truthfulness. "Steadfast love" is more complicated, as is suggested by the varying English translations of the Hebrew word,

---

For Marianne, with appreciation.

hesed. Constant love, loving kindness, kindness, mercy, or simply love are all attempts to translate *hesed*. It denotes the commitment that someone shows when they have no reason to make a commitment (so it overlaps with grace, John's word) or when the person to whom they show it has forfeited all right to it (so it overlaps with *mercy*, the Septuagint's word). In my view "commitment" is the nearest English equivalent. But given that John never refers to mercy, and that "grace" features prominently in Christian parlance,[3] "grace and truth" is a fair equivalent of *hesed wā'ĕmet*. It does deserve noting that as well as never referring to mercy, only in 1:14–17 does John refer to grace, though he often talks about truth (e.g., 8:32; 14:6; 17:17). He prefers to speak about love (e.g., 3:16; 13:1; 15:9), light (1:4–9; 8:12; 9:5), and judgment (!) (5:22; 9:39; 12:31). In words, then, the Scriptures and the Gospel differ. But in substance, they compare.

And steadfast love and faithfulness or commitment and truthfulness or grace and truth do sum up the character of Yahweh. To say that the *logos* became flesh, and as such was full of grace and truth, is therefore to say that the Jesus who had become flesh was someone who was like Yahweh in his essential nature.

Now Jesus can issue the challenge or rebuke, "You people search the Scriptures . . . and they testify about me" (5:39). Occasionally they testify about him by promising the coming of a new David (we will consider John 10 in due course), but John's opening paragraphs point in a different direction for this testimony. Those opening paragraphs invite his readers to see Jesus not as a new David but as the embodiment of God, of the God of Israel, of God as Israel's Scriptures speak of him. And the Scriptures testify more widely and deeply of Jesus in their talk about Yahweh than they do in their talk about David. While Jesus made a point of distinguishing himself from the Father, he also declared that the Father was in him (10:38). People who saw him saw the one who sent him (12:45). They saw the Father (14:9). His accusers who said he was implying that he was equal to God (5:18) were onto something. In retrospect, his followers realized that he was indeed the embodiment of God. At the time, they had not realized that "the arm of the Lord [had] been revealed" in him (12:38). But it had been. As he himself puts it a page later, it is in the process that would lead to his death that "God has been glorified in him" (13:31).

If we start, then, from the fact that Jesus is the embodiment of the God who is grace and truth, that he is the Son of God, that he and the Father are one, it should enable us both to see things about Jesus and to see things about that God, about Yahweh. We will not be surprised to find that there are things that the scriptural account of Yahweh helps us to see about John's Jesus, and that there are things that John's account of Jesus enables us to see in the scriptural account of Yahweh. To put it another way, one can approach John and the Scriptures in an intertextual fashion. There may be only a little by way of the intertextuality that spots allusions to the Scriptures in John (once again, John 10 will be a standout example). But there will be more of the kind of intertextuality that perceives things such as neither the Scriptures nor John were conscious of, but perceives things about Yahweh and about Jesus through setting the Scriptures and John alongside each other.

So how does John's Jesus show himself as like Yahweh? We will approach this question by considering what Yahweh is like as the God of grace and truth. First, Israel's story is, all the way through, a story of God's grace and truth. Second, this story is then the context for accounts in the Torah in which God expresses his grace and truth in laying down his expectations of his people's relationship with him in worship and everyday life, expectations that express his vision for their life but also make allowance for their stubbornness. That is an expression of grace and truth, too. Third, so is his speaking through prophets. Through them he directly confronts his people with warnings about where their stubbornness will lead, and with promises about where his grace will lead. Fourth, in the Psalms his grace and truth find expression in his openness to his people's protests about their experience as well as their enthusiasm for his generosity and championing.

To that portrait of grace and truth, at each point we may juxtapose what John's Jesus is like.

Working and Not Giving Up

First, running through and fundamental to the scriptural story is the fact that Yahweh was committed to Israel. It is key to the framework of the Scriptures. It is expounded from the beginning in the Torah and the Former Prophets, and it is reaffirmed at the end in the works that close the Writings in the usual Jewish order, Ezra, Nehemiah, and Chronicles. The Scriptures do start with Yahweh as the creator of the entire world, but they focus on Yahweh's involvement with Israel. He initiated that involvement with Israel's ancestors, made promises to them of increase and a land and blessing, and fulfilled those promises. Israel's response to him was at best patchy, and he thus found himself in an up-and-down relationship with them that made no progress through their story, from Abraham and Sarah through Moses and Joshua, Saul and David, Hezekiah and Josiah, Joshua and Zerubbabel, Ezra and Nehemiah. Eventually the story stops rather than finishes, as if there could have been another series of the drama, but another series did not get made.

How does John's Jesus embody this Yahweh? John begins with creation, like the Torah, with that midrash about the *logos*, asserting not only that the *logos* was with God at the beginning but that that the *logos was* God (1:1). But like the Torah, John soon leaves creation behind, to focus on Jesus's relationship with the Jewish people.

Ironically, John has the reputation for being the most anti-Judaic of the Gospels,[4] but John's Jesus comes to be revealed to Israel (1:31). "Come and see," he says to the Jewish Andrew and Peter, "Follow me," he says to Jewish Philip, and "truly an Israelite," he says to his brother Nathanael: "You will see greater things" (1:39, 43, 47, 50). "Do you want to be made well," he asks a disabled Jew, and then tells him he can walk (5:5–9). He takes pity on five thousand Jewish people and feeds them, then urges them to come to him for real food, based on the fact that they can all be taught by God (6:45; cf. Isa 54:13). As Jews, they can know the truth and find that it makes them free (John 8:32). As long as he is in the world, he is the light of the world (9:5)—the Jewish world. When he prays out loud to the Father as he bids Lazarus to come out of his tomb, he does so in order that the Jewish crowd may believe that God sent him, and many of them do (11:41–45; cf. 12:11, 17).

From the beginning, however, interwoven with this demonstration of grace and truth to Jewish people is a confrontational stance against Jewish people, such as an individual Jew like poor, clueless Nicodemus (3:1–10) and "the Jews" who oppose Jesus (e.g., 5:16–18). While there are many Jews who come to believe in him because he bids Lazarus to come out from the tomb and Lazarus does, some of the Jews who are there go to tell the Pharisees (11:46). Apparently, it is not so that they will also come to believe, but as part of the process that will lead to their working together with gentiles to get Jesus killed (there is a parallel with Israelite leaders and ordinary people unconsciously working together with gentile leaders such as Nebuchadnezzar for the downfall of Israel). Jesus comes into this (Jewish) world for judgment, so that people who did not see might see and people who did see might become blind (9:39). He manifests grace and truth toward Israel in an open and in a confrontational way, and thus he operates as someone who is the embodiment of Yahweh. He is Godlike in his reaching out to the Jewish people and in his hostility to the Jewish people. He continues to relate to Jews in the same way to the end. From the beginning, he loved his own people who were in the world (1:11) and he loves them to the end, to the ultimate (13:1), in Yahweh-like fashion.

Isaiah 53:1 asks rhetorically, "To whom has Yahweh's arm been revealed?" Yahweh's arm stands for Yahweh's power, but Isaiah 52:13–53:12 sees Yahweh's power embodied in a servant of his whom people dismissed. Reading the story of Yahweh's relationship with his people in light of the rhetorical question in Isaiah 53:1 makes one read Israel's story as an account of his people's dismissal of him. But Yahweh promises this will not be the end of his servant's story, and the long haul of the story of Yahweh and Israel suggests that it will not be the end of Yahweh's story either. It fits that John will apply Isaiah 53:1 to Jesus (John 12:38). In my NRSV, John's further comment that Jesus loves his people to the end (13:1) comes lower down in the same column of text. And for Jesus, as for Yahweh's servant and for Yahweh, the dismissal will not be the end.

Both versions of the story of Yahweh and Israel make the point. The Torah–Former Prophets narrative ends not with the 587 BCE events of the destruction of Jerusalem and the temple, and the blinding and deportation of King Zedekiah, but with the 562 event of the release and elevation of David's descendant, King Jehoiachin. The Ezra-Nehemiah-Chronicles sequence similarly but differently looks beyond those 587 events to the 537 event of Cyrus's declaring that Yahweh has charged him to commission Judahites to return to Jerusalem to rebuild the temple. Yes, Yahweh will love his people to the end, and Jesus will do the same. "Every Christological affirmation has a theological correlate,"[5] and every theological affirmation has a christological correlate, too.

Laying the Law Down

In the Torah, there is an essential relationship between God's being at work with and for his people, and his expecting them to live in light of what he does, what he says, and who he is. The same is true of John's Jesus. John's Jesus is Godlike in laying the law down. There is another slightly more puzzling similarity. When the Hebrew Scriptures tell Yahweh's story, it is Yahweh's followers who tell it. It is not Yahweh's memoir. Similarly, in John it is not Jesus who tells his story, but one of his followers who does so. It is also not a memoir. But in the Torah, much of the time, Yahweh himself speaks to lay the law down, and in John, Jesus speaks to lay the law down. Yahweh's story and Jesus's story work by having the people who listen to them use their imagination, but the storytellers also work by quoting Yahweh's biddings and quoting Jesus's biddings in a way that puts their listeners close to being Yahweh's addressees and Jesus's addressees, with results that are often uncomfortable.

"I am Yahweh your God who got you out of the country of Egypt, from a household of servants. There will not be other gods for you, over against me" (Exod 20:2–3). "You are to be sacred people, because I, Yahweh your God, am sacred" (Lev 19:2). "Listen, Israel: Yahweh our God, Yahweh one" (the Hebrew clause or clauses have no verb, and it is hard to know where to put a verb or two to make an English sentence out of it). "You will commit yourselves to Yahweh your God with all your mind, and with all your spirit, and with all your energy" (Deut 6:4–5). In contrast to Exodus and Leviticus, admittedly, in Deuteronomy, it is mostly Moses speaking and referring to Yahweh in the third person.

The logic in the Torah is not that people are to live a certain way, and then will earn the right to belong to Yahweh, as if law comes before gospel. It is that Yahweh has lived in a certain way in relation to them and has earned the right to expect them to live a certain way. Each of those three versions of what he expects, in Exodus, Leviticus, and Deuteronomy, is a headline for the spelling out of these expectations in that which follows. The first leads into commands about abjuring the manufacture of images, keeping Sabbath, revering parents, telling the truth, resisting the temptation to want someone else's spouse, being generous rather than grasping with one's property, loving people one could be tempted to hate, and so on. But the Exodus headline speaks of how Yahweh's action came first. Indeed, there is hardly any expression of expectation in the entirety of Genesis 1 to Exodus 19. It is all about Yahweh's action toward people who are often stupidly resistant. Expectation only follows the action. The second headline, in Leviticus 19, leads into some similar commands, and some complementary ones relating to matters such as the sacredness of worship, honesty, fairness in the community court, and loving the people toward whom one might be inclined to harbor resentment. The third headline, in Deuteronomy, leads into some commands that Jesus directly takes up, not in John but in Matthew 4 and Luke 4.

In Matthew and Luke, that story of Jesus's needing to quote Deuteronomy leads soon into the Sermon on the Mount and the Sermon on the Plain, but there is no such block of teaching early on in John. John focuses on Jesus's direct dealings with people who are often also stupidly resistant, as he looks for people who are sensible enough to trust in him. It is a theme that also runs through the Former and Latter Prophets because Israel found it hard to live life on that basis.

John's Jesus talks about expectations not at the beginning of his story, but when he knows that he has more or less completed his task in relation to his people. "If I have washed your feet, as lord and teacher, you ought to wash one another's feet, too. Because I have given you an example, so that you should also do as I have done to you" (John 13:14–15). To this implausible requirement he adds that they should love one another as he has loved them (13:34). That expectation corresponds to Yahweh's expectation that Israelites should show mutual commitment and concern. But there is a novelty in Jesus's formulation, in his anticipating their following his example of love. Perhaps Peter perceives the horrifying nature of this expectation, given that he immediately changes the subject (13:36).

Like Yahweh, then, Jesus lays the law down in terms that find limited response. Keep my commandments, keep my word, he keeps saying (14:15, 21, 23, 24; 15:7, 10, 12, 14, 17), just like Yahweh. He is disappointed that it does not work, but he is not surprised (16:32), and that is like Yahweh, too. Yahweh's first set of teachings, in Exodus, leads into an account of his people's flouting his first commands (Exod 32). And it is after this episode that he offers his self-revelation as "Yahweh, God compassionate and gracious, long-tempered and big in commitment and truth" (Exod 34:6). The revelation goes on less comfortably. While he does "carry" people's wrongdoing" (the literal meaning of the word conventionally translated "forgive"), "he definitely does not treat people as innocent" (Exod 34:7). Perhaps the implication is that they must repent if they are to have their wrongdoing carried (synagogue worship makes this inference), or that they will still pay a price for their wrongdoing (as Exodus implies, and David's story shows). The sets of teaching in Leviticus and Deuteronomy close with hair-raising threats of the consequences of such flouting (Lev 26; Deut 28–29). Fortunately, the story in the Hebrew Scriptures shows that Yahweh's bark is regularly worse than his bite. Is that also true of Jesus (John 15:4)?

Threatening and Promising

The Latter Prophets (approximately Isaiah to Malachi) spend their time being confrontational. Through them, Yahweh is critiquing Israel—especially its leaders, its pastors, its heads of families, and its other prophets—when things are going well, for their politics, their theology, and their indulgence, and warning them that they are going to pay a price for their waywardness. Or, when things are going badly, he is promising them that he has not finished with them, contrary to the way things look and to the gloomy expectations they not unreasonably have. A time of shalom will come, a time when Yahweh makes Jerusalem a glorious city, when a Davidic king reigns there, when he himself betroths the nation as bride again, when he renews his covenant, when the empires no longer control them, when he rebuilds his sanctuary among them, when they see such blessing that the nations will come to them and ask if they can join them, when he brings a change to the way they work as human beings that means they worship him and serve him in accordance with the Torah.

Either way, Yahweh is unfailingly confrontational. He never lets them settle where they are. That is why he commissions prophets, actually. Their vocation is never to confirm the way people are thinking. It is always to challenge it.

John's Jesus is also unfailingly confrontational and never lets people settle where they are. He tackles them antagonistically when they are being positive and think that they are serving God and that they are responding positively to him. "Stop making my Father's house a market place" (2:16). "You worship what you do not know. We worship what we know" (4:22). "Unless you see signs you will not believe" (4:48). "You do not have God's love in you" (5:42). "You are only looking for me because I provided you with food" (6:26). "One of you is a devil" (6:70). "None of you keeps the law" (7:19). "You judge by human standards" (8:15). "Why do I speak to you at all?" (8:25). "You are from your father the devil" (8:44). "Do you now believe?" (16:31).

He also meets them head on when they look as if they need their horizon broadened and their hopes raised. "No one who comes to me will ever be hungry" (6:35). "Anyone who believes in me will have eternal life. I will raise him up at the last day" (6:40). "Anyone who follows me will walk in the light" (8:12). "You will know the truth and the truth will free you" (8:32). "People who believe in me will live, even though they die" (11:25). "I go to prepare a place for you" (14:3). "I will not leave you orphaned" (14:18). "The Holy Spirit will teach you everything" (14:26). "Peace I leave with you" (14:27). "Ask and you will receive" (16:24).

In connection with the two-sided confrontational stance that both Yahweh and Jesus take toward their people, Ezekiel 34 and John 10 are intriguing. The NT never quotes Ezekiel, but Revelation could not exist without it, and perhaps neither could John 10. The context in Ezekiel is the aftermath of the Babylonian destruction of the temple and the city of Jerusalem in 587, its people's subjugation, the transportation of its king and many of the Judahite people, and the flight into self-imposed exile of many others. Yet the context in Ezekiel 33 is also a conviction on the part of the people who remain that Abraham's once having gained possession of the land surely means that they can regain it. This two-sided context is one for Yahweh to manifest his two-sided confrontational stance. No, the disaster is not the end. No, their conviction that they can regain possession of the land is not realistic—for religious and ethical reasons.

While the problem is not only the people's leadership, the problem of its leadership is central to the people's predicament. Given the unreliable nature of Israel's shepherds, in Ezekiel 34, Yahweh declares that he will shepherd Israel himself: seek them out, rescue them, feed them, bind up their broken limbs. He indeed makes clear that the problem is not only the people's leadership but also the people themselves: he will also judge between sheep and sheep. Yet, he also says that he will set up a new David over them as their shepherd. So he is ambiguous about how this shepherding will work. "I will shepherd my sheep" (34:11–16). But also, "I will set up over them one shepherd and he will shepherd them, my servant David. He is the one who will shepherd them. He will be a shepherd for them" (34:23). So will Yahweh shepherd them, or will a new David?

The ambiguity of Yahweh's words suits John 10. Here, too, Jesus confronts Israel's spiritual leaders. And "while this discourse contains no direct Old Testament citations, it nevertheless draws on the extensive scriptural imagery for both God and the king as Israel's shepherd."[6] In Ezekiel 34, Yahweh is Israel's shepherd, and the king is also Israel's shepherd. In John 10, Jesus is the good shepherd, fulfilling the role that Yahweh promised that he would fulfill and that he also promised that a new David would fulfill. It is in that context that Jesus declares that he and his Father are one, and that no one will take his sheep away from him (John 10:29–30).

Approachable and Interactive

The Psalter comprises 150 indications of Yahweh's being easy to talk to. In 130 or so of these psalms, Israelites address Yahweh; in the remaining ones, Yahweh addresses them or one Israelite addresses others. I assume the Israelites were not deceiving themselves in supposing that they were free to tell Yahweh how much they admired him, how grateful they were for what he had done for them, and how agonized and puzzled they were when he let things go wrong in their lives.

The nature of such prayers and praises (like the ones we use in church) is not usually to incorporate Yahweh's possible responses (the same applies to Lamentations). But the prayers and praises incorporate many references to Yahweh's having been known to respond and to the expectation that he will respond, and occasionally they include a response: Psalm 12 is an example. More thought-provoking are interactive moments outside the Psalter, when people protest to Yahweh in psalm-like manner, and in response he gives as good as he gets. "Serving you is pointless." "Okay, I will give you a bigger job" (Isa 49:4–6). "Why do you not pay any heed to us in our need?" "You have got some hutzpah, considering the way I have been reaching out to you" (Isa 63:15–65:7). Most spectacular is the book of Job, where Job works hard for chapter after chapter, trying to needle Yahweh into responding to him, and eventually succeeds in provoking a rejoinder that makes him wish he had kept his mouth shut, yet which becomes a rejoinder that congratulates him for speaking the truth (Job 38–42).

In the Torah, the Prophets, and the Writings, there is no doubt that Yahweh is Lord, but there is also no doubt that he is approachable. He is the monarch living in a castle at the top of the hill, but the drawbridge is down, no security men stand on guard, and one can go and knock on his door. He may respond uncompromisingly, but his forcefulness will be combined with faithfulness, and it may change one's thinking in a way that one needed, and that would never have happened if one had not gone through the combative interactive process.

John's Jesus is God-like in letting people come to him with questions and affirmations and in responding in ways that may challenge their presuppositions. "Where are you staying?" "Come and see" (John 1:38–39). "They have no wine." "What does that have to do with us?" (2:3–4). "You are a teacher sent from God." "You need to be born again—you are a teacher, and you are so ignorant" (3:2–3, 10). "I do not have a husband." "What about the previous five?" (4:17–18). "Have something to eat." "I have food you do not know about" (4:31–32). "You should not be doctoring on the Sabbath." "My Father is still working, and so am I" (5:16–17). "When did you come here?" "You are just interested in gifts of food" (6:25–26). "Go to Judea so people can see you act." "You cannot tell the time" (7:3–6). "This woman was caught in the act of adultery." "The one among you who is sinless should be the one to start throwing rocks" (8:4, 7). "Abraham is our father." "The devil is your father" (8:39, 44). "Who sinned, this man or his parents?" "Neither" (9:2–3). "You are making yourself God." "Have you not read Psalm 82?" (10:33–34).[7] "Lazarus is ill." "I am staying here" (11:1–6). "She is wasting money that could be given to the poor." "Leave her alone" (12:5–7). "You cannot wash my feet." "You had better let me, otherwise you are screwed" (13:8). "Show us the Father." "You ask that, after all you have seen?" (14:8–9). "Now we believe." "Really?" (16:30–31). "So you are a king?" "Those are your words" (18:37). "I can kill you or release you." "You have no such power" (19:10–11).

"My Lord and my God." "Do you believe because you have seen?" (20:28–29). "What about him?" "That's nothing to do with you" (21:21–22).[8]

Modern readers may find it a surprise that Yahweh is so accessible but not that he can be combative in his responses. They may not be surprised that John's Jesus is so approachable, but be shocked by the pugnacious nature of many of his responses. Like Yahweh, Jesus is approachable, but like Yahweh, he is also mind-expanding, unsettling, disconcerting, enigmatic, mysterious.

Conclusion

The *logos* was God, but he became flesh and came to live among us. He was like Yahweh, then. He continued to work on his people and not give up on them. He laid the law down in a way that reflected who he was but made allowance for who they were. He set before them the existential and eternal dangers they were putting themselves in and the existential and eternal promises that he wanted to fulfill for them. He was always open to their approaching him but always prepared to mess with the framework of their thinking.

CHAPTER FIVE

Seeing Jesus, Seeing God

Theophany and Divine Visibility in the Gospel of John

Brittany E. Wilson

AMONG SCHOLARS WHO work on early Christology, there is a growing recognition that visionary experiences of the divine play an important role in how NT texts portray Jesus in relation to God.[1] This tradition of people who encounter God through visions and theophanies finds its roots in Jewish Scripture but continues throughout the Second Temple period and finds its way onto the pages of the NT.[2] Many early Christian texts, especially of the apocalyptic variety, apply the trope of "seeing God" to Jesus himself, as when John of Patmos sees a vision of Jesus sharing God's throne in the book of Revelation (Rev 22:3–4). Such visions participate in early attempts to express Jesus's divinity and relationship with God, but we see NT texts applying the trope of divine visibility to Jesus in other ways too. Paul's letters, for example, associate Jesus with the divine *kavod*, or God's "Glory" (δόξα) (e.g., Phil 3:21; 1 Cor 2:8; 2 Cor 3:7–18; 4:4), an expression of God's visible presence according to many scriptural texts.[3] The Synoptic Gospels also famously portray Jesus's visual transformation when he is transfigured on a mountaintop before the disciples' very eyes (Matt 17:1–13; Mark 9:2–8; Luke 9:28–36), an episode that finds affinity with accounts of epiphanies and apocalyptic visions and that subtly associates Jesus with God's own anthropomorphic *kavod* on Sinai.[4] With such examples, we see the NT portraying Jesus in a manner akin to how people visually encounter God in scriptural and apocalyptic texts and, in doing so, contributing to the emergence of an early "high" Christology.

In this essay, I will join this wider discussion concerning NT Christology by focusing specifically on how the Gospel of John incorporates the visual experience of seeing God in its portrayal of Jesus. My focus on John, however, may seem like an odd choice, for John has long been read as rejecting the tradition of seeing God. John's prologue famously concludes with the words "no one has ever seen God" (John 1:18), and a few chapters later, Jesus accuses his Jewish interlocutors of never having seen God's form (5:37), a comment that could be

---

I thank Laura Holmes, Luke Irwin, Alicia Myers, Catrin Williams, and the editors of this volume for their helpful feedback on this essay.

heard as affirming God's invisibility (or that God does not have a form to see).[5] With these statements, John also seems to deny that anyone from Israel's history, including Moses himself, ever saw God, especially since he alludes to Sinai in the immediate contexts of both statements (John 1:14–18; 5:37–47; cf. Exod 33–34; Deut 4:12 LXX) (and Moses, of course, famously spoke to God face to face on Sinai [e.g., Exod 24:12–34:35]).[6] Similarly, John seems to reject the Jewish apocalyptic claim that certain individuals such as Abraham, Moses, Isaiah, and Enoch ascended to heaven and experienced visions of God.[7] Despite this tradition of heavenly ascent, John not only claims that no one has seen God (John 1:18) but that "no one has ascended into heaven except the one who descended from heaven, the Son of Man" (3:13). What is more, John never includes theophanies in his Gospel, or, that is to say, John never depicts God directly entering into the narrative as a visible character. Though an argument from silence, this lacuna is striking since God does become visually manifest in the three other canonical Gospels (Matt 3:16; 17:5; Mark 1:10; 9:7; Luke 2:9; 3:21–22; 9:34–35; cf. Acts 7:2, 30–34, 55–56), as well as the book of Revelation (e.g., Rev 4:2–11; 5:1–14; 7:9–17; 19:4–5; 20:11–15; 21:3–8; 22:1–5), which has long been associated with John's Gospel in Christian tradition.[8] Yet in contrast to these theophanies in some of the Fourth Gospel's closest literary counterparts, the only time God directly intervenes in John's narrative is strictly as an audible voice: God speaks from heaven using direct discourse but there is no visionary element (John 12:28–30).

When we look at all these details together, it appears that visionary experiences do not play an important role in John's Christology since John eschews the very notion that God can be seen. Instead of continuing the scriptural tradition of God's encountering people through visions and theophanies, John's Gospel, so many commentators surmise, instead aligns with a more platonically informed, Philonic understanding of God's visibility, or lack thereof.[9] Like the Jewish philosopher Philo, so the argument goes, John views God as being fully transcendent and beyond human sight; God is ontologically invisible and thus not subject to the bodily senses.[10] This more Platonic view of God's "essential" invisibility explains why John claims that no one has ever seen God, and it also explains why he does not include theophanies in his Gospel. On the question of whether God can be seen, therefore, John aligns less with texts like Revelation and the Synoptic Gospels and more with texts like Colossians 1:15, 1 Timothy 1:17, and Hebrews 11:27, which call God "invisible" (ἀόρατος).[11] According to this interpretation, John particularly aligns with texts that favor philosophical understandings of God, such as those written by Philo and the later church fathers, who had to rely on creative interpretative strategies in order to reconcile scriptural accounts of theophany with their belief in God's essential invisibility.[12]

However, despite this common perspective on God's invisibility in John, an increasing number of scholars, including this volume's honoree, insist that the tradition of seeing God does in fact play an important role in John's Gospel.[13]

John may not draw on this tradition in the same way as NT texts like the Synoptics and Revelation, but he does still harness the power of sight and theophany in order to cultivate belief in Jesus. Along with this line of interpretation, I will argue that John incorporates the scriptural pattern of theophany and that he primarily does so in order to communicate Jesus's own visible divinity and unique relationship with God. To make this argument, I will first problematize the assumption that the Johannine God is "invisible" by demonstrating how John's portrayal of God sits uncomfortably alongside Platonic notions of divine invisibility. I will then discuss how precisely John depicts God as a visible deity before concluding with how John incorporates the notion of God's visibility to further his wider christological aims. In the end, I will maintain that while John stands out from many NT texts by circumscribing divine visibility primarily to the person of Jesus, he still incorporates the theme of seeing God in order to communicate the inextricable relationship between Jesus and the God of Israel.

Seeing and Not Seeing God in John

Before turning to how John applies the language of divine visibility to Jesus, it is first important to demonstrate that John does not present God as an invisible entity in a strictly Platonic sense.[14] Although John does arguably adapt Platonic principles when it suits his purposes, on the whole, he seems unconcerned to craft his portrayal of God in accordance with firm Platonic notions of divine transcendence and invisibility.[15] For one, John never calls God "invisible" (ἀόρατος), unlike Philo who frequently speaks of God's invisibility, or even unlike texts such as Colossians 1:15, 1 Timothy 1:17, and Hebrews 11:27. Moreover, the statement at the end of John's prologue, which is echoed in 1 John (1 John 4:12, 20), does not claim that God *cannot* be seen (cf. 1 Tim 6:16). Instead, John 1:18 simply says that "no one has ever seen God." In other words, John 1:18 says that God is unseen by human eyes, not that God is invisible in an ontological sense or that God is empirically unavailable to human sight.[16] Jesus's statement in chapter 5 about how his interlocuters have never seen God's form reflects a similar idea, for Jesus does not claim that God *lacks* a form. He instead continues his critique of his Jewish interlocuters by asserting that they have never seen God's form, nor heard God's voice (5:37). The fact that he even mentions God's "form" (εἶδος) suggests that God does have a form that can be seen, just as God has a voice that can be heard.[17] Again, his point is that his hearers simply have not seen that form.

Second, John's ostensible denial that specific people from Israel's past saw God does not "prove" God's invisibility in the Fourth Gospel. As I noted earlier, John situates his two references to people not seeing God within the context of Sinai allusions. John mentions Moses and the law (which was given to Moses on Sinai) in both of these contexts (John 1:17; 5:45–47), and in his prologue, he says that "we have seen his Glory [δόξαν]" (1:14), referring, however, not to

God's Glory, which was seen on Sinai, but to "the Word's" Glory.[18] In chapter 5, John's statement that Jesus's Jewish hearers have never heard God's voice nor seen God's form may also allude to Deuteronomy 4:12 LXX, where Moses explains to the Israelites that they are prohibited from making "idols" because "you saw no likeness [ὁμοίωμα] when the Lord spoke to you at Horeb [or Mount Sinai] out of the fire." With this latter potential allusion to Deuteronomy 4:12, it is important to note that, once again, the text does not say that God lacks a form. Moses instead claims that the Israelites did not *see* God's form, or more precisely, God's "likeness" (ὁμοίωμα). According to Moses and Jesus, God may be hidden from their hearers' eyes, but this does not mean there is nothing to see. More importantly, with both of the allusions to Sinai in the prologue and in chapter 5, John seems less concerned to refute the idea that Moses and the Israelites saw God and more concerned to situate Moses as a witness to Jesus, or someone who can testify to Jesus's claims. Moses's role as a witness to Jesus is especially clear in chapter 5, since Jesus says, "If you believed Moses, you would believe me, for he wrote about me" (John 5:46), and the reference to the law being given through Moses in the prologue may serve a similar function (1:17).[19] It is not necessarily the case, then, that John is rejecting scriptural accounts of seeing God, for he marshals Moses and Scripture (e.g., 10:35) in an effort to support Jesus's claims about himself.[20]

Third, and finally, the fact that God only becomes verbally—and not visually—manifest in John's Gospel does not evince God's intrinsic invisibility, for God's direct discourse in 12:28 is still a theophany of sorts. In the ancient world, including the world of Scripture, visions and epiphanies typically include both visual and verbal elements, and in many cases, they feature one element over the other, or only occur on an aural level (hence the classification "divine audition").[21] Thus while God enters John's narrative only as a voice from heaven, this entrance nevertheless complicates the notion that God is fully transcendent and beyond sensory engagement in John's Gospel.[22] Instead, God speaks into the earthly realm; God is not a remote, metaphysically absent entity, but one who directly engages fellow characters in the narrative, as well as us as readers, when God responds to Jesus by saying, "I have glorified it [i.e., God's name], and I will glorify it again" (12:28). Furthermore, while it is true that this is the only occurrence when God directly enters the narrative as a fellow character, John, like his synoptic counterparts, does depict the visual manifestation of God's Spirit along with God's words at Jesus's baptism (1:32–34; cf. Matt 3:16–17; Mark 1:10–11; Luke 3:21–22). John only discloses this incident in retrospect via the discourse of John the Baptist, but he still depicts the intersection of the visual and verbal in God's endorsement of Jesus. According to John, God's Spirit can be seen descending from heaven like a dove and resting on Jesus, even if we as readers do not witness it firsthand.[23] In this way, as with God's audition, John depicts God engaging God's people in the manner of scriptural theophanies; God visually and verbally confirms Jesus's status to John the Baptist, and God audibly responds to Jesus so that all those who are gathered can hear.

Of course, just because God speaks does not mean that God is understood. While the reader is privy to God's actual words during the divine audition in chapter 12, aside from Jesus, the narrative audience does not recognize that God is the one speaking. Some listeners mistake God's words for thunder and others for an angel who is speaking to Jesus (John 12:29). My point, though, is that this narrative audience still hears God's speech (John says that "the crowd standing there *heard* [ἀκούσας]"), even if they incorrectly identify the source of this speech (or in the case of some, do not even recognize God's speech *as* speech but as thunder).[24] John's depiction of the crowd hearing but not understanding furthers his wider theme of recognition and misrecognition concerning Jesus.[25] But this episode also depicts God as directly intervening in the earthly realm on behalf of God's people in the way that God has always done: as Jesus tells his audience, "This voice has come for your sake, not for mine" (12:30). John's reference to the crowd identifying God's voice as thunder particularly places this divine incursion within the trajectory of the Sinai theophany, since God answers Moses in thunder in Exodus 19:19.[26] By including this "theophany," then, John seems less concerned with establishing Platonic notions of transcendence and more concerned with underscoring how God is the same God of Israel who has always intervened for the sake of God's people, even if that intervention is misunderstood. God may be "unseen" in this theophany, as well as misheard, but this does not mean that God is invisible in a Platonic or Philonic sense.

Divine Visibility
God as the Object of Sight in John

As John's Gospel unfolds, it becomes clear that John highlights God's hiddenness from human eyes because he wants to underscore the uniqueness of Jesus's own ability to see God—an ability, of course, that also speaks against the notion that God is somehow ontologically invisible in John. Indeed, God is not invisible according to John because Jesus himself can see God.[27] Jesus is the one who reveals his unique purview of the divine in chapter 6 when he says the following: "Everyone who has heard and learned from the Father comes to me. Not that anyone has seen [ἑώρακεν] the Father except the one who is from God; he has seen [ἑώρακεν] the Father" (John 6:45–46). As "the one who is from God" (cf. 9:33; 17:8), Jesus maintains that he has seen the Father, and he uses the word ὁράω to describe this sight, the same word that appears elsewhere in John's Gospel to depict physical sight, along with the words βλέπω, θεάομαι, and θεωρέω.[28] Given the conceptual and etymological overlap between "seeing" and "knowing" (or physical sight and cognitive insight), John may certainly mean that Jesus "sees" God in a cognitive sense, but he makes no effort (here or elsewhere) to differentiate between the different valences of the word.[29]

John's point, rather, seems to be that Jesus can see God because he has special access to God. Jesus's access to God—and the visual apprehension associated with that access—emerges at various places in John's Gospel. John, for example, indicates that Jesus testifies to what he has seen and heard in the heavenly realm (3:31–32; cf. 3:11), and he further indicates that Jesus currently sees all that God does since the Father shows him (5:19–20). Akin to 6:45–46, Jesus also distinguishes between people's ability to hear from God and his own ability to see from God when he says: "I declare what I have seen [ἑώρακα] from the Father; as for you, you should do what you have heard from the Father" (8:38). In other words, John indicates in his Gospel that because Jesus has been in God's presence, Jesus has seen God; his unique relationship with God gives him a direct line of sight to the divine that distinguishes him from others who only hear God.

The fact that Jesus has direct access to the sight of God and God's deeds—both in the past when he was in heaven and in the present when he is on earth—may also explain why John says that no one has ever seen God: unlike Jesus, no one has ever seen God *fully*. While Marianne Meye Thompson observes that Jesus has seen God because he has been with God, she also highlights how Jesus's vision of God is particularly direct.[30] In chapter 6, Jesus explicitly says that he has seen "the Father" (6:46) and, in doing so, positions God as the direct object of sight (indeed, "the Father" is the direct object of the verb "to see"). Jesus does not just see God's Spirit or God's Glory or a cloud that descends on a mountaintop. Jesus instead directly sees *God* (or "the Father") in a way, according to John, that no one else has. When read in these terms, John is not necessarily contradicting Jewish Scripture when he says that "no one has ever seen *God*" (and note, once again, that God is the direct object of "to see") (1:18). John may instead be interpreting scriptural theophanies as episodes in which people only saw God in part.[31] Although such an interpretation does not seem to account for those rare occasions when God speaks to people "face to face" (e.g., Gen 32:30; Exod 33:11; Num 12:8; Deut 34:10), it does capture the mystery and veiled nature of divine revelation that permeates all scriptural theophanies, and it may also explain why John's prologue makes a statement that, on the surface, seems to fly in the face of Scripture's witness to God's visual manifestations.[32]

Yet while John claims that Jesus sees God in a way that differentiates Jesus from all others, John ultimately does not limit divine visibility to Jesus's eyes alone. Instead, after revealing that Jesus can see God (John 6:46), John goes on to explain that God can be seen in Jesus himself. Jesus, once again, is the one who discloses this information, doing so first at the conclusion of his public ministry when he says, "Whoever sees [ὁ θεωρῶν] me sees [θεωρεῖ] the one who sent me"

(12:45), and then again during his farewell discourse when he says "whoever has seen [ὁ ἑωρακώς] me has seen [ἑώρακεν] the Father" (14:9; cf. 14:7). On one level, these statements continue to complicate, or at least qualify, the prologue's declaration that "no one has ever seen God" (1:18). Though John's Gospel opens with this assertion, as the narrative progresses, we learn that Jesus can see God and that, by extension, others can see God in Jesus. (This is why Luke Irwin argues that the meaning of 1:18 draws closer to "no one has ever [fully] seen God [yet]," especially since this statement occurs at the outset of the narrative before we learn how exactly God becomes visible in John's narrative.[33])

On another level, these statements also continue to complicate the Platonic notion that God is a fully transcendent being who never becomes available to sensual sight or manifests in the form of human flesh (cf. 1:14).[34] To be sure, interpreters have long argued that those who encounter Jesus in John's Gospel do not "really" see God, claiming that God's visibility in Jesus is indirect or purely cognitive.[35] Such readings are of course possible, but John's language itself resists such attempts to deflect the prospect of directly seeing the divine in Jesus. In both of Jesus's declarations, God once again emerges as the direct object of the verb "to see," and the action of seeing Jesus directly parallels the action of seeing God (e.g., "whoever has seen *me*" // "has seen *the Father*" in 14:9). John, therefore, seems to suggest that seeing Jesus is tantamount to seeing God, a correlation that should perhaps not be too surprising since Jesus claims that "the Father and I are one" (10:30) and that "I am in the Father and the Father is in me" (14:11) and since the disciple Thomas declares Jesus to be "my Lord and my God [θεός]" (20:28; cf. 1:1). John does not make the metaphysics of this seeing clear, but he nonetheless maintains that to see the Son is to see the Father. Indeed, John does not readily align with accounts of God's ontological invisibility, for God somehow becomes visible in the Word made flesh (cf. 1:14). While 1 John indicates that seeing God will be a future reality (1 John 3:1–2), the Gospel of John indicates that seeing God is also a present reality in Jesus.[36] By seeing Jesus, characters in John's narrative see God, and in this way, John is not so different from other NT texts that also adapt visionary experiences of God to express Jesus's divinity.

Jesus *as* Theophany
Seeing Jesus in John

By equating the sight of Jesus with the sight of God, John incorporates the tradition of seeing God in a manner that furthers his high christological claims. Thus while John does not include the theophanic tradition in the same manner as the Synoptics and Revelation, he does still rely on this tradition, and he even takes it a step further.[37] Indeed, for John, people do not only experience Jesus along the lines of a theophany for a brief moment in time (as during the transfiguration in the Synoptics), but they also encounter the whole of Jesus's earthly life—or his fleshly manifestation—as a theophany. To put it differently, John asserts that Jesus himself is in effect an enfleshed theophany. John makes this clear from the very outset of his Gospel when he correlates Jesus's becoming "flesh" (σάρξ) with the divine *kavod*, saying, "the Word became flesh [σὰρξ ἐγένετο] and tabernacled [ἐσκήνωσεν] among us, and we have seen his Glory [δόξαν]" (John 1:14).[38] Through the prologue's network of allusions to Sinai, including the tabernacle language here in v. 14, John casts Jesus as God's Glory, indicating that Jesus is God's visible presence who can be seen and who simultaneously makes God known (1:18).[39] As in Luke's transfiguration account, people see "his Glory" (John 1:14; cf. Luke 9:32), but the visibility of the Johannine Jesus's Glory is more than a momentary mountaintop glimpse, for it is linked to his own fleshly manifestation. In this way, John correlates God's visibility to Jesus, and he does so by connecting it to Jesus's earthly existence.

In addition to linking Jesus with the divine Glory, John also portrays Jesus as a theophany through his christological interpretation of scriptural theophanies. In other words, John interprets at least some theophanies from Jewish Scripture as being "Christophanies," or instances in which people saw Jesus. The clearest example of this Johannine tendency emerges in chapter 12, directly before Jesus summarizes his ministry with the words "whoever sees me sees the one who sent me" (John 12:45).[40] Jesus's words follow on the heels of the narrator's comment that the prophet Isaiah saw "his Glory" (12:41), which is an allusion to Isaiah's famous theophanic encounter in Isaiah 6.[41] (At the beginning of this encounter, which became foundational in Jewish apocalyptic and mystical traditions, Isaiah says that "I saw the Lord [κύριον] sitting upon a throne, high and lifted up, and the house was full of his Glory [δόξης αὐτοῦ]" [Isa 6:1 LXX].[42]) Yet while the prophet sees God's anthropomorphic form and Glory in Isaiah 6, John interprets Isaiah's vision to suggest that he actually saw Jesus. In this reinterpretation, John includes the prophet's words in Isaiah 53:1 and 6:10 to explain why people do not believe in Jesus (John 12:37–40), and he claims that, unlike those who cannot "see" Jesus (12:40; cf. Isa 6:10), Isaiah "saw his Glory and spoke about him" (John 12:41). Even though people saw Jesus perform "many signs in their presence" (12:37), Isaiah is the one who is able to see Jesus's Glory. John thus applies Isaiah's words and vision in his summative reflection on the rejection of Jesus and his ministry, and in doing so, suggests that "the Lord" (κύριος) whom Isaiah sees is in fact "the Lord" Jesus (John 12:41; cf. Isa 6:1 LXX).[43] When John says that Isaiah saw "his Glory," then, he means that Isaiah saw Jesus's Glory, especially since Jesus is the referent of the pronoun "his" (αὐτοῦ) in the surrounding comments (John 12:37, 42).[44] Just as John claims in his prologue that we have seen "his Glory [τὴν δόξαν αὐτοῦ]" (1:14), so too does he suggest that Isaiah saw "his Glory [τὴν δόξαν αὐτοῦ]" (12:41).

Because of John's suggestion that Isaiah saw Jesus when he saw "his Glory," many commentators claim that this sight involved Isaiah's vision of the preexistent Jesus (cf. John 17:5).[45] The interpretation of "Old Testament" theophanies as instances in which people saw "the Son" or the preexistent "Word" (and not God) can be found as early as Justin Martyr and became a popular tradition among the church fathers in particular up until the fifth century CE.[46] Such interpretations enabled at least some early Christians to preserve their belief in God's essential invisibility by redirecting the object of sight in theophanies to Jesus in his preexistent state. As Catrin Williams observes, however, it is difficult to restrict Isaiah's view of Jesus's "Glory" in 12:41 to only the preexistent Word.[47] Instead, it may be that Isaiah had a vision of future events, a vision that involved Isaiah foreseeing Jesus's *incarnate* divine Glory.[48] (Again, just as John claims that we have seen "his Glory" in the flesh [1:14], so too may Isaiah have seen this future fleshly reality when he saw "his Glory.") This interpretation finds corroboration in 8:56 when Jesus says that Abraham saw "my day," a reference to Abraham foreseeing Jesus's earthly ministry ("Abraham rejoiced that he would see [ἴδη] my day; he saw [εἶδεν] it and was glad").[49] Like Abraham, Isaiah is a visual witness to Jesus, and like Abraham's vision, Isaiah's vision likely involves foresight into Jesus's future ministry and earthly existence, an interpretation that is all the more plausible since John situates Isaiah's vision within his summary of Jesus's ministry (12:36b–50), and since he interprets Jesus's rejection as a fulfillment of Isaiah's words (12:38).[50] With this reading, then, John maintains that Isaiah's vision of Jesus's Glory involves a vision of the earthly Jesus. John interprets Isaiah's theophany as a vision of Jesus's future Glory and earthly ministry, and in doing so, suggests that seeing the fleshly Jesus is tantamount to experiencing a theophany.

Yet while it is likely that John reads Isaiah's theophany in Isaiah 6 as a Christophany, it is not necessarily the case that John wholly replaces Isaiah's vision of God with a vision of Jesus. Instead, the very ambiguity of John's language suggests that it can be read in reference to both Jesus *and* God: the title "Lord" (κύριος) often applies to both God and Jesus, and the pronoun "his" (αὐτοῦ) could technically apply to both God and Jesus as well (i.e., the narrator does not specifically say that it is "Jesus's Glory" but only "his Glory").[51] John's statement that Isaiah "saw his Glory," therefore, could be read in relation to Jesus and God simultaneously. As Irwin explains, John is not necessarily contradicting Jewish Scripture by intimating that Isaiah saw Jesus during his theophanic encounter. Instead, "if Jesus is the subject of the theophanies and if one understands that Jesus is God, then no contradiction need exist. . . . Jesus does not replace God in the theophanies; rather, he is present because God is present."[52] Williams further explains that John's interpretation of scriptural theophanies may also illuminate his rejection of Jewish apocalyptic claims that individuals such as

Abraham and Isaiah ascended into heaven and experienced visions of God (cf.
John 1:18; 3:13). She writes that, for John, "it is a real 'seeing' of the earthly Jesus,
not heavenly ascents and visions, that is required in order to experience a 'vision'
of God's glory."[53] Thus instead of rejecting the tradition of visionary experiences
wholesale, John redirects this tradition to Jesus himself (see also, e.g., 1:51). To
see the earthly Jesus, John claims, is to have a vision of God, and in this sense, the
patriarchs and prophets like Abraham and Isaiah did experience a vision of God.
Once again, seeing Jesus and seeing God overlap; one does not replace the other.

Conclusion

In sum, John continues scriptural and apocalyptic traditions concerning God's
visibility but circumscribes that visibility to the person of Jesus. He thus incorporates traditions concerning God's visibility in service to his high Christology,
and he does so by directly overlapping God's visibility with Jesus's visibility. It is
not necessarily the case, then, that God's mediation in Jesus somehow dispels the
directness of God's visibility in Jesus. As recent work on theophanies (and their
connection with divine embodiment) has argued, God can become manifest in
different entities without always lessening the divine fullness of that manifestation, mainly because some strands of Scripture testify to God's ability to be
present simultaneously in different locations (e.g., God can be both in heaven
and on earth at the same time but still remain the one God of Israel and be really
present in each location).[54] When read through this lens, seeing Jesus in John
does not become yet another indirect way of seeing God but a way to see God
fully. Jesus is not only privileged because of his ability to see God directly, but
God can be seen directly in Jesus himself. In this way, John goes beyond other
NT accounts of Jesus's divine visuality, as in Revelation and the Synoptics, for
he indicates that the incarnation itself equates to a sustained theophany. Unlike
other NT texts, Jesus does not appear with God in heaven in visions (e.g., Rev
22:3–4; Acts 7:55–56) or only become visually manifest for brief moments
in a manner akin to God's theophanic manifestations in Scripture (e.g., Matt
17:1–13; Mark 9:2–8; Luke 9:28–36). Instead, seeing God and seeing Jesus is
one and the same in John's Gospel, even as Jesus is also clearly distinct from
God. For John, therefore, God's visibility becomes a means to express Jesus's
shared identity with the God of Israel. According to John, Jesus is the site—and
sight—where God is most fully visible.

CHAPTER SIX

Jesus's Humanity and Ours

John's Christology and Ancient Views of the Self

Wil Rogan

THE FOURTH GOSPEL'S Christology has proved to be a liability for the humanity of the Fourth Gospel's Christ. Having identified Jesus as the ever-existent Word through which God made the world, the Fourth Gospel narrates his earthly life as the revelation of God in his words and works. No small measure of difficulty that interpreters have had with Jesus's humanity is due to the thought that humanity and divinity are incompatible. Already in the second century, drawing on the association between divinity and incorruptibility, Valentinus supposed that Jesus ate and drank without his body producing waste (Clement of Alexandria, *Strom.* 3.59.3; cf. John 4:31–34) and Ignatius of Antioch wrote against those who believed, perhaps out of convictions about divine impassibility, that Jesus only appeared to suffer in the flesh (*Smyrn.* 2.1–7.2; cf. 2 John 7). In the last century, however, the most powerful argument against Jesus's humanity in the Fourth Gospel was expressed in terms of the disparity between Jesus's humanity and ours.[1] Ernst Käsemann famously contended that the evangelist could answer the question of Jesus's identity only "in the form of naïve docetism."[2] Käsemann asks: "In what sense is he flesh, who walks on the water and through closed doors, who cannot be captured by his enemies, who at the well of Samaria is tired and desires a drink, yet has no need of drink and has food different from that which his disciples seek?"[3] In calling the Fourth Gospel's apparently less-than-human portrait of Jesus "naïve," Käsemann construed its docetism as the unintended outcome of how its Christology displaced its apocalyptic eschatology.[4] Without

---

Throughout this essay I try to make explicit the immense intellectual debt that I owe to my doctoral mentor Marianne Meye Thompson. I must make explicit the personal debt I owe her, which can largely be summed up in something she once told me. In my first year as an assistant professor, I asked her if there was anything she wished she knew at the beginning of teaching that she would impart to me. She said, "One thing I really learned is that, in many ways, you teach yourself—not just your understanding of a text, but your understanding of God, life, salvation, church. Students remember the class, but they remember your passion, your love for Jesus, your care for them. These are the lasting legacies. Much that they need, especially a living faith, you cannot give them, but you can walk alongside of them and be a witness to it." By God, I hope my life can be such a witness as Marianne's has been to me.

apocalyptic eschatology, the glory of the risen Jesus collapsed into his earthly life, leaving us with the "absolute minimum of the costume designed for the one who dwelt for a little while among men, appearing to be one of them, yet without himself being subjected to earthly conditions."[5]

In *The Humanity of Jesus in the Fourth Gospel,* her spirited rejoinder to Käsemann's argument, Marianne Meye Thompson finds that John's Christology assumes and even depends on Jesus's human origins, his life in the flesh, the materiality of his signs, and the brutal reality of his death. Without these, she argues, no ground is left to explain the christological conflict that develops in the Fourth Gospel, where the offense is not that God becomes human but that "one who is flesh, who lived and died among them, claims to be the Word from heaven."[6] For Thompson, John's Gospel does not so much argue for Jesus's humanity as assume it. Its christological concern is not whether Jesus is human, but whether "in the flesh of Jesus, *God* is revealed."[7] Even so, or precisely for that reason, Jesus's humanity does not look quite like ours in John's Gospel. In the final paragraph of her book, Thompson calls the unlikeness of Jesus to us "disconcerting" and raises the question: "For Jesus to be truly human must he be exactly and only like all other humans?"[8] She contends that the Fourth Gospel would offer the answer *no,* because the humanity of Jesus is an uncancellable feature of its claims about his distinctive identity as the Messiah and Son of God. Jesus is human even if he is uniquely human. Thompson acknowledges Jesus's unlikeness to us but rules out Käsemann's conclusion that Jesus is less than human in John's Gospel. In a way, then, Thompson ends where Käsemann begins—with the distinctiveness of Jesus.

The distinctiveness of Jesus as a human being in John's Gospel is the point of departure for this essay. Simply put, given that Jesus is human just like us, what makes him so different from us? This way of putting the question locates our christological inquiry within ancient discourses on selfhood. As it so happens, John's Gospel was written during what Richard Sorabji has described as an "explosion of new ideas about the Self."[9] Explosion is a fitting metaphor for the power—as well as the chaos, disorder, and divergence—of ancient reflection on the Self, observable in the writings of Lucretius, Cicero, Seneca, Epictetus, and Plutarch among others, as well as ancient Jewish writings like the works of Philo.[10] For Sorabji, inquiry about the antique Self is inquiry about "an embodied individual whose existence is plain to see" that can "relate itself to the world in terms of me and me again."[11] As such, ancient discourses about selfhood may illuminate the distinctiveness of Jesus as a human being. But, first, some account of that distinctiveness is in order.

The Distinctiveness of Jesus

The distinctiveness of Jesus as a human being in the Fourth Gospel is not a product of deficient narration, as though the evangelist accidently splattered divinity on his otherwise human portrait of Jesus.[12] Interestingly, the features of the Fourth Gospel that make Jesus's humanity incredible to Käsemann are also found in the Synoptic Gospels, but Jesus's fast in the wilderness (Matt 4:1–2), stroll across the water (Mark 6:47–52), evasion of his opponents (Luke 4:28–30), and mighty deeds among crowds (Matt 8–9), to take several examples, are seldom thought to impugn his humanity in those writings. Why should they in the Fourth Gospel? Even so, whereas in the Synoptic Gospels the mighty deeds of Jesus cause offense in view of his human origins (Matt 13:54–58; Mark 6:1–6), in the Fourth Gospel, the signs of Jesus mark him out as an exceptional human being (John 3:1–2; 7:31; 9:30–33; 11:37). The evangelist would not be surprised to learn that we find Jesus to be, in certain respects, unlike us. As Grant Macaskill writes, "The experience and identity of believers is derived from Jesus, rather than being identical to his, as it would be if he were merely the prototypical believer. . . . [W]hile he is the Good Shepherd, they are the sheep (John 10:11)."[13] Or, to adapt a sentence from Karl Barth, the Fourth Evangelist cannot speak of Jesus simply by speaking of humanity in a loud voice.[14] Jesus's unlikeness to us is part of the Fourth Gospel's rhetorical design, particularly with respect to Jesus's signs, Jesus's agency in God's saving work, and Jesus's unique relation to God, as God's Son. As will be seen, in these matters Jesus is singular, nearly inimitable.

No one has, does, or will perform the signs that Jesus performed, at least, according to the man born blind (9:30–33), the teacher of Israel (3:1–2), and the believing crowd (7:31). The evangelist narrates these signs of Jesus in order to elicit trust in him among his readers (20:30–31; cf. 2:11; 12:37). In the Fourth Gospel, Jesus's humanity made possible material signs that reveal who he is, and John's writing makes it possible for his flesh-and-blood readers to reckon with those signs and entrust themselves to Jesus.[15] As such, the signs of Jesus are not given as ethical models for believers to imitate or even approximate within our own limited abilities, as though doctors, bakers, and wine-makers are more closely imitating Jesus than those in other vocations.[16] This is most evident in Jesus's discourse on the bread of life, which interprets the sign in which he feeds a hungry crowd with a few fish and loaves and then gathers up the leftovers (6:1–71). When the crowd asks Jesus what to do to do God's work, Jesus answers, "This is the work of God, that you trust in him whom God sent" (6:28–29, my translation).[17] Commending the practice of giving food to those who need it is simply not the point of the sign with the bread, even if elsewhere we do learn that Jesus's disciples were supposed to practice material care for those in need (12:6; 13:29). The discourse following the sign is rather concerned with how Jesus is the bread of life given by the Father (6:30–59). The discourse gives way to two responses among his disciples: either distrust or trust in Jesus (6:60–71). The sign is not meant to be imitated so much as it is meant to evoke trust. The same rhetoric is operative in other signs of Jesus: water made wine elicits trust from his disciples (2:11), the giving of sight to the man born blind is met with the man's trust (9:38), and Jesus expects that Lazarus's death will occasion trust from his disciples (11:15, 25–27, 40; cf. 4:50; 20:30–31).[18] All this to say, the signs of Jesus are inimitable not only because we are not Jesus, but also because we are not supposed to be. The signs do not show us what exactly we are to do, so much as they show us whom we are to trust.

Not all the works of Jesus are presented as inimitable in the Fourth Gospel, but even where Jesus's human life is the pattern for ours, our actions are inconsequential by comparison. Nowhere is this discrepancy clearer than in the double interpretation of the footwashing, which for Jesus is both a figure of his lowly death for those he loves (13:5–11) and a moral pattern of life that his disciples are to replicate with each other (13:12–20). In what sense are these interpretations of the footwashing commensurable, when the first signifies how the life-giving love of Jesus is actualized in his singular, saving death and the second instructs the disciples to practice love for one another in continuous lowliness and service?[19] The two interpretations cohere not in the effects a pattern of life has in the world, but in the pattern itself: a pattern embodied by Jesus to which the disciples are to conform, a pattern weaving together love, life, and lowly service in God's presence and in human community.[20] Together, the two interpretations of the footwashing reflect "the intrinsic connection between God's action in Christ, which constitutes the community of his followers, and the life of that community."[21] When Jesus's disciples practice the lowly, life-giving love of Jesus among one another, it means they are blessed (13:17). And when Jesus does it, it means God's life for the world (3:16). In dying, Peter would glorify God and do so as one who follows after Jesus (21:19), whose own death glorified God even as God glorified him (17:1–5). But it is Jesus, not Peter, who gives his flesh for the world's life (6:51–58; cf. 3:14–15), who dies for the regathering of a dispersed nation (11:47–53), and who, lifted up onto a cross, draws all people to himself (12:32–33). In a sense, then, the practice of love that makes us most like Jesus is the one that makes him most unlike us.

Jesus's relation to God is unlike ours because he is the only Son of God. The Fourth Gospel presents Jesus's human relationship to God as unmediated, whereas ours is mediated through Jesus. An asymmetry is at play between our relation to God and Jesus's, which comes through in a number of his succinct statements:

- "I know my own and my own know me, just as the Father knows me and I know the Father" (10:14–15).
- "I am in my Father, and you in me, and I in you" (14:20).
- "As the Father has loved me, so I have loved you" (15:9).
- "The glory that you have given me I have given them, so that they may be one, as we are one" (17:22).
- "As the Father has sent me, so I send you" (20:21).

This asymmetric dynamic is also at play with respect to seeing God. Jesus alone has seen the Father and sees what the Father is doing (5:19; 6:46), whereas we see the Father only by seeing Jesus (14:7–9; cf. 1:18; 17:24). It is not quite correct to say of these relational dynamics that what Jesus is to the Father, we are to Jesus. We are not called children of Jesus but children of God (1:13), with Jesus referring to us as brothers and sisters (20:17). Rather, as a human being, Jesus's unique relation to the Father makes room for us to know God as Jesus does (1:18), because we know Jesus as God does, as the one whom the Father sent to give life and light to all that would not have been made without him (17:3; 1:1–5). Jesus does not blot out the face of God. Instead, the Fourth Gospel challenges its readers to see the glory of God in the flesh of Jesus (1:14).[22]

So there is a disparity between Jesus's humanity and ours, and that disparity is not simply a matter of what we suppose humanity is in contrast to how John represents Jesus as human. The Fourth Gospel itself presents Jesus in his unlikeness to us as he performs signs, imparts eternal life through his death and resurrection, and relates to the Father. In these respects, Jesus is singular among human beings, and his singularity owes to what he is to God and what God is to him. Having created all things through the Word, God elects to give eternal life to creatures through the flesh of Jesus, a divine act signified in the signs of Jesus, actualized in his glorification, and made possible by the Father sending him into the world. Jesus's humanity is unlike ours in his actions and their magnitude, but our human lives come to depend on Jesus's, because the Fourth Gospel would have it that we are made alive through trust in him.

But if John's strange Christology makes Jesus inimitable in every important sense, then in what meaningful sense is he human? Or, if we are to suppose that Jesus is the true human being, then in what sense are we human who cannot be wholly like Jesus? The problem is ameliorated (but not eliminated) by recent scholarship on the ethics of John's Gospel. Whereas an older consensus suspected that the Fourth Gospel sacrificed ethics on the altar of its Christology, a newer consensus is emerging that attends to the ethics implied by its Christology.[23] As Lindsey Trozzo argues, even where he appears most elevated and strange, the Fourth Gospel presents the way Jesus relates to the Father as a model for how we are to relate to Jesus, and so to God. That is, Jesus is inimitable save for his responsiveness to God.[24] If in saying "I can do nothing on my own" (5:30) Jesus characterizes his words and works as "transparent to God's act and power," then in telling us "apart from me you can do nothing" (15:5) we might come to understand our works as transparent to Jesus's act and power, like a fruit-bearing branch is to the vine (15:1–8; cf. 3:21; 14:12–14).[25] So the divine act in Jesus is determinative for the shape of his human life and ours. This is why the basis of ethics in the Fourth Gospel is trust in Jesus (6:28–29).[26] Even in his unlikeness to us, Jesus's responsiveness to the Father shows us what is possible for us when through trust in him we have life from God. Because the Fourth Gospel is written from the perspective that Jesus is alive, we do not need to be Jesus to be like him or to participate in his work. Jesus's humanity makes ours possible.[27]

What to Make of Oneself?

Having established how Jesus's singularity as a human being is an element of the Fourth Gospel's narrative design, we might attempt to account for Jesus's distinctiveness. Although the concept of divine identity has proven helpful in articulating just what kind of oneness Jesus has with God in John's Gospel and other writings in the NT, it is less helpful for conceptualizing Jesus's solidarity with and distinctiveness among human beings.[28] For that, we do well to turn to ancient discourses of selfhood, especially those that focus on how each person can work on themselves to become like gods (or like God's). The Fourth Gospel reflects engagement with questions of the Self with respect to its Christology. Notably, the question "What do you make of yourself?" (τίνα σεαυτὸν ποιεῖς, 8:53) is addressed to Jesus in the middle of a series of christological conflicts in John 5–10, the beginning and end of which are marked by the supposition that Jesus makes himself something he is not:[29]

> [Jesus] "was also calling God his own Father, thereby making himself equal to God" (ἴσον ἑαυτὸν ποιῶν τῷ θεῷ, 5:18).

> "You, though only a human being, are making yourself God" (σὺ ἄνθρωπος ὢν ποιεῖς σεαυτὸν θεόν, 10:33; cf. 19:7, 12).

The charge is that Jesus is engaged in a perverse project of self-fashioning, not unlike what Gaius did when he wore winged sandals and assumed the name Mercury (Philo, *Embassy* 101–102; cf. 77–78; 162) or what Antiochus did as he donned the name Epiphanes (2 Macc 9:8–12).[30] Focus on what Jesus makes of himself in John's Gospel converges at the points where his oneness with God is at stake. By making this charge about self-fashioning constitutive of the christological conflict in the feast cycle, the Fourth Gospel relates what it has to say about Jesus to an expansive ancient discourse about the Self. Stated differently, when John's Gospel works out what kind of human being Jesus is, it does so with reference to what one makes of oneself, given what one is in relation to others.

Ancient discourses on selfhood involved reflection on how human beings could (and could not) become like god(s). Owing in no small measure to Socrates, the question "What do you make of yourself?" came into theological articulation among the Platonic, Aristotelian, Epicurean, and Stoic philosophical schools.[31] Socrates tells Phaedrus that he has no time for traditional myths because he does not yet understand himself: "I'm unable as yet to know myself, as the inscription at Delphi says. . . . I shall examine not them [i.e., the traditional myths] but myself [ἐμαυτόν], to see if I really am either some monster more tangled up and more raging than Typhon, or a tamer and simpler animal with some natural share of the divine [θείας] and calm" (Plato, *Phaed*. 230a [Emlyn-Jones and Preddy]). One classicist regards this inquiry into the self as "ancient philosophy's hardest question" because of the way it binds together understandings of humanity, divinity, and "long-term happiness," all of which were controverted matters among ancient Greco-Roman thinkers.[32] Whereas Platonists and Aristotelians viewed human beings as an aggregation of distinct parts with a core that could be identified as the Self, Stoics and Epicureans understood human beings as physical, psychological wholes, irreducible to parts, but having a constitution that cohered with a larger ethical order, what Christopher Gill refers to as the "structured self."[33] These views of human beings interfaced differently with how a human being could become like god. Plato and Aristotle identified the intellect as the core of the Self as well as the most divine faculty, the part by which one could make oneself godlike. So, for them, godlikeness consisted in pure contemplation, an activity by which humans could approach immortality and self-sufficiency. Even so, Plato and Aristotle qualify their claims about the extent to which one can become godlike. Aristotle writes, "We ought *so far as possible* to achieve immortality" (ἐφ᾽ ὅσον ἐνδέχεται ἀθανατίζειν, Aristotle, *Eth. nic.* 1177b 30–36 [Rackham]; cf. Plato, *Tim.* 90C).[34] By contrast, Stoics like Epictetus treat the whole person as "a fragment of God," so that one's reflexive actions are undertaken both with respect to oneself and to God (*Diatr.* 2.8.11–14).[35] Knowledge that "God himself is present within you" ought to make one godlike through ethical conduct. Pointing readers to the statue of Zeus at Olympia, Epictetus writes, "That is how I'd like to show myself to you: faithful, modest, noble-minded, imperturbable" (*Diatr.* 2.8.27). Epictetus asks whether in being godlike he is "immortal too, and eternally young, and immune from disease," and continues, "No, but [I'd like to show myself to you] as one who can die in a god-like way, who can endure disease in a god-like way. That lies in my power, that I can do, but the rest is not in my power, nor can I do it" (*Diatr.* 2.8.28). Even as these thinkers make sense of themselves with recourse to divinity, they guard against a sense that all that can be predicated of gods can be predicated of humans without remainder.

The question of what one makes of oneself becomes even more difficult when one considers how ancient Jews constructed the Self in relation to God through the interpretation of Israel's Scripture and their practices of piety. For instance, in his youth Philo of Alexandria was among Plato's heirs on the matter of the Self, even quoting his famous digression in *Theaetetus*: "We ought to fly away from earth to heaven as quickly as we can; and to fly away is to become like God, as far as this is possible [ὁμοίωσις θεῷ κατὰ τὸ δυνατόν]; and to become like Him is to become holy, just, and wise" (Philo, *Flight* 63 [Colson and Whitaker]). But Philo was not an uncritical reader of Plato, as he makes the knowledge of God more central to the understanding of the Self than Plato does and develops his concept of the Self through biblical exegesis.[36] In supposing that Abraham and Moses did not apprehend God with their outward senses, as Maren Niehoff observes, "Philo suggests that preparing for the approach of God is best done by turning inward and knowing oneself."[37] In quite a different way, as Mira Balberg argues, the Tannaitic rabbis expanded the realm of ritual impurity (and undertook other innovations in the observance of purity) with the result that daily life came to involve attentiveness to one's Self—one's own body and one's relations to others—out of regard for the law. Engaging a widespread cultural concern about selfhood through the observance of ritual purity, in the Mishnah "the rabbinic self is defined by subordination to the Torah."[38] The diversity of understandings of Self—even with respect to which concepts or practices were most important to take into account—was grounded in a diversity of understandings about god(s), human beings, ethics, and teleology.

To make matters more complicated, even as the Self was being conceived intellectually, ethically, and legally with reference to fundamental ideas about humanity and divinity, concepts began to emerge about individual differentiation within these larger cultural frameworks.[39] Philo, for example, allegorically identifies the cities of refuge as six divine powers (the highest of which is God's unseen Logos), and he suggests that the particular manifestation of divine power that a person might come to know has everything to do with the kind of person they are (*Flight* 94–99; cf. *Abraham* 124–130; Num 35:11–28 LXX; Exod 21:12–14 LXX). Elsewhere, Philo takes Abraham, Isaac, and Jacob to represent three different ways persons might come to attain virtue (*Dreams* 1.167–171). While the goal of human life was common to all human beings, the path toward virtue and the resulting knowledge of God's power would differ depending on a person's disposition and character (*Flight* 102). Philo leaves it to each of his readers to discern what sort of people they are as they aim to attain virtue and the knowledge of God.

But most important for emerging ideas of individual differentiation within the realm of ethics, according to Richard Sorabji, is Cicero's interpretation of Cato's suicide.[40] Cicero adapted an earlier Stoic "theory of personae" that viewed all human beings as having a common rational character but also conceived of each human being as having peculiarities in their character and will that informed the shape of their moral actions. Cicero writes, "For we must so act as not to oppose the universal laws of human nature, but, while safeguarding those, to follow the bent of our own particular nature.... we may ... regulate our own pursuits by the standard of our own nature [*nostrae naturae regula*]" (*Off.* 1.110 [Miller]). Cato's suicide illustrates this concept:

> Indeed, such diversity of character [*differentia naturarum*] carries with it
> so great significance that suicide may be for one man a duty, for another

[under the same circumstances] a crime. Did Marcus Cato find himself
in one predicament, and were the others, who surrendered to Caesar in
Africa, in another? And yet, perhaps, they would have been condemned,
if they had taken their lives; for their mode of life had been less austere
and their characters more pliable. But Cato had been endowed by nature
with an austerity beyond belief, and he himself had strengthened it by
unswerving consistency and had remained ever true to his purpose and
fixed resolve; and it was for him to die rather than to look upon the face
of a tyrant. (*Off.* 1.112 [Miller])

Unlike a modern European concept of Self that envisions a "buffer" between
one's Self, one's body, and the world outside—a concept of Self that disembeds
individuals from a larger ethical and social frame so that they are first and foremost individuals—ancient ideas about differentiated individuality were envel-
oped within larger convictions about humans and god(s).[41] The question about
what one makes of oneself came to involve not only considerations about the
common lot of humanity but also about how one's acts could be consistent with
one's own character.

What to Make of Jesus?

Despite the complexity of ancient reflection on the Self, we may now be in a
somewhat better position to appreciate the peculiarity and distinctiveness of
Jesus in the Fourth Gospel as a function of his humanity rather than a diminu-
tion of it. Jesus's dialogue with the *Ioudaioi* at the Feast of Dedication reflects
concerns about what Jesus makes of himself with reference both to Jesus's oneness
with God and to what sort of creatures human beings are (John 10:22–39). After
Jesus says, "The Father and I are one" (10:30), the *Ioudaioi* charge Jesus with
slandering God "because you, though only a human being, are making yourself
God" (σὺ ἄνθρωπος ὢν ποιεῖς σεαυτὸν θεόν, 10:33). Two matters integral to the
Fourth Gospel's Christology are at stake in this charge. The first is the conception, indicated by the concessive participle (ὢν), that a human being cannot be
God. The second is the charge that in claiming oneness with the Father, Jesus
makes himself something he is not. As will be seen, Jesus's answer about himself
can be understood as an assertion about humanity and the sense in which human
beings can be like gods, an answer that also establishes grounds to recognize the
peculiar way in which he is one with the Father (10:34–36). But this exchange
about what Jesus makes of himself is embedded in a discussion of Jesus's works,
which we do well to address first.

Jesus answers the request "If you are the Messiah, tell us plainly" (10:24)
with reference to the works he does in the Father's name (10:25, 32–33): works
that actualize Jesus's oneness with God (10:30) and enable apprehension of

Jesus's unique relation to the Father (10:37–39).⁴² As David Litwa wryly observes, however, Jesus's works of healing are part of the problem he has gotten into with the *Ioudaioi*. By performing his works on the Sabbath, he transgressed the law (5:9–18; 9:14–16).⁴³ Answering the contention that he broke the Sabbath by healing a paralyzed man, Jesus tells the *Ioudaioi*, "My Father is still working, and I also am working," prompting the first charge that he made himself equal to God (5:17–18). Jesus's ethical defense is not universalizable, such that all humans can work on the Sabbath if God does. Neither is there any straightforward indication that Jesus has abolished the fourth commandment. Instead, the claim about working on the Sabbath is peculiar to who and what Jesus is in relation to God and to others. Jesus makes an ethical argument for the validity of his work that is in keeping with what Cicero might call "the standard of his own character" (*naturae regula, Off.* 1.110). It is not that Jesus needed an excuse for working on the Sabbath, which his identity with God conveniently supplied. The work that Jesus does in enabling a paralyzed man to walk, rather, is exactly the kind of work that he does whenever God gives life and renders judgment (John 5:19–30). In healing on the Sabbath, Jesus undertakes an action that some regarded as a crime, but which was consistent with himself as one who does God's works, which do not cease on the Sabbath. Jesus's healing on the Sabbath, however, is not as exceptional as Cato's suicide. The narrator does not concede that Jesus broke the Sabbath. Jesus later argues that performing works of healing on the Sabbath is lawful because performing eighth-day circumcision on the Sabbath is lawful (7:21–24). Jesus adjures his hearers to "judge with right judgment" (7:24), a theme that recurs with respect to his works at the Feast of Dedication.

Unique to the charge that Jesus makes himself God at the Feast of Dedication is the implication that a human being cannot be God. In answering his interlocutors, Jesus says that Scripture says that God says, "You are gods," a response that has embarrassed or discountenanced recent commentators on John because of how Jesus seems to equivocate on the meaning of god (θεός). It is as though he predicates deity of human beings generally to evade the charge that he deifies himself in a peculiar (and apparently blasphemous) way:⁴⁴ "Jesus answered them, 'Is it not written in your law, "I said you are gods" [ἐγὼ εἶπα· θεοί ἐστε]? If [God] called (εἶπεν) them to whom the word of God came *gods*—and the Scripture cannot be broken—are you saying of him whom the Father consecrated and sent into the world "you are speaking impiously," because I said "I am God's son"?'" (10:34–36, my translation). Even the interpretation that Jesus's response works as an *a fortiori* argument—if *god* can be predicated of humans, all the more so can *son of god* be predicated of Jesus—leaves one with the impression that Jesus's response is no more than a rhetorical trick, if not a "rhetorical trap."⁴⁵ It is inescapable that the question's rhetoric is meant to establish a basic compatibility between human beings and God, but it is often overlooked that the analogy depends on God's action in both cases. God is twice the subject of the speech-act whereby humans are called gods, and humans are so called because God's word came to them, presumably another act of God. God's action, moreover, is the basis of what Jesus has to say about himself. So, if God makes humans out to be gods by giving them the word of God, then God can make one human out to be God's Son by consecrating and sending him. As Thompson writes, "The christological scandal of John is not that Jesus has made himself equal or one with God, but that God has chosen to make himself one with Jesus."[46] The anthropological surprise, we might add, is that God made humans out to be gods.

The fact that reflection on the sense in which humans are like gods attended questions about selfhood among ancient Romans and Jews alike suggests that Jesus's response has more conceptual density than may otherwise be presumed. What does Jesus think God predicates of human beings by calling us gods? Although early rabbinic interpretation understood this to indicate that Israel became immortal in receiving the law at Sinai (until, that is, the incident with the golden calf; cf. Ps 82:7), Jesus implies that these human beings are gods because the word of God came to them.[47] In this context, the "word of God" seems to refer not to the law or Scripture as such (though Jesus refers to both in the same sentence as the word of God), so much as to the godlike way of thinking inscribed in them that affords wisdom, knowledge, and right judgment to human beings.[48] In Psalm 81 LXX (82 MT), God exercises right judgment (διακρίνει) over those mortal gods who judge unjustly (κρίνετε ἀδικίαν, 81:1–2). In their moral deliberation and injustice, they are judged as neither knowing nor understanding (οὐκ ἔγνωσαν οὐδὲ συνῆκαν, 81:5). That is, these gods are like God in rendering judgment but are unlike God in that their judgment is wrongful. By bringing the theme of judgment and godlikeness from Psalm 81 LXX into connection with receiving the word of God, the law becomes a way into moral deliberation, judging with right judgment. It is unsurprising, then, that Nicodemus presumes the law judges people only by giving them a hearing (John 7:51; cf. 7:24). And there is surely an irony intended by the implied author in Pilate's words about judging Jesus according to the law (κατὰ τὸν νόμον ὑμῶν κρίνατε αὐτόν, 18:31). Given that the law in John's Gospel is one of Jesus's witnesses *and* that which enables humans to exercise the godlike faculty of judgment, to judge Jesus by the law would be to see him as one with God. That is, in the Fourth Gospel, we are most like gods when, in exercising right judgment about Jesus's works, we make him out to be God's Son. In trusting and knowing this about Jesus, we also become like gods in having eternal life (17:3; cf. 10:28–29).

But Jesus's quotation of Psalm 81 LXX works not only to show the compatibility of humanity with divinity, but also of divinity with mortality.[49] The fragment of God's speech Jesus quotes is from the sentence: "I said, 'Gods you are [ἐγὼ εἶπα Θεοί ἐστε], and sons of the Most High, but you all are dying like human beings, and like one of the rulers you fall'" (81:6–7 LXX).[50] The sentence is jarring because gods are not usually mortal. But in the same breath that Jesus identifies himself as "God's Son" he refers to himself as "him whom the Father consecrated and sent into the world" (John 10:36). Richard Bauckham has argued that the language of consecration, used as it is during the Feast of Dedication, is about how God sets Jesus apart for sacrifice, just as new altars are set apart for sacrifice (Num 7:1–11; 1 Kgs 8:63–64).[51] What is astonishing, then, is that what distinguishes Jesus as God's Son, what makes Jesus singular among human beings because of his unity with the Father, is how God sets him apart for death (John 10:36; cf. 3:16–17), a death that, to be sure, Jesus also sets himself apart for (17:17–19), a death through which Jesus brings God's work to completion (19:30).[52] Jesus's mortality makes it possible for us to die in a godlike way even as we live (always) with Jesus. So in the Fourth Gospel's ideological perspective, humanity and divinity are not finally incompatible and Jesus does not make himself God. Jesus is most singular in his oneness with the Father at just the point he is in most solidarity with us, namely, in being mortal.

Conclusion

The difference that emerges between Jesus's humanity and ours in John's Gospel is not by mistake but by design. The Fourth Gospel presents us with Jesus in his singularity among human beings, as his life-giving power is reflected in his signs and actualized in his glorification. At the same time, the act and power that distinguish Jesus as a human being become the basis of our lives as human beings. Having been made alive by trust, our lives might be laid bare to Jesus's works in the way that his life is laid bare to the Father's. The ancient preoccupation with what to make of oneself informs both John's Christology and anthropology. Jesus answers the charge that he, a human being, makes himself God with reference to the works of the Father that he does. He asks those who have seen his works to be gods, rendering right judgment about those works (10:22–39; cf. 7:21–24). Jesus knows himself as one who is utterly "transparent to God's act and power," as one who does not speak or act "from himself" but only from the Father whom he alone sees (5:19; 6:46). The distinctiveness of Jesus impugns neither his humanity nor ours. In the Fourth Gospel, Jesus is different than us not because Jesus is more or less human, but because Jesus is Jesus.

CHAPTER SEVEN

Jesus's Apotropaic Theophany

Guarding and Sanctifying Believers in John's Gospel

Alicia D. Myers

IN HER EXTENSIVE and enduring interpretations of the Gospel of John, Marianne Meye Thompson has explored various facets of the Gospel's portrayal of Jesus as well as its depictions of God as his Father.[1] For Thompson, neither the human nor divine aspects of Jesus's person should be overlooked, for it is in the unique blending of these two identities that God reveals the extent of his love for creation (3:14–21). Moreover, it is the Father's will and at his initiative that Jesus acts. As a human being, the Word made *flesh*, Jesus is mortal; he experiences the precariousness and eventual destruction that comes with mortality. As the Word, however, he is victorious over death (16:33), resurrecting himself to rejoin his disciples and gift them with the Spirit (20:19–23). Rather than arguing for Jesus's humanity, then, the Gospel presupposes his humanity, often characterizing it as a "stumbling block to accepting the claims that he makes (6:42, 52)."[2] As Thompson notes, this stumbling block is the foundation for the Gospel narrative, setting its claims apart from contemporaneous Jewish and Greco-Roman literature that clearly delineated immortal divinity from mortal human flesh.[3] As the incarnate Word, Jesus reveals God's love to creation in a tactile and never-before-seen way. Thus, the prologue claims, "No one has seen God before; it is the Unique God (μονογενὴς θεός), the one being in the Father's bosom, that one showed the way" (1:18).

Jesus's "showing," or "interpreting" (ἐξηγήσατο), God happens throughout his ministry, as he gathers disciples, restores bodies, and gives life to various individuals with his works and his words.[4] In addition to these signs and teachings, Jesus also shows who God is by protecting those who remain with him throughout his lifetime. In fact, Jesus claims this is part of the will of God that feeds him (4:34) and which he lives to fulfill (5:30; 7:17). In 6:38–40 he explains, "I have descended from heaven, not that I might do my will but the will of the one who sent me. And this is the will of the one who sent me, that I should not lose anything from which he has given me, but that I should raise it on the last day. For this is the will of my Father, that each one who sees the Son and believes in him should have eternal life, and I will raise him on the last day." In John 10 and

17, Jesus makes similar claims of protection that unite him with the Father and, in John 18:9, the narrator draws attention to how Jesus fulfills this protective work during his arrest.[5]

This essay adds to these discussions by showing how this protection participates with the larger themes of Jesus's manifestation of God's presence on earth as the "Holy One of God" (6:69) and his triumph over "the ruler of this world" (12:31–32; 14:31; 16:11) that sets the stage for the Holy Spirit's continued work among and through believers. Contextualizing the theme of Jesus's embodying God's holiness, I argue that John's Gospel tells the story of Jesus's apocalyptic victory over the ruler of this world. While this victory is especially emphasized in his exorcistic death, his protective, and thus apotropaic, presence is also at work during his ministry and offered to his disciples through the gift of the Holy Spirit after his resurrection. As an apotropaic presence, Jesus keeps his followers from direct attacks and, eventually, succeeds in casting out the ruler of this world from their midst by means of his death and resurrection.[6] This presentation risks leaving believers unprotected after Jesus's departure. Although Jesus's enfleshed revelation is gone, however, the Fourth Gospel argues that God's holiness is accessible *and* protective through the Holy Spirit even when that protection does not prevent persecution and even death (15:18–25; 16:2). In this way, the Gospel progresses from the corporeal apotropaism of Jesus's theophanic presence to the Spirit, whose apotropaism extends to all believers regardless of physical or temporal distance from their incarnate Savior.

Jesus as the Holy One of God

The understanding of Jesus embodying God's presence and holiness is well-established among Johannine interpreters. Although Johannine scholarship has moved past Rudolf Bultmann's readings in a number of ways, scholars still acknowledge the importance of Jesus's work of self-revelation. He makes God's glory visible, audible, and tactile in ways not previously possible.[7] The Word's incarnation as Jesus, God's Son and Christ, bridges the gap, bringing humanity into direct contact with the divine with both scandalous and miraculous consequences. Mary L. Coloe notes, as the embodiment of God's glory and holiness, Jesus acts as a mobile temple—a tabernacle—who dwells among humanity and travels throughout Judea, Samaria, and Galilee.[8] When people encounter Jesus, then, they meet a living sanctuary who is not tied to one physical location (4:23–24). The conflicts that result when people encounter the person Jesus are because they cannot recognize the holiness standing before them; he does not *look* or *sound* like what they expect from God. Yet, the Gospel insists, because of Jesus's origins from, and unity with, God, he *is* holy (6:69). But what is God's holiness and what does it do?

According to Jacob Milgrom and Mary Douglas, God's holiness is both protective and dangerous.[9] Holiness is God's creative force that makes, protects, and preserves life, but it is dangerous because when it encounters mortality (e.g., impurity or profanity) it "breaks out," either with destructive power or by withdrawing and leaving people bereft of God's protection (cf. Exod 19:21–23).[10] Thus, the Levitical code prescribes various rituals to cleanse people from everyday (thus not sinful) impurities as well as atonement rituals to reconcile them to God after committing moral impurities (e.g., idolatry, murder, adultery), either individually or as a collective people. In the Second Temple period, the Jerusalem temple had different boundaries with specific requirements that needed to be met in order for one to cross and, therefore, be closer to God's holy presence. Greek and Roman temples were similarly set off from the rest of the city with a border marking the τέμενος, whether it included temple precincts or holy groves.[11] To cross these boundaries flagrantly risked the deities' wrath, bringing judgment on the individual *and* to the city or people.

Examples of God's holiness breaking out are found throughout the OT as well as in Second Temple Jewish literature. Indeed, this understanding explains Ezekiel's portrayal of God's glory leaving Jerusalem, thus leading to the city's and temple's destruction by the Babylonians. According to Ezekiel, a key reason for this departure was the priests' failure to maintain the boundaries between holy and profane because they were either no longer able to distinguish pure from impure, or they were unwilling to do so (8:7–18; 22:26–31). The result has been the suffering of innocent people who are victimized by both princes and priests, who attack them rather than protect them as good shepherds ought to do (22:6–31; 34:1–10). For this reason, God uses Babylon as the instrument of judgment and, after withdrawing from the temple, God allows Babylon to attack and destroy Jerusalem and the sanctuary within it (10:18–11:25; 17:12–21).

Brian Neil Peterson and, more recently, Josiah Hall have argued that Ezekiel's portrayal of God's departure from the temple resonates with John's Gospel.[12] Peterson highlights the priests' defilement of the sanctuary with idolatry in Ezekiel 8:6–18. In 8:6, the Lord proclaims to Ezekiel that these "great abominations" will drive him from the sanctuary. This parallel informs Peterson's interpretation of Jesus's temple action in John 2:13–22 as a prophecy of the temple's destruction and replacement. Peterson is right to note the violent reaction of Jesus to the sight of merchants and moneychangers in the temple precincts. As one who has just revealed his glory in 2:11, his entrance into the temple in 2:13–17 reflects expectations of holiness breaking out with destructive results (cf. 2 Macc 3). Yet, Jesus undercuts the expectation of the destruction that results from unrecognized holiness and profaned spaces. Instead of condemning the temple, he predicts the destruction of his own body that is a "sanctuary" (ναός), or a dwelling place of God (John 2:22).[13] As the Gospel continues, Jesus repeatedly notes that he has not come to judge the world, but rather to reveal the world's own judgment (3:17); people will show the truth of themselves based on their reactions to him. Either they will come to the light despite their shortcomings and impurities to receive healing and life, or they will remain in darkness and experience wrath and its consequence of death (3:18–21).

According to Hall, this judgment comes in the form of Jesus's departure, which is simultaneously the moment of rescue and blessing for believers. In his reading of Ezekiel 8–10, Hall focuses more on how Ezekiel and John console their audiences by explaining God's absence and pointing toward restoration.[14] Noting that Ezekiel and John were composed after destructions of Jerusalem and the temple, Hall argues that these writings explain *how* God could allow such things to happen and when the suffering would end. In Ezekiel 40–44, God departs and uses the Babylonians for a time of judgment but will restore Israel with a new temple in the end. In John's Gospel, however, the crisis is less the Jerusalem temple's destruction than it is Jesus's departure after his resurrection.[15] This departure is both the result of the world's (and especially the religious authorities') inability to decipher Jesus's holiness *and* the judgment against them. Having failed to recognize the divine visitation, the world faces divine wrath.[16] At the same time, however, this judgment does not extend to believers. Instead of judgment, Jesus's death enables the gift of the Holy Spirit after his resurrection. In this way, the Gospel assures its audiences that they have not been abandoned, even though the world has been and continues to be judged. Indeed, given the Holy Spirit, believers continue Jesus's work by receiving and remembering his words *and* judging the world as it now turns to reject them (16:2–11).

Jesus's Death as John's Exorcism

The connection between holiness and judgment, particularly from the work of Hall, helps to bridge the gap between how Jesus's holiness connects to his exorcistic work. In John 12:27–32, Jesus links these ideas as he reflects on his choice to follow God's will despite the troubling it causes in his soul. In John's recasting of the Gethsemane scene, Jesus acknowledges the pain he experiences but confidently declares that it "was for this reason I came for this hour. Father, glorify your name!" (12:27b–28a). Assured of his mission, Jesus tells the confused crowd:

> Now is the judgment of this world,
> > now the ruler of this world will be cast out outside.
> And I, if I am lifted up from the earth,
> > I will draw all things[17] to myself. (12:31–32)

The narrator then helpfully clarifies that Jesus "was saying this to signify the type of death he was about to die" (12:33). According to John, therefore, Jesus's manifestation of God's holiness is not simply rejected by people who do not recognize him. Instead, he faces direct and diabolical opposition from "the ruler of this world." Moreover, because Jesus chooses to die in accordance with the Father's will (laying his life down for his sheep, 10:17–18), he confirms his identity as God's Son and Holy One. When the crowd surrounding him accuses him of blasphemy in John 10, Jesus responds: "Can you say to the one whom the Father consecrated (ἡγίασεν) and sent into the world, 'You are blaspheming,' because I said, 'I am the Son of God'? If I am not doing my Father's works, do not believe me. But if I am doing [them] and if you should not believe me, believe the works so that you might know and recognize that the Father is in me and I am in the Father" (10:36–38). Jesus is God's Holy One not only because he embodies God's glory, but also because he fulfills the task for which he was consecrated (or "sanctified"): he dies on behalf of others in order to bring people back to God (11:51–52).[18] Jesus's death, then, is not just a judgment that leads to his departure (and, thus, the departure of God's holiness) from the world; it is the completion of God's will and, therefore, the moment at which Jesus's victory over the false ruler is assured.

In 1995, Judith L. Kovacs published an article that focuses on John 12:31–32 as the key to understanding John's presentation of Jesus's death.[19] Kovacs notes the similarities between 12:31–32 and 16:11 to suggest that Jesus's judgment of the world is the same as that of the ruler of this world. Rather than just a symbolic idea, Kovacs argues that this ruler is the devil, whom the Gospel depicts as a "liar and murderer from the beginning" (8:44). Indeed, Kovacs notes, this struggle is precisely what 1:1–5 describes as "darkness" seeking impotently to overcome the light (cf. 12:35–36). Comparing John's pervasive dualistic imagery of light versus darkness with apocalyptic writings from the Second Temple period, Kovacs argues that John's Gospel was influenced by these apocalyptic ideas, particularly in its depiction of Jesus as "*the* Son of Man." For Kovacs, then, Jesus's death on the cross is not an awkward add-on to the Gospel (e.g., Bultmann, Käsemann) or a sacrifice, but rather it "is the locus of a cosmic battle, in which Jesus achieves a decisive victory over Satan."[20]

Building on Kovacs's work, Jutta Leonhardt-Balzer argues that Jesus's death is better described as an exorcism than a battle.[21] According to Leonhardt-Balzer, Jesus's death "casts out" the ruler not from the entire cosmos, but from the midst of believers who cling to Jesus's word. Freed from the ruler by means of Jesus's victorious exorcism, believers are now given the Holy Spirit who protects them from the evil one (17:15).[22] Rather than being enthralled or possessed by the ruler, believers are now possessed and enlivened by the Spirit.[23] While I agree with much of Leonhardt-Balzer's conclusions, her emphasis on Jesus's death and resurrection overlooks the protective work he has already done throughout his life. Indeed, when we recognize the interrelationship of holiness, exorcism, and protection in John's Gospel, we can see the apotropaic aspects of his ministry from which believers continue to benefit after his departure.

God's Protective Will
From Corporeal to Spiritual Apotropaism in John

The interrelationship between Jesus's embodiment of God's holiness and the exorcism accomplished by his death indicates a subtle presence of apotropaic thought in the Gospel of John. Apotropaism was a common element of exorcism throughout the larger Greco-Roman world since exorcists warded off malevolent spirits. Most often, apotropaism was expressed through rituals that involved prayers, incantations, or lullabies, as well as material objects (e.g., *amuleta* or φυλακτήρια) that could absorb the wrath of an evil spirit or convey the protective power of a benevolent spirit or deity.[24] In the Roman world, for example, young sons wore amulets called *bullae* to protect them until they reached manhood, and Pliny the Elder describes the phylactic powers of amber.[25]

Apotropaic ideas exist in ancient Jewish literature and the NT as well, although in distinct ways. In Jewish writings, the one who protects Israel and the Jews is God, who is petitioned through prayer and whose presence is maintained through covenantal obedience and ritual purifications. God's holy presence provides protection from threats, but when God's glory withdraws, it leaves Jerusalem open to attack (Ezek 8–10). Jesus's exorcisms in the synoptic traditions have also been interpreted as apotropaic, though Clint Wahlen is careful to emphasize that Jesus liberates people not with magical objects but with his words.[26] In this way, Wahlen suggests, Jesus mirrors the intercessory work of Abraham and Moses, who appealed to God not to abandon the people and thus leave them open to destruction.[27] According to Graham Twelftree, Jesus's exorcistic activity was not unusual in the Greco-Roman world, but the Gospels' depictions of these exorcisms as evidence of God's victory over Satan was unique.[28] In these conflicts, Jesus continually demonstrates the power of God's Holy Spirit to expel the demonic spirits of Beelzebub, the "ruler of demons" (Mark 3:22; Matt 12:24; Luke 11:15).

Rather than multiple individual exorcisms, John's Gospel depicts Jesus's victory over the ruler with the single exorcism caused by his death and resurrection. Having cast out the ruler, Jesus gives the Holy Spirit to continue his protective and instructive work (John 20:19–23). While apotropaism is more subtle in John's Gospel, I argue that it is nevertheless present. The apotropaic motif is perhaps most visible in Jesus's final prayer to the Father before his arrest. In John 17:11–19, Jesus prays for the continued protection of his disciples. My translation below breaks these verses into two main sections to highlight the parallelism between vv. 11b–13 and vv. 14–19.

> And I am no longer in the world, but they are in the world, and I am coming to you. Holy Father, keep the ones you have given me in your name so that they might be one just like us. When I was with them, *I kept* (ἐτήρουν) the ones you have given me in your name, and *I guarded* [them] (ἐφύλαξα), and I lost no one from them except *the son of destruction,* so that the Scripture might be fulfilled. But now I am coming to you and I am saying these things so that they might have my joy completed in them. (17:11b–13)

> I have given them your word and the world hated them because they are not from the world, just as I am not from the world. I do not ask that you take them from the world, but that *you should keep* (τηρήσῃς) *them from the evil one.* They are not from the world just as I am not from the world. Consecrate them in the truth; your word is truth. Just as you sent me into the world, I myself sent them into the world. And on behalf of them I am consecrating myself, so that they might be consecrated in truth. (17:14–19)

In his prayer, Jesus includes the apotropaic themes of keeping (τηρέω) and guarding (φυλάσσω), equating the two in v. 12. In vv. 14–19, Jesus creates a parallel between this protective work and his request for the Father to continue it after his departure. Jesus has preserved everyone except "the son of destruction," whom most scholars interpret as Judas, the disciple Jesus sent out into the night to initiate his betrayal (13:29–30). Jesus calls Judas "a devil" in 6:70, while John's narrator informs readers of his lying thievery in 12:1–8 and his possession by Satan in 13:2 and 27. John's Gospel, therefore, characterizes Judas as an agent of the devil, whom Jesus describes as metaphorically fathering those intent on lies and murder in 8:44. When Jesus asks his Father to keep the disciples from "the evil one" in 17:15, the parallelism implies this is another title for Jesus's primary opponent in the Gospel who is variously called darkness, the devil, Satan, and the ruler of this world.

In his analysis of Jesus's prayer, Loren Stuckenbruck notes the protective motif of Jesus's request, finding resonance with similar prayers from the Dead Sea Scrolls and Jubilees.[29] Stuckenbruck argues that these prayers for protection are rooted in a belief that God's final victory is assured in the eschaton. Michael J. Morris explicitly argues that Jesus's prayer is like those from Qumran, which are apotropaic prayers insofar as they ask for protection from an evil power.[30] While Stuckenbruck is right to emphasize the protective element of Jesus's prayer,

I agree with Morris's conclusion that "apotropaic" is a more precise designation, not because Jesus's prayer is in some way seeking to manipulate and control God's response, but because it asks for protection from an evil power.[31] This apotropaic protection, I argue, is provided by means of the Holy Spirit's continued presence.

As noted above, the Gospel of John is emphatic that Jesus follows the Father's will alone, in accordance with his consecrated task of loving the world and laying his life down on behalf of his disciples (cf. 3:16–18; 10:17–18, 36; 17:19). Jesus's prayer in 17:15 does not seek to control God or use a talisman to guarantee protection. Instead, Jesus's confident request is made because of his unique relationship with the Father that results in God's always hearing his prayers (11:41; cf. 9:31). Jesus prays for the disciples' protection in 17:11–19 because he is about to leave them in the world and will no longer be physically present to protect them as he has in the past. Throughout his ministry, Jesus's physical presence is apotropaic because he protects the ones the Father has given to him. For example, Jesus protects his disciples from threats such as hunger (6:1–14) and sea travel (6:19–21), but the Gospel likewise implies Jesus's protection during his conflicts with the Jewish authorities and crowds. The disciples are explicitly present for Jesus's initial confrontation with the Jewish authorities in 2:13–22, and his teaching in the synagogue later in 6:51–58, but their presence is implied at other times as well. Thus 9:1–5 indicates that the disciples are present during Jesus's teaching in the temple during Tabernacles, which culminates in the crowd's attempt to stone him (8:58–59). In all his conflicts, however, Jesus alone remains the target of violence, rather than his disciples. During his lifetime, Jesus's disciples are not permitted to experience violence on his behalf, even when they suggest it; neither Thomas's cry for the disciples to return to Judea to "die with him" (11:16) nor Peter's claim that "I will lay down my life for you" (13:37) is realized. Instead, it is Jesus who is targeted after his raising of Lazarus in 11:43–52, and he steps in to ensure his disciples' safe escape during his arrest. In 18:8 Jesus surrenders himself and instructs his captors to "release these ones to depart" (ἄφετε τούτους ὑπάγειν), which the narrator interjects to interpret as the fulfillment of Jesus's word that "I did not lose any of the ones you have given to me" (οὓς δέδωκάς μοι οὐκ ἀπώλεσα ἐξ αὐτῶν οὐδένα, 18:9). When Peter disobeys Jesus by striking Malchus with his sword, Jesus reprimands him with an allusion back to 12:27–33: "Put the sword in the sheath; shall I not drink the cup which my Father has given to me?" (18:11). The casting out of the ruler of this world is not accomplished in a violent revolt, or even with a disciple's personal sacrifice, but in Jesus's death that leads to his resurrection.

Although Jesus does not perform various exorcisms in the Gospel of John, he nevertheless keeps those physically with him from experiencing darkness and death during his lifetime.[32] Jesus's protection does not prevent *every* person who expresses some belief in him from departing (6:66; 17:12), nor does it prevent death for Lazarus while Jesus is absent. Yet, the Gospel emphasizes that those the Father has given to Jesus will remain in his word and, therefore, experience eternal life. Indeed, Jesus's return to and the raising of Lazarus offer hope for the crisis caused by Jesus's return to the Father that threatens to end his apotropaic reach, since he will no longer be physically present to intercede for believers. Jesus, the Gospel narrates, will return (cf. 14:1–7).

At the same time, however, during his farewell discourse, Jesus promises not to leave his disciples without protection in the interim. In so doing, the Gospel flips the crisis of Jesus's departure into a moment of victory and transition from corporeal to spiritual apotropaism. Jesus promises he will send the Spirit as "another Paraclete" who will remind and instruct the disciples even while continuing the world's judgment (14:16; 16:7–11). This Paraclete is the "Spirit of truth" (14:17; 15:26; 16:13) or the "Holy Spirit" (14:26), who will teach the disciples everything and remind them of Jesus's words. The Gospel itself testifies to the Spirit's presence among the believers with its post-Easter perspective and remembrances that interpret Jesus's words and actions (2:17, 22; 12:16). Jesus emphasizes that the Spirit's coming is only possible after his death and resurrection—that is, after his exorcizing the ruler of this world from their midst. Thus, in 14:16, Jesus assures his disciples, "I will ask the Father and he will give you the Paraclete," while in 16:7 he says, "I am telling you the truth, it is better for you that I go away, for if I do not go away, the Paraclete will not come to you. But if I depart, I will send him to you." Jesus ties the Spirit's presence with the "peace" he gives that counteracts the "troubling" and "fear" they experience because of his departure (14:26–27; cf. 12:27). Just as the ruler of the world has no authority over Jesus (14:31), his death and resurrection free the disciples from the ruler's control (12:31–32), thereby allowing them to receive the Spirit. Indeed, in 16:11 Jesus includes the ruler's condemnation as part of the Spirit's work as judge.

When Jesus prays to the Father in John 17, he already begins to fulfill this promise by asking the Father to protect believers from the evil one who continues to exist in the world (17:3, 8, 11, 15). Even though Jesus does not call for the Spirit in these verses, he does mention "truth." Moreover, this truth is found in Jesus's words, which were given to him by the Father (17:6–8, 14). Believers know that Jesus was "truly" sent from the Father (17:8) and have received Jesus's word that is "truth" (17:17). After Jesus's death, believers continue to have access to truth through the "Spirit of truth," as described above. In 17:18–19, Jesus asks God to "consecrate them in truth," and describes the disciples whom he will commission as ones sent into the world, thereby blending the temporal horizons of the present narrative moment with the future reality of his victory that is characteristic of the farewell discourse.[33] The disciples will be consecrated and commissioned with the gift of the Spirit in 20:19–23. But first, Jesus indicates, he must consecrate himself "so that they might be consecrated in truth" (17:19). While this may seem to contradict his statement of having been consecrated by the Father in 10:36–38, Jesus's comment here emphasizes his own agency in choosing to lay down his life and take it back up again "on behalf of the sheep" in 10:14–18.[34] When the risen Jesus returns to the fearful disciples in John 20, they look nothing like victors. But it is in this moment that Jesus gives them his peace, breathes the Holy Spirit upon them, and commissions them to continue his work. Jesus's consecration, which was the completion of the work God gave him to do, is now transferred to the disciples by means of the gift of the Spirit of truth. This Spirit keeps believers connected to God and, therefore, protected from the schemes of the ruler of this world. Now inspired, the disciples no longer need fear disconnection from Jesus or the Father because they have the ongoing apotropaic protection of the Spirit as long as they remain in Jesus's word (15:1–14). Their unity and their participation in eternal life are assured, regardless of what the ruler of this world may continue to do.

This protection, however, should not be understood as necessarily physical protection, but spiritual protection. Indeed, Jesus's own death demonstrates that the apotropaism of his presence and that of the Spirit do not guarantee physical safety. Rather, Jesus warns the disciples that the world will hate, persecute, and even kill them just as it does him (15:18–16:4). What is protected is not one's earthly life, but believers' connections to the God who is life. Jesus's physical protection of the disciples during his lifetime is, therefore, another sign of his identity as the incarnation of light and life from 1:1–5. This does not mean they will experience physical protection after his departure; Lazarus's life is almost immediately threatened after his having been raised (12:9–11) and, in 21:18–19, Jesus returns to tell Peter of his coming martyrdom. True and eternal life is not found in surviving in the world by acquiescing to the devil's evil schemes, but in resisting this ruler by clinging to the truth revealed in Jesus, God's Son and Christ (20:31). Thus, in 12:24–26 Jesus teaches: "Amen, amen I am saying to you, unless a seed should fall to the earth and die, it will remain alone. But if it should die, then it will bear fruit. The one who loves their life will lose it, but the one who hates his life in this world guards (φυλάξει) it for eternal life. If someone should serve me, let him follow me, and where I am there also my servant will be. If someone should serve me, the Father will honor him." In Jesus's death, he initiates the fruitful production by ensuring the disciples' continued connection to the Father by means of the Spirit. By following his model to love others in the same way, Jesus commands believers to be willing to die so that others might also have access to eternal life. Physical suffering and death do not separate believers from God, but when experienced in obedience to Jesus's commands, they demonstrate the continued guarding that keeps believers from the evil one. Moreover, because of Jesus's death and resurrection, this protection is no longer limited only to those who remain with his corporeal form, but it is available to all believers regardless of their temporal or physical distance from him (cf. 17:20–26; 20:29–31).

Conclusion

In the Gospel of John, Jesus makes God's presence accessible in his physical form. This revelation scandalizes a number of people throughout his ministry, ultimately leading to his rejection and crucifixion. For the disciples left behind by his departure, however, the crisis is magnified. Throughout the Gospel, Jesus's holy presence has protected his disciples from a variety of physical threats. The physical protection is apotropaic, but it points to the superior protection that will be given to believers after Jesus's death and resurrection. In his farewell discourse and final prayer to the Father, Jesus promises the gift of the Holy Spirit, the Spirit of truth, who will remind, instruct, and comfort the disciples in Jesus's place, thereby continuing their connection to God and the Father. As Thompson notes, the Spirit not only does the same work as Jesus, but also that of the Father, thereby demonstrating the divine unity to which believers are also connected.[35] This connection, I suggest, is also apotropaic because it protects believers from the evil one who continues lying and murdering in the world. Even though they suffer physically, Jesus assures them that they are spiritually protected and have guarded their being (ψυχή) for "eternal life" (12:25).

In this way, Spirit-filled believers are not only connected to Jesus and the Father, but they are God's continued apotropaic presence in the world. When they live out Jesus's command to love one another and to continue his mission of revelation and judgment in the world, they are evidence of his victory over the ruler of this world who uses fear to tell lies about how to preserve life (11:48–52). In contrast to having pain-filled and troubled hearts, the gift of the Spirit comes alongside Jesus's enduring and true peace even in the face of the world's continued attacks. Living out God's love by following Jesus's model with the help of the Holy Spirit, believers are thus able to bear witness in the world and even draw others to God by continuing to share the word given to them (17:20). In the Gospel of John, Jesus scandalizes by existing as God's incarnate and Holy Word, but the corporeal scandal continues after his departure in the form of newly born children of God (1:12–13; 3:3–8). With the gift of the Holy Spirit, John depicts believers as Spirit-filled, corporeal apotropaic presence in the world who face continued attacks from the ruler and the world that remains beholden to him. Nevertheless, believers remain protected and consecrated, assured of their place in God's household and their participation in the divine unity regardless of their physical distance from Jesus himself.

CHAPTER EIGHT

The Messiah of Life

Johannine Christology and the Theme of Life

Jeannine K. Brown and Jenelle Lemons

ἐν αὐτῷ ζωὴ ἦν, καὶ ἡ ζωὴ ἦν τὸ φῶς τῶν ἀνθρώπων·
Life existed in the Word, and that life was the light for humanity.

[John 1:4, AT]

"The final victory of the God of life requires the elimination of [God's] great foe, death."

[Jon D. Levenson, *Resurrection and the Restoration of Israel*]

THE FAITH EXPRESSED in the Jewish Scriptures sets its sights on the God of life. The psalmist expresses this yearning, "My soul thirsts for God, *for the living God*" (Ps 42:2). The NT is no different (e.g., Acts 14:15; Rom 9:26; 1 Tim 4:10). Our goal in this essay is to explore this theological theme as it is applied to Christology in the Gospel of John. In other words, we are interested in the Johannine portrait of the Messiah of life, in conversation with the Jewish affirmation of Yahweh as the God of life.

Our inspiration for this analysis comes from the work of Marianne Meye Thompson and especially her work on God and on Christology in the Gospel of John.[1] We have appreciated her approach to reading John and the other Gospels that combines nuanced narrative sensibilities and thoughtful theological engagement.[2] We have also appreciated the ways she has been a role model for many women (and men) in biblical studies by generating stellar scholarship on a wide array of topics and texts that are both of keen interest to the guild and of deep importance for the church. We dedicate this chapter to her on the occasion of her retirement.

God as *the God of Life* in John

In order to consider Jesus as the *Messiah of life* in John's Gospel, it is necessary to begin with John's broader theological vision. For John, as for his Jewish predecessors, Israel's God is the God of life. This affirmation means both that life is a characteristic of God and that God is the only one who can bestow life. As Thompson affirms, in the Johannine portrait, God is "the living life-giver."[3]

It is certainly the case that life is *a characteristic of salvation* in John; in other words, life describes what God gives to humanity (God is the "life-giver"). This connection between salvation and life resonates with many facets of the motif of life across the Gospel (e.g., John 10:10; 20:31). Yet the theme of life goes further in John, as Thompson so ably uncovers. *Life is itself a defining characteristic of God*, who can be identified rightly as the God of life. In 6:57, God is referred to as "the living Father."[4] Life is a quality that is constitutive of God and not only the gifts of God.[5]

The Jewish Scriptures attest to Israel's God as the "living God," often in relation to other gods and in contexts where worship of idols is decried. For example, in Jeremiah 10:1–16, we hear affirmations of Yahweh as the true and living God in the midst of a polemic against idols that "cannot speak" or "do any good" (10:5) and that "have no breath in them" (10:14). In contrast to these "worthless wooden idols" (10:8), "the Lord is the true God; . . . the living God, the eternal King" (10:10). While pagan gods "did not make the heavens and the earth" (10:11), Israel's "God made the earth by his power; he founded the world by his wisdom and stretched out the heavens by his understanding" (10:12). Yahweh "is the maker of all things, including Israel, the people of his inheritance" (10:16).[6]

This vision of God as "the living God" (Jer 10:10) is tied to Yahweh as creator and to Yahweh as Israel's God (10:16). And in John, the vision of God as "the living Father"[7] (John 6:57) is tied to God as the origin of life, a connection already apparent in the opening lines of the Gospel, where references to God, to the act of creation and giving life, and to the Word are thoroughly intertwined (1:1–5). Thompson locates the notion of the God who is life not only in texts like 6:57, but also in John's ubiquitous use of the Father/Son pairing for identifying Israel's God.[8] John's identification of God as "Father" is integrally tied to God as the source of life—as the One who is living and eternal. As Thompson argues, "The affirmation that God is 'Father' cannot be separated from the affirmation that God is the source of life, nor from the conviction that the life of the Father has been given to, and comes to human beings through, the Son."[9] She also highlights that John's "Father" language should not be read apart from its pairing with the Messiah as "Son": "it is only in relation to the Son that God is 'Father.' It is not merely the designation of God as 'Father' but the corollary reference to Jesus as 'Son' that delineates the meaning of each."[10]

We can see this integral connection between Father and Son and in relation to the theme of life in 5:25–26: "Very truly I tell you, a time is coming and has now come when the dead will hear the voice of the Son of God and those who hear will live. For as the Father has life in himself, so he has granted the Son also to have life in himself." John distinguishes that, while those who trust in God (5:24) will be given life (5:25), the Father has granted to the Son the status of life-giver, so that the Son is able to offer life as the Father does (5:26). In a striking correspondence, "life-giving prerogatives" of the Father belong to the Son as well.[11]

This brief review of the Johannine theological portrait of God as the God of life, with the help of Thompson's insightful work, provides a foundation for the christological exploration of Jesus as the Messiah of life in John's Gospel, to which we now turn.

Jesus as *the Messiah of Life* in John

The Johannine Jesus is presented as the Messiah of life in explicit ways (e.g., 5:25–26). Yet often, as one would expect in a narrative genre, themes are identified indirectly and implicitly. This is true of the motif of the life-giving identity of the Son, which is often communicated using indirect means and, frequently, through intertextuality. Strategically for the theme of the Messiah of life, John frames his entire Gospel with a literary *inclusio* distinguished by intertextual allusions and echoes taken from Genesis 1–2.[12]

The Use of Genesis 1–2 in John

The opening words of the Johannine hymnic prologue mirror Genesis 1:1 (cf. John 1:1), and then continue with creation-centered themes (1:1–5). Similarly, John concludes his Gospel by drawing on language from Genesis 1–2 in the climactic passion, crucifixion, and resurrection narratives.[13] As Jan Du Rand suggests, this *inclusio* invites the reader to view "the entire fourth Gospel . . . from a creation perspective."[14] The intertextual echoes found in this *inclusio* enrich the Gospel's Christology and present Jesus to the reader as the divine agent of both creation and creation's renewal, as well as the second Adam tending over God's new creation. The use of the creation/new creation motif at pivotal moments in the Gospel signals to the reader its central significance.

The evangelist anchors his Gospel firmly to the creation account in the very first words: "in the beginning" (ἐν ἀρχῇ; John 1:1). This phrase is a direct allusion to the opening line of Genesis 1:1 (LXX: ἐν ἀρχῇ). The prologue goes on to introduce themes of life (ζωή) and light (φῶς) in John 1:4–5, similarly derived from Genesis 1 (1:3, 14, 20, 24 LXX).[15] The evangelist's use of λόγος, "the word," also recalls the verbal refrain from Genesis 1 of "God said" (εἶπεν ὁ θεός) to signal the divine creative activity (1:3, 6, 9, 11, 14, 20, 24, 26, 29 LXX).[16] John begins the Messiah's story in the soil of Genesis 1, evoking with it the context of the creation story and suggesting to the reader that Jesus's life and ministry are embedded in the ongoing story of God's creative work and purposes. The Word of God, the agent of that first creation, has now come in the flesh to complete God's creative work and to inaugurate God's new creation.[17] As Du Rand offers, "The Creator who creates has departed on a 'new creation' journey in the Fourth Gospel."[18]

The companion bookend to this set of Genesis allusions is found at the conclusion of the Fourth Gospel in John 19–20. In these climactic chapters, which narrate Jesus's passion, death and resurrection, the gospel writer frequently and thoughtfully weaves in allusions to the creation accounts of Genesis 1–2.

We begin with the most clearly intentional allusion to Genesis in John 19–20. The allusion to Genesis 2:7 in John 20:22 is almost universally recognized by commentators.[19] Here, the evangelist uses the verb ἐμφυσάω to describe Jesus's act of breathing on his disciples, by which he imparts to them the Holy Spirit (πνεῦμα ἅγιον). The evangelist is alluding to Genesis 2:7 LXX, a scene in which God breathes (ἐμφυσάω) the breath of life (πνοὴν ζωῆς) into the first human.[20] The strength of this single-word allusion is augmented when we consider that ἐμφυσάω is not a common term, occurring in the Septuagint fewer than a dozen times.[21]

The use of ἐμφυσάω in Ezekiel 37 also connects the term to the breath of Yahweh from Genesis 2. In Ezekiel 37:9 LXX, the divine life-giving breath is envisioned as resurrecting and regenerating the people of God.[22] This image and word choice resonate with John 20:22: As Jesus breathes on his disciples, the reader can pick up the echo of humanity's inaugural enlivenment reverberating from Genesis to Ezekiel to the Fourth Gospel. At the climax of the Gospel, when the disciples are hiding in fear (20:19), the Messiah appears and imparts new life.[23] Through this intertextual allusion, John depicts the Messiah as the long-anticipated, divine life-giver, who is now inaugurating creation's renewal.[24] From the beginning to the end of John (1:1–5; 20:22), the christological portrait that emerges is one of the preexistent Word who was the agent of the first creation, took on human flesh, and is now the one who inaugurates the renewal of creation and offers the divine breath of life to his followers. The emphasis in what we have explored so far is decidedly on what we might refer to as John's divine Christology.

Another set of Genesis allusions in John 18–20 that contributes to the author's divine Christology revolves around the garden setting.[25] John is the only evangelist to specify the location of the crucifixion, burial, and resurrection accounts in a "garden" (κῆπος; 18:1, 26; 19:41 [bis]; cf. 20:15). The evangelist begins the passion narrative with Jesus's arrest in a garden (18:1), an identification reiterated in 18:26. In 19:41, immediately following the crucifixion, the narrator mentions "the garden" twice, this time with reference to the location of Jesus's tomb.[26] The garden setting resurfaces for a fifth time in the resurrection scene when Mary supposes Jesus to be the gardener (ὁ κηπουρός; 20:15), a detail only included in the Fourth Gospel. We understand the garden motif in these passages to be an intertextual nod to the Garden of Eden, tethered to the story of creation and directing the reader's gaze to that original creation account for the purpose of shaping the theological significance of these Gospel events.[27]

Mary's identification of Jesus as "the gardener," along with the prominent garden setting for John 19–20, suggests a christological affirmation. Although, on one level, the reader hears Mary's words as a case of mistaken identity, on another level, John may be inviting his audience to hear truth in her supposition. The narrator makes it clear that, on the story level, Mary understands Jesus to be a gardener. "The real question is, is she right or wrong?"[28] We suggest that the evangelist harnesses this misidentification on the story level to express christological truth on the discourse level.[29] Jesus's identity as gardener provides an echo of that first gardener of the Genesis creation narratives. Jamie Clark-Soles suggests that the article is important here (*the* gardener, ὁ κηπουρός): "The fact that Mary supposes Jesus to be not *a* gardener but *the* Gardener cues us to think of Genesis and the original garden of Eden."[30] Especially given John's propensity to emphasize the misunderstanding of various characters in response to Jesus and his teachings (e.g., 3:3–10: 4:10–15),[31] it would be unsurprising for the author to employ this misunderstanding to further highlight Jesus's true identity. As Lightfoot proposes, characters like Caiaphas (11:49–53), Pilate (19:5), and Mary (20:15) sometimes speak "more truly than [they] knew."[32]

Yet there is ambiguity in identifying Jesus as "the gardener." Is Jesus the divine Gardener, "who 'planted a garden in Eden, in the east' (Gen 2:8) and, like a gardener, cultivated it (Gen 2:9) and walked in it (3:8)," as Mary Coloe suggests?[33] Or, does John hint that it is Adam, that first human gardener, who is a type for the Messiah?[34] Given where John's Gospel begins (with the Word as divine agent in creation), there is good reason to see John tapping into a divine Christology in Mary's words.[35] Nevertheless, there is also support from another Genesis allusion in John to see an Adam typology at work here.

Earlier, in John 19:5, an Adamic allusion has surfaced during Pilate's interrogation of Jesus. Pilate presents Jesus to the crowd declaring, "Behold, the man!" (Ἰδοὺ ὁ ἄνθρωπος). Although it is possible to understand this verse as functioning primarily or solely at a story level (with Pilate referring to and deriding Jesus's person and humanity), a number of scholars also understand this allusion to be a comparison to the first human (the first Adam).[36] As with Mary's assumption that Jesus is the gardener (20:15), a case of mistaken identity by a Johannine character presents an opportunity for the evangelist to highlight and augment his christological portrait. In this light (and on the discourse level), the Messiah is revealed to be a new or second Adam, who ushers in the renewal of creation.[37]

Given that allusions often suggest more than one potential referent, we propose that the garden setting for the Johannine passion narrative and Mary's (mis)identification of Jesus as "the gardener" may signal that Jesus embodies the roles of both Yahewh and Adam from that first creation story, in his inauguration of creation's renewal. Another intertextual connection in John's passion narrative, one that subtly contributes to this both–and portrait, comes in Jesus's final words before his death: "Jesus said, 'It is finished.' With that, he bowed his head and gave up his spirit" (19:30). The verb, τετέλεσται ("it is finished": from τελέω; also in 19:28), corresponds to language from Genesis 2 that highlights God's completion of the work of creation and the divine blessing of the seventh day as sabbath because the work was finished. Genesis 2:2 reads, "And God finished (συντελέω) on the sixth day his work, which he accomplished, and he rested on the seventh day from all his work, which he accomplished" (LXX; AT). John could be intimating that God's creative, life-giving work, begun in Genesis, finds its ultimate completion at the death of Jesus the Messiah.[38] Here, John portrays Jesus as the one who finishes God's work on God's behalf (cf. John 4:34; 5:16–18). And here we see that it is precisely in his death—that reality that joins Jesus most intimately with humanity, with *Adam*—that Jesus completes the work of God, and paradoxically, opens the way for life for humanity (cf. 1:4; 3:14–15; 5:26). Thompson captures this irony when she writes: "Jesus alone is life; but he is life for the world because, and only because, he dies."[39] Christologically, Jesus's words, "It is finished," display the continuity between the Father's creative, life-giving endeavors and the Son's vocation and prerogatives. The work of the living Father and the Messiah of life are in lockstep.

To summarize our discussion in this section, allusions from Genesis 1–2 that bookend the Fourth Gospel are significant in John's development of both an Adamic and divine Christology.[40] On the one hand, these echoes of the creation account show Jesus to be the *Logos*, the divine agent of creation, intimately linking the Messiah of life with the living God. As God imparted the breath of life to the first human being, the Johannine Jesus breathes on his disciples, bestowing the Holy Spirit (John 20:22). John implies that, as God planted and cultivated the first garden, Jesus, who is the embodiment of that original gardener, tends the dawn of renewed creation. On the other hand, the Edenic allusions shed light on Christ's identity as the second Adam, that first human gardener. "Christ thus fulfills both the role of God the Creator . . . and that of the new Adam."[41] In John, the *Logos* becomes flesh and reverses the induction of death that the first Adam had provoked, thereby offering life in the Father's kingdom to all who would receive it. John communicates through these various touchpoints with Genesis 1–2 that Jesus is the Messiah of life.

Christology and the Theme of Life in John

Along with fostering connections between Genesis 1–2 and his portrait of Jesus, the author of the Fourth Gospel aligns his prominent theme of life with Jesus's identity and mission as the Messiah of life.[42] At the beginning of his Gospel, as he is echoing Genesis 1, the evangelist makes the assertion that "Life [ζωή] existed in the Word, and that life [ζωή] was the light for humanity" (John 1:4; AT). Given the affirmation that "the Word [λόγος] became flesh" in 1:14, already by the end of the prologue the reader will recognize that it is Messiah Jesus who has life in himself. Jesus, the Word, is able to provide life for humanity, since life is a constituent part of his being. This life-giving quality that belongs to Jesus as the Word will be narrated across the Fourth Gospel. As Craig Koester frames it, "The hallmark of God's Word is the ability to give life (1:3–4). . . . Readers [of John] are therefore to look for this in the Word made flesh. . . . Jesus the Word gives life physically when he heals the sick, opens the eyes of the blind, feeds people with bread, and raises the dead. He also promises that those who come to know and believe in him enter the relationship with God that is true life."[43]

The truth that Jesus is the one *who has life in himself* is further affirmed in 5:25–26. We have already accented this important text in our discussion of God as the God of life. As we turn to consider more fully what this passage affirms about Jesus, we notice that these verses are part of a larger discussion by Jesus defending his "work" of healing on the Sabbath (5:16–30). Jesus's defense begins, "My Father is always at his work to this very day, and I too am working" (5:17). As Koester notes, this point may initially seem to be at cross purposes with what Jesus is trying to defend, but Koester goes on to suggest that Jewish teachers would concur that God does "work" at all times.[44] In rabbinic literature, the affirmation of God's ongoing activity on the Sabbath focuses on God's work of giving life and of judgment (cf. 5:21–22).[45]

Jesus goes on to assert that, not only does the Son work in concert with the Father in the activities of giving life and of judging (5:19–23), but the Father "has granted the Son . . . to have life in himself" just as the Father "has life in himself" (5:26). This quality of Jesus as Son sets him apart from all of his human sisters and brothers. While life is given as a gift to any and all who trust in God (5:24–25), the Father has "gifted" to the Son "life in himself" (5:26). As Thompson observes, "The parallel clauses in these verses assert life-giving prerogatives of both the Father and the Son," a stunning declaration considering that "in biblical thought the power to give life is attributed to God alone."[46] For John, Jesus truly is the Messiah of life, because only he and the Father can fulfill the role of "life-giver."[47]

The attribution not only of life but of life-giving prerogatives to Messiah Jesus is also intimated in the concluding words of John 20, where the evangelist provides the explicit purpose statement of the Gospel: "Jesus performed many other signs in the presence of his disciples, which are not recorded in this book. But these are written that you may believe that Jesus is the Messiah, the Son of God, and that by believing you may have life in his name" (20:30–31). The ultimate purpose of the Gospel is to impart life to those who trust in Jesus as

Messiah. This life is described as "life in his name" (20:31). One's "name" in this historical setting could stand in for the entire person, so that "abundant life . . . is connected with the very person of Christ."[48]

The evangelist also identifies Jesus as the Messiah of life through other claims that the Johannine Jesus makes about himself. Specifically, two of the "I am" statements center on Jesus as the Messiah of life—Jesus claims to be "the bread of life" (6:35, 48) and "the resurrection and the life" (11:25).[49] The first affirmation, "I am the bread of life," comes in the middle of an extended discourse set during Passover, a festival that draws on the symbol of bread (e.g., Exod 12:17–20). The Johannine Jesus compares himself to the manna that God provided for Israel in the wilderness (John 6:30–33) and claims that, in contrast to manna that did not result in eternal life, he is the "true bread from heaven" (6:32) and "the living bread that came down from heaven" (6:51). Jesus then explains his life-giving prerogatives: "Just as the living Father sent me and I live because of the Father, so the one who feeds on me will live because of me. This is the bread that came down from heaven. Your ancestors ate manna and died, but whoever feeds on this bread will live forever" (6:57–58). The Son lives because of "the living Father," who gives the Son authority to give life to others; and they will live because of the Son and the life the Son has *in himself* (cf. 5:26).[50]

At the conclusion to the book of signs, Jesus raises Lazarus from the dead (11:1–44); and it is during that episode that Jesus claims, "I am the resurrection and the life" (11:25).[51] Martha has just affirmed her confidence in her brother's "resurrection at the last day" (11:24), and Jesus responds by turning her eschatological focus toward his own person: "I am the resurrection and the life. The one who believes in me will live, even though they die; and whoever lives by believing in me will never die" (11:25–26a). Jesus is "the life," by which John means "Jesus has the power to call the dead from the tombs, both now and at the last day; he has the power to grant them eternal life, anticipated and enjoyed now, and fully experienced with the resurrection at the last day."[52] It is no accident that Jesus raises Lazarus to life immediately after he prays to his Father, acknowledging that the Father hears him "always." It is in his relational unity with the Father that Jesus is able to impart life. And Jesus not only offers life; he has life in himself, because *the Messiah is life.*

Conclusion

The Fourth Gospel presents Jesus, by nature of his unique relationship with the Father, as having been granted life as an integral part of his identity and, consequentially, his vocation. Drawing intertextual allusions from Genesis 1–2, the evangelist forms a creation-centered *inclusio* in John 1:1–18 and John 19–20, portraying Jesus as the source of all life. He is the one who, as the *Logos*, presided over creation's genesis, and, as the Messiah, inaugurates its renewal. This intertextual pattern from Genesis provides a lens through which the reader is meant to interpret the ministry of Messiah Jesus. As Thompson affirms, "From creation, through the revelation in word and deed, to his death and resurrection, the Son is the means through which God gives life in and to the world."[53] Through explicit declarations (e.g., the "I am" statements, John's purpose statement, and the direct pronouncement in 5:25–26) and also via the motif of life permeating the Gospel, divine life is reinforced as being integral to the vocation and character of Jesus in John. It is this Messiah of life who is able to grant life to God's people, delivering them from death into restored relationship with the living Father and the life-giving Son. Life is the mission of the Johannine Jesus; and even more so, Jesus is the Messiah of life.

CHAPTER NINE

The Glory of John

Carey C. Newman

Odd Glory

GLORY THUNDERED OVER the waters, ensuring victory over Yahweh's ancient foe, ever slippery chaos. Glory appeared in the wilderness, a visible beacon of Yahweh's presence to guide the children of Israel along their way. Glory appeared on the mountain, overshadowing all, a visible sign of Yahweh's legitimation of Moses as prophet and lawgiver. Glory appeared in tabernacle and, subsequently, in temple, filling each to the brim, to mark both as Yahweh's singular, sacred spaces of choice. Yahweh, acclaimed as cosmic King of Glory, transformed earth to temple by flooding it with Glory, marking city Zion the cosmic epicenter of Glory, and the royal, messianic scion the unique bearer of Glory. The scarcity of Glory, signaled by Glory's staged withdrawal from temple and city, pronounced Yahweh's judgment on a recalcitrant people. Glory confronted and commissioned Israel's prophets, tasking them to be Yahweh's special messengers of Glory to Yahweh's people. Glory filled prophetic preaching, pointing to the specific and definite Day when Glory will usher in Yahweh's long-awaited kingdom, will reverse Israel's fortunes in the exchange of Glory for suffering, and Jerusalem/ Zion will become the reconstituted city of Glory. Glory continued the imagination of Israel's many seers, pulling the curtain back on the heavenly throne room to reveal it as a place of Glory, the God of such visions as the Great Glory, and a human-shaped figure of Glory whose entitlements included sitting upon the throne of Glory. Yahweh's Glory, Yahweh's visible, movable presence, binds Israel's testimony about Yahweh—be it in ancient theophany, coronation hymns, prophetic call narrative, eschatological hope, or apocalyptic throne vision—into a luminous whole.[1]

Yahweh's Glory did not long remain tucked behind clouds or sequestered in distant rooms. The decidedly earthly theophany of Glory ratified the angelic

---

It is an honor to record in print my respect of, lasting debt to, and deep affection for Marianne Meye Thompson. Over many decades I have had the joy of knowing her as a scholarly colleague, an author, a co-conspirator in all sorts of EHCC mirth; and, most importantly, as a wise and faithful friend in good times and bad.

announcement of Jesus's miraculous birth.[2] Moses, Elijah, and the transfigured Jesus, all bathed in Glory, appeared in concert atop the mountain to converse about Jesus's impending destiny.[3] Stephen, having delivered his full-throated witness, was permitted a vision of Glory.[4] Glory figured the future dreams of the earliest followers of Jesus, just as it had, and still did, for their former co-religionists—a new temple, a new city, and a refashioned earth, each to be places of overflowing Glory.[5] Glory, too, the promise of a new people: those who follow Jesus are called to Glory,[6] to stand in Glory,[7] and to be crowned with Glory.[8] Glory such ubiquitous shorthand for divine presence that the earliest followers of Jesus styled any appearance of Yahweh as Glory.[9] No wonder Glory named among Israel's most cherished, and exclusive, privileges to which those who followed Jesus laid fervent claim.[10]

But those who dared to follow Jesus did not do Glory by the book. They improvised. They innovated. They rewrote. Recklessly so. Their Glory inventions stressed the bindings of scriptural tradition about Yahweh's Glory. They put Glory to novel ends. The earliest followers of Jesus not only claimed Jesus to be the bearer of Yahweh's Glory—comparable to other mediatorial figures—but that Jesus *was* Yahweh's Glory.[11] Jesus proved meritorious of veneration right alongside Yahweh, and the praxis of Christ devotion both shaped and was rooted in the confession "Jesus (the) Christ is the Lord"[12]—i.e., Jesus is Yahweh, Jesus is the Glory—proved too scandalous, too contentious a provocation for the earliest followers of Jesus to remain within the prescribed bounds of their co-religionists.[13] A parting of the ways inevitable.[14] The confession of Jesus as Yahweh's Glory was triggered by—and entailed in—Jesus's resurrection. The resurrection of Jesus was interpreted as an apocalypse of Yahweh's Glory, an apocalyptic invasion of Glory that spelled the end of one age and the beginning of another. This apocalyptic reading of Jesus's resurrection as an apocalypse of Yahweh's Glory was, no doubt, encouraged by the enigmatic statements found on the lips of Jesus himself: that he, as the Son of Man, would come in/with Glory, to occupy the destined throne of Glory, to vanquish all enemies, and to establish a cosmic kingdom of Glory. The story of Yahweh's Glory had taken a dramatic turn.[15]

Glory everywhere in John.[16] Glory at narrative's beginning. Glory at narrative's end.[17] Yet, John's Glory does not ride the clouds or shake the earth. Glory does not appear,[18] commission, or guide. Glory does not overshadow or hover. No visions of Glory, thrones of Glory, figures of Glory. Glory does not paint the future. Unlike other early followers of Jesus, John does not use Israel's vast scriptural encyclopedia to identify Jesus as Yahweh's Glory or interpret Jesus's resurrection as an invasion of future Glory. For all of John's weighty Glory talk—and indeed it is substantial—there are no glowing faces, no temple fillings, no Glory apocalypses.[19] Like a letter that is never read, John features a Glory that never appears.[20] More אִי־כָבוֹד than כבוד.[21] Odd indeed.[22]

Glory Games

John's Jesus enters the fray. That he does, no mistake. The struggle inevitable, so Jesus wades in—and plays for keeps.[23]

The contest is one of appraisal, of estimation, of judgment, of allegiance—with Glory both medium and measure. Mutual Glory, singular Glory, unified Glory. Disclosed Glory, recognized Glory, allied Glory. Blinded Glory, jealous Glory, repudiated Glory.[24] Glory at every turn. Glory between God and Jesus, between Jesus and his disciples, between Jesus and his adversaries.[25]

Jesus's opponents barter and bicker over traded Glory. Jesus flatly rejects their Glory ploy.

> I neither seize nor accept Glory from anyone. (John 5:41)[26]

Their debased Glory leaves Jesus cold, incredulous.

> How can you believe when you seize and accept Glory from one another, especially when you do not seek the Glory that is from the only God? (John 5:44)[27]

Theirs a demanded Glory, a stolen Glory, a Glory taken by one, robbed from another. Back and forth the Glory goes. Superficial. Perfunctory. Exhausted. The glib exchanges empty Glory of its *substantia*. Their Glory asseverations render Glory's properties inert. They rent Glory asunder from belief.

Theirs a thin Glory, a blinded Glory, an entrapped Glory.

> The one who speaks on his own authority seeks his own Glory. But the one who seeks the Glory of the one who sent him, he is true, and there is no unrighteousness in Him. (John 7:18)

Self-referential Glory, egocentric Glory, first lusts for and then obsesses over self, confounding the pursuit of true Glory.

A Glory game rigged from the start. To them the public miracle of recovered sight of no consequence, other than to remind they suffer constant Glory anxiety. Their sham piety commands the ascription "Glory to God" only as a safeguard to their own Glory.[28] Their fear of an uncontrolled Glory bleed leads them to demonize any who threatens its loss.[29] They cannot admit another Glory. They Glory hound, coercing those who know the truth to cower, to deny—or face the reprisal of exclusion.[30] The reason for their Glory mongering arises out of misplaced affections rather than sincere devotion.

> For they loved the Glory from each other more than the Glory of God.
> (John 12:43)[31]

Their choices Glory poor.

Jesus does not need nor crave their Glory. He decries their Glory shilling. He refuses the pursuit of selfish Glory.

> But I am not seeking my Glory. There is one who seeks it—and judges.
> (John 8:50)

He instead chooses hard Glory, heavy Glory, a dependent Glory. Jesus recognizes the self-deception in the parade of self-aggrandizement. He sees through vain Glory's many disguises. He knows inwardly obsessed, self-fashioned Glory always but sounding brass.

> Jesus answered, "If I Glory myself, my Glory is nothing." (John 8:54a)

Jesus instinctively looks elsewhere. He prizes a different Glory, a worthy Glory, the right kind of Glory—the only kind that really matters, a Glory that forges different Glory relations, a Glory with uncommon Glory assignations.

> My Father is the One who Glories me. (John 8:54b)

> This . . . (is) for the Glory of God, so that the Son of God may be Gloried by it. (John 11:4)

> Father, Glory Your name . . . "I have both Gloried it, and will Glory it again." (John 12:28)

> The Son of Man has been Gloried, and God is Gloried in Him; if God is Gloried in Him, God will also Glory Him in Himself, and will Glory Him immediately. (John 13:31–32)

> So that the Father may be Gloried in the Son. (John 14:13)

> Glory your Son, so that the Son may Glory you back. (John 17:1)

Jesus rejects Glory solitaire. The Father Glories the Son, and the Son follows suit. Father Glories Son. Son Glories Father. Son Glories Father when Father Glories Son. Father Gloried in Son when Son Glories Father. Round and round the Glory goes. Just as the Son Glories Father, the Spirit will Glory the Son.

But when the Spirit of truth comes … He will Glory me. (John 16:13, 14)

Glory, true Glory, always shared Glory, a conveyed and a connected Glory. Shared Glory forges Glory bonds.

All that are mine are yours, and yours are mine, and I have been Gloried in them. (John 17:10)

Shared Glory a catholic Glory.

The Glory that you have given me I have given them, so that they may be one, as we are one. (John 17:22)

Those who oppose refuse to share. They only know taking, and keeping, and wasting. Allied Glory a mutual Glory. Mutual Glory an inclusive Glory. Inclusive Glory a singular Glory. All hinges on Glory. Noble Glory determinative, determinative for alliances—Jesus with God, Jesus with Spirit, Jesus with disciples. Debased Glory divisive Glory. Those who resist and reject, blinded to noble Glory by their many Glory gambits. They play their Glory game day by day. Pure sport. But Jesus plays just once. For everything. Forever. For all the Glory.

Glory Clock

Glory marks time. Glory keeps time. Glory knows the day. Glory knows the hour. Glory, from Κανά to Κρανίον—from Γαλιλαία to a grim τόπον.

Just how a shortage of wine at a wedding escalates to the apocalyptic "my hour has not yet come" requires supplying a lack.[32] The impertinent "what to me and to you?" only muddles.[33] The enigmatic, so it seems, requires imagination to attend this wedding as well. Jesus's elaborate parlor trick left a befuddled host to wonder about who does such a thing.[34] Mounting ambiguity demanded clarification: This impromptu sign was the beginning of all signs. No turning back time. No more killing time. The time of Jesus's Glory had arrived.

Jesus performed this [i.e, turning water to wine] in Cana of Galilee [to signal the] beginning of signs. And [through this sign Jesus] he revealed his Glory—and [because Jesus manifested his Glory in the sign] his disciples believed in him. (John 2:11)

Though Glory as indeterminant as the sign itself, Glory singularizes to Jesus. Glory unique to him. His Glory[35]—and Jesus the sole agent who manifests his own Glory.[36] Jesus incarnates his own Glory in the sign.

Mary's forcing of Jesus's hand pushed him onto the stage, along with his hour, the sign, and his Glory. Time began its procession: Glory as signifier marching toward Glory as signified. But until that hour's end, Glory consigned to the time in between. Liminal Glory—the Glory between Glory's onset and Glory's hour.

Liminal Glory, always ambiguous Glory. Ambiguous Glory always needs more words. Liminal Glory required editorial postscript, after-hour exegesis. Liminal Glory begs hermeneutical Glory.

> But he said this concerning the Spirit, which those who believed in him were about to receive. For the Spirt had not yet [been given], because Jesus had not been Gloried. (John 7:39)

> When the Spirit of truth comes, this one will guide you in all truth. For [the Spirit] will not speak from himself, but [the Spirit] will speak [only that] which [the Spirit] hears and will announce to you all the things that are coming. This one will Glory me because he will receive what is mine and announce it to you. (John 16:13–14)

The memory of a time without Spirit demanded explanation: It was a time before, a time of promise, a time in between, a time of Glory's not yet. To understand the not yet required a something else. Glory, Spirit's something else. Glory's moment, once realized, makes Spirit possible: δόξα to πνεύμα, πνεύμα to πάση. Glory's not yet reveals that the ambiguities of Glory as signifier must be endured until the revelation of Glory as the signified.

Liminal Glory, always anticipatory Glory. Never in full, always in part. The fate of Lazarus, a John the Baptist to Glory's hour, bound tight to that of Jesus. Lazarus anticipatory, partial.

Glory entombed with Lazarus—waiting patiently, for days. But death was not to make an end of Lazarus. Glory denied death the last word. Lazarus's fortune wrapped by a different cloth.

> But when Jesus heard it, he said,
> "This sickness is not for (πρός) death
> But is for (ὑπέρ) the Glory of God,
>   so that the Son of God may be Gloried through it." (John 11:4)

The Glory attending to Lazarus not an earthy Glory, a tainted, a bartered Glory. Weightier matters at work. Primal matters. Sickness and death on one side, God, the Son, and Glory on the other. Lazarus's sickness led Glory into the realm of darkness—and back again. Lazarus's death made Glory purposeful, for God, for the Son. Doxology lowered into death but raised as prophecy. Jesus's declaration vindicated in Glory's end.

> And Jesus said to her, "Did I not say to you that if you believe you will see (ὄψῃ) the Glory of God?" (John 11:40)

No earthly tremors or temple fillings. No theophanies. No glowing faces. No angelic figures beside a heavenly throne. Glory appears in the enacted, Λάζαρε, δεῦρο ἔξω. Glory, come out.[37] Jesus makes of Lazarus a walking, talking Glory parable. The raising of one signed the lifting of another. The Glory in the death of one epiphanic for the Glory in the death of another—partial signifier reaching forward to ultimate signified.[38]

Liminal Glory always a riddled Glory. No amount of prophecy, no amount of enacted parable, orders the disarray of Glory's alterity. Even hearing the messianic cries "Hosanna" and witnessing the parade of Solomon's son left those present perplexed. Neither Scripture nor event sufficient, even if necessary. Mystery prevailed, prevailed until Glory's moment. Then, and only then, words and deeds remembered, recollected, and their presaged correspondences discerned.

> His disciples did not understand these things at first, but when Jesus was Gloried, then they remembered that these things had been written of him and had been done to him. (John 12:16)

Glory's hour stirs memory, enables a knowing backwards, and authorizes the reading in reverse.[39] Liminal Glory, a confounding signifier; Glory's hour, a signified beset only by clarity, assignation, comprehension. Liminal Glory always indeterminate Glory. Indeterminate Glory persists right to the moment of Glory's end. Some Greeks. Ἕλληνές τινες.[40] Surely not the first or only. Why just τινες? Why not a lot, most, or all? Aporia prevails. Ἕλληνές τινες a sure sign that something else is afoot. But isolated, they appear as misplaced signifiers in desperate search of their signified. Their who, their why lost to the indeterminate. But, for Jesus, semiotic clarity: Their simple request triggered the most ominous of pronouncements.

> "We desire to see Jesus.". . . Jesus answered them, "The hour has come for the Son of Man to be Gloried." (John 12:21, 23)

Jesus explains one mysterious sign, Ἕλληνές τινες, by another equally so, the Son of Man. But the hour is not a time in which the Son of Man rides the clouds, puts right all wrongs, and ushers in a kingdom. It is instead the time of the passive, the tragic. The hour's arrival means the Son of Man is to be Gloried, to die.[41] Three mysteries compound to form a single sign, *the* sign that *his* hour, the Son of Man's hour, Glory's hour has finally arrived.

This hour's knowledge a burden. Its arrival a test, a singular and solitary test. The hour's arrival vexed. The temptation to shrink answered by resolve, resolve and a petition for Glory.

> Father, "Glory your name." (John 12:28a)

An epiphanic voice of confirmation answered,[42] declaring Glory has already—and Glory will yet again. The Father fully invested in the Glorying of Jesus.

> Then a voice came from heaven, "I have Gloried it, and I will Glory it again." (John 12:28b–c)

Glory's storied past throws fresh light on the Glory coming into view. But past Glory, even its freighted exemplars, still too indeterminate, too debatable, despite divine assurance and promise. Jesus himself senses the lack. Jesus prompted, compelled, to clarify the voice out of heaven.

> Now judgment is upon this world; now the ruler of this world will be cast out. And I, if I am lifted up (ἐὰν ὑψωθῶ) from the earth, will draw all to myself. (John 12:32)

Glory's hour entails the apocalyptic despoiling of the powers. Glory's hour begins the grand covenantal ingathering. Glory's hour coincides with Jesus's lifting up. To be lifted up a powerful but still too indistinct, too slippery, too veiled. Naming the signified to this evocative signifier left to another:

> Now he [Jesus] was saying this to indicate what kind of death He was going to die. (John 12:33)

Hour inexorable to death; death inexorable to crucifixion; crucifixion inexorable to Glory.[43] Hour, death, crucifixion, Glory. But death and Glory arrived as already scripted concurrence. John saw the prophet Isaiah's words about death and Glory come to life in Jesus.[44]

> After Jesus had said this, he departed and hid from them. Although he had performed so many signs in their presence, they did not believe in him. This was to fulfill the word spoken by the prophet Isaiah:

"Lord, who has believed our message,
 and to whom has the arm of the Lord been revealed?"

And so they could not believe, because Isaiah also said,

"He has blinded their eyes
and hardened their heart,
so that they might not look with their eyes
and understand with their heart and turn—
and I would heal them."

Isaiah said this because he saw his Glory—and spoke about him. (John 12:36b–41)

The prophet's warnings came to tragic realization in the staggering unbelief by those who should have believed. Isaiah's perspicacity remarkable. But the rationale for Isaiah's prophecy about ironic unbelief even more so. Isaiah said what he said because (ὅτι) Isaiah saw what he saw.[45] He said what he said about unbelief because he saw what he saw—the Glory of Jesus.

Isaiah knew theophanic Glory, the Glory that fills temples and shakes the earth. Isaiah also knew royal Glory, the Glory of kings, their thrones, and their kingdoms. But, according to John, Isaiah saw another Glory, one to be distinguished from Yahweh's Glory and not to be confused with it.[46] Isaiah, John says, saw a Jesus Glory, and Isaiah's Glory prescience prompted Isaiah to speak about him.

Behold, my servant (ὁ παῖς μου) will understand, and he will be lifted up (ὑψωθήσεται) and Gloried (δοξασθήσεται) exceedingly. (Isa 52:13 LXX)

Isaiah had foreseen Jesus's lifting up, his crucifixion, and then foreseen in that death the coincidence of Jesus's Glory that requires imagination. The servant is Jesus. His lifting up is the cross. Glory entwined with the two. To construe rightly the hour's last sign depends on the very same interpretive competency to decode the hour's first. The Gospel reads the prophet backwards; Isaiah, the prophet, preaches the gospel forward. The Glory of Isaiah's servant presages the Glory of John's Jesus.

But Prophet and the Gospel haggle—former suggestive of latter, latter finding pretext in former. Words of a prophet juxtaposed with words of a messiah. The two speak to one another, creating by their conversation a new webwork of Glory figuration.[47]

And He said to me,

"you are my servant Israel,
and in you (ἐν σοί)
I will be Gloried (δοξασθήσομαι)." (Isa 49:3 LXX)

"Shine, Shine Jerusalem; for your light has come,
        and the Glory of Yahweh has risen on you (ἐπὶ σέ).
Behold, darkness and gloom will cover the earth,
        upon the nations.
But Yahweh will appear to you (σέ),
        and his Glory will appear upon (ἐπί) you." (Isa 60:1–2 LXX)

Therefore, when he had left, Jesus said,

"Now the Son of Man is Gloried (νῦν ἐδοξάσθη ὁ υἱὸς τοῦ ἀνθρώπου),
and God is Gloried in Him (ὁ θεὸς ἐδοξάσθη ἐν αὐτῷ);
if God is Gloried in Him (εἰ ὁ θεὸς ἐδοξάσθη ἐν αὐτῷ),
God will also Glory him in himself (ὁ θεὸς δοξάσει αὐτὸν ἐν αὐτῷ),
and will Glory him immediately (καὶ εὐθὺς δοξάσει αὐτόν)." (John
        13:31–32)

Like water to wine, Isaiah's ἐν σοί has, over time, become the John's ἐν αὐτῷ. The best saved for last. The Glory Isaiah lauded proves far more than ocular drama or, even, noetic insight. The Glory only seen and known falls short. Isaiah's Glory embodied. Isaiah's Glory *in* the servant. And Glory in the servant prefigures Glory in the Son. The Glory in Isaiah's servant through lifting up becomes the Glory in John's *Christos* through lifting up. Glory from the Father (παρὰ πατρός) became Glory with the Father (παρὰ πατρί) by Glory in the Son (ἐν αὐτῷ). The mystery of Jesus's hour dissolves into death; and the death of Jesus re-mystified as Glory. Glory as signifier finally reaches Glory as signified. Embodied Glory. Cruciform Glory. Glory nailed to a cross. Glory takes a full measure of death in the Son. Death, Glory's embodied plentitude.

Singular Glory

Glory dances between verb and noun. Each polysemantic. Each beckoning to the other. Verb to noun, noun to verb. Glory Glorying the Gloried; and the Gloried Glorying back. Slippage and play prevail. Slippage and play and implicature. Glory defies assignation. Yet, Glory a one.

That John's Jesus refuses the Glory game played by the feckless points to the prizing of other Glory, a stubborn other Glory, one whose inflection parsed hard, one not subject to the easy whims of empty, shameful honor. Jesus refuses, revalues. Jesus's iterative deeds, instead, witness to the glorious contradictions inherent in other Glory. Other Glory never as simple as appearances. Miracle made Glory always a signifier pointing forward. And when right hour arrived, Jesus's death—the deed of all deeds—divulged the riddled significance of other Glory.[48] The brooding thickness of other Glory revealed in its shocking concurrency with death. Other Glory unveiled as cruciform Glory, and other Glory's disfigurement refigured all of Glory's previous revelations.

Glory marked the path from Cana to crucifixion: Glory signs pointing the way to other Glory. The Glory of Cana, and all the Glory in between, signifiers reaching for their destined, defaced signified. This, the journey of other Glory. This, John's Glory diegesis. But a prequel to the other Glory's plot. Other Glory arrives with a past—and one not analogic to the Glory of theophanies, tents, temples, or thrones, kings, and kingdoms. Crucified Glory stirs a different, more distant memory. Crucifixion completes one Glory script only to invoke another, more ancient recital.

> Jesus spoke these things; and raising His eyes to heaven, He said, "Father, the hour has come; Glory your Son, so that the Son may Glory you." (John 17:1)

> And Father, you Glory me now. (John 17:5)

"Glory your Son," "Glory me now." Requested. Demanded. Glory the Son because the Son now stands at death's door. The Father's Glorying the Son occasioned by death—and occurred in death. But death no dead end. Parsimony rules the grave. The Father's Glorying never wasted, as the Glory from Father to Son permits the Glory from Son to Father. Glory's seeming end merely Glory's prelude. Crucified Glory transubstantiated into reciprocal Glory.

> I Gloried you on the earth by completing the work you gave me to do. (John 17:4)

The Son's Glory a dutiful Glory. Dutiful Glory a resolute Glory, a Glory heavy with ballast of the particular, the specific, the non-repeatable. Confident Glory travels Glory's one path. Jesus faithful to Glory's one τέλος. Dutiful Glory the singular predicate for cruciform Glory. Cruciform Glory the singular predicate for reciprocal Glory. But dutiful Glory, cruciform Glory, reciprocal Glory the combined τέλος of Glory's ἀρχή.

> And Father, you Glory me now (νῦν) with (παρά) yourself, with the Glory I had with you before (πρό) the world existed. (John 17:5)

Glory νῦν is Glory πρό. The bloody Glory fated to hang on a Roman cross precedes time and place.[49] The Glory that submits to the world's chaos is the one and same Glory that existed before the world and its chaos came to be. Cruciform Glory, the incarnation of a long antecedent Glory. But Glory πρό and Glory νῦν equally a self-conscious Glory, an ἐγώ Glory—a Glory "which I had" (ἣ εἶχον). Father differentiated from this ἐγώ Glory. Jesus Glory distinct. Jesus Glory independent. Jesus Glory a Glory παρά, a Glory alongside. Glory πρό, Glory νῦν, and Glory εγώ concordant with Glory παρά. Glory's present imperative stirs inklings of Glory then. But memory betrays absence. Recollection of Glory πρό makes present lack more desperate. Jesus cries for the Father to Glory him with the same (τῇ δόξῃ) he had. Desire now for the Glory of then.

Jesus's Glory a gift to be given because it a gift received. In the same way cruciform Glory unites Father to Son so too cruciform Glory unites Jesus to his disciples.

> The Glory that you have given me I have given them, so that they may be one, as we are one. (John 17:22)

Jesus desires that his disciples see his Glory (ἵνα θεωρῶσιν τὴν δόξαν τὴν ἐμή), the Glory the Father gave to him πρό.

> Father, I desire that those also, whom you have given me, may be with me where I am, to see my Glory, which you have given me because you loved me before the foundation of the world. (John 17:24)

No theophany. No throne vision. No transfiguration. No resurrection. No parousia. Only the Glory of the cross. Jesus loved before the foundation of the world. Jesus Gloried before the foundation of the world.[50]

Glory always incarnated. Glory only incarnated. Glory always gritty. Glory only gritty.

> In the beginning was the Word. The Word was with God. The Word was God. And the Word became Flesh, and lived among us, and we beheld his Glory, Glory as the only begotten with the Father, full of Grace and Truth. (John 1:1, 14)

Glory did not become Word, nor did Word become Glory. Word became Flesh, and enfleshed Word revealed gritty Glory.[51] Gritty Glory a signifier of the singular (μονογενοῦς). Gritty Glory superlative (πλήρης).[52]

For John, Glory present in the beginning, not revealed in theophany,[53] throne vision,[54] or at the parousia.[55] For John, this ancient Glory manifested by incarnation, not future Glory's prolepsis in transfiguration.[56] For John, Glory realized in gritty crucifixion, not discovered in resurrection.[57] For John, Glory a mapping of unique relations rather than ontological assertions and predications.[58] For John, the Glory Jesus had with the Father destined for the Glory of incarnation. For John, the Glory of incarnation destined for the Glory of the signs. For John, the Glory of the signs destined for the Glory in crucifixion. For John, crucifixion, the deed of all deeds—Glory, for all eyes to behold. For John, Glory hermeneutical—a signifier and signified constituting a sign, the sign. Glory reaching for Glorified. This Glory unique because the Son's deed unique. This Glory singular because the Son an only. For John, Glory the true measure of christological monotheism. For John, the Glory of the Son's one cross exegesis of the Glory of the one God.[59]

Part Two

John and Other
New Testament Christologies

CHAPTER TEN

Davidic Messianism in Matthew and John

R. Alan Culpepper

THE PREVAILING CONSENSUS has been that the Gospel of John shows little or no interest in Jesus's fulfillment of the expectation of a Davidic messiah. Jesus is never called "Son of David," and "David" appears in the Gospel only in John 7:42, where some in the crowd ask, "Has not the scripture said that the Messiah is descended from David and comes from Bethlehem, the village where David lived?" Moody Smith noted that John "makes nothing of Jesus's Davidic sonship, not even to call him Son of David," although "at the same time no Gospel is more clearly in touch with Jewish, traditional roots."[1]

Recent scholarship has reopened this issue in response to work on postexilic Jewish messianism. We will proceed by summarizing expressions of Davidic messianism in Second Temple Jewish literature, especially the Dead Sea Scrolls and Psalms of Solomon, noting common motifs. Then, we will compare the ways Matthew and John engage this tradition. Although there are three primary strands of Jewish messianism, royal, priestly, and prophetic,[2] often associated with David, Aaron, and Moses or Elijah respectively, our attention here will be restricted to the first: expectations regarding a royal and specifically Davidic messiah.

The Expectation of a Davidic Messiah

The expectation of a messiah from the lineage of David arose from the promise in 2 Samuel 7:11–16 that David's son would build "a house for my name" and "his kingdom would endure forever," which is echoed in Psalm 89:3–4, 19–37; Isaiah 9:7; 11:1–5; Ezekiel 34:23–24; 37:24–25; Jeremiah (passim); and Zechariah 12:7–13:1. Andrew Chester reviews the debate between the minimalist position represented by Kenneth Pomykala, who argues that the hope for a Davidic messiah was not revived until the Hasmonean and Herodian-Roman periods, and the maximalist view of Antti Laato and William Horbury, who argue that

---

Marianne Meye Thompson and I have shared not only our common interest in the Gospel of John, our graduate experience at Duke (at different times), our affection for Moody Smith, and writing commentaries for the New Testament Library series, but also seminars, conversations, meals, and excursions at more conferences than we can count. This essay is a token of my gratitude to Marianne for her friendship through the years and her contributions to my understanding of John and its Christology.

the hope for a Davidic king arose early and was sustained throughout the post-exilic period.³ Pomykala defends three conclusions:

1. There is little evidence from the early postexilic period for an expectation of the re-establishment of a specifically Davidic monarchy or hope for a specifically Davidic messiah. Thus, at the dawn of the early Jewish period, there existed no dominant and widespread expectation of a Davidic messiah that early Jewish authors could inherit and carry on.⁴
2. Early Jewish writers who took up the Davidic dynasty tradition possessed a rich fund of concepts, images, and terms from which to draw.⁵
3. One must ask *how* early Jewish writers employed and adapted the biblical traditions about Davidic figures and the Davidic dynasty.⁶

When we turn to the Gospels, we will take up the third point directly.

Davidic Messianism and the Hasmoneans

The period of the Maccabees and the Hasmoneans was formative for Jewish messianism, with the Maccabees driving out the Seleucids and the Hasmoneans combining the offices of king and high priest. These developments provided models for conceptualizing the role of an apocalyptic messiah. Apocalyptic groups emerged, the Essenes withdrew to Qumran, and the literature they produced provides the earliest clear evidence of Davidic messianism. As Johannes Tromp observes, "The name of David apparently stood for the king of the Judeans par excellence; only when in eschatological circles the idea of a future ideal king arose was this name associated with future expectations."⁷

The Testament of Judah (probably late 2nd c. BCE)⁸ affirms that the messiah will come from the tribe of Judah, while assimilating "a mosaic of eschatological expectations."⁹

> This is the Shoot of God Most High; this is the fountain for the life of humanity. Then he will illumine the scepter of my kingdom, and from your root will arise the Shoot, and through it will arise the rod of righteousness for the nation, to judge and to save all that call on the Lord. (T. Jud. 24:4–6; *OTP* 1:801)

First Maccabees (late 2nd–early 1st c. BCE) seems to profess the expectation of a Davidic king: "David, because he was merciful, inherited the throne of the kingdom forever" (2:57). Apparently, when 1 Maccabees was written, the author, an apologist for the Hasmonean dynasty, could still maintain the hope that the dynasty would endure "forever."[10]

Davidic Messianism at Qumran

Our interest in this section is in the roles and functions of the Davidic messiah in the Qumran scrolls and whether they are representative of Davidic messianism in Judaism at this time or unique to the Essenes. Pomykala cautions that each text must be taken as a potentially distinct expression of Qumranic eschatological expectations: "One cannot assume a unified messianic expectation at Qumran."[11] We will survey key texts, then gather the common threads.

4Q161 (4QpIsaᵃ) 8–10 III, 11–24

> [A shoot will issue from the stu]mp of Jesse. . . . Over him [will be placed] the spi[rit of the Lord; a spirit] of discretion and wisdom. . . . [He will not judge] by appearances. . . . [Isa 11:1–5]. [The interpretation of the word concerns the shoot] of David which will sprout [in the final days]. . . . His sword will judge all the peoples. And as for what he says: "He will not [judge by appearances] or give verdicts on hearsay. . . ." (García Martínez, 186[12])

All the commentary (pesher) texts date from the first century BCE or CE, and many are autographs. As in the other *pesharim*, the interpretation concerns the conflict between the faithful of Israel and the Romans (the Kittim).[13] The Davidic messiah will be a just judge. He will not judge "with the sight of his eyes nor with the hearing of his ears" but with righteous judgments, apparently as he is instructed by the priests (cf. Isa 11:3b; 4 Ezra 12:32–34). This messianic interpretation of Isaiah 11 is also attested in the Psalms of Solomon 17, and hence was current beyond the Qumran community.[14]

4Q174 (4QFlor) 1–3 I, 10–13

> And "YHWH de[clares] to you that he will build you a house. I will raise up your seed after you and establish the throne of his kingdom [for ev]er. I will be a father to him and he will be a son to me" [2 Sam 7:12–14]. This (refers to the) "branch of David," who will arise with the Interpreter of the law [cf. CD VI, 7; VII, 18] who [will rise up] in Zi[on in] the last days, as it is written: "I will raise up the hut of David which has fallen" [Amos 9:11]. This (refers to) "the hut of David who has fallen," who will arise to save Israel." (García Martínez, 136)

CD VII, 15–21 also quotes Amos 9:11, the promise to raise up the house of David that has fallen, but there it means the books of the law and not the reestablishment of Davidic sovereignty.[15] 4Q174, which dates from the end of 1st c. BCE or 1st c. CE,[16] is particularly important because it not only links 2 Samuel 7:12–14 and Amos 9:11 but connects these texts with Exodus 15:17–18 and the expectation of one who will build an eschatological temple. In addition, it attributes a salvific role to the branch of David, who will appear with the Interpreter of the Law in the last days. Moreover, "the messiah, like the king in 2 Samuel 7, could be regarded as a son of God, in some sense."[17] Matthew 1:21 echoes the expectation of a Davidic messiah who will save Israel.

4Q246 (4QAramaic Apocalypse) II, 1–8

> Son of God he shall be called, and they will name him "Son of the Most High". . . . His (or its) kingdom is an everlasting kingdom, and all his ways truth. He will judge the earth with truth, and all will make peace. . . . [God] will make war on his behalf, give nations into his hand, and cast them all down before him. His sovereignty is everlasting. . . ."[18]

Sometimes called "the Son of God" text, this text has been widely debated.[19] At a minimum, its language echoes Psalm 2 and 2 Samuel 7, although it does not use the term "messiah." Yarbro Collins and Collins find that "the depiction of the 'son of God' in 4Q246 fits nicely with the portrayal of the Davidic/royal messiah in the scrolls,"[20] and Chester notes that this figure has "very clear messianic traits on the pattern of what may be expected of a messianic king: that is, an eternal rule of peace in truth, the function of sitting in judgment, military authority to bring about a time of peace, divine support, and giving help to the people of God."[21]

4Q252 (4QpGen^a) V, 1–4

> A sovereign shall [not] be removed from the tribe of Judah [Gen 49:10]. While Israel has the dominion, there will [not] lack someone who sits on the throne of David [Jer 33:17; 1 Kgs 2:4; 11QTemple^a LIX, 17]. . . . Until the messiah of justice [i.e., righteousness; Jer 23:5–6; 33:15–17] comes, the branch of David. For to him and his descendants has been given the covenant of royalty over his people for all everlasting generations. (García Martínez, 215)

Appeal to the coming of a righteous, Davidic king challenges the legitimacy of a reigning king, whether Hasmonean, as may be the case in Psalms of Solomon 17, or a Herodian or Roman king, as in 4QpGen^a, as its date (mid-1st c.

BCE–mid-1st c. CE) suggests.[22] The War Scroll (1QM I, 5; XVII, 7–8) asserts that Israel will be victorious in the final eschatological battle between the Sons of Light and the Sons of Darkness. When the righteous messiah comes, there will be a Davidic king forever. In contrast to the illegitimate kings who preceded him, righteousness will mark his reign. Again, this hope could be relevant for Matthew's Emmanuel theme, "I will be with you always" (28:20).

4Q285 (4QWar Scroll[g]?) V, 1–4

This text has been restored in different ways. Below, the first translation accentuates its fragmentary condition, the second its probable meaning.

> A shoot will emerge from the stump of Jesse [. . .] the bud of David will go into battle with [. . .] and the Prince of the Congregation will kill him, the b[ud of David . . .] and with wounds. And a priest will command [. . .] the destruction of the Kittim. (García Martínez, 124)

> "A shoot shall come out from the stump of Jesse [and a branch shall grow out of his roots" (Isa 10:34–11:1). This is the] branch of David. Then [all the forces of Belial] shall be judged, [and the king of the Kittim shall stand for judgment] and the prince of the community—the bra[nch of David]—will have him put to death. [Then all Israel shall come out with timbrel]s and dancers [Exod 15:20; Judg 21:23], and the [high] priest shall order [them to cleanse their bodies from the guilty blood of the c] orpse[s of] the Kittim.[23]

This text, which comes from the Herodian period,[24] attributes a more significant role to the Davidic messiah than does 1QM, although both affirm God's ultimate triumph over the forces of evil—an apocalyptic theme that appears in both Matthew and John.[25] It has understandably raised questions: How is the Prince of the Congregation related to the bud of David, and does the Davidic messiah slay or is he slain?[26] The most natural interpretation is that the Prince of the Congregation is a royal figure, the Davidic Messiah (CD VII, 15–21)[27] and that he will slay the leader of the Kittim. Elsewhere, the War Scroll refers to "the severely wounded of the Kittim" (1QM XVI, 8) and "the dead of the Kittim" (XIX, 13). "The real problem for the 'slain messiah' view," Chester contends, "lies in the immediate context of Frag. 5 and the overall thrust of 4Q285 as a whole. . . . What it portrays is not a messiah who is killed, but the Prince— as military leader in the final battle—now identified with the Davidic royal messiah."[28] Laato further identifies "the Branch of David" and "the Prince of the Congregation" in this text with the "righteous Messiah" based on 4Q252.[29]

4Q369 (4QPrayer of Enoch) 1 II, 4–12

> for his seed for their generations, an eternal possession, and al[l] . . . and
> your good judgments you have explained to him . . . in eternal light,
> and you have made him for you as a first-born son . . . like him, to be
> a prince and ruler in all your inhabited world . . . the heavens, and the
> glory of the clouds you have supported . . . and the angel of your peace
> in his congregation, and . . . to him righteous rules, as a father to his
> son . . . you have loved him (/his love), your soul clings . . . for in them
> you [have set] your glory.[30]

Although the designation, "firstborn son," refers to Israel in Exodus 4:22, in
Psalm 89:20, 26–27, David is called God's "firstborn." The psalm declares that
the Lord has anointed David, who will cry, "You are my Father, my God, and the
Rock of my salvation!" and the Lord "will make him the firstborn, the highest of
the kings of the earth." Evans and Chester maintain that God's firstborn is the
Davidic messiah.[31] The Lord will explain his righteous judgments to the messiah,
who will inaugurate the kingdom of peace on the earth.[32] Alternatively, James
Kugel favors the view that the "firstborn son" is Israel,[33] and Benjamin Wold,
that in 4Q369, the son is a holy teacher (*maskil*) with great authority based on
the occurrence of "firstborn son" in 4QInstruction, where "God relates to the
addressee as a son who in turn is like a father to others in his community."[34]
Whether this figure is messianic or not, the importance of divine instruction is
nevertheless clear. The same can be said of 4Q381 (4QNon-Canonical Psalms
B), which says, "and I, your anointed, have gained understanding (?) (. . .) for I
have made known and teach. For you have taught me (. . .)."[35] Chester concludes
that the speaker in this psalm "sees himself as having been given instruction by
God, and hence is now able to instruct others. Whether he should be seen as a
'messiah' is a more complex issue."[36]

Summary of Davidic Messianism at Qumran

Davidic messianism was muted prior to the Hasmoneans. The striking developments in Jewish messianic expectations in the scrolls suggest that they reflect the
period in which they were written.[37] The Hasmoneans had been anointed kings
of Israel, although they were not of the Davidic line, and they had combined the
royal office with the office of high priest. The Essenes and perhaps others also
found one or both developments sufficiently scandalous to render the Hasmonean
dynasty illegitimate. By advancing hope for the coming of a Davidic king and
by separating the functions of a royal messiah from those of a priestly messiah
(1QS IX, 11; 1QSa II, 11–22) they exposed the offenses of the Hasmonean kings.

These expectations continued into the Roman and Herodian periods,[38] when the hope for a Davidic messiah was widely held.[39]

The texts surveyed above quote or echo what appear to be a common repertoire of scriptural references that included Genesis 49:10–12 (4Q174, 4Q252), Numbers 24:17 (4Q174; cf. 1QM XI, 4–7), 2 Samuel 7:12–14 (4Q174, 4Q246), Psalm 2 (4Q246), Psalm 89:20, 26–27 (4Q369), Isaiah 11:1–5 (4Q161; 4Q285; cf. 1Q28b V, 23), Jeremiah 23:5–6; 33:15–17 (4Q252), and Amos 9:11 (4Q174).

The royal messiah exhibits both apocalyptic and wisdom traits.[40] He will deliver Israel, or at least the pious remnant of Israel, from its enemies, the Romans and those who support them (4Q285), reestablish the house of David, judge the nations with righteous judgment, and be a shepherd to Israel. Some texts also emphasize that the royal messiah will execute judgment as he has been instructed by the Lord or by the priests or the priestly messiah, or that the king will also teach (4Q381), fulfilling a role typically assigned to the priests.[41]

Psalms of Solomon 17

The most significant statement of Davidic messianism not found among the Dead Sea Scrolls is in Psalms of Solomon 17.[42] Apparent allusions to Pompey in Jerusalem in 63 BCE (Pss. Sol. 2:2; 8:15–21) and his murder in 48 BCE (Pss. Sol. 2:26–27) point to a date of late first century BCE or shortly thereafter,[43] and Kenneth Atkinson has argued that the setting of Psalms of Solomon 17 is Herodian, specifically 37–30 BCE.[44] In response to Herod's atrocities or earlier Hasmonean propaganda, the Psalms of Solomon look forward to the advent of a Davidic king.[45]

The chapter opens with a strong affirmation of God's everlasting kingship. It continues: "And the kingdom of our God is forever over the nations in judgment. Lord, you chose David to be king over Israel, and swore to him about his descendants forever, that his kingdom should not fail before you" (Pss. Sol. 17:4, *OTP* 2:665). When David's successors "set up a monarchy because of their arrogance" and "despoiled the throne of David with arrogant shouting," God overthrew them and allowed "a man alien to our race" (Pompey?) to rise up against them (Pss. Sol. 17:6–7). Jerusalem was defiled.

> For there was no one among them [the citizens of Jerusalem]
> Who practiced righteousness or justice:
> From their leader to the commonest of the people, (they were) in
>   every kind of sin:
> The king was a criminal,
> and the judge disobedient;
> (and) the people sinners. (Pss. Sol. 17:19–20, *OTP* 2:666)

The psalmist pleads for a rightful, Davidic king: "See, Lord, and raise up for them their king, the son of David, to rule over your servant Israel in the time known to you, O God" (Pss. Sol. 17:21, *OTP* 2:667). This is the only occurrence of the designation "the son of David" in reference to a messianic figure in early Jewish literature.[46] The rest of the psalm longingly looks forward to the restoration of a Davidic king, whose activities and attributes it describes:

> "He will gather a holy people" (17:26),
> "He will judge the tribes of the people" (17:26),
> "For he shall know them that they are all children of their God"
> (17:27),
> "He will judge peoples and nations" (17:29),
> "And he will be a righteous king over them, taught by God" (17:32),
> "He shall be compassionate to all the nations (who) reverently (stand)
> before him" (17:34),
> "He will bless the Lord's people with wisdom and happiness" (17:35;
> cf. 4 Ezra 12:32–34),
> "For God made him powerful in the holy spirit and wise in the
> counsel of understanding" (17:37),
> "Faithfully and righteously shepherding the Lord's flock,
> He will not let any of them stumble in their pasture.
> He will lead them in all holiness" (17:40–41).

As in the scrolls, the son of David will be a military leader (17:22–25; cf. 4Q161 8–10 III, 21–22; 1Q28b V, 24–29, CD VII, 20–21; 4Q285 V, 4) who will drive out Israel's enemies, then establish righteousness (4Q252 V, 3; 1Q28b V, 20–23; 4Q161 8–10 III, 23–24).[47] As the righteous messiah, "he will not rely on horse and rider and bow" (Pss. Sol. 17:33) but "he will strike the earth with the word of his mouth forever" (17:35); i.e., by his wisdom and righteousness (17:23; cf. Isa 11:2; Jer 23:5).[48] As in the Qumran documents, the Davidic messiah's rule will extend over all the nations,[49] and he will be Israel's shepherd: "Faithfully and righteously shepherding the Lord's flock, he will not let any of them stumble in their pasture. He will lead them in all holiness" (Pss. Sol. 17:40–41).[50]

The Davidic King in Jewish Messianism

The texts surveyed above exhibit remarkable fluidity and adaptability regarding the expectation of a Davidic king, whether in the near or eschatological future, messianic or not.[51] Typically, however, the expected figure fulfills various scriptural references, especially 2 Samuel 7 and Isaiah 11. He will deliver Israel, or at least the faithful remnant, from its enemies and judge the nations with righteousness. This expectation was maintained by opponents of the Hasmoneans and by their anti-Roman and anti-Herodian successors, marking a renewal of hope, albeit apocalyptic hope, in God's providence and faithfulness to Israel.

The common metaphor of king as shepherd, which was current in other cultures also, was a typical trait of the Davidic king. The Words of the Luminaries (4Q504) speaks of David as a "princely shepherd" and emphasizes his chosenness, but it is not clearly messianic.[52]

> And you chose the land of Judah, and established your covenant with
> David so that he would be like a shepherd, a prince over your people,
> and would sit in front of you on the throne of Israel for ever. (4Q504
> 1–2 IV, 5–8; García Martínez, 415)

Nevertheless, this text "reinforces the tradition of Davidic promise and expectation very powerfully, and introduces titles for David (Shepherd and, especially, Prince) that have very obvious potential messianic resonance."[53] Other traits are also prominent. The Davidic messiah will judge the nations. He will be wise, taught by God, and he will establish justice, righteousness, and peace.

Emphasizing the diversity of expectations rather than the common core of Davidic messianism, Pomykala offers a challenge to future scholarship: "Scholars will have to investigate specifically how the Davidic dynasty tradition was interpreted and applied in various early Christian and rabbinic texts in terms of the particular characterizations and functions ascribed to the Davidic messiah."[54] So, with the preceding survey of key texts in view, we turn to the Gospels of Matthew and John, to explore how they appropriate and adapt the traditions of Davidic messianism current in Second Temple Judaism, giving particular attention to its common themes: fulfilling the Davidic covenant, delivering Israel, shepherding Israel, and judging the nations with righteousness.

Davidic Messianism in Matthew

The Gospel of Matthew announces the coming of the Son of David in the first verse, then traces Jesus's genealogy from Abraham, to David, and through the Babylonian exile in three series of fourteen generations. Although the last sequence contains only thirteen generations, Matthew underscores the significance of there being three sets of fourteen generations (Matt 1:17), and David is the fourteenth name in the genealogy.[55] Each Hebrew letter had a numerical value, and the numerical value of "David" is fourteen (*dvd* = 4 + 6 + 4 = 14). The appellation "son of David" occurs only three times in Mark but ten times in Matthew (1:1; 9:27; 12:23; 15:22; 20:30, 31; 21:9, 14; 22:42, 45). In a dream, an angel addresses Joseph as "son of David," and Jesus is born in Bethlehem, fulfilling the prophecy in Micah 5:2.

> "From you shall come forth for me one who is to rule in Israel, whose origin is from of old, from ancient days." (Mic 5:2)

> "From you shall come a ruler who is to shepherd my people Israel." (Matt 2:6)

Matthew quotes Micah 5:2–3 but inserts the reference to "shepherd" from the anointing of David in 2 Samuel 5:2 and 1 Chronicles 11:2.[56] As we have seen, the connection between kingship and shepherding, while common, also appears in texts from Qumran and Psalms of Solomon 17:40–41.

The shepherd motif reappears in Matthew 9:36: "When he saw the crowds, he had compassion [Pss. Sol. 17:34] for them, because they were harassed and helpless, like sheep without a shepherd." The Matthean Jesus is therefore cast as the Davidic Messiah, Israel's shepherd, echoing Psalm 78:70–71: "[The Lord] chose his servant David, and took him from the sheepfolds; from tending the nursing ewes he brought him to be the shepherd of his people Jacob, of Israel, his inheritance." Jesus's compassion (Matt 14:14; 15:32; 18:27; 20:34) is emphasized by the allusion to Israel as "sheep without a shepherd" (Num 27:17; 1 Kgs 22:17; 2 Chr 18:16). By implication, Jesus is Israel's Davidic shepherd, and Jesus's healing activity is connected to his role as the "Son of David."

Dennis Duling, advancing the work of Christoph Burger, argues that Matthew 22:41–46 softens "the apparent polemic against the Son of David title" in Mark 12:35–37 while drawing on "the Markan Son of David who heals."[57] Matthew 22:41–46 skillfully redacts Mark 12:35–37 so that the first two questions Jesus poses are: "What do you think of the Messiah? Whose son is he?" (Matt 22:42). When they answer, "The son of David," Jesus presses them to explain how, then, David can call him "Lord" and quotes Psalm 110:1. Jesus's fourth question returns to the main issue: "How can he [the Messiah] be his [David's] son?" From the birth account at the beginning of the Gospel, Matthew has been showing how Jesus is both the anticipated son of David yet greater than David's son; Jesus is the Son of God.[58]

As Lidjia Novakovic notes, apart from Matthew 1 and 22:41–46, other occurrences of the title "Son of David," with the exception of 21:1–11, are found in healing contexts,[59] and William Loader interprets Matthew's use of the title as affirming that as the Davidic Messiah, Jesus will deliver Israel from its blindness and demon-possession.[60] Wayne Baxter traces the connection between healing and the Son of David in Matthew to Ezekiel 34:16, which promises, "I will bind up the injured, and I will strengthen the weak."[61] Matthew adds that Jesus sent his disciples only "to the lost sheep of the house of Israel" (10:6; cf. 15:24). When Jesus heals on the Sabbath, he is doing no more than the Pharisees would do if their sheep fell into a pit on the Sabbath (12:11–12).

When Jesus cast out a demon that made a man blind and mute, "the crowds were amazed and said, 'Can this be the Son of David?'" (12:23). Although the Pharisees, the chief priests, and the scribes remain blind to Jesus's messianic identity, when he cured the blind and the lame in the temple, the children cried out, "Hosanna to the Son of David" (21:14–15).[62] The truth is revealed through the mouths of babes (Ps 8:3).

Among the Gospels, only Matthew includes a description of the messianic king judging the nations, separating the sheep from the goats (25:31–46), which echoes the recurring references to judging in the messianic texts discussed above, drawing on Isaiah 11 (4Q161; 4Q246; Pss. Sol. 17:4, 29).[63] The establishment of righteousness is another prominent theme in Matthew. The lemma *dikaio-* occurs twenty-two times in Matthew. Joseph is righteous (1:19). John baptizes Jesus "to fulfill all righteousness" (3:15). Those who "hunger and thirst for righteousness" are blessed (5:6), as are "those who are persecuted for righteousness' sake" (5:10). "Whoever welcomes a righteous person in the name of a righteous person will receive the reward of the righteous" (10:41), and "the righteous will shine like the sun in the kingdom of their Father" (13:43; cf. 25:46).

God will do for Israel what a faithful shepherd does for the flock, and "they shall know that I . . . am with them" (Ezek 34:30; cf. Matt 1:23; 28:20). Moses, who had been a shepherd, served as Israel's shepherd. Later, this role was assigned to David and his descendants, and by extension to the messiah.[64]

Matthew therefore seizes on Davidic messianism at the outset of the Gospel and develops it throughout, weaving other themes into it. As the righteous, Davidic Messiah, Jesus teaches a new standard of righteousness, and notably there is no hint of his subordination to a priestly messiah. He gives a new interpretation of the Law and the Prophets in the Sermon on the Mount and when he is interrogated in the temple (22:34–40).[65] His healings validate his role as Israel's shepherd. He judges Israel and the nations with righteousness, and his reign and his presence will be forever ("Emmanuel"). Clearly, Matthew draws deeply from contemporary Davidic messianism, but Piotrowski is correct when he asserts, "Matthew *is* unique among late Second Temple literature, however, in the explicit force with which the eschatological Davidide is put front and center."[66]

Davidic Messianism in John

While Matthew recasts Mark to show that Jesus fulfilled the expectations for a Davidic messiah, John routinely avoids portraying Jesus as the Davidic Messiah.

David appears only once in the Gospel (John 7:42), there is no Davidic genealogy or birth narrative, Jesus is never called "Son of David," and the question of the interpretation of Psalm 110:1 is not found in John. The reference to the expectation that the Messiah would be born in Bethlehem in John 7:42 is problematic because it is raised by some of the crowd who do not really know where Jesus is from, so it advances John's insistence that Jesus is "from above," the one sent by the Father. Any significance related to Davidic descent is secondary.[67]

This absence of explicit references to David, however, has not deterred some recent interpreters from finding Davidic messianism in John. Margaret Daly-Denton contends "the 'Davidlikeness' of Jesus is, perhaps, a neglected strand in the multihued texture of the Fourth Gospel."[68] She argues that because Davidic authorship of the Psalms was assumed, where they are quoted, they echo David's voice. John avoided Psalm 110:1, Daly-Denton explains, because of the evangelist's Christology of "the descent from heaven of the pre-existent Word and his return to where he was before."[69] Similarly, "recourse to messianic interpretations of the Davidic materials in the early attempts of Christians to express their understanding of Jesus seems to have aroused serious misgivings within the Johannine circle, to the point where the Evangelist has decided to avoid reference to David."[70]

Still, "while [John's] portrayal of Jesus never refers to him as 'Son of David,' it draws extensively on the multifaceted richness which the figure of David had acquired in Second Temple Judaism."[71] "Shepherding," she notes, "is a Davidic role in Jewish tradition."[72] A clue to the association between David and Jesus as "the good shepherd" (ὁ ποιμὴν ὁ καλός) appears in the description of the young shepherd anointed by Samuel in 1 Samuel 16:12: "and he was ruddy, with beautiful (κάλλους) eyes, and good (ἀγαθός) in the sight of the Lord, and the Lord said to Samuel, 'Arise and anoint David, for he is good (ἀγαθός).'"[73] Daly-Denton also connects the hearing of the shepherd's voice in John 10:27 with Psalm 94:7:

> For he is our God,
> And we are the people of his pasture,
> And the sheep of his hand.
> O that today you would listen to his voice!

In contrast to thieves who kill and destroy, the good shepherd gives life (John 10:10), and the giving of (eternal) life is ultimately related to his laying down his life for the sheep (cf. 10:27–28). Kirsten Nielsen likewise contends that "what is new in John 10 and far beyond the Old Testament is the idea that the good shepherd lays down his life for his flock,"[74] but again Daly-Denton argues that the David narrative offers a hint of this facet of the shepherd metaphor because David risked his life for the people on many occasions, and when they were being killed, he offered himself in their place (2 Sam 24:17).[75] Cumulatively, she concludes, the interpretation of the Psalms and allusions to David establish a "paradigmatic role in relation to Jesus in the Fourth Gospel."[76]

Several essays in *Reading the Gospel of John's Christology as Jewish Messianism* take up the argument that John draws on Davidic messianism. Drawing on "conceptual blending theory," Beth Stovell notes John's claims of Jesus's kingship in John 1:49 and 12:13 and the blending of "priestly and kingly depictions of Jesus" through Jesus as the new temple.[77] She builds the case by identifying elements in John that are identified elsewhere with David, especially anointing and the anointed one, shepherd, Son of God, king and kingdom, and temple and divine presence, which as we have seen also appear in 4Q174, 4Q252, 4Q504, and 11QPsalms[a]. Stovell concludes, "While at times John's Gospel represents new blendings of these messianic conceptions in creative ways, many of the essential ingredients for these blends themselves find precedence in their counterparts within Second Temple Judaism."[78]

Joel Willitts approaches John's dearth of references to David in another way: "The argument of this essay is that John's understanding of Jesus's messiahship is a sophisticated Davidic messianism which subverts and subsumes, or what I will call 'sublates,' other early Jewish messianic expectations. . . . To put my hypothesis plainly: John's positive interest in Moses and Jesus's superiority over Moses as the Son of God is consistent with the Chronicler's Davidic perspective and narrative strategy. The sublation of Moses by David is a feature of early Davidic tradition."[79] The argument requires two steps, showing first that for the Chronicler Moses's importance is "subsumed by David" with the result that while Moses is great David is greater, then that John did likewise, producing "a sophisticated and complex Davidic Christology, one that traffics below the surface at deeper levels of imagination and conceptual structure."[80]

Caution is in order. Daly-Denton, Stovell, and Willitts find Davidic messianism in John by identifying facades behind which David allegedly appears in the Gospel: the Psalms, concepts and roles related to David, and Moses's greatness telegraphing the greater importance of David. The problem remains that while John repeatedly contrasts Jesus with Moses and asserts that Moses bears witness to Jesus, the same cannot be said for David. Marida Nicolaci, in the same volume, argues with more restraint that in the context of Jewish messianism (including Pss. Sol. 17, 1 En. 37–71, and 4Q491), John portrays a "royal Davidic Messiah" whose "'royalty of nature' . . . extends well beyond his 'Davidic' descent."[81] John Lierman's observation that the evidence for Davidic messianism in John is all indirect and deductive remains the challenge all interpreters face, because although Jesus's roles as king, judge, and shepherd are important in John, it is less clear that John understands them as associated with David. Lierman's conclusion, therefore, remains to be refuted: "Nothing in the

Fourth Gospel itself indicates that John had the slightest interest in advancing
a Davidic appraisal of the Messiah Jesus."[82]

Marianne Meye Thompson states the situation clearly and repeatedly:
"While Jesus is the Messiah, the King of Israel, John highlights his identity as
Son of God, not as a son of David."[83] Jesus is not the Messiah who builds the
temple; he "zealously purifies his Father's house."[84] Even if Jesus is from Bethlehem of Judea, "that, for John, would not explain the kind of Messiah that Jesus
is; he is the Messiah and 'King of Israel' as the Son of God."[85] Similarly, for John,
Jesus's role as shepherd is based not on David but God's role as shepherd of the
people of Israel.[86] At Hanukkah, in the temple, "rather than presenting himself
as the son of David, Jesus presents himself as the Son of God, who does the works
of God," and it will be his death that "protects and unifies God's people."[87] In
John's account of Jesus's triumphal entry, "there is no mention of David, David's
kingdom, or Jesus as the son of David."[88] Contrary to the expectation of a Davidic
messiah who will "remain forever" (2 Sam 7:13; 4Q252; Pss. Sol. 17:35), Jesus
announces that he will die, and "his mission will be accomplished by means of
his death on a cross: a Roman instrument of political subjugation and torture."[89]
When Jesus is anointed, he is anointed for his burial.[90] His kingdom is "not of
this world"; that is, "it cannot be identified with any earthly kingdom: Jewish,
Davidic, or otherwise."[91] Finally, although the Psalms "provide the texture of
the Passion Narrative" in the Gospels, "John never states that these quotations
come from the Psalms . . . , nor does he make reference to David, their alleged
author . . . . For John, these passages are important because they are *Scripture*."[92]

Conclusion

In sum, the Dead Sea Scrolls and Psalms of Solomon 17 provide indisputable
evidence of the currency of Davidic messianism in the first century, and Matthew
recasts Mark's Jesus to show that Jesus fulfilled Jewish hopes for a Davidic
messiah. Nevertheless, John never identifies Jesus as Son of David. Elements of
Davidic messianism in other texts, especially the roles of shepherd, king, and
judge, are not associated with David. Instead, for John, these roles confirm Jesus's
divine sonship. As strong as "the Davidic-centered eschatological outlook in the
late Second Temple period" may have been,[93] John insists that Jesus be seen not
in the context of Davidic expectations but as the culmination and fulfillment
of God's revelatory and redemptive work since the creation of the world. The
question remains: Why did these two Gospels take such different stances in
regard to Davidic messianism?

CHAPTER ELEVEN

The High Christology of the Lowly Jesus

The Johannine Thunderbolt in Matthew

Tommy Givens

> All things were handed over to me by my Father. No one knows the Son
> except the Father, nor does anyone know the Father except the Son and
> any to whom the Son desires to reveal [him].
>
> (Matt 11:27)[1]

THE "JOHANNINE THUNDERBOLT" of Matthew (11:27) has been construed as
Johannine for its supposedly high Christology, which is considered typical of the
Gospel of John. It is thought uncharacteristic of the otherwise lower Christology
of Matthew's Gospel or the rest of the synoptic tradition.[2] So uncharacteristic,
according to some modern scholars, that Matthew 11:27 must be a meteoric
invasion of Matthew from a Johannine imagination.[3] But Mark Goodacre has
claimed that it is not in fact so alien to Matthew and has briefly documented that
claim.[4] He suggests that Gospel scholars have overdrawn christological distinctions between Matthew and John and have "been misreading the Synoptics in
light of our familiarity with John." Rather than interpret the words of Matthew
11:27 as a Johannine invasion of Matthew, we should, he urges, recognize them
as native to Matthew's Gospel and inspirational for John's later Christology. "The
language and theology of the thunderbolt, with its underlining of Jesus' divine
authority, and its stress on the father and the son, is at home in Matthew where
it had its genesis."[5] It "is not so much a bolt from the Johannine blue as it was
the Synoptic platform from which John launched his Christological rocket."[6]

With appreciation for the corrective offered by Goodacre, I propose a somewhat more radical reassessment of the words of Matthew 11:27, one that draws
from their force in the immediate context of Matthew's narrative. This reassessment problematizes the distinction between low and high Christology and thus
any Christology or interpretation of Gospel texts that is overly determined by
that distinction. It highlights the liability latent in "partitive exegesis," which
crystallized in a broad stream of patristic biblical interpretation and anticipated
the terms whereby Gospel Christology has been defined by modern scholars

as lower or higher. Taking this liability into account, I then point to neglected features of John's "high" Christology and to an example of their wise consideration in Marianne Meye Thompson's magisterial commentary on the Gospel of John. I begin with a brief account of how debate over "the Johannine thunderbolt" in Matthew has led to the distortion of the Christology of Matthew and other Gospels such as John in relation to Jesus's "divinity."

The Problem of Jesus's "Divinity"

It is not only scholars' familiarity with John that has prompted poor readings of synoptic words like those of Jesus in Matthew 11:27 (cf. Luke 10:22). It is also their familiarity with classic, ecumenical Christian creeds and corresponding streams of Christian and post-Christian doctrinal discourse that have misleadingly determined debates about early Christology according to canonical Gospel testimony. Such creedal formulations, dependent as they are on the Gospel of John, have been conceived widely as themselves the force of biblical teaching in Christian and post-Christian understanding. This has encouraged exegesis that treats divinity as a flattened abstraction, one that is conjured in opposition to a similarly abstract humanity.[7]

Under the pressure of creedal formulations thus conceived, and without sufficient attention to literary and background considerations, a driving critical question of Matthew 11:27 has come to be *whether* Jesus is presented as divine or as "merely human."[8] In relation to John's Gospel, the question is whether 11:27 is somehow peculiarly Johannine because it "underlines Jesus's divine authority" or otherwise anticipates John's "high" Christology. Even if it is not an invasive Johannine meteor but a piece of the synoptic platform of a Johannine christological rocket, its interpretation is made a matter of whether Jesus is divine and thus of the relative "height" of synoptic Christology. Accordingly, in 11:27 we supposedly find a high synoptic Christology in relation to a still higher Johannine Christology. Via the higher Christology of John, then, "the Father" and "the Son" of 11:27 are thus haunted by a certain specter of later Trinitarian and christological doctrine,[9] whose principal deliverance, like that of 11:27, is reduced to the highly abstract "divinity" or "divine authority" of Jesus.[10]

If such creedal formulations are conceived as themselves the force of teaching like 11:27, then Gospel scholars are right to guard such teaching against "orthodox" Christian corruption in its reception history. But this scholarly criticism has commonly assumed the abstract divinity of Christ in Christian creedal doctrine—and supposedly in John—as what must be denied in the historically sound interpretation of Matthew, some scholars famously construing it as an alien, Johannine thunderbolt.[11]

We are helped some, but only a little, by a corrective claim that Jesus is in fact divine according to the breadth of Matthew, whose Christology, as expressed in 11:27, is thus deemed consonant with the later narrative of John that it perhaps inspired. We are helped only a little because the crucial question of *what constitutes divinity* in the respective narratives is begged. Whether in defense or denial of the divinity of Jesus according to Matthew, whether for or against the christological consonance between Matthew and John, debate about the meaning of 11:27 and its "high" Christology traffics in the same flattened abstraction of divinity characteristic of Christian creedal formulations. What divinity *is* according to such Gospel testimony is passed over. And the problem is only compounded by theories or assumptions of development from earlier, "lower" Christology, to later, "higher" Christology.

Whether the presentation of Jesus in a Gospel narrative predicates of him an abstraction of divinity or divine authority, or even whether it conforms to such an abstraction, is arguably not a relevant exegetical question. A relevant exegetical question is instead *who* a Gospel narrative presents Jesus to be, including *who* it attests God to be in relation to Jesus. And that question must be addressed with caution about abstractions of divinity that we inevitably bring to the study of the narrative, even if, according to such abstractions, the exegetical judgment is that a text does not teach that Jesus is divine.

This caution is especially in order if the narrative in question claims, as the canonical Gospels do, to attest to an apocalypse of Israel's God and not simply to confirm an already available and stable concept of divinity. More especially still, if, as we might expect of something genuinely revelatory, it is somehow subversive of prevalent understandings of divinity, even of Israel's God. That is why simply *whether* Jesus is divine or bears divine authority is arguably not itself a question relevant to the interpretation of 11:27 or to its relation to John. Moreover, merely *that* Jesus is divine is not the point of 11:27 or the rest of Matthew or even of John, despite what creedal gleanings from such Gospel testimony and other Christian interpretation have induced many to assume.[12]

Sensibly, Goodacre suggests that "so much of what he [the Fourth Evangelist] finds in the Synoptics is oblique, subtle, suggestive," although this is putatively in contrast to the "clear, unambiguous Christological claim" of Matthew 11:27, which "becomes a central source of reflection" for John.[13] Yet, this is to assume that all of that obliqueness, subtlety, and suggestiveness is pointing to something that could in fact be presented more flatly and unambiguously, as John supposedly does under the inspiration of texts like Matthew 11:27. But what if a certain ambiguity is in fact constitutive of who Jesus is according to Matthew, as well as John for that matter? What if such ambiguity is constitutive of whatever divinity each presents Jesus as disclosing, ambiguity that is perhaps key to the knowledge of the one God who is? Why is it, after all, that neither Matthew nor

John simply says, at some juncture, "Jesus is God," as Christian creedal doctrine is taken to do? Is it possible that divinity, as Matthew and John variously present it, is such that Jesus's being divine, whatever that might mean, is not simply one fact among others to be asserted?[14]

The Lowly Son of Matthew 11:25–27

If the supposedly Johannine Christology of the confession of Matthew 11:27 is to be discerned in terms of its relative "height," one cannot but be struck by the words that lead directly to it in Matthew's narrative, words about the lowliness of God's revelation in Jesus:

> At that time, Jesus continued, "I confess to you, Father, Lord of heaven and earth, that you hid these things from wise and discerning people and revealed (ἀπεκάλυψας) them to little children. Yes, Father, for thus took place [your] choice pleasure (εὐδοκία) before you." (11:25–26)

"At that time," "continued," and "these things" in v. 25 indicate that the meaning of what Jesus says here and in the Johannine thunderbolt that follows in v. 27 is constrained and focused by the preceding narrative, to which I will turn shortly. But it is already clear enough that whatever Christology we are to attribute to the words of v. 27, in Matthew it is an expression of the apocalypse of the presumably "high" Lord of heaven and earth *to little children*, which is hidden from wise and discerning people. In fact, arguably, hiding from such people is here a key mode of the apocalypse of the Lord of heaven and earth, not merely its attendant condition. Jesus, according to Matthew, is hardly making a claim to divinity or divine authority as mere abstraction, with which wise and discerning people have proven characteristically comfortable. He speaks of the apocalypse of God such that it renders a stable distinction between high and low dubious at best; the revelation of God operates precisely by disturbing such a distinction, insisting that God, the "highest" Lord of all, is revealed in and through what is low.

What is more, this apocalypse—as disruptive to the distribution of power on the earth as it is correspondingly to the powerful minds of the learned—is the occurrence of God's "choice pleasure" (εὐδοκία). Matthew employs this noun only here, the related verb (εὐδοκέω) only at Jesus's baptism (3:17) and its echo on the Mount of Transfiguration (17:5).[15] In Jesus's vision at the Jordan, the voice of Israel's God in heaven expressed choice pleasure in him as he joined his people in a baptism of confessing their sins. In that moment of solidarity with his broken people, the vision revealed to Jesus his anointing as Son, the messianic king of Israel, the human heir of God's rule. And this only after, to wise John, Jesus insisted on his subordination to the Baptizer; John, knowing himself as the lowly herald of the coming king, thought Jesus too high for his baptism, saying that instead he needed to be baptized by Jesus (3:14–15).

Later in Matthew, when Jesus is transfigured before his three closest disciples in a vision on a high mountain, God's expression of choice pleasure in his Son to them is followed by a command that they listen to him (17:5). They must listen to him because, for them, his highness and lowness do not compute, we might say; in Matthew Jesus has just begun teaching them that he will come to power as Messiah by a lowly death at the hands of the corrupt regime in Jerusalem—an impenetrable scandal to Peter, to other disciples, and to human canons of power generally. In fact, if his disciples are to follow Jesus as Messiah, they should not declare him so, deny themselves, and live so as to be in danger of crucifixion themselves (16:20–28). Then, on the Mount of Transfiguration, this Son is the one to whom Peter, James, and John are commanded to listen. In him as Son is the choice pleasure of the God who is unveiled by disclosing himself to little children and, accordingly, veiled to wise and discerning people. Can the Christology of such a Son be categorized as high or low without betraying him?

Consider, again, the words of 11:27, which culminate Jesus's confession of the lowliness of God's revelation according to God's choice pleasure: "All things were handed over to me by my Father. No one knows the Son except the Father, nor does anyone know the Father except the Son and any to whom the Son desires to reveal [him]." Notice that a predicate of divinity is not explicit in 11:27 but inferred by exegetes from Jesus's being entrusted "all things" as Son by God as his Father and thus from Jesus's exclusive mediation of the knowledge of God. I suspect that exegetes are prompted to construe Jesus's words as a claim to divinity because "Son of God" denotes the unique divinity of Jesus in standard Christian teaching and because of the resonance of the verse with the language of John's Gospel. But what sort of divinity Jesus's words here imply is scarcely clear.

Within the confines of the narrative drama, in which Jesus is making a confessional declaration in the hearing of crowds, including his ambitious disciples, surely the words of 11:27 mean something rather cryptic. They mean something that extends beyond the horizon of the narrative itself, it seems, something that grows with the retrospection available to readers and hearers, even if their immediate force for the characters of the narrative must not be circumvented. In any case, the words are not a bald and flat declaration that Jesus *is* the Son of God, however much that may be thought implicit. Jesus has made no such declaration to this point in the narrative. He has heard himself described as such only in a vision—at his baptism—and only the devil and demons have spoken of him in such terms since (4:3, 6; 8:29). And he will soon tell his disciples not to tell others he is the messianic Son (16:16, 20). I suggest that the narrative's purpose is not simply to declare *that* Jesus is the Son of God, as if the audience of the narrative already knew who the Son of God is and simply needed to be shown that Jesus is a match—that would not be testimony to any apocalypse of God. Its purpose is instead to *tell who* Jesus is *as* Son of God and therefore who and what the Son of God is.

Jesus's words in 11:27, then, are less a plain, freestanding assertion about himself and more the climax of his confession to God as his Father about how God has been revealed according to the preceding section of the narrative. While his sonship is implicitly unique, we should remember that, to this point in the narrative, Jesus has said that peacemakers are to be blessed because they will be called "sons of God" (5:9). He has assumed that his people know God as their Father and urged them to pray and live accordingly (5:16, 45, 48; 6:1–18, 26, 32; 7:11, 21; 10:20, 29, 32–33); his own sonship, thus, a sharing in theirs. He is Son of the God who is Father to little children in defiance of wise and discerning people, and thus made known to and through the lowly according to his Father's "choice pleasure."

But what, precisely, has God revealed to little children and hidden from wise and discerning people? What, in 11:25, are "these things" that "at that time" Jesus "continued" speaking about, such that we might clarify what it means for "all things" to have been handed over to Jesus as Son by the Father such that he is *the* mediator of the knowledge of God as Father?[16]

The Christology of the Johannine Thunderbolt in Light of Matthew 11:2–26

"At that time" in Matthew, bellwether towns of Galilee, where Jesus and his newly chosen twelve apostles have focused their proclamation and works of the kingdom of heaven, have recently refused to receive them. Under hypocritical and fearful authorities, Chorazin, Bethsaida, and even Capernaum where Jesus lives, have generally refused to repent of the patterns of injustice they have inherited and thus to live hospitably into the kingdom as Jesus and his apostles have taught it. The generation coursing through such towns has been unmoved, even offended, by the unimpressive appearance of the kingdom in John the Baptist, Jesus, and Jesus's twelve apostles (10:14–15; 11:16–24).

To their generation in the land, Jesus and these apostles have been presenting the kingdom of heaven as powerful through humble seeds of hospitality to unimpressive, needy messengers and the ways of sharing that they can inspire (10:5–14, 40–42). The patterns of life and perception that offer no welcome to such a kingdom, Jesus foretells, are leading to a catastrophic judgment coming to his unrepentant generation. It is coming particularly to the intergenerational life and memory of Chorazin, Bethsaida, and Capernaum, for whom the nearness and familiarity of the kingdom seem to have thickened its formative disguise.[17]

Led by wise and discerning people, Jesus's generation in these towns is captive to an unjust rule that impresses them enough to maintain the status quo and thus disempowers them. They are left, then, with "hope" only for more of the power they already see and hear, which is not enough power to enter the kingdom coming from heaven or avert destruction in the judgment coming to their generation. Striving for high prominence, they are headed for oblivion beneath the earth, Jesus warns (11:22–24).

Yet, we should not jump to the conclusion that this generation's suffering the consequences of entrenched injustice under shepherds leading them astray is a blow to the kingdom of heaven. It is instead the horrifying revelation of its God, an act of his awaited government, borne witness by little children, the childlike who can see the unimpressive kingdom for the power from heaven that it is. Per the climax of Jesus's words in 11:27, the living and generative relation between the underwhelming Jesus as Son and Israel's God as Father is the lowly height of this earth-shattering apocalypse, its disturbingly divine power in the unseemly human on the earth.

John the Baptist has already proven a disappointment by being imprisoned by Herod Antipas after drawing masses to his kingdom proclamation at the Jordan (4:12). Now, the very prophet who announced the coming ruler of the kingdom of heaven has sent disciples from prison to ask whether Jesus is the one he was proclaiming (11:2–3). And to that prophet who publicly does not know if Jesus fulfills his prophecy, Jesus has not answered that he is the one John predicted would come to power. He has instead publicly indicated the present signs of Israel's healing foretold by Isaiah and pronounced blessing on those who are not insulted by such powerfully humble signs from him (11:4–6). Then, rather than distancing himself from John's unimpressive prophetic authority, Jesus goes on to declare to the listening crowds that John is the greatest person yet born, the prophet who has prepared Israel for the great and terrible day of the Lord, which has already dawned; John the Baptist, Jesus announces, is Elijah who was to come (11:7–15; cf. Mal 3–4).

John is not a lower prophet of God because of his imprisonment by a corrupt ruler and ignorance about his own prophecy, then. Precisely as such he is the highest prophet of all in the face of the heavenly kingdom that shatters the human tower of high and low on the earth. That his generation found John's prophetic dance insufficiently festive and the Son of Man, with his sordid associations, the wrong kind of man is itself apocalyptic (Matt 11:16–19). That their bellwether towns in Galilee have not repented at the proliferation of humbly potent kingdom healing in them is a signature of the disturbing power of heaven's rule, attested by the healed and the humble, who can see and hear the unfolding redemption that Isaiah foretold. To them, to those who see and hear meekly amidst such widespread blindness and deafness, God has revealed how the strongholds of hypocritical and self-righteous power are already crumbling. Such things, Jesus confesses publicly to the Father, are "these things" (11:25) that the Father has hidden from wise and discerning people while revealing them to little children. "Wise and discerning people" are many of the authorities of Jesus's generation and the people charmed by them, and they have tried to outsmart the kingdom of heaven. Meanwhile, to those who would not presume to know, God has revealed how the kingdom is coming.

In 11:25–27, this scandal, this choice pleasure of God as Father, extends from God's revealing "these things" to little children to God's handing "all things" over to Jesus as Son, the lowest Child of all, we might say. To the hearing crowds, this is only for Jesus to deepen the scandal of the apocalypse of God he has been describing, not to resolve it or decode it. For all of his failure to seem the bearer of the kingdom from heaven to the authorities and prominent Galilean towns of his generation under their governance, the work of his life is in fact where and how God has hidden "all things"; his is the contagious life that somehow inherits the whole world, in all its future unfolding. God has thus hidden that life from other, apparently powerful people who would presume to be the heirs of God's rule of the world. Preposterously, the Father of Israel has hidden all things in one who, whatever healing power and teaching authority can be attributed to him, gives his power away (10:1), parties with the reprobate (11:19), and cannot even get his own town to repent, for which it is doomed (11:23–24).[18] This is not simply what God has done; it is a disclosure of who God is. It is what divinity is *as* Israel's Father who is particularly the Father of Jesus.

The subject of the words of 11:27, then, is not some kind of easily intelligible divine sonship. Only the Father can know this Son as the living, incomprehensible revelation he is. And since God is this way, entrusting all things to this Son on the earth, the Father is finally the One whom only the Son knows, such that the Son is the ultimate mediator of the Father to others, whether they know it or not. God is fully revealed as Father, welcoming people into the fullness of his Son's inheritance, as his choice pleasure spills over in the desire of his Son for others.

In this eschatological context of the hidden nearness of the kingdom of heaven, the dawn of the day of the Lord with Elijah's coming, Jesus is not laying claim to some highly abstract divinity or divine authority. Nor is he indicating himself as some isolated, remote, and exclusive means of generic access to God— certainly not something that comes by "believing in him" as such, about which he says nothing. He simply does not speak of himself as an abstract object of faith. He expresses the hidden nearness of Israel's Father in him as ignoble heir among the heirs of Israel.

This is a disturbing nearness that arouses hostility in those who hunger for heroic spectacle and that as such conveys the inheritance of the kingdom to people as they are transformed by lowliness, by divine welcome. It is not a nearness that conforms to a stable concept of divinity; it constantly disturbs what human beings associate concretely with a "God" who is higher than they and as such a tool for their rule over others and for their own captivity. Thus, for the knowledge of Israel's God to be mediated by Jesus is for it to be hidden, more hidden from some than from others, more hidden from those who presume to know than from those who do not know to presume.

After the Johannine thunderbolt of 11:27, Jesus goes on to appeal to his listening generation, who have been toiling under the burdens of their wise and discerning guides (11:28–30). Following them, their tendency so far is to refuse to repent. So Jesus offers them rest from the strains imposed by teachers who presume to know and so spread blindness and deafness to the lowly kingdom power of justice and healing. Such teachers have fostered a tattered fabric of relations in which people must labor for a seat at the table, sacrificing the justice of God's law and trafficking in self-righteousness as capital, imitating their impressive guides. To such burdened lives of his generation Jesus offers a yoke that is restful, teaching gentleness and lowliness in heart; in these ways of living God has hidden heaven's rule from wise and discerning people. As a scandal to the exhausting appetites of his generation trained by these presumptuous guides, Jesus offers a yoke of learning, but one that is light, shepherding the weary to a life of rest. And then the narrative turns to show how Jesus gives disturbing relief from the heavy burdens imposed by wise and discerning people on the Sabbath day of rest (12:1–14).[19]

The Liability of Partitive Exegesis for Gospel Interpretation

We are now in a position to observe a clarifying, patristic antecedent for the modern scholarly tendency to neglect the force of the narrative for the meaning of the Johannine thunderbolt of Matthew 11:27. This modern tendency reduces its interpretation to overly abstract terms of divinity and humanity. What was perhaps more a potential liability in patristic exegesis and Christology has become actual in modern scholarship that makes the interpretation of 11:27 a matter of whether it implicitly attributes divinity or divine authority to Jesus or presents him as "merely human." This liability is actual and manifest in the conception of Gospel Christology as on a spectrum between low and high and in the treatment of divinity and humanity as opposing abstractions, as supposedly enshrined in ecumenical Christian creeds.

Defending the divinity of Christ as outlined in those creeds, influential patristic teachers combatted interpretations of Gospel passages that attributed to Jesus, without qualification, what could not be predicated of God according to their understanding of divinity. In short, they combatted Christian interpretations that implied Jesus is not God. Such interpretations held that certain Gospel passages present Jesus as a clearly sub-divine being. They present him as, for example, tired, hungry, weeping, and ignorant of the day and hour of his coming to power as Son. In response, the likes of Athanasius, Cyril of Alexandria, and Gregory of Nazianzus interpreted such passages *partitively*. They said that these fleshly limits could indeed be attributed to the Son's incarnation as a human being but not to his divine nature, while such activities as forgiving sins or miraculously feeding multitudes, which were more intuitively divine for them, should be attributed to his divinity.[20]

Athanasius articulates the rule for partitive exegesis this way: "When he is said to hunger, to thirst, to tire, not to know, to sleep, to cry, to ask, to flee, to be born, to avoid the cup, and, simply, all the things of the flesh, let it be said that . . . [it is] not in divinity but 'for us in the flesh,' that these sufferings should be recognized not as his own as of the Word according to nature but rather as his own as of the nature of the flesh."[21] When, in 24:36, Jesus says to his disciples that no one knows the day or the hour of the Son of Man's coming to power, "neither the angels of heaven, nor the Son, but only the Father," Cyril of Alexandria interprets: "From which it is plainly to be understood that he indeed knows the day and the hour as God, even if, showing the human in himself, he says he does not know. . . . For it is proper to the order of the human for him not to know the things that are to come."[22] Gregory of Nazianzus sums up the hermeneutical sensibility of partitive exegesis strikingly:

> In one summary statement: apply the high things to the nature that is divine and superior to what is of sufferings and of body. The low things [apply] to that which is composite—indeed to that which was for you emptied and enfleshed, and to say nothing worse, humanized, yet also exalted, so that you, by destroying that which of your decrees [i.e., what directs you as a human being] is fleshly and lowly, might learn to be exalted, even to ascend to divinity, not remaining with the visible things but rather rising with the noumenal things, and might also know what word is about [the divine] nature and what word is about economy.[23]

Such patristic writers were, for good reason, seeking to sustain the claim that Jesus was the scandalous apocalypse of God, rather than the manifestation of a created being who was not God and who thus left the human perception of divinity unchallenged. And one must attend carefully to their insistence that the impassible God was revealed in Christ by assuming the passibility of the flesh into his divine life, the economic expression of God's immanent and eternal love poured out for all created life.[24] But their exegesis would have been truer to this insistence, and more responsive to the Gospel narratives, had they not divided the narratives into what could be predicated of the divine nature versus what could be predicated of the nature of humanity in which Christ shared.[25]

One regrettable effect of this division of the personal narrative subject into two, as opposed to respecting a singular narrative subject who can be said to embody the communication between divine and human natures, is resistance to the lowliness of God as revealed in Christ according to the Gospels.[26] It often involves the reification of notions of divinity and humanity established independently of scriptural testimony, typically at the expense of the uncomely and the bodily, rather than dogged openness to God's revelation of God and of the human, which unfolds as God in the human as Jesus.

That some Gospel words about Jesus can be conceived as about Jesus as divine, while others are about him only as human, depends on abstractions of divinity and humanity that are insufficiently open to Gospel testimony. Gospel testimony is not about one nature or another but about the one person Jesus as "God with us" (1:23). The associated concretions of those divided abstractions in the minds and social fabric of exegetes are thus reinforced as such when they should be tested (e.g., the emerging metaphysical substance of the bodily and the visible). The exegetical question is reduced to whether the text speaks of Jesus's divinity or something sub-divine, created, or human. It is thus allowed to say less about who the person Jesus is or who he reveals God to be, or what corresponding call is delivered to readers and hearers of Gospel testimony. The same reduction by abstraction and division has emerged in modern Gospel scholarship that makes the question of 11:27 whether it presents Jesus as divine or bearing divine authority. It sees in 11:27 a Johannine thunderbolt or the platform of a Johannine rocket. It imagines Christology as on a two-dimensional scale stretched between low and high as opposing poles.

But the Gospels are not so cavalier about the mystery of God. They assume that the revelation of God must be *told*, and incompletely so, not claimed or defined with summary abstractions. True to their singular subject, they are "oblique, subtle, suggestive."[27] What human beings are apt to imagine as powerful or divine is not reliably so, especially in relation to what they imagine as human. And to the imagination and experience of the human, insofar as it is not reliable, the revelation of God involves God's hiding from human beings. Not hiding as absence, but hiding as presence in what human beings—especially governing human beings—are apt to despise, with a view to forming all of the human into knowing participants in that presence together, for their healing. This hiding as unperceived presence, in the Gospels, is the coming of the kingdom of God to the human. It is the coming of the kingdom of heaven to the earth, the dramatic incarnation of the Word.

It may come as a surprise that, for Athanasius, at least in one place, the Johannine thunderbolt is not to be predicated of Jesus as divine but of Jesus as human. He takes Jesus to be describing what the Father has given him as incarnate Son rather than what Jesus always enjoyed as divine Son.[28] It may also come as a surprise that "orthodox" patristic writers who were moved to interpret the Gospels partitively did not find John to be reliably higher in its Christology than the Synoptics. Instead, John furnished for them a plethora of passages that, because of how their opponents were interpreting them, required that they defend the divinity of an evidently lowly Christ. Apparently, they could not have conceived of John as a reliably high source of a bolt in an otherwise lowly Gospel of Matthew, nor as a rocket that had soared from a lower Synoptic platform. In the controversies in which they were embroiled, John had too many christological vulnerabilities of its own.

The High Christology of the Lowly Jesus in John

As a literary whole, John can be conceived as presenting a "high" or "higher" Christology only by ignoring the many low moments of Jesus in it. It seems that attributing to it a "high" Christology is not commentary on the Gospel but on particular moments in it that speak directly of the preincarnate life of the person enfleshed as Jesus, the unique relation between God as Father and Jesus as Son, or something else that smacks of Jesus's divinity in one way or another.[29] Insofar as such moments are construed as presenting Jesus as straightforwardly divine, the patristic tendency I have illustrated takes them as testimony to his divine nature rather than his incarnate life, and modern scholars often interpret them as evidence of a "high" Christology.[30]

But whatever the divinity of such a person might mean, for John the same person wept, grew tired, otherwise suffered, and died, even shamefully so. And in the climax of the opening, programmatic sequence of John's narrative, "Son of God" is appositional to "the King of Israel" (1:49), who is the Messiah (1:41).[31] The Gospel makes no effort to minimize its lowly moments of Jesus or otherwise shield divinity from them; quite the contrary. It will not do, then, to attribute "to the Gospel of John" some generally "high" or "higher" Christology. One could only attribute a certain, questionable abstraction of divinity to certain moments of John and at the expense of others.

Marianne Meye Thompson's magisterial commentary on the Gospel of John is delightfully free of the tendency to divide the central personal subject of the narrative into two natures, one divine and one human. She does not find in John's Gospel a Christology that is somehow "high" and not "low," or one that is "higher" than that of the Synoptic Gospels. Her comments on Jesus's weeping, weeping that many have found to be distinctly human such that it is not divine, are illustrative. She emphasizes, as revelation of God in Johannine terms, Jesus's sharing in the grief of others he loves and his grief at the death of his beloved Lazarus. "That Jesus will soon raise Lazarus to life, and *so manifest God's glory*, does not mute the genuine sorrow that he experiences and expresses."[32] She then elaborates, "While the story is sometimes read as a demonstration of Jesus' human nature, 'humanity' and 'divinity' are not separable aspects of Jesus' identity in John: he is always the incarnate Word of God, and it is the Word-made-flesh, the life-giving Son confronted by death, who weeps at the tomb of his friend."[33] Thompson thus refuses the patristic and modern impulse to render the humanity of Jesus as effectively competitive with his divinity. Instead, she reads in John a word about *who* Jesus is and therefore *who* the divine Word is. The divine Word, as revealed, is One who weeps at the tomb of his friend. However divinity and humanity must be mutually distinguished, so as to avoid their conceptual collapse into one another, in the Gospels they are revealed for who and what they are by the embodied communication between them. This communication is presented as ultimately a revelatory person in the flesh shaped by others, and not a hollow person who manifests overly abstracted divine or human attributes derived otherwise. As communication between God and the human, that person has a long history in Israel and beyond.[34] His is the life of the Word without beginning by whom God gave life in the beginning. He is the Word who, as flesh, according to John, unfolds in the full drama of a concrete, apocalyptic life whose light is the life of all others.

CHAPTER TWELVE

The Waves, the Wind, and the Wilderness

Some High Christological Narratives in Mark and John

Richard Bauckham

High Christology in Mark's Gospel

PROBABLY THE MOST popular understanding of Mark's Christology is that he sees Jesus as a human Messiah exercising a delegated authority to speak and act on God's behalf. In my view, this is too superficial a reading of Mark.[1] Undoubtedly, Jesus is the expected Messiah, the son of David. This is what Peter concludes on the basis of the events he witnesses in the first half of the Gospel (8:29). It is this messianic identity that Jesus requires the disciples to keep secret. But, beginning with Bartimaeus's public recognition of Jesus as son of David (10:47–48), the secret is out. Jesus himself affirms this royal messianic identity by riding into Jerusalem on a donkey (11:1–10), though characteristically he thereby performs an action from which people can draw that conclusion rather than explicitly claiming to be the Messiah. However, the adequacy of such a category to plumb the true depth of Jesus's personal identity is thrown radically into doubt when Jesus himself, referring to Psalm 110:1, asks how then it can be that David there calls the Messiah "Lord" (12:35–37). This is not a repudiation of Davidic messianic identity but an indication that there is more to be said about who Jesus is. At this point in the narrative, Jesus's probing question goes unanswered. As such, it is one of a series of "leading questions" about Jesus's identity that run through the Gospel and point to Jesus's truly divine identity. That Jesus, undoubtedly a human, is also included in the unique identity of the one God of Israel is the deeper secret of Jesus's identity that Mark discloses for the most part only by way of questions and suggestive hints.[2]

The seven "leading questions" are only one of the ways Mark indicates Jesus's divine identity, but their cumulative impact is important and has not been fully appreciated because they have not been recognized as a series. They are all questions about Jesus's identity that go unanswered until a direct question, the high priest's, is directly answered by Jesus himself, in a way that in effect answers all eight questions.[3] The questions are not rhetorical questions that do not require an answer. Nor are they open questions to which there might be many answers. They are questions that expect a certain sort of response. The characters in the story may not know the answers, but Mark's readers should, if they have properly understood the questions. Though asked within the story, they are really addressed to readers. Mark expects competent readers to answer in a certain way. If they cannot do so, the answer will emerge as the story proceeds and provides them with more data to consider.

The seven "leading questions" are:

1. The question about Jesus's authority, asked by the crowd (1:27);
2. The question about forgiving sins, asked by the scribes (2:7);
3. The question about stilling the storm, asked by the disciples (4:41);
4. The question about Jesus's background, asked by the Nazarenes (6:2–3);
5. The question about the goodness of God, asked by Jesus (10:18);
6. The question about Jesus's authority over the temple, asked by the chief priests and others (11:28); and
7. The question about the Messiah and David, asked by Jesus (12:35–37).

These seven questions lead up to an eighth, which is the direct question about Jesus's messianic identity, asked by the high priest (14:61) and answered by Jesus (14:62).

Not all of the questions point as clearly as others to Jesus's divine identity, but seen as a series they can all be seen to point in the same direction. Particularly significant are the questions that allude to the Shema (2 and 5), suggesting that the secret of Jesus's true identity is his inclusion in the unique identity of the one God.[4] Similarly important are the accusations of blasphemy made in the context of question 2 and in response to Jesus's answer to the high priest (14:64). That final answer to all the questions, with its claim that Jesus will sit with God on the divine throne (Ps 110[109]:1), amounts to a claim to share the unique divine identity. I have argued at length elsewhere that Psalm 110:1 was the keystone of the earliest high Christology.[5]

In this essay I shall be concerned with only one of these questions, the third one, about the stilling of the storm (4:41), but I shall link that question with three other Markan narratives: the walking on the water and the two feeding miracles. This will bring to light the high Christology of all four of these narratives and enable us to compare it with John's versions of two of them.

Stilling a Storm at Sea (Mark 4:35–41)

The story is a realistic one. On the lake of Galilee storms can blow up quickly and be a real danger to the lives of fishermen in small boats. But Mark's use of the term "sea" (θάλασσα), his regular usage for the "sea" of Galilee, echoing Semitic terminology,[6] allows him to evoke passages in the Jewish Scriptures that speak of God's unique authority to command and subdue the sea.[7] The most relevant are these (given here in translations of the Old Greek version):[8]

> At your *rebuke* (ἐπιτιμήσεως) they [the waters] will flee;
> at the sound of your thunder they shall panic (Ps 103[104]:7 OG).

> Those who go down to the sea in *boats* (πλοίοις),
> doing business on the great ocean,
> they saw the Lord's works,
> and his wonders in the deep.
> He spoke and the stormy wind arose;
> and its *waves* (κύματα) were lifted up.
> They go up to the heavens, and down to the depths;
> their soul melted because of their troubles. . . .
> Then they cried out to the Lord in their afflictions;
> and he led them out from their distress.
> He commanded the storm and it stood still, turned into a breeze;
> and its *waves* (κύματα) were silenced (Ps 106[107]:23–26, 28–29
>   OG).

> Lord, God of hosts, who is like you?
> You are powerful, O Lord, and your truth surrounds you.
> You are master of the sea,
> and you calm the surge of its *waves* (κυμάτων) (Ps 88:9–10[89:8–9]
>   OG).

These passages provide some very close parallels to what happens in Mark's story (with Jesus taking YHWH's place), but there is very little verbal correspondence. (Significant words Mark 4:35–41 has in common with these passages are printed in italic along with the Greek word.) This may indicate that their influence on the story derived from the Hebrew text, or that Mark did not have any of these passages specifically in mind but was influenced by their general theme while writing in his own words. In all of them it is clear that it is the unique authority of the creator that he exercises when he commands the sea and stills its raging. Psalm 88(89), in particular, with its acclamation of the incomparability of YHWH, brings this theme into connection with a monotheistic understanding of the powers and prerogatives of the one and only God.

There is one significant exception to the lack of verbal correspondence between these passages and Mark's text. This is the word "rebuke" (Mark 4:39;

Ps 103[104]:7), for which Mark uses the verb ἐπιτιμάω and the psalm the cognate noun ἐπιτίμησις. These terms are the equivalent of the Hebrew גער, which is regularly used in the Hebrew Bible of God's power to rebuke and to subdue the cosmic elements, especially the sea imagined as a hostile force (2 Sam 22:16; Job 26:10–11; Pss 18:15; 104:7; 106:9; Isa 17:13; 50:2; Nah 1:4). Used in that sense, only God appears as the subject of this verb.[9] In the Qumran literature, the word is used of God's powerful rebuke to the spirits of evil (1QM XIV, 10), while in the Genesis Apocryphon, it describes an exorcism that occurs when Abraham prays to God (1QapGen XX, 28–29). At later periods, Aramaic incantation bowls frequently quote Zechariah 3:2 ("the Lord rebuke you, Satan!"), and one amulet invokes God's protection by quoting Nahum 1:4 ("he rebukes the sea and makes it dry").[10] Even in such contexts of magic spells, it is always God who is expected to do the rebuking. What evidently made Jesus's exorcisms remarkable was that he did not invoke the name of God or employ techniques such as reciting incantations, but simply commanded the demons, assuming for himself the divine authority to do so.

Mark uses ἐπιτιμάω twice with reference to Jesus's exorcisms (Mark 1:25; 9:25). In the first of these cases, Jesus not only "rebukes" the demon, but also tells it to "be silent" (1:25), and the crowd marvels that the demons "obey" Jesus's commands (1:27). The same vocabulary is used when Jesus stills the storm (4:39) and the disciples wonder that the winds and the waves "obey" him (4:41). These are the first and third of Mark's seven "leading questions." The parallel does not mean that the stilling of the storm is an exorcism, but that in both cases Jesus exerts the divine authority to command and subdue.

So what is the implied answer to the disciples' question, "Who then is this that even the wind and the sea obey him?" (4:41)? Is it that Jesus himself is divine, included in the unique identity of God, or that he is, as Messiah, acting on God's behalf with delegated authority to command the elements? Is the implicit Christology what I have called "divine identity Christology" or what Daniel Kirk calls "high human Christology"?[11] Kirk and Stephen Young have proposed that the key to the answer is a neglected text in the idealized portrayal of the Davidic king in Psalm 88(89):[12]

> I shall place his hand on (ἐν) the sea;
> and his right hand on (ἐν) the rivers. (Ps 88:26[89:25] OG)

Kirk and Young argue that YHWH's mastery over the sea, portrayed in v. 10(9) of the psalm, is here shared with his deputy on earth, the Davidic ruler. They are right to think that this portrayal of the Davidic ruler would have been understood, in the late Second Temple period, to refer to the messianic king to come. But their interpretation of v. 26(25) is very dubious. They do not even mention other interpretations of the verse that are to be found in the literature. They relegate discussion of the problematic preposition ἐν to a footnote, where they admit that "the use of ἐν to designate what a royal figure has authority over is surprising."[13] They themselves give the plausible translation:

> And I will set his hand to the sea,
> and his right hand to the rivers.[14]

This gives a good meaning, which they do not even consider: that the king's authority will extend right up to the sea and the rivers. The Greek is a literal translation of the Hebrew, where the preposition is ב. This too can readily be understood as indicating the extreme limits of the king's rule, rather than its object. Robert Alter translates the verse:

> And I shall put his hand to the sea,
> and his right hand to the rivers.[15]

The most plausible interpretation of both the Hebrew and the Greek seems to be that the verse describes the extent of David's empire, stretching from the Mediterranean Sea to the Euphrates and its northern tributaries or perhaps to the Euphrates and the Nile.[16] Just such an exaggerated picture of the realm of David is found in Psalm 71(72), with reference to Solomon:

> And he shall have dominion, from sea to sea,
> and from the Nile to the ends of the world. (Ps 71[72]:8 OG)[17]

(The Greek translator has interpreted "the river" of the Hebrew text as the Nile, though originally it is more likely to have referred to the Euphrates.) This psalm would also have been understood messianically in the late Second Temple period. The references to David's "hand" and "right hand" in Psalm 88:26(89:25) are certainly metaphors for his power, but the psalmist means that David's power stretches as far as the very shores of the Mediterranean and as far the area of northern Mesopotamia defined by the Euphrates and its tributaries. This power derives from God, but, rather than v. 10(9), the description of God's own power to which it alludes is more likely v. 14(13):

> Yours is the arm with power;
> may your hand be strengthened, your right hand be exalted. (OG)

Here the reference to God's "hand" and "right hand" corresponds to his promise in v. 26(25) to extend David's "hand" and his "right hand" over the realm he has given him. But such power bestowed on God's anointed king is not a participation in God's incomparable powers as creator of the heavens and the earth, described in vv. 9–13(8–12).

It would, of course, be possible for an exegete in Mark's time to have understood the verse differently. I know of no evidence of interpretation from that period, but later Jewish literature offers two different interpretations. Midrash Rabbah (on Num 12:12) takes it to mean that the King Messiah will hold sway over the sea, just as he will over the land, but the meaning is that he will control the shipping routes and have ships bringing goods from everywhere, just as Solomon did (1 Kgs 10:11, 22). In effect, this is an aspect of his power over people, not power to command the winds and the waves as God can. The second attested exegesis of this verse is in the Targum to Psalms, which reads it quite similarly to the way I have suggested (though without the specific geographical references):

> And I will set his dominion upon the harbors of the sea,
> and the might of his right hand upon those who dwell along the
> rivers.[18]

These examples of interpretation are much later than the Second Temple period, but they do illustrate the possibilities available to Jewish exegetes. Neither expects the King Messiah to participate in the special prerogatives of the creator. The attempt of Kirk and Young to make Psalm 88:26(89:25) relevant to Mark's Christology has proved completely unsuccessful.

The disciples' question should be read in its place in the narrative Christology of the Gospel. It is the third of the "leading questions," and its adequate and conclusive answer will be given in Jesus's reply to the high priest (Mark 14:62). But I want to suggest now that it receives an answer of sorts, for those who have ears to hear, in Mark's second narrative of a miracle at sea.

Walking on Water (Mark 6:45–52)

The two sea miracles in Mark have significant resemblances, but each story has its own integrity and coherence. In the first the disciples are in serious danger and fear for their lives (4:35–41). In the second they are not in danger, but are simply unable to make progress across the lake in the face of an adverse wind (6:45–52).[19] They are not afraid of the conditions on the lake, but of the spectral figure who turns out to be Jesus. Therefore, in the first of the two miracles Jesus saves them from danger to life, but in the second he enables them to make progress to their destination on the far side of the lake. Jesus's command over the sea and the wind is evident in both cases, but whereas in the first miracle the christological focus is on his exercise of it in order to rescue the disciples, in the second the christological focus is on his mysterious appearance, which takes the form of an epiphany.[20] Since this is emphasized at the expense of what the story has in common with the first sea miracle (Jesus subdues the wind), we should expect it to represent an advance in what is revealed about Jesus's identity.

Some details of the narrative need to be briefly addressed. The disciples, rowing, are of course facing in the opposite direction to the direction they wish the boat to travel. So they see Jesus walking across the lake in the same direction. Mark's information that Jesus "intended (ἤθελεν) to pass them by" (6:48) has usually been considered problematic. The meaning cannot be that he seemed to the disciples to be intending to walk past them,[21] because this statement belongs to the part of the narrative that Mark tells from Jesus's perspective (6:47–48). Only after this statement are we told that the disciples saw him and the perspective shifts to theirs. Some commentators refer to Exodus 33:19, 22; 34:6, where YHWH's glory "passes by" Moses, and 1 Kings 19:11, where YHWH "passes by" Elijah. Mark's statement is therefore indicative of a theophany. But in that case the meaning would be that Jesus intended a fuller disclosure of his divine identity, but was distracted from this by the disciples' terror and instead got into the boat in order to help them.[22] But this seems an odd way to read a narrative in which, surely, we are to suppose that a theophany actually takes place.[23]

The difficulty commentators find with the statement that Jesus "intended to pass them by" derives from an assumption that Jesus can only help them if he gets into the boat, as he eventually does. But we can easily suppose that Jesus intended to help them by overtaking the boat and taking up a position in front of it. In that position he might have commanded the wind to cease, or, perhaps more probably, he would have walked ahead of the boat clearing a safe way for it through the wind in order to bring it to land. Jesus changes his intention when the disciples cry out in terror at the sight of him and he needs to reassure them. He then quietens the wind from inside the boat, as we already know from the first sea miracle he can do.

What the disciples see, in the dim light before dawn ("the fourth watch of the night"), is an "apparition." The word φάντασμα is usually translated as "ghost," but there is no reason to be so specific. Unlike the disciples in Luke 24:37, the disciples in this story had no reason to think that Jesus had died and was appearing as a ghost. The figure might be a ghost or some kind of spirit, ill-intentioned or otherwise. The last thing they would have expected to see was a living human walking over the deep waters of the lake. Had they not been Jews, they might have thought of a god or a deified human, like Pythagoras.[24] But in Mark's Gospel we should rather consider a scriptural background. Significantly, there is no reference in the Jewish Scriptures to a human walking on water, but there is one reference to God that many commentators have found relevant to

Mark's story.[25] We should consider both the Hebrew and the rather different Old Greek versions of Job 9:8:

> who alone stretched out the heavens
> and trampled the waves of the Sea. (NRSV)

> God who alone stretched out the heaven,
> and who *walks on the sea* (περιπατῶν … ἐπὶ θαλάσσης) as on dry
>   land. (OG)[26]

The context is an extended account of God's unique power over the whole created world (Job 9:4–10). In the Hebrew, v. 8b describes God's subduing of the rebellious "Chaos monster" or primeval ocean (the correct translation could be "back" rather than "waves"). But the Old Greek (which may well represent how Jewish readers in the late Second Temple period would have understood the Hebrew) "demythologizes" the text and makes walking on water a characteristic and unique divine activity. It also has a precise verbal parallel to the phrase that occurs twice in Mark's account.[27] Mark's emphasis on this phrase, "walking on the water," may indicate a deliberate allusion to this passage. If so, he is rather clearly stating that Jesus relates to the sea as only the creator of all things does.[28] However, this passage in Job is not likely to have been a well-known part of the Jewish Scriptures for Mark's readers. The Psalms (probably evoked by Mark's first story of a miracle at sea) would have been much better known.

Passages that refer to God making a path *through* the waters and leading his people through them, whether at the time of the exodus from Egypt (Ps 76:17–21[77:16–20]; Isa 43:16; 51:10) or perhaps in a new exodus of the future (Isa 43:2), are less precisely apposite, but they may contribute an additional resonance to Mark's story, especially if my suggestion that Jesus intended to walk ahead of the boat, making a way for it to the shore, is correct. It would cohere with the "new exodus" theme that can be seen elsewhere in Mark.[29] It is of particular interest that Psalm 76:17–21(77:16–20) describes the crossing of the Red Sea, a great event of salvation for God's people, in language that is unparalleled in Exodus 14–15, and makes the event a theophany. Similarly, in Mark 6:45–52 Jesus comes to the aid of the disciples, but the focus is on his epiphany, which we can now confidently also call a theophany.

If we recognize the scene as a theophany, in which Jesus appears as God, then great significance attaches to his words to the disciples in v. 50. The words ἐγώ εἰμι can, of course, be understood as a simple self-identification, "It is I," with which Jesus assures the disciples that the figure they see is Jesus. But there is a problem, not usually noticed, with understanding how such a self-identification can function in the context. At a distance and in low light, the disciples cannot see Jesus's face or features. Presumably he has to shout to them against the noise of the wind and the waves. Can he expect them to recognize his voice? In such a situation, to identify himself clearly, Jesus should have used his name, as he does in Acts 9:5, when he appears unrecognizably to Saul.[30] The context in Mark is different from that in Luke 24:39, where the disciples think the risen Jesus is a ghost. There Jesus invites them to "see my hands and my feet, that it is I myself (ἐγώ εἰμι αὐτός)." The disciples on that occasion are in a much better position to recognize Jesus than the disciples in the boat in Mark's story.

Mark has used a phrase that is not natural in the context in order to hide within this seemingly ordinary self-identification the secret of Jesus's divine identity. Although scholars continue to say that ἐγώ εἰμι is the divine name, it is not, nor even a translation of the name. "I am" occurs only once in Jewish literature as a version of the name: in Exodus 3:14 (MT) it serves as an abbreviation of the full explanation of the name, "I am who I am" (or "I will be who I will be"). But in the Septuagint ἐγώ εἰμι is not used here. The full interpretation is given as "I am the one who is" (ἐγώ εἰμι ὁ ὤν), and the abbreviated version is not "I am" (ἐγώ εἰμι), but "the one who is" (ὁ ὤν). When ἐγώ εἰμι appears in the Septuagint/Old Greek as a divine self-declaration (in the absolute, without a complement) it translates the Hebrew אני הוא (and its variations אני אני הוא and אנכי אנכי הוא), which means "I am he." This declaration by God appears nine times in the Hebrew Bible (Deut 32:39; Isa 41:4; 43:10, 13, 25; 46:4; 48:12; 51:12; 52:6). In the Septuagint/Old Greek ἐγώ εἰμι or the double form ἐγώ εἰμι ἐγώ εἰμι appears as its equivalent seven times (Deut 32:39; Isa 41:4; 43:10, 25; 45:18; 46:4; 51:12).[31] If ἐγώ εἰμι in Mark 6:50 is to be understood as a divine self-identification, then its background lies in this usage, not in Exodus 3:14. Catrin Williams has shown conclusively that this is the case with the absolute "I am" sayings in John.[32] Only the unique God can identify himself in this absolute way, without even a name: "I am he." The contexts of the expression in Isaiah 40–52 are emphatically monotheistic. Jesus's usage in Mark 6:50 unequivocally identifies him with the one God of Israel. But Mark has hidden this significance in a *double entendre* that makes it possible not to perceive this meaning.

The fact that the story focuses on Jesus's epiphany rather than his pacification of the wind requires that it say something very special about him, more than the stilling of the storm in the earlier story or the pacification of the wind in this story. By itself, the walking on the water, despite its strong allusion to Job 9:8 (OG), probably does not say enough. Job 9:8 is a relatively obscure text and, in this respect, an isolated one. It underlines Jesus's exercise of the creator's unique powers over creation. But for its full significance, it depends on what Jesus says: "I am he." Now Jesus does not just do what God does. He identifies himself as God does. "I am he" is the answer to the leading question with which the first miracle at sea left us: "Who then is this. . . ?" But the secret is hidden from those who do not understand the significance of what Jesus says. They include the disciples.

The Incomprehension of the Disciples (Mark 6:51b–52)

Throughout Mark's Gospel people are amazed at Jesus's deeds and words, and Mark uses a variety of verbs to convey that (ἐκπλήσω: 1:22; 6:2; 7:37; 10:26; 11:18; θαμβέω: 1:27; 10:32; ἐξίστημι: 2:12; 5:42; 6:51; θαυμάζω: 5:20; 15:5; ἐκθαυμάζω: 12:17).[33] But the two miracles at sea, which only the disciples witness, are distinctive. In the first case, Mark uses a Semitism (literally "they feared a great fear") deriving from Jonah 1:16 (OG), for the distinctive recognition of a peculiarly divine act, which gives rise to their question, "Who then is this. . . ?" (4:41). This great awe is a completely appropriate reaction. In the story of Jesus walking on water, the disciples are in the first place "terrified" or "shaken with fear" (6:50: ταράσσω, used only here in Mark), before they know that the apparition is Jesus, and then they are "utterly astounded" (NRSV). The verb (ἐξίστημι) is the strongest of Mark's words for astonishment (also used in 2:12; 5:42). A better translation might be "confounded." Literally, it means that they were out of their minds, in a mental state in which their reason was not operating. In other words, they were not just amazed, but had no idea what to make of what they had seen and heard. With λίαν ("very") and, in some manuscripts, ἐκ περισσοῦ ("excessively"), the meaning is that it was way beyond their ability to understand. Mark adds ἐν ἑαυτοῖς ("in themselves") to indicate that, unlike their state in 4:41, they were unable to talk about it. In the original meaning of the English word, they were "dumbfounded." (Note that in 2:12, the people were "confounded" [ἐξίστασθαι] but were able to speak. In 5:42, the only other occurrence of this verb in this sense in Mark, as a reaction to a miracle, it is the people who saw Jairus's daughter brought back to life who were "utterly confounded" [ἐξέστησαν ἐκστάσει μεγάλῃ].) The state of the disciples in 6:51 is probably the most extreme state of bewilderment that Mark attributes to anyone in his Gospel. The extraordinary nature of Jesus's "I am he" declaration helps to explain this.

But Mark himself explains it in a rather surprising way: "for they did not understand about the loaves" (6:52). That Mark refers to the feeding miracle rather than to the stilling of the storm is not a problem in itself. The feeding miracle had only just happened. Its significance, had they grasped it, would have been fresh in the disciples' minds. But the implication must be that, like the two miracles at sea, the feeding miracle was a disclosure to the disciples of Jesus's divine identity. They could have learned from it enough to make them more able to understand the theophany at sea than in the event they were.

Feeding Five Thousand Men (Mark 6:30–44)

It is widely recognized that this story, with its emphasis on its location in the wilderness (6:31, 32, 35), presents Jesus's miraculous feeding of a large crowd as analogous to the provision of manna to the people of Israel in the wilderness

(Exod 16). It is easy to relate this to the theme of the new exodus that runs through Mark's Gospel. Rikki Watts, following Madeleine Boucher, explains the importance Mark evidently attributes to this story (along with the second feeding miracle in 8:1–9): "of all the 'signs' which Jesus performs [this] should have been the clearest indication that the NE [new exodus] was beginning."[34]

Along with its evocation of the manna in the wilderness, it is often claimed that the story portrays Jesus as the new Moses. Joel Marcus speaks of the "pronounced Mosaic and eschatological features" of the story.[35] Yet there is a rather obvious reason for doubting whether the analogy with the story of the manna puts Jesus in the role of a new Moses. It was God who gave the manna. Moses had nothing to do with it other than conveying God's messages to the people. He did not even ask God to provide it. That the manna came from God is very clear not only in Exodus 16, but also in Psalm 78(77):23–25 and Nehemiah 9:15. Nowhere is Moses credited with providing the manna. Similarly, in the one reference we have in Jewish literature of the Second Temple period to a new bestowal of manna in the paradisal age to come, it descends from heaven again, with no human mediation (2 Bar. 29:8).

The case for a Mosaic portrayal of Jesus in this story has been argued especially on the basis of the motif of the shepherd that appears in Mark 6:34. The words, "like sheep without a shepherd," could be an allusion to Numbers 27:17, where Moses, having learned that he will die before he can lead the people into the land, asks God that they "may not be like sheep who have no shepherd." God's response is to appoint Joshua as his successor. This is a slender basis on which to postulate a Moses typology in Mark's story. The comparison of Moses with a shepherd is almost incidental and the possibility that the people be left without a shepherd is only hypothetical. Moses appears to be called the shepherd of Israel in Isaiah 63:11 (OG; MT is different), but nowhere else in the Jewish Scriptures. According to Psalm 76:21(77:20), at the time of the exodus, it was God "who guided your people like sheep, by the hand of Moses and Aaron." According to Isaiah 40:11, in the new exodus also it will be God who shepherds the flock of Israel.

Moreover, the simile, "like sheep without a shepherd," appears to be a stereotyped one: it appears in almost the same words in 3 Kingdoms(1 Kings) 22:17 (with a parallel in 2 Chr 18:16) and in rather similar words in Isaiah 13:14 and Ezekiel 34:5, 8 (cf. also Matt 9:15). It is, as Richard France observes, "an obvious metaphor for lack of care and leadership."[36] While Mark's exact words are closest to Numbers 27:17 and 3 Kingdoms(1 Kings) 22:17, there is a good deal to suggest that his story is intended to evoke Ezekiel 34. This chapter is a prophecy of the eschatological regathering and restoration of scattered Israel. They are pictured as sheep scattered and vulnerable because those who should have been their shepherds have neglected and exploited them. They have no shepherd. So God intervenes and takes on the role of Israel's shepherd himself, regathering the scattered sheep and caring for them as a shepherd should. He will feed them in good pastures where they will lie down and have rest (Ezek 34:1–16). There is a strong emphasis in this passage on feeding the sheep, which is precisely what Jesus does in Mark's story. It is possible that in speaking of the people as "sheep without a shepherd," Mark implies that, as in Ezekiel 34, they have been abandoned and exploited by those who should have been their shepherd, including Herod as depicted in Mark just before the feeding miracle (Mark 6:14–29). It is also possible that the gathering up of the leftovers in twelve baskets (6:42) symbolizes the eschatological regathering of the people of Israel.

Ezekiel 34 goes on to predict that God will raise up David to shepherd his people, presumably after God himself has gathered the flock and restored them to safety and wellbeing. Only two verses describe David's role (Ezek 34:23–24). Does Mark depict Jesus as the Davidic Messiah or as God himself? Perhaps the answer is both. Mark's Jesus is the Messiah, son of David, and probably this is as much as Peter was eventually able to conclude from the two feeding miracles (Mark 8:29). But greater attention to the scriptural background of these miracles suggests a more profound level of meaning: Jesus's divine identity. Of course, in Mark's Gospel, Jesus is not simply identified with God; he also relates to God as his Father. He shares the divine identity without exhausting it, and he shares it without detriment to his human identity.[37] Perhaps Mark saw this paradox in the alternation of God and David in the shepherding role in Ezekiel 34.

That Jesus in this story acts as the divine shepherd of Israel can be confirmed by its allusions to Psalm 22(23):[38]

> The Lord shepherds me;
> and there shall be nothing lacking for me.
> Into a place of green grass (τόπον χλόης), there he has made me rest.[39]
> Beside[40] the water of repose he has fed me.
> He has restored my soul;
> he has guided me on the paths of righteousness,
> for the sake of his name. (Ps 22[23]:1–3 OG)

There have been several suggestions as to why Mark notes that the people were to recline (ἀνακλῖναι) on the green grass (ἐπὶ τῷ χλωρῷ χόρτῳ), but an allusion to Psalm 22(23):2 is the most plausible. Mark could also have associated v. 3 of the psalm ("guided me on the paths of righteousness") with his statement that Jesus, having observed that the people were like sheep without a shepherd, taught them (Mark 6:34). We should note that there are strong similarities between Psalm 22(23):1–2 and Ezekiel 34:13–15. In Jewish exegesis the two passages could easily have been brought together.

Once Again, the Incomprehension
of the Disciples (Mark 8:14–20)

It is a very remarkable feature of Mark's two stories of miraculous feeding that he says nothing whatsoever about the people's reaction. Among Jesus's public miracles, they are almost unique in that respect. In almost every other case, Mark records the amazement of the crowds (exceptions are 3:1–6; 9:14–28; 10:46–52). Yet, these are stupendous miracles witnessed by thousands of people. The reason must be that in both cases Mark is focused on the disciples. They play an unusually large role in both stories, and probably we should suppose that only they knew about the remarkable quantities of leftovers they gathered in baskets. Mark delays commenting on their reactions until, in both of the boat scenes that follow the two feeding miracles, we learn that they did not understand (6:53; 8:17–21). In the second case Jesus reminds them of both feeding miracles and their own special knowledge of the superabundance of the provision in both cases (8:19–20). With Jesus's final question, "Do you not yet understand?" (8:21), the disciples' incomprehension reaches a peak.

Yet, almost immediately, there follows Peter's confession. Has he suddenly understood what he failed to understand? This apparent aporia is explained by the one narrative that intervenes: the healing of a blind man in two stages (8:22–26). It takes place in private and we are not even told that the disciples are present. Mark tells this story for the benefit of his readers. The two stages in which the man regains his sight suggest that, for disciples and readers alike, there are two levels of insight into Jesus's identity.[41] Peter grasps his messianic identity. But, although the two miracles at sea and the two feeding miracles have given the strongest indications of it, he does not grasp Jesus's divine identity. The first half of this Gospel can be read as providing the basis for believing, as Peter does, that Jesus is the Messiah. But a reading that is attentive to leading questions, scriptural allusions, and suggestive ambiguities can discern a secret more profound than the messianic secret.

John's Appropriation of Mark's Christology (John 6)

I have argued elsewhere that John not only knew Mark's Gospel, but also that he expected many, if not all, of his readers to know it. For the most part he avoids repeating Mark's narratives. He retells only those for which he has a specific reason to do so.[42] They include the feeding of the five thousand (John 6:1–15) and the walking on the water (6:15–21). They are linked in chronological succession as they are in Mark. John's Gospel is as focused on the identity of Jesus as Mark's is. I think he saw these two Markan stories as of great christological significance, correctly recognizing that in Mark's Gospel itself they are presented as narratives in which the disclosure of Jesus's divine identity reaches a climax. John recognized here in Mark the indications of the high Christology that John develops in a more explicit fashion throughout his Gospel.

By comparison with Mark 6:45–52, John's narrative of the miracle at sea is so brief as to be obscure.[43] Is the sea so rough that the disciples are in danger, as in Mark's story of the stilling of the storm? Or are they merely unable to make progress? The latter is probably implied by the statement that they are halfway across the lake (agreeing with Mark, though differently expressed) along with the concluding statement that "immediately the boat reached the land toward which they were going" (John 6:21). We are not told how this happened. Unlike Mark, John does not say that Jesus stilled the wind, though this may be implied. Perhaps "immediately" suggests no more than that they were no longer impeded by the storm, which Jesus had pacified, and so made rapid progress. There may be an allusion to Psalm 106(107):30 (OG: "he led them to the harbour they longed for"). Another difference from Mark is that John does not say that they thought what they saw was an "apparition." So the reason why they were "terrified" is not clear. We might suppose that they intuited divinity, so that their fear was awe in the presence of God. In that case, Jesus's words assure them that in his divine presence they need have no fear.

I have suggested that in Mark's account the focus is on the epiphany rather than the stilling of the wind. This is even more the case in John. If John did not understand Jesus's appearance as a theophany, a disclosure of Jesus's divine identity, then it is hard to see why he chose to narrate this story at all. So it is remarkable that some commentators see Jesus's self-identification (ἐγώ εἰμι) as meaning no more than that he is Jesus ("It is I").[44] Most likely John intends a *double entendre* of the same kind as I have argued Mark does. But he may attribute a more adequate understanding of it to the disciples than Mark does. In John's account, it is on the following day that Peter declares Jesus to be "the Holy One of God" (John 6:60). In disagreement with most commentators, I would suggest that the meaning of this title is not "the one who is consecrated to God" (cf. 17:19), but "the one who participates in the holiness of God." (It is what the demons, with their supernatural knowledge, declare Jesus to be, according to Mark 1:24, and it is why they fear him.) It may be that we should understand Peter's confession in John 6:69 to be based on the theophany the disciples witnessed on the lake the night before. Like the demons in Mark 1:24, they recognized and feared the holiness of the divine presence (cf. Exod 3:5–6) until reassured by Jesus.

That the ἐγώ εἰμι of John 6:20 has fully divine significance, recalling the divine self-identification "I am he" in Deuteronomy and Isaiah, is confirmed by the fact that it is the second of a series of seven such occurrences of ἐγώ εἰμι on the lips of Jesus in the Gospel of John.[45] The Gospel in fact contains two series of "I am" sayings, each a series of seven. John 6:20 belongs to the series of absolute "I am" sayings (4:26; 6:20; 8:24, 28, 58; 13:19; 18:5, 6, 8, treating the three occurrences in chapter 18 as a single saying repeated). The other series is of "I am" sayings with predicates:

> I am the bread of life. (6:35, 41, 48)
> I am the light of the world. (8:12; cf. 9:5)
> I am the gate for the sheep. (10:7, 9)
> I am the good shepherd. (10:11, 14)
> I am the resurrection and the life. (11:25)
> I am the way and the truth and the life. (14:6)
> I am the true vine. (15:1)

The two series should not be confused. The words "I am" (ἐγώ εἰμι) function differently in the two different contexts, though it is significant that in both cases the pronoun is used to identify Jesus, even where it might not be necessary in Greek. The "I am" sayings with predicates disclose what Jesus is for those who believe in him, his saving significance. The absolute "I am" sayings disclose Jesus's divine identity, which is the basis for his provision of salvation (or "eternal life" as John most often calls it in nonmetaphorical language).

Rather like Mark's seven "leading questions," John's series of absolute "I am" sayings needs to be recognized as a series if they are to be fully appreciated. The words ἐγώ εἰμι, used without an explicit predicate, can have a predicate implied by the context. This makes some of the absolute "I am" sayings ambiguous (4:26; 18:5, 6, 8). We have also seen that the phrase is ambiguous in 6:20, as it is in Mark 6:50. It could be a simple self-identification by Jesus of himself as Jesus. In these three cases out of the seven, an ordinary meaning is possible and may even be superficially the obvious meaning, but in the remaining four cases (8:24, 28, 58; 13:19) no such ordinary meaning is available, and the phrase "I am" is as strangely incomplete in the Greek as it is in literal English translation. In these cases, the only adequate interpretation is that Jesus is using the uniquely divine self-declaration, "I am he." (I repeat, as I explained above with reference to Mark 6:50, that this is not the divine name.) So it makes good sense, in a Gospel full of double meanings, to understand the ambiguous cases as deliberately ambiguous, concealing a declaration of divine identity in words that could be otherwise understood. It is probably significant that the first absolute "I am" saying (4:26) is the most ambiguous. Both the Samaritan woman within the story and the first-time reader are likely to understand this "I am" as having an implied predicate ("the Messiah," just mentioned by the woman). The first of the sayings that cannot be understood in an ordinary sense is 8:24. Between them is 6:20, which could be understood as "It is I." But here the context (Jesus walking on the sea) is a clue for an appropriately informed reader to suspect the more profound meaning, a declaration of Jesus's divine identity. The first three of the sayings therefore present a gradation from the most ambiguous to the least ambiguous. John is revealing in three steps the potential significance of this portentous phrase. It may have been significant for John that the second occurrence of the phrase would already have been known to many of his readers in the Gospel of Mark. It roots the wider usage in his Gospel in this already well-established usage in what his readers probably knew as the first Gospel. (If they knew Matthew's Gospel, they would have found it there in Matt 14:27.)

We can understand why John thought the second of Mark's stories of a miracle at sea was important enough for him to retell it. But we should also notice that he has placed it before the first occurrence of an "I am" saying with a predicate: "I am the bread of life" (6:35, 41, 48). This is the declaration of Jesus around which the whole of his dialogue discourse in 6:25–58 revolves. It is John's interpretation of the significance of the other narrative John has repeated from Mark: the feeding of the five thousand (6:1–15).[46]

Comparing John's narrative with Mark's, there are at least three significant differences: (1) John lacks Mark's allusions to scriptural "shepherd" passages. It is notable that, like Matthew, he refers to the "grass" but omits Mark's adjective "green," with its likely allusion to Psalm 23. We do not see John's Jesus here playing the part of the divine shepherd of the people. (2) John emphasizes the significance of the gathering of the leftovers by giving Jesus a command to the disciples: "Gather up the fragments left over, that nothing may be lost" (John 6:12). This is evidently to prepare for the interpretation of this feature of the miracle in 6:39. The bread represents the eternal life that Jesus will give to all who believe in him, none of whom will be lost. (3) Unlike Mark, John focuses on the reaction of the crowd to the miracle (6:15–16), which leads into Jesus's discussion with them in Capernaum the following day.

That the miracle does recall the gift of the manna in the wilderness emerges in the crowd's reaction. John lacks Mark's references to a "wilderness" location, but when the crowd suppose Jesus to be "the prophet who is to come into the world" (6:14), they are identifying him as the new Moses. This figure would be a "king" (6:15) in the sense of a leader, as Moses was.[47] But the people are wrong because they fail to see that the miracle is a sign that, like all the "signs" in John's Gospel, points to Jesus's gift of eternal life. Like so many of the modern commentators on Mark, they even get the story of the manna wrong by supposing that it was Moses who gave their ancestors the manna as a sign (6:31). Jesus points out that it was not Moses but Jesus's Father who gave the manna, as the very text they quote makes clear: "He [God] gave them bread from heaven" (6:31–32, quoting Ps 77:24 OG). Jesus himself is not a new Moses, but the true "bread from heaven" that his Father gives to those who believe in him (6:33). Jesus is both the one who gives eternal life (6:27) and the "bread of life" that the Father gives. As Jesus explained in chapter 5, the Father, the source of eternal life, has granted to the Son also to be a source of eternal life to others (5:21, 26).

We need not pursue further the way the discourse unpacks the image of Jesus as the bread of life. John's development of the symbolism of the miracle is different from Mark's, as well as explicit, where Mark's is implicit. But we should note that in neither case is Jesus a prophet like Moses, a merely human agent of God.

Conclusion

My account of "high Christology" in John's narratives of the feeding miracle and the walking on the water is in general agreement with a broad consensus in the commentaries and studies on John. What I have endeavored to show in this essay is that Mark conveys, in questions, allusions, and suggestive hints, just as "high" a Christology, i.e., a Christology of divine identity. Like Mark, John employs *double entendre*, questions, and even riddles in his complex presentation of Jesus's identity, but he also brings to the surface what lies largely hidden in Mark. For both evangelists, the feeding miracle(s) and the miracle(s) on the lake are high points in the disclosure of Jesus's divine identity and its salvific significance.

CHAPTER THIRTEEN

High Christology in the Gospel of John and Book of Revelation

Craig R. Koester

THE GOSPEL OF John and the book of Revelation are alike in that they develop high Christologies in which the distinctive powers of God are exercised by Jesus and God's presence is revealed in Jesus, so that Jesus is included in the identity of the one God. Comparisons of the Gospel and Revelation often focus on questions of composition, and whether both were written by the same author or came from the same circle of early Christians.[1] Here, however, we treat each book in its own right, asking how christological claims are made within the texts. For comparison, we select elements that occur in each book, noting both similarities and differences.

Certain assumptions are made by both the Gospel and Revelation.[2] First, there is only one true God, to whom the Scriptures of Israel bear witness. Second, Jesus is God's Messiah, who was crucified and is now risen. Third, understanding the relationship of Jesus to the one God involves the revelatory action of God's Spirit, who works among Jesus's followers after his resurrection. In the Gospel, the Spirit guides reflections on the meaning of Jesus's earthly ministry, providing insights that were not available prior to his death and resurrection (John 14:26; 16:13–15; cf. 2:22; 12:16; 20:9). In Revelation, the Spirit inspires visions of the risen and exalted Jesus, as well as scenes of heaven, the future, and the cosmic conflict now unfolding (Rev 1:10; 4:2; 17:3; 21:10). The Spirit mediates the words of the exalted Jesus rather than informing accounts of his past ministry (e.g., 2:1, 7; 2:12, 17).[3]

The Gospel develops its high Christology in part by narrating debates about Jesus's relationship to the one true God. Everyone in the Gospel, whether a friend or foe of Jesus, recognizes that he is human; the question is what more can be said about him. Each aspect of his identity is disputed: whether he is a legitimate Jewish teacher, a prophet, or Messiah, and whether he can rightly claim to be God's Son. There is a collision between two frames of reference. For Jesus's opponents, his claims make it sound like he is a human being elevating himself to divine status, making himself the Son of God (John 19:7), a person equal to God (5:18), and indeed making himself God (10:33). In response, the Gospel argues that the movement is the opposite. Jesus is not elevating himself to divine status but has come down from above and is carrying out his Father's work in complete unity with his Father.[4]

In Revelation, the question of Christology and monotheism is framed differently. While there is some tension between the followers of Jesus and local Jewish communities (Rev 2:9; 3:9), the primary issue is Greco-Roman polytheism, which some followers of Jesus seem to accommodate by eating meat that had been offered to idols (2:14, 20). For the writer, idolatry included practices linked to traditional Greco-Roman deities and the imperial cults.[5] In response, the book depicts a cosmic conflict in which Satan's power is exercised through the ruler of the empire, who is pictured as a beast, so that worshiping the ruler means worshiping Satan. Conversely, the power of God the creator is exercised through Jesus the Lamb, who shares God's throne and is honored and worshiped within the worship rightly given to the one God.

Word and Wisdom

John and Revelation both depict Jesus as the Word (λόγος) of God. The Gospel begins with God, whose Word comes into the world and becomes flesh in Jesus. This sets a direction that implicitly counters the idea that Jesus is a human being trying to become God. The prologue creates a tension by saying, "the Word was *with* God," which presupposes a difference between them, then adds, "the Word *was* God," which identifies them (John 1:1). Ordinarily one indicates either who someone "is," or whom someone is "with," but the prologue's paradoxical claim is that both statements are true at the same time. At the level of experience, the speaker has priority. The word is dependent on and can be distinguished from the one who utters it, yet to hear the word is to hear the person, and when the word effects something, the speaker effects it. The word and the speaker can be differentiated but not separated. By analogy, that is the case with God and the Word.

The prologue relates the Word to creation: "All things came into being through him" (1:3). The language recalls Genesis 1:1–3, where "in the beginning . . . God said," and thereby "created the heavens and the earth." The Word was the way God's creative power was exercised (Ps 33:6; cf. Wis 9:1), and John 1:3 can say that through the Word "all things were made." The focus of the Word's activity is "life," for "in him was life and the life was the light for people" (1:4). In the Gospel, "life" is multidimensional, including animate life and life in relationship with God through Jesus, which is the "eternal life" that begins in the present through faith and continues beyond bodily death through the promise of resurrection. God's Word is also revelatory, so that when "the word of the Lord came to" various people, it made the will of God known.[6] In the Gospel, revelation occurs when the Word becomes flesh, revealing divine glory and the "grace and truth" that characterize God himself (1:14–18; cf.

Exod 34:6). The paradox is that "flesh" (σάρξ) connotes limitation and mortality (John 3:6; 6:51; 8:15), anticipating that revelation will occur not only in Jesus's human life but in his death.[7] John's characterization of the Word also recalls divine wisdom, which was personified and preexistent, working with God in creation (Prov 8:22–31; Wis 7:22; 9:9; Sir 24:1–3, 9), revealing divine glory (Wis 7:25–26), and providing life (Prov 8:35; Bar 4:1). According to Sirach 24:8–10, wisdom made her tent or tabernacle in Jacob, while in John 1:14, the Word's tabernacle is the flesh of Jesus.[8]

The prologue orients readers to consider how the traits of God are revealed in Jesus in the narrative that follows. It does not provide an argument in which points are made in a logical sequence with supporting material included. Instead, its imagery offers a way of seeing that can lead to understanding. The Gospel recognizes that people see things differently, depending on where they are standing, so it begins by positioning readers on an elevated plane, enabling them better to discern how the lifegiving work of God is exercised through Jesus, the incarnate Word. God speaks to the world through the words Jesus speaks and the actions he performs, through the death that he dies and the resurrection and giving of the Spirit that follow. The Gospel will seek to show that Jesus is not asserting himself against God but has come from God to act on God's behalf and to reveal God's purpose and presence.

Revelation identifies Jesus as the Word of God, who is the agent of God's eschatological reign. The expression "word of God" is initially used for the message that is revealed to the seer (Rev 1:2; cf. 19:9) and the message that Jesus's followers are to hold on to in the face of conflict and death (1:9; 6:9; 20:4). As "the Word of God," Christ appears on a white horse to defeat God's adversaries with the "sword" from his mouth, an image for Christ's own word, which wins the victory (19:11–15).

Depicting Christ as the Word who brings judgment recalls biblical texts that were read messianically. In Isaiah 11:1–5, the coming Davidic king is to judge the poor with righteousness, to strike the earth with the rod of his mouth, and to slay the wicked with the breath of his lips. In Revelation 19:11–15 Jesus does this by judging and making war with righteousness, and striking down the nations with the sword from his mouth.[9] He also rules the nations with a rod of iron, an image drawn from Psalm 2:9 LXX, which depicts God's anointed king doing battle with hostile nations.[10] Christ appears when heaven is opened (Rev 19:11), and his role in the battle has affinities with the way God's wisdom could be portrayed. In Wisdom 9:1–4, wisdom is beside God's throne, and in 11:15–16 this wisdom becomes God's "word," carrying out judgment on the Egyptians at the time of the exodus: "Your all-powerful word leaped from heaven, from the royal throne, into the midst of the land that was doomed, a stern warrior carrying the sharp sword of your authentic command, and stood and filled all things with death, and touched heaven while standing on the earth."

Yet, Revelation goes further by including traits of God in the description of Jesus the Word. He is "faithful and true" (Rev 19:11; cf. 3:14). While some of Jesus's followers were faithful (2:10, 13; 17:14), "true" characterizes God, his words, and his judgments (6:10; 15:3; 16:7; 19:2). The Word's eyes are like a flame of fire, a detail suggesting divine power (19:12).[11] God was called the King of kings (2 Macc 13:4; 3 Macc 5:35; Philo, *QG* 4.76) and Lord of lords (Deut 10:17; Ps 136:3), and both titles could be used together (1 En. 9:4; Dan 4:37 LXX). In Revelation 19:16, these titles are used for Christ the Word, who is not a rival to God but the one through whom God's lordship is exercised.

Finally, this portrayal of Christ the Word, whose traits include those of deity, is shaped by the key role of his death. The passage recalls Isaiah 63:1–6, where God is described as a warrior, whose robe is stained red with the blood of those he trampled in the winepress of his wrath. Christ, the Word, also wears a robe dipped in blood, but in his case the blood is his own, not the blood of his adversaries. He is stained with blood *before* the battle begins, *before* he treads the winepress of God's wrath (Rev 19:13), recalling that Revelation introduced Jesus as the slaughtered Lamb, whose own blood was shed to redeem people of every nation (5:6; 7:14), which is the way he conquered (5:5). God's own truth and faithfulness have already been conveyed in Christ's death and will be again through the final defeat of evil forces.[12]

Son of Man

In John's Gospel, Jesus refers to himself as "the Son of Man," and in Revelation, the writer sees visions of the glorified Jesus, who is "like a son of man." In the OT, "son of man" commonly referred to a human being. A significant development occurred in Daniel 7:13–14, however, where "one like a son of man" comes on the clouds of heaven to receive everlasting dominion, glory, and kingship, so that all nations should serve him. Other apocalyptic texts considered this son of man figure to be the Messiah, a preexistent heavenly being, who sits on a throne of glory, which is God's throne, and will be the agent of judgment in the end time.[13] In the Synoptic Gospels, Jesus refers to himself as "the Son of Man." Although the meaning of the expression in the Synoptics is disputed, three aspects are notable. First, the Son of Man has authority to forgive sins, which listeners consider divine authority (Mark 2:7–10). Second, in his passion predictions, Jesus says the Son of Man must suffer, die, and be raised (8:31; 9:31; 10:33–34). Third, Jesus envisions himself as the Son of Man, who is to come in power on the clouds (14:61–62) and will serve as eschatological judge (Matt 25:31).

John draws on traditions concerning the Son of Man to emphasize Jesus's heavenly origin and preexistence, presenting him as the one through whom God's eschatological judgment occurs, and the one who reveals God's glory on earth through his crucifixion. Like "Word," the title "Son of Man" follows a movement from heaven to earth, countering the idea that Jesus is a human striving upward to usurp God's prerogatives. In apocalyptic texts, the Son of Man comes on the clouds of heaven or is revealed in heaven, but in John 1:51, Jesus promises that his followers will see "heaven opened" and "the angels of God ascending and descending upon the Son of Man," for he is the locus of God's self-revelation to human beings. In 3:13, he identifies himself as the Son of Man who descends from heaven and can therefore reveal heavenly things to human beings (3:12) before ascending again to heaven (3:13; 6:62). His preexistence and descent set him apart from those who purportedly made visionary ascents in order to learn heavenly secrets.[14]

The revelatory movement leads to Jesus's crucifixion, where the Son of Man is glorified and manifests the glory of God. Jesus says three times that the Son of Man must be "lifted up," sayings comparable to the three passion predictions in Mark. In John, "lift up" ($\dot{\upsilon}\psi\acute{o}\omega$) has the dual sense of physical elevation on the cross and exaltation in honor. Although some think the verb includes Jesus's resurrection and ascension, it is best understood as an interpretation of the crucifixion itself, as seen from a postresurrection perspective.[15] In 3:14, Jesus compares the Son of Man's being "lifted up" to Moses's lifting up the serpent in the wilderness (Num 21:4–8). Both actions involve physical elevation on a pole or cross and provide life for those who are perishing. In 8:28, Jesus tells his opponents, "When you have lifted up the Son of Man, then you will know that I am ($\dot{\varepsilon}\gamma\acute{\omega}$ $\varepsilon\dot{\iota}\mu\iota$), and that I do nothing on my own, but speak as the Father taught me." This passage assumes that being lifted up in crucifixion will be accomplished by Jesus's adversaries, and yet postresurrection it will become apparent that his death reveals his identity as "I am," an expression recalling the self-revelation of God, as discussed below. Finally, the narrator explains that being "lifted up" signifies the manner of Jesus's death (12:32–33). Elsewhere Jesus says that the Son of Man gives food that endures to eternal life (6:27), which one receives by consuming the flesh and blood of the Son of Man, that is, by receiving the benefits of his death (6:53).

In apocalyptic texts, the Son of Man is glorified by being given a place on a throne of glory in God's presence.[16] John, however, brings the glory of the Son of Man into the work of the earthly Jesus and his crucifixion. It is through his death that the Son of Man is "glorified" and in him, God is glorified (12:23; 13:31–32). In the Gospel, "glory" ($\delta\acute{o}\xi\alpha$) connotes both honor and the revelation of divine power and presence. During his ministry, Jesus reveals divine glory by signs that give life (2:11; 11:40) and by his crucifixion, for he lays down his life in order that the world might know of his love for God and God's love for the world, and thereby receive eternal life (3:16; 14:31). By his resurrection and ascension Jesus returns to the heavenly glory he has in the Father's love, and he prays that his followers will one day join him to share in that glory and love (17:5, 24, 26). Yet through the Spirit, who glorifies Jesus after his return to the Father (16:14), believers can already discern the glory of divine love revealed in the crucified Son of Man.[17]

As an apocalyptic figure, the Son of Man is linked to eschatological judgment. The Gospel assumes that the power to judge belongs to God and emphasizes that, as the Son of Man, Jesus judges only because the Father has entrusted that authority to him (5:22, 27). As judge, Jesus is not a rival to God but the agent of God. He is not honored instead of God but along with God, whose work he is doing (5:23).[18] Such a response will be exhibited by the blind man who was healed, as he worships Jesus as the Son of Man, who carries out the work of the Father who sent him (9:35–38; see below).

Revelation differs from the Gospel in that it refers to the risen Jesus as "one *like* a son of man," preserving the idiom used in Daniel 7:13 (Rev 1:13; 14:14). Yet the apocalyptic language is adapted to fit Jesus, who was crucified, and who now as the risen one has traits of an angel and of God. Revelation recalls Daniel 7:13 by saying, "he is coming with the clouds," then paraphrasing Zechariah 12:10 to identify the coming one as the crucified one, for people "will see him, even those who pierced him" (Rev 1:7). Next the seer recounts a vision of "one like a son of man," whose features are like those of an angel who appeared to Daniel (Dan 10:5–6; Rev 1:12–16). He is girded with a golden belt, and has blazing eyes, a radiant face, and feet like bronze. In Revelation, however, the traits of the son of man figure go further and include those of God, making him more than an angel. In Daniel 7:9, God is depicted as the enthroned Ancient of Days, whose clothing is white as snow and whose hair is like pure wool. In Revelation 1:14, it is the son of man figure whose hair is white as wool or snow. Where the angel's voice in Daniel 10:7 is like that of a crowd, the voice in Revelation 1:15 is like rushing water, which may signal the approach of God (Ezek 1:24; 43:2).

In what follows, the divine traits of the exalted Jesus, the one "like a son of man," are amplified, further distinguishing him from an angel. He says, "I am and first and the last" (Rev 1:17), recalling God's own self-identification in 1:8, where he said, "I am the Alpha and the Omega," a pattern discussed below. Here the one like a son of man says he was dead, but came to life, so that he is "the living one" (1:17–18), as is God (7:2), and he "lives forever and ever," as God does (4:9–10; 10:6; 15:7). When addressing each of the seven churches, he begins, "Thus says" (τάδε λέγει), a formula often used for God's speech in the prophets (2:1, 8, 12, etc.).[19] When the one "like a son of man" appears again to oversee the eschatological judgment, he wears a golden crown, whereas the angels who carry out the judgment do not (14:14). The role of the son of man figure in judgment is not limited to the future, since he already walks among the lampstands that symbolize the churches (1:12, 20; 2:1) and warns of judgments against those who do not repent (2:5, 16, 21–23; 3:3, 19). Moreover, he does not participate in God's endless life only through resurrection, since like God, his existence extends from the first to the last (1:17).

Son of God

Jesus's identity as "the Son of God" has a central place in John's Gospel (John 20:31) and corresponds to Jesus's practice of referring to God as his Father and to himself as the Son.[20] This way of identifying himself was offensive to his opponents, who considered it a blasphemous attempt to elevate himself to divine status (5:17–18; 10:33, 36; 19:7). Yet the Gospel inverts that perspective by elaborating the priority of the Father as the one who gives life and entrusts responsibilities to the Son, and Jesus as the Son who receives life from the Father and faithfully carries out his Father's will. The passion narrative also suggests an ironic judgment against Jesus's accusers, who finally declare that they have no king but the emperor—a human being who was considered "son of god."

The Gospel depicts some characters calling Jesus the "Son of God" in a messianic sense (1:49; 11:27). In Scripture God said of the heir to David's throne, "I will be his father and he will be my son" (2 Sam 7:14), and told his anointed king, "You are my son; today I have begotten you" (Ps 2:2, 6, 7; cf. 89:20, 26–27).[21] Traditionally, the king's identity as "son" of God was not construed ontically but in terms of the distinctive status a ruler had in relation to God and other people. Notably, it was a status given by God, which was to be carried out in obedience to God.[22]

The Gospel goes further by invoking the idea that God "the Father has life in himself" (John 5:26). Because life is inherent in who God is, God the Father is the source of life for others.[23] He is the creator of all things and has the power to raise the dead and give them life (5:21; cf. 7:11; 2 Macc 7:23). As Father, God is the source of life for Jesus his Son, for "just as the Father has life in himself, he has given the Son also to have life in himself" (John 5:26). The Son has life on the same terms as the Father has it, but only because the Father has "given" it to him. The same idea is repeated when Jesus calls God "the living Father" (6:57), which is a variation of the common reference to him as "the living God."[24] In contrast to idols, which have no life, and to mortals, who perish, God is "the living one" (2 Bar. 21:9–10), who "is life" (Sib. Or. frag. 3:34) and "lives forever."[25] Accordingly, Jesus can say, "The living Father sent me, and I live because of (διά) the Father, so whoever eats me will live because of me" (John 6:57). Marianne Meye Thompson commented, "Such predications assume and are dependent upon the conviction that there is but one God, one source of life. Jesus is not a second source of life, standing alongside the Father. Rather, the Son confers the Father's life, which he *has in himself*. . . . Precisely in holding together the affirmations that the Son has 'life in himself' with the affirmation that he has 'been *given*' such life by the Father, we find the uniquely Johannine characterization of the relationship of the Father and the Son."[26] These same affirmations attest the unique status of Jesus as the "only" Son (μονογενής) of the Father (1:14, 18; 3:16, 18). Others are begotten as children of God through the Spirit, who engenders faith, through which they receive eternal life (1:12–13; 3:3, 5, 15–16), but they do not have life in themselves as the Son does.

Jesus appeals to the familiar idea that a son was to honor and obey his father by saying that he did only what the Father wanted him to do. His signs attest to this relationship because they exhibit power to give life by feeding, healing, and raising the dead. Since giving life is consistent with God's will and creative action, it shows that Jesus's claim to divine sonship does not mean he is working against his Father but in concert with his Father, even laying down his life to carry out his Father's command (10:17–18). "Hence, arguments for the Son's dependence on the Father are ultimately arguments for the unity of the Son with the Father," enabling him to say, "I and the Father are one" (10:30).[27] "The christological scandal of John is not that Jesus has made himself equal to or one with God, but that God has chosen to make himself one with Jesus."[28]

Revelation develops Jesus's identity as "the Son of God" in terms of participating in God's sovereignty. It adapts the traditional idea that God's "son" was the anointed king, whom God empowered to rule, but it goes beyond the tradition in depicting them ruling as one. God's sovereignty is regularly associated with God's throne in Revelation, and this ruling power is exercised by Jesus, the firstborn of the dead, who is "the ruler of the kings of the earth" (Rev 1:4–5). The writer paraphrases Exodus 19:6, where God said that his intent was that Israel be "a kingdom of priests," by saying that Jesus, through his death, redeemed people to become "a kingdom, priests serving his God and Father" (Rev 1:5–6). The Father's intent to form a kingdom is carried out by the crucified and risen Jesus, who is implicitly his Son. The title "Son of God" is used for Jesus in the message to Thyatira (2:18), where he has the blazing eyes and bronze feet of the son of man figure (1:14–15). The writer paraphrases Psalm 2:6–8, where God's son, the anointed king, is given power over the nations. Jesus has been given that authority by his Father and mediates it to his followers, who "conquer" the nations by remaining faithful to Jesus and thereby participate in his rule (Rev 2:26–29).

In the message to Laodicea he adds, "To the one who conquers, I will give a place with me on my throne, just as I myself conquered and sat down with my Father on his throne" (3:21). Here again Jesus is the mediator of divine sovereignty. Others may share his throne, but only he shares his Father's throne. Where Psalm 110:1 depicted the one called "lord" being seated at the right hand of God—a text read messianically elsewhere in the NT—Revelation depicts Jesus on God's throne.[29] Later visions depict Christ as the slaughtered and now living Lamb, who alone is in the middle "by" or in the middle "of" God's throne (Rev 5:6; 7:17). In the new Jerusalem there is only the one throne, shared by God and the Lamb, who reign and are worshiped as one (22:1, 3). By way of contrast, the heavenly elders and resurrected martyrs sit on multiple thrones, which are around God's throne, but they do not share God's throne as Christ does (4:4; 20:4).[30] Later, a heavenly company declares that the "kingdom of the world has become the kingdom of our Lord *and* of his Messiah," followed by the singular verb, "*he* will reign forever and ever." That may reflect the idea that their sovereignty is exercised as one.[31]

"I Am" Sayings

The Gospel of John and book of Revelation both use the expression "I am" (ἐγώ εἰμι) to portray Jesus as the one in whom God is uniquely present and revealed. The expression draws on the biblical use of "I am" for God. When Moses asked God to identify himself, God replied, "I am who I am" (Exod 3:14), which the LXX translated, "I am the one who is" (ἐγώ εἰμι ὁ ὤν). The "I am" sometimes included a predicate, like "I am the Lord your God" (Exod 20:2), and Deuteronomy 32:39 used the "I am" for God's sole claim to deity: "I am and there is no god beside me." That usage also appears in Isaiah, where God intends "that you may know and believe me and understand that I am. Before me no god was formed, nor shall there be any after me" (Isa 43:10). "I am first and I am last" (48:12).[32]

The "I am" (ἐγώ εἰμι) in John's Gospel has connotations of divine self-identification, yet it occurs in texts that also differentiate Jesus from his Father. The tension is like that in the prologue, where the Word was "with God" and also "was God" (John 1:2). Some occurrences of "I am" have been called "absolute," since they are grammatically awkward, calling attention to their function as a divine claim. Jesus tells his opponents that "you will die in your sins, unless you believe that I am" (8:24), and that "when you have lifted up the Son of Man, then you will know that I am" (8:28). These passages recall the "I am" of Isaiah 43:10, quoted above, where God asserts his sole claim to deity. Later Jesus says, "Before Abraham was, I am" (John 8:58), and his opponents attempt to stone him, apparently thinking he is negating God's singular status by claiming deity for himself. But in the Gospel, Jesus is not a second god but the one whom God has sent, who speaks and acts only as the Father has instructed him, whose Father is always "with" him, and indeed is present and revealed in him (8:26–29). The unity of Father and Son is ultimately manifested in Jesus being "lifted up" in crucifixion, which conveys God's love and brings life to the world.

Other occurrences of ἐγώ εἰμι have an implied predicate, often translated, "I am he" or "It is I," but here too the sense of deity is apparent.[33] When Jesus walks on the sea, he tells the disciples, "It is I. Do not be afraid" (6:20). The scene has qualities of a theophany, for in Israel's tradition it is God who makes his way on the sea (Isa 43:16; Job 9:8; Ps 77:19), yet incarnation is apparent in the wider context, for God is revealed in a person who will give his flesh for the life of the world (John 6:19, 51). Later Jesus tells those who are seeking to arrest Jesus of Nazareth, "I am (he)," and they fall to the ground, as people do when encountering a divine being (18:5–8). Yet Jesus uses the divine power that is evident only to secure the release of those entrusted to him by God, before drinking the cup of suffering that his Father had given him (18:9–11).

Finally, there are "I am" sayings with a stated predicate. Although the "I am" has divine connotations, these passages do differentiate Jesus from his Father. While Jesus is the bread of life, the Father is the giver (6:32–35); Jesus is way to the Father (14:6); Jesus is the vine and his Father is the vine grower (15:1). Yet some of the images also integrate Jesus's identity with God's identity.[34] For example, he says, "I am the light of the world" (8:12), in part recalling that God's servant was to be a light to the nations (Isa 42:6–7; 49:6), yet light imagery was also used for God himself (Ps 27:1; Isa 60:1–2, 19–20; 1 John 1:5), and the prologue identifies light with the Word, who was with God and was God (John 1:1–5). Saying, "I am the good shepherd" (10:11, 14) fits Jesus's identity as God's Messiah (cf. Ezek 34:23; Pss. Sol. 17:40), but God too was depicted as the good shepherd (Ezek 34:11–16; Ps 23:1).

The book of Revelation is framed by "I am" sayings that assert the unique deity of God and include Jesus within it. These passages again recall Isaiah, where God said, "I am the first and the last; besides me there is no god" (Isa 44:6). "I am he; I am the first and I am the last" (48:12; cf. 41:4). Like the Gospel, Revelation paraphrases Isaiah's language, but in a different way:

God: I am the Alpha and the Omega (Rev 1:8).

Christ: I am the first and the last (1:17; cf. 2:8).

God: I am the Alpha and the Omega, the beginning and the end (21:6).

Christ: I am the Alpha and the Omega, the first and the last, the beginning and the end (22:13).

In Isaiah such passages assert the true and enduring existence of the one God, who is the Creator and the one to whom all nations are ultimately subject. The contexts in which these claims are made also reject the claims made about other gods. In Revelation this same emphasis continues, as Richard Bauckham has commented: "God precedes all things as their Creator and he will bring all things to their eschatological fulfillment. He is the origin and goal of all history. He has the first word, in creation, and the last word, in new creation."[35] The trajectory of the book reflects the lordship of God the creator, who at the outset is depicted as the one who has made all things and, in the end, makes all things new (4:11; 21:5).

What is startling is that the crucified and risen Jesus uses God's self-identification for himself. After saying, "I am the first and the last," he adds that he is the "living one," who "was dead" and is now "alive forever and ever" (1:17–18). Christ has endless life, as God does (4:9–10; 10:6; 15:7), not only because he has been raised from the dead, but because he has shared the eternal life of God from "the first," and because of that has triumphed over death.[36] Depicting Christ as "the Alpha and the Omega, the first and the last, the beginning and the end" (22:13) assumes that he and God his Father are one in the role of creation. Revelation does not say that Christ was "with" God at the beginning, in the manner of personified wisdom, but has him declare, "I am" the beginning, so that he participates in the eternal being, work, and reign of God.

Revelation elaborates God's identity as the Alpha and Omega by saying that he is "the one who is and who was and who is to come, the Almighty" (1:4, 8; 4:8). The expression "the one who is" (ὁ ὤν) reflects God's self-identification in Exodus 3:14 LXX, and this is expanded to include both the past and the future. Rather than saying that God "was" and "will be," however, Revelation refers to his past existence and future coming (1:4, 8; 4:8). God was expected to come, bringing salvation and judgment, and that purpose is fulfilled through Christ, who repeatedly says, "I am coming" (2:5, 16; 3:1; 16:15; 22:6, 12, 20). In Christ's coming, God comes.[37]

Worship of God in and through Jesus

The corollary to the high Christologies of John and Revelation is that in both books people worship God in or through Jesus—not in a manner contrary to monotheism but within the tradition of monotheism. In the Gospel, worship is given to God, the Father of Jesus. The Samaritan woman frames the question of worship as one of location, that is, whether people are to worship God on the mountain in Samaria or in Jerusalem (John 4:20). Jesus redefines the issue by declaring that in the coming hour, worship will not be centered in either location. Rather, "the hour is coming and is now here, when the true worshipers will worship the Father in Spirit and truth, for the Father is seeking such people to worship him. God is Spirit, and those who worship him must worship in Spirit and truth" (4:23–24). The dialogue is not arguing for a purely interior spiritualized worship, as opposed to the external rites linked to holy places. Rather, it speaks of worship engendered by God's Spirit, which will be given after the coming "hour" of Jesus's death, resurrection, and return to the Father (7:37–39; 20:22). The Spirit of truth (14:17; 15:26; 16:13) will enable people to know the God who is true, and thereby to worship him in Spirit and truth.[38]

The Gospel also depicts Jesus as the sanctuary where God's truth is embodied and revealed, so that believers worship the Father through Jesus. The prologue says that the Word that was with God and was God became flesh in Jesus and "tabernacled" (ἐσκήνωσεν) among people, revealing divine glory, and was full of "grace and truth" (1:14). The imagery recalls that God, who was full of steadfast love and truth (Exod 34:6), formerly revealed his glory to Israel in the "tabernacle" (σκηνή; 40:34–38). By adapting that imagery, the Gospel shows that true worship of God is centered in the place of his self-revelation, and that place is now a person—Jesus, God's only Son, in whose flesh God's glory and truth are revealed.

John's Gospel assumes that in the early first century, the Jerusalem temple was the focal point for worship of Israel's God. It was the place where God was uniquely present and was the sole place where sacrifices could be offered. Jesus affirms the temple's validity as a place of worship by referring to it as his Father's house (John 2:16). The Gospel was composed after the temple was destroyed in 70 CE, but it depicts the functions of the temple as fulfilled in the crucified and risen body of Jesus (2:19–22). He is the "temple" in whom God is uniquely present, as well as the sacrificial Lamb of God, who takes away the world's sin (1:29), so that the focus for true worship of God is Jesus, who is God's temple.[39]

The story of the blind man who was healed by Jesus anticipates the way true worship of God will focus on Jesus. The man is enabled to see physically and then comes to greater insight into who Jesus is, until he is cast out of the synagogue for his testimony. When Jesus finds him, he discloses that he is the Son of Man, and the former blind man confesses his faith and worships Jesus (9:35–38). Readers know that true worship is directed toward God the Father, and that the Son of Man is the one in whom God's presence is revealed, as discussed above. Accordingly, to worship Jesus is ultimately to worship the God who sent him (9:4; 12:44).[40] The man's action anticipates the post-Easter recognition of God in the crucified and risen Jesus, which becomes explicit in Thomas's confession, "My Lord and my God" (20:28).

Revelation also brings the worship of Jesus into the monotheistic worship of God. In Revelation 4:1–11, the seer describes a scene of heavenly worship, in which God the creator is seated on his throne, while four living creatures acclaim his holiness and twenty-four elders fall before the throne to worship the one who lives forever and ever. The elders declare God worthy to receive glory, honor, and power because he has created all things, and by casting their golden crowns before him, the elders acknowledge God's rightful reign.

As the scene continues, Jesus the Lamb takes a scroll from God's hand in order to break its seals and make the will of God known (5:1–7). Then the living creatures and elders fall down before the Lamb, just as they did before the creator, and they hold bowls full of incense, which signify the prayers of the saints (5:8). Traditionally, prayers and incense were offered to God, yet here they are presented to Christ. The heavenly company sings a "new song," an expression used in the Psalms for the praise of God, but here the "new song" celebrates the redemptive work of the Lamb (5:9–10).[41] As the worshipers told God, "You are worthy" of glory, honor, and power, they say the same of the Lamb (5:9–11). Yet, in the end, the praise of God and the Lamb becomes one, as all creation blesses God and the Lamb together, and the elders worship them as one (5:13). The idea is not that the Lamb is a second deity, worshiped alongside God, for the Lamb redeemed people of every nation to serve as priests *of God* (5:10). Rather, worship of the Lamb is brought within the worship of the one God, since the Lamb is the one through whom God's redemptive purpose is accomplished.[42]

The same dynamics are portrayed in the vision of new Jerusalem, where it says, "I saw no temple in the city, for its temple is the Lord God Almighty and the Lamb" (21:22). Where the Gospel indicated that the new temple would be the body of the crucified and risen Jesus, Revelation envisions it as the presence of God and the Lamb together. They share the same throne, not two different thrones, and they seem to be worshiped as one. The writer says the redeemed will worship "him" and see "his face," and "his name" will be on their foreheads (22:3–4). Although the shift to the singular could reflect the writer's sometimes peculiar syntax, there are good reasons to think that it reflects the idea that worship of the Lamb is included in the worship of the one God. The redeemed bear "his name" on their foreheads, recalling that Israel's high priest bore God's name on the turban over his forehead (Exod 28:38). Yet in Revelation 14:1, the foreheads of the redeemed are inscribed with the names of both the Lamb and his Father, and in 22:4 the two names apparently become one. It was the Lamb who redeemed people for priestly service to God (1:5–6; 5:9), and they in turn include the Lamb within the worship they offer to the one God.

Jesus the Lamb is the only one who can rightly be worshiped in this way, according to Revelation. On two occasions, the writer falls before an angel in order to worship him, but the angel tells him not to do so. Instead, the angel places himself alongside the writer's fellow believers and says, "Worship God!" (19:10; 22:8–9). There is an even sharper polemic against the worship practiced in the imperial cults, which is portrayed as demonic. Where emperors were said to have been granted power by the gods to rule, Revelation says that Satan the dragon gave the throne and ruling authority to the tyrant, pictured as a beast, so when people worshiped the ruler, they actually worshiped Satan (13:2, 4).

Conclusion

John's Gospel and the book of Revelation embed high Christology in their narratives. Each is framed by announcements that the one God is present and revealed in Jesus, who uniquely shares God's endless life and deity. The Gospel opens by announcing that the Word, who was with God and was God at the beginning, tabernacled in the mortal flesh in Jesus (John 1:1–18), and it culminates with Thomas's confession that in the risen Jesus, who bears the scars of crucifixion, he recognizes, "My Lord and my God" (20:28). In Revelation's introduction and conclusion, both God and Jesus utter a form of the statement, "I am the Alpha and the Omega, the first and the last, the beginning and the end" (Rev 22:13: cf. 1:8, 17; 21:6). In each book, Jesus is the one in whom God uniquely speaks, acts, and is revealed, so that people are to relate to God in and through Jesus. Each also maintains the tension in that Jesus is one with God and yet differentiated from God, and the even more profound tension in which God is present and revealed in the human being who was crucified. These tensions shape the readers' perceptions of who Jesus is and who God is, for God's power to give life, to judge, and to reign are exercised through the suffering, death, and resurrection of the Lamb, with whom God is one (John 1:29; 10:17–18, 30; Rev 5:5–6; 22:1–5).

CHAPTER FOURTEEN

Jesus the Door

*Gate Christology in the Gospel of John
and in Second-Century Christianity*

David J. Downs

It is a great privilege to have studied under Marianne Meye Thompson when I was an MDiv student at Fuller Theological Seminary and to have known Marianne as a friend and mentor when I later served on the faculty of Fuller for over a decade. One of the many things I came to appreciate about Marianne, first as my professor, and then as a trusted colleague, is her love of hymns in the evangelical tradition. Whether in the classroom, in faculty meetings, in conversations over a meal, or in her office in Payton Hall, Marianne has always been quick to cite a line from a beloved hymn.

Hymns are meaningful vessels of theological tradition. They capture, reinforce, and shape the beliefs and practices of those who sing them.[1] Part of the power of hymns to effect the theological and moral formation of congregants lies in the ways hymns, as lyrical poetry, employ metaphorical language to praise the one whom Christians worship as "God in three persons, blessed Trinity."[2] Whether in hymns or in other sorts of confessional texts, Christians have found no shortage of metaphors to apply to Jesus. In just the first three chapters of the Gospel of John, for example, Jesus is imaged as the Word, light, the Lamb of God, the temple, and a bridegroom.[3] Among the most popular English-language hymns, Christ appears as a solid rock, an anchor, a shield, a refuge, a branch, a key, the morning star, and the rock of ages.[4]

This essay is not about hymns but about one particular christological image in the early church, namely, Jesus as the door or gate. The metaphor of Jesus as a door or gate is not particularly prominent in English-language hymnody.[5] Yet in the early centuries of the Christian movement, Jesus was not infrequently imaged as a door or gate. The most well-known instance, of course, comes from the Gospel of John, where Jesus says to some Pharisees, "Very truly, I tell you, I am the gate for the sheep (ἡ θύρα τῶν προβάτων). All who came before me are thieves and bandits; but the sheep did not listen to them. I am the gate (ἐγώ εἰμι ἡ θύρα). Whoever enters by me will be saved, and will come in and go out and find pasture" (10:7–9 NRSV).[6] Outside of the Fourth Gospel, several Christian texts from the second century that do not betray direct influence from the Gospel of John also employ the image of Jesus as the door/gate. The aim of this essay is to explore, roughly in chronological order, some key expressions of what might be called "gate Christology" in the early church, beginning with the Gospel of John and concluding with Hegesippus's account of the martyrdom of James. Although we will consider instances of gate Christology from the Fourth Gospel, 1 Clement, Ignatius's letter to the Philadelphians, the Shepherd of Hermas, and some extant fragments of Hegesippus's *Hypomnemata*, there is little evidence to suggest literary relationships among any of these texts.[7] Thus, to call Jesus the gate (πύλη) or door (θύρα) in the late-first or second century appears to have been a relatively well-attested theological confession, independently found among a diverse collection of literary witnesses.[8]

The Gospel of John

In one of the seven "I am" formulations followed by a predicate in the Gospel of John, Jesus says, "I am the gate for the sheep" (ἐγώ εἰμι ἡ θύρα τῶν προβάτων, 10:7; cf. 6:35; 8:12; 9:5; 10:11, 14; 11:25; 14:6; 15:1). He then repeats this declaration without the qualifier "for the sheep": "I am the gate (ἐγώ εἰμι ἡ θύρα). Whoever enters by me will be saved, and will come in and go out and find pasture" (10:9).[9] These "I am" statements come in the context of a parable in which Jesus images himself both as a good shepherd who safeguards his sheep and sacrifices his life for his sheep (esp. 10:11–18) and as the gate through which the sheep enter into and out of the sheepfold, allowing the sheep to find deliverance from threats and land for grazing (esp. 10:1–10).

As has often been observed, while no OT texts are explicitly cited in the discourse (called a παροιμία, or "parable," in 10:6) in John 10, the passage is rich with scriptural imagery, for biblical authors commonly depict God's people as sheep and both God (e.g., Gen 48:15; 49:24; Pss 23; 28:9; 78:52–53; 80:1; Isa 40:11; Ezek 34:11–24; Mic 7:14) and Israel's leaders (e.g., Num 27:17; 2 Sam 5:2; 7:7; 1 Kgs 22:17; 1 Chr 11:2; 17:6; Ps 78:71; Jer 23:1–4; Ezek 34:1–10) as shepherds. For the present purposes, we may briefly consider the possible scriptural background of Jesus's assertion that he is the gate to the sheepfold (vv. 7, 9). In her monumental commentary on the Gospel of John, Marianne Meye Thompson suggests that the image of Jesus as the gate in John 10 may evoke Ps 118:19–20:

> [19] Open to me the gates of righteousness,
>   when I enter in them,
>   I will acknowledge the Lord.
> [20] This is the gate of the Lord;
>   righteous ones shall enter in it. (NETS)[10]

Thompson writes, "The depiction of Jesus as a door by which one 'comes in and goes out' may recall promises found in the Psalms: the righteous enter into salvation through the 'gate of the Lord' (*pylē tou kyriou*, 118:20–21 [117:20–21 LXX])."[11] The possibility that the metaphor of Jesus as a door (θύρα) evokes the gate imagery from Psalm 118:20–21 is perhaps weakened by the fact that the author of John employs a different word than that found in the LXX version of the psalm (i.e., πύλη). Yet, the author of John certainly knows Psalm 118, material from which is explicitly cited in the Johannine account of Jesus's final entry into Jerusalem (Ps 118:26 in John 12:13) and perhaps alluded to elsewhere in the Fourth Gospel.[12]

Regardless of possible allusions to the gate imagery of Psalm 118, the depiction of Jesus as the door relates to a cluster of themes developed elsewhere in the Fourth Gospel. First, Jesus is the exclusive gate. At the beginning of the parable, Jesus imagines that there are other illicit ways into the sheepfold than through the gate, but those who enter the sheep pen by any other means than the gate are identified as thieves and bandits (John 10:1). Later, Jesus will equate these thieves and bandits with "all who came before me" (10:8), which seems to function as a reference to his opponents. Jesus is both the shepherd of the sheep and the gate through which the sheep enter the protection of the pen (10:2). And the sheep belong to no one and heed the commands of no one but the good shepherd (10:3–5). As Jesus will go on to say in a later discourse to his disciples, "I am the way, and the truth, and the life. No one comes to the Father except through me" (14:6). The image of Jesus as the door to the sheepfold serves the christological exclusivism that runs through the entire narrative, an exclusivism rooted in the high Christology of the Fourth Gospel.[13] Because Jesus is the Word made flesh, the only Son who has seen God and has made God known (1:18), the only one who has ascended into heaven (3:13), he is the only gate through which the sheep may enter into salvation and find good pasture.[14]

Second, and relatedly, Jesus as the gate is the means of salvation and flourishing for God's flock. Not only does the parable stress that whoever enters the sheepfold by Jesus the gate will be saved (10:9), but here Jesus provides a brief image of what "salvation" looks like. In contrast to the thief, who comes to steal and destroy, Jesus has come to give the sheep abundant life (10:10). As Thompson aptly remarks:

Even as Jesus provided wine (2:1–12) and bread (6:1–14) in abundance, so he generously provides abundant pasture, once again illustrating the Gospel's affirmation "from his fullness we have all received" (1:16). Such abundant life consists of fellowship with God (17:3) and others (17:20–26) that issues in fullness of love (13:34–35; 15:13; 17:26), joy (3:29; 15:11; 16:24; 17:13), and peace (14:27; 16:33). This "abundant life" is what created life ought to be (1:3–4), and it anticipates the blessings of eternal life (3:16–17). Abundant life is found at the intersection of created life and eternal life: each is given by God through the Son (or Word) and experienced as knowledge of and union with God (17:3).[15]

According to the Gospel of John, abundant life is only available through the Son of God. Jesus is the gate through which all sheep must pass in order find salvation and good pasture. As we shall see, this exclusivist soteriology is paralleled in a number of second-century texts that also employ the image of Jesus as a door/gate.[16]

1 Clement

We turn now to a second-century text that undoubtedly cites Psalm 118 in connecting gate imagery with being "in Christ." In a letter from the church in Rome to Christ-followers in Corinth, an epistle aimed at exhorting the Corinthians to end a schism that has led certain elders to be removed from their positions, the authors of 1 Clement lament that news of the shameful behavior of the divisive Corinthians has not only reached the Roman believers but is now also known among pagans, "with the result that you heap blasphemies upon the name of the Lord because of your stupidity, and create danger for yourselves as well" (1 Clem. 47.7).[17] The Roman authors of 1 Clement then make the following plea to their Corinthian readers:

> [1] Therefore, let us remove this problem quickly, and let us fall down before the Master and weep, begging him to be merciful and to be reconciled to us and to restore us to the honorable and pure way of life, seen in love for others. [2] For this gate of righteousness is open for life, as it is written: "Open to me the gates of righteousness, so that I may enter through them and praise the Lord. [3] This is the gate of the Lord; the righteous shall enter through it." [4] Although many gates are open, this gate is the gate that leads to righteousness, the gate that is in Christ, by which are blessed all who enter in and keep their path straight in piety and righteousness, accomplishing everything without disturbance. (48.1–4)

A plaintive summons to repentance and the end of division comes with the hope of mercy from and reconciliation to God, along with the restoration of honorable and pure conduct, which is seen in love for others (48.1).[18] This exhortation is rooted in the claim that a response of repentance, reconciliation, and restoration of good conduct is a way into righteousness that leads to life, a contention that the authors support with a marked quotation (γέγραπται) of Psalm 118:19–20.[19] As is the case elsewhere in 1 Clement, the scriptural text is interpreted with reference to Christ, although the authors of 1 Clement do not directly identify Jesus himself as the gate, as is seen in John 10.[20] Instead, they refer to "the gate that is *in Christ*" (ἡ ἐν Χριστῷ), or, perhaps more expansively, "the gate that is [open] in Christ." Presumably this means that honorable and pure conduct, demonstrated by mutual love for one another, is the gate that leads to righteousness, and that gate is open to those who are united with Christ or who follow his example of humility (1 Clem 16.1–17).

Christological exegesis of Psalm 118 played a key role in early Christian confession of Jesus as Lord.[21] The psalm recounts the thanksgiving of a king who has been delivered by God from a near-death experience at the hands of his enemies. At one point, the king enters the temple to give thanks to the Lord (vv. 19–20). Among other things, the king praises God that "the stone that the builders rejected has become the chief cornerstone" (v. 22 NRSV), a saying interpreted christologically by a number of early Christian authors (Matt 21:42 // Mark 12:10 // Luke 20:17; Acts 4:11; Barn. 6.2–4; cf. Eph 2:20; 1 Pet 2:6). Toward the end of the psalm, a chorus of voices in the temple proclaims, "Blessed is the one who comes in the name of the Lord. We bless you from the house of the Lord" (Ps 118:26 NRSV). This confession, too, features prominently in the Gospel traditions regarding Jesus's entry into Jerusalem before the passion (Matt 21:9 // Mark 11:9 // Luke 19:38 // John 12:13; Matt 23:39 // Luke 13:35; cf. Did. 12.1). Although the authors of 1 Clement do not interpret the righteous gates of Psalm 118:19 as a reference to Christ himself, their reading of 118:19–20 with reference to the righteous behavior of those in Christ represents an appeal for the Corinthians to end their factious conflict, rooted in their strategy of citing the OT with direct reference to the lives of their readers.

The authors of 1 Clement grant that "many gates are open" (48.4). It is unlikely that this statement is fundamentally at odds with the christological exclusivist soteriology associated with the door imagery in John 10. Although articulating a doctrine of salvation is far from the main goal of the authors of 1 Clement, an earlier explicit reflection on salvation (σωτήριον) in 1 Clement 36 indicates that "Jesus Christ, the high priest of our offerings, the benefactor and helper of our weakness" is the way (ἡ ὁδός) of salvation and the one through whom readers are able to look into the heights of heaven (36.1–2). In the context of 1 Clement 48, the notion that there might be other "gates" that lead to righteousness and life likely means that other kinds of life-giving behavior—aside from the specific repentance, reconciliation, and restoration of good conduct that the authors are recommending here—are ways to righteousness. It is precisely the restoration of an honorable and pure way of life, through the cessation of conflict, that the authors of 1 Clement declare to be "the gate that is in Christ, by which are blessed all who enter in and keep their path straight in piety and righteousness, accomplishing everything without disturbance" (48.4). Those who enter through this gate will be blessed (48.4). As the authors go on to indicate, in language that evokes Paul's discourse regarding spiritual gifts in 1 Corinthians 12–14, the exercise of gifts for the benefit of others is the key to a flourishing community: "For the more one appears to be great, the more one should be humble, and the more one should seek the common good for all, and not of oneself" (1 Clem 48.6).

Ignatius of Antioch

The next example of gate Christology comes from the letters of Ignatius, second-century bishop of Antioch. It has sometimes been alleged that Ignatius was not well acquainted with Israel's Scriptures and/or that Jewish Scriptures played little to no role in the formulation of the seven-letter corpus that survives under his name.[22] A better interpretation of the evidence, however, is that Ignatius deeply valued the Scriptures, yet advocates a resolutely christological interpretation of these sacred writings.[23] This is the point that Ignatius makes in recounting in his letter to the Philadelphians the story of an earlier dispute regarding Scripture he had engaged in with some who were saying, "If I do not find it in the ancient records (τὰ ἀρχεῖα), I do not believe it in the gospel" (*Phld.* 8.2). As Ignatius goes on to insist, proper understanding of "the archives" must begin "with Jesus and [work] backward to the way in which his life and death fulfil the archives."[24] Thus, Ignatius declaims, "But to me the 'ancient records' are Jesus Christ, the inviolable ancient records are his cross and death and his resurrection and the faith that is through him. By these things I want, through your prayers, to be justified" (8.2). Elsewhere Ignatius emphasizes that the prophets anticipated the gospel (5.2; 9.2) and that Jesus is the true high priest (9.1). Moreover, while he does not cite Scripture extensively in his letters, he does quote and appeal to the authority of Jewish scriptural texts on several occasions (i.e., Prov 3:34 in *Eph.* 5.3; Prov 18:17 LXX in *Magn.* 12; and Isa 52:5 in *Trall.* 8.2; cf. possible allusions to Isa 5:2 in *Smyrn.* 1.2 and Ps 32:9 LXX in *Eph.* 15.1).

This scriptural context is relevant when it comes to Ignatius's claim, advanced just after recounting the hermeneutical dispute he had had with some opponents in Philadelphia, that Jesus is the high priest and the door of the Father:

[1] The priests, too, were good, but the high priest, entrusted with the Holy of Holies, is better; he alone has been entrusted with the hidden things of God, for he himself is the door of the Father (αὐτὸς ὢν θύρα τοῦ πατρός), through which Abraham and Isaac and Jacob and the prophets and the apostles and the church enter in. All these come together in the

unity of God. ² But the gospel possesses something distinctive, namely, the coming of the Savior, our Lord Jesus Christ, his suffering, and the resurrection. For the beloved prophets preached in anticipation of him, but the gospel is the imperishable finished work. All these things together are good, if you believe with love. (*Phld.* 9.1–2)[25]

Ignatius claims that Jesus, the high priest, is superior to the Levitical priests, though the priests are good. Jesus's superiority rests in part on the fact that he has been entrusted with the holy of holies and with the hidden things of God. Although Ignatius may be referring to the christological interpretation of scripture that he discussed in the section immediately before this one (8.2), he probably also has in mind the extent to which Jesus is the center of God's revelation to the world (cf. *Eph.* 19.2–3; *Magn.* 8.2; *Rom.* 8.2). Because of the unity that the Son shares with the Father, only the Son, the true high priest, can enter the holy of holies and share the hidden things of God with humanity.

Moreover, Ignatius declares that Jesus the high priest has this mediatory role because "he himself is the door of the Father" (*Phld.* 9.1).[26] Playing on the image of the door, Ignatius indicates that the patriarchs, the prophets, the apostles, and the church all enter through the door of Jesus Christ and, therefore, are all bound together in the unity of God (εἰς ἑνότητα θεοῦ). Although it has been suggested that Ignatius's claim that Jesus is the door of the Father draws on Psalm 118:20, it is difficult to discern a particular scriptural antecedent for this image. Yet Ignatius ties his depiction of Jesus as "the door of the Father" to a similar kind of christological exclusivist soteriology as found in the Gospel of John, even while Ignatius is more explicit regarding the fact that even the patriarchs Abraham, Isaac, and Jacob, along with the OT prophets, enter the door of the Father and join in the unity of God *through* Jesus the high priest. Indeed, Ignatius goes on to insist that the prophets preached in anticipation of Christ, but the gospel—that is, the coming, suffering, and resurrection of the Lord Jesus Christ—is "the completion of immortality" (*Phld.* 9.2). Thus, we find in Ignatius a use of gate Christology similar to that found in the Fourth Gospel: Jesus is *the* door that leads to the Father. In some ways, Ignatius's use of the door imagery is more explicitly inclusive than the door and sheepfold metaphor in John 10, for Ignatius notes that even individuals before Christ—notably the patriarchs and the prophets—come to the Father through Jesus the door. Yet for Ignatius, as for the author of John, Jesus is *the* door to the Father, and even the patriarchs and prophets must pass through this door.

Shepherd of Hermas

The next example of gate Christology is found in the enigmatic second-century apocalypse from Rome called the Shepherd of Hermas. In the ninth parable of the Shepherd of Hermas, the protagonist, Hermas, is given a vision of a large square white rock that is ancient and higher than the mountains; the rock is large enough to hold the entire world (Herm. 79.1–7). Out of this rock has been carved a new radiant gate (πύλη) surrounded by twelve glorious virgins (79.2–5). After receiving this vision, Hermas asks his guide, a figure called the Shepherd, about the identity of the rock and the gate: "First of all, sir, who is the rock and the gate?" (89.1). The Shepherd responds to Hermas, "This rock and the gate (ἡ πύλη) are the Son of God" (89.1). The rock is old, Hermas is told, because "the Son of God is far older than all his creation, with the result that he was the Father's counsellor in his creation" (89.2). And the gate is new, explains the Shepherd, "because [the Son of God] was revealed in the last days of the consummation; that is why the gate is new, in order that those who are going to be saved may enter the kingdom of God through it" (89.3).

The Shepherd goes on to illuminate some of the imagery in light of this motif of christological exclusivism. He asks Hermas if Hermas had noticed that stones that have passed through the gate have become part of the construction of a large tower, which is soon revealed to be the church (90.1), whereas stones that did not come through the gate have been returned, and thus excluded from the church. The Shepherd then expounds, "In the same way, no one will enter the kingdom of God unless he receives the name of his Son. For if you want to enter into a certain city, and that city is walled and has only one gate (μίαν ἔχει πύλην), you can't enter into the city except through the gate it has, right?" (89.5). When Hermas agrees, the Shepherd continues to expound the imagery: "If, therefore, you cannot enter into the city except through its gate, so also no one can enter the kingdom of God except through the name of his Son, who was loved by him" (89.5). To emphasize the point again, the Shepherd notes there are angels guarding the Lord, "but the gate is the Son of God; there is only this one entrance to the Lord. No one, therefore, will go in to him in any other way than through his Son" (89.6).

As is characteristic of the Shepherd of Hermas, this passage contains no explicit references to Jewish Scripture. What is clearest in the gate Christology of the Shepherd of Hermas is that the Son of God is the only means through which people may enter the kingdom of God. As in the Gospel of John, so also in the Shepherd of Hermas, this exclusivist soteriology is rooted partly in the Son's preexistence. The antiquity of the rock in Hermas's vision is explained on the basis of the Son's preexistence: "The Son of God is far older than all his creation, with the result that he was the Father's counsellor in his creation" (89.2; cf. 91.5). Thus, for the author of the Shepherd of Hermas, one may only enter the kingdom of God through Jesus the door.

Hegesippus

As a final example, gate Christology plays a key role in one of the earliest Christian martyrological accounts, namely, Hegesippus's narrative of the death of James, the brother of Jesus. Hegesippus was the author of the *Hypomnemata*, probably written sometime in the latter decades of the second century, portions of which are preserved by the fourth-century historian Eusebius.[27] According to Hegesippus, James is asked by some of the "seven sects among the people" who "the gate of Jesus" (ἡ θύρα τοῦ Ἰησοῦ) was, a query to which James replies that the gate is the Savior (τοῦτον εἶναι τὸν σωτῆρα; Eusebius, *Hist. eccl.* 2.23.7–9). Later, after the scribes and the Pharisees have made James stand on the highest point of the temple, they cry out to him, again inquiring about the gate of Jesus, "Oh, just one, to whom we all owe obedience, since the people are straying after Jesus who was crucified, tell us who is the gate of Jesus?" (2.23.12). James answers with an allusion to the synoptic tradition of Jesus's own evocation of Daniel 7 and Psalm 110 at his trial (Matt 26:64 // Mark 14:62; cf. Matt 24:30 // Mark 13:26 // Luke 21:27): "Why do you ask me concerning the Son of Man? He is sitting in heaven on the right hand of the great power, and he will come on the clouds of heaven" (Eusebius, *Hist. eccl.* 2.23.13). Although many in the crowd are convinced by James's testimony, the scribes and the Pharisees throw him down from the temple and stone him before he is clubbed to death by one of the laundry workers (2.23.14–18).

In a perceptive study, Richard Bauckham has shown that Hegesippus's account of James's death is deeply shaped by the language and imagery of Psalm 118, especially vv. 19–20.[28] James, the righteous one, is framed as the speaker of the psalm. He acknowledges the Lord (Jesus), the gate of the Lord (Jesus) is opened to him, and he enters into it. Thus, Bauckham suggests that at the core of Hegesippus's narrative is a christological interpretation of the phrase "gate of Yahweh" in Psalm 118:20. In this tradition, Jesus is interpreted as the Lord (κύριος) from Psalm 118:20, and, through his martyrdom, James becomes one of the righteous ones who enter into salvation through Jesus the gate. As Bauckham concludes, "The gate of YHWH/Jesus is Jesus himself as the gate of the eschatological Temple, the one through whom the righteous (with James the Righteous at their head) enter the presence of God in the midst of his people, the messianically renewed Israel. Some such exegesis of Psalm 118:20, expounded in James' preaching, could well have been understood to associate Jesus so closely with YHWH as to be evidence that James was leading the people into apostasy."[29]

At issue in Hegesippus's account of James's death is the question of Jesus's identity and whether people should obey him. When James is taken up to the rampart of the temple, the scribes and the Pharisees ask him whether followers of Jesus have been misled: "Oh, just one, to whom we all owe obedience, since the people are straying after Jesus who was crucified, tell us who is the gate of Jesus?"

(Eusebius, *Hist. eccl.* 2.23.12). This prompts James's response that the Son of Man is sitting at the right hand of God, a reply that leads to James being thrown down from the temple. Thus, although James does not explicitly indicate that Jesus is the only gate through which the righteous may pass, his willingness to die for his conviction that Jesus is "the gate of the Lord" would seem to indicate a belief in the exclusive nature of this christological confession.

Conclusion

The metaphor of Jesus as a door or gate is found in several early Christian texts from the first and second centuries. Jesus is portrayed as a door or gate (or mentioned in close association with this imagery) in the Gospel of John, 1 Clement, Ignatius's letter to the Philadelphians, the Shepherd of Hermas, and Hegesippus's *Hypomnemata*. It does not appear that the Fourth Gospel's claim that Jesus is the gate to the sheepfold shaped these second-century images of Christ as the door or gate. That there is not likely a literary relationship between any of these texts is an indication that the depiction of Jesus as a door or gate was a popular christological image in the early church. Thus, this essay is not a study in the early reception of a Johannine metaphor. Yet, for that reason the ways in which gate Christology is developed independently among second-century Christian authors may shed some light on the theology of the Gospel of John.

It was argued above that the claim of the Johannine Jesus to be "the gate for the sheep," the only means by which the sheep enter into salvation and obtain good pasture, is part of the exclusivist soteriology characteristic of the Fourth Gospel. The notion that Jesus might be the only way to salvation has, however, troubled many interpreters of the Gospel of John. One signal example of this discomfort is found in an essay by James Charlesworth, who devotes significant attention to Jesus's assertion, "I am the way, and the truth, and the life. No one comes to the Father except through me" (John 14:6).[30] Charlesworth calls this text "an exceptional embarrassment to Christians who are seeking a fruitful dialogue with persons of other religions, especially Jews."[31] On the basis of his analysis of this verse, Charlesworth declares Jesus's statement in John 14:6 to be a "later [expansion] and [corruption] in the development of Jesus' traditions."[32] According to Charlesworth, the claim that no one can come to the Father except through Jesus "seems to reflect and thus derive from the problems and perspectives of the second generation of Jesus' followers. . . . Thus, John 14:6b is a relic of the past. It is not the Word of God for our time."[33]

Charlesworth's interpretation is illuminating particularly because of his explicit rejection of Johannine exclusivist soteriology. Yet, many other scholars, perhaps less directly strident in their objection to the Fourth Gospel's claim that no one comes to the Father except through Jesus but equally uncomfortable with it, agree with Charlesworth in this strategy of explaining Johannine christological exclusivism in light of a particular historical context that allegedly gave rise to the sectarianism of the so-called Johannine community. As D. Moody Smith, for example, explains in his commentary on John 14:6: "This statement reflects a severe exclusivity, even intolerance. It should, however, be seen in light of John's presupposing a bitter polemic between Christ-confessing and Christ-denying Jews, in which confessors are being expelled from synagogues for their belief (9:22). Moreover, such polemic and mutual rejection were not unprecedented within ancient Judaism."[34] Thus, one strategy for dealing with the difficulties posed by an ostensibly exclusive christological claim like "No one comes to the Father except through me" is to locate this assertion in the historical experience of a community of Christ-followers that was itself marginalized and perhaps persecuted. Johannine exclusivist soteriology, then, becomes a byproduct of Johannine sectarianism.

There are reasons to doubt the specificity of many hypotheses regarding the so-called Johannine community, and this essay does not pretend to engage that debate.[35] There are also significant theological, ethical, and political challenges raised by the exclusive christological claims made by the Gospel of John, and this is not the context to address, let alone attempt to resolve, those difficulties. What this study of the image of Jesus as door/gate in first- and second-century Christian writings does suggest, however, is that the Fourth Gospel is far from the only writing to employ the metaphor "Jesus is the door" in order to emphasize that salvation, or entry into the kingdom of God, is available only through Jesus. The image of Jesus as door/gate is, of course, deployed in diverse ways in different contexts. Yet, some form of exclusivist soteriology is explicitly associated with the gate imagery in the Shepherd of Hermas, and christological exclusivism is linked with gate imagery in Ignatius's *Letter to the Philadelphians* and in Hegesippus's account of James's martyrdom. Few would suggest that these second-century writings are representatives of "sectarian" Christianity. Instead, there seems to have been a fairly widespread belief among nascent Jesus followers that salvation is mediated through Jesus alone. And several early Christian writers found the image of Jesus as door/gate conducive to their exclusivist soteriologies.

Part Three

John's Voice and the Church's Witness

CHAPTER FIFTEEN

Conversing with the Word

Homiletical Reflections on Incarnation

Michael Pasquarello III

"The Church exists, with all its human and material elements because God loves His creation, particularly his human creation, and communicates with us in our own language. What is more typical of the divine communication in human language than the Divine Word made man?"[1]

I AM GRATEFUL to the editors for the invitation to contribute this essay in honor of Dr. Marianne Meye Thompson, who for a time was my colleague and dean in the Fuller Seminary School of Theology. My first brief introduction to Marianne (and John) occurred more than forty years ago, when I, an MDiv student at Duke Divinity School, was enrolled in a PhD seminar taught by the late Dr. David Steinmetz. Marianne and John were doctoral students working in their respective disciplines, which led both toward a theological reading of Scripture in service of the church. Since those early days at Duke, I have benefited from Marianne's work in the study of the NT, and especially the Gospel of John. First as a preacher and later as a teacher of preaching, I found her interpretation of Scripture to be the kind of work necessary for the church to recover its voice for speaking of God present and active in Jesus Christ, the Word made flesh. What follows is offered with gratitude to God for Marianne's exemplary life, leadership, teaching, and scholarship as witness to the Word and Wisdom of God incarnate in Jesus.

Homiletical Minimalism and Excarnation

In a highly acclaimed work, *A Secular Age*, philosopher Charles Taylor writes of how western culture has, in practice, largely excluded God from its "social imaginary." In using the term "social imaginary," Taylor is not referring to theories or ideas of God, particularly doctrine, but of the images, pictures, people, and stories that fire the imagination and shape sensibilities—in other words, those shared understandings and practices that continue to make belief plausible in a time when many consider it either no longer possible or even desirable.[2]

Taylor's extensive narrative of the west shows how a predominate social imaginary, pervaded with a sense of God's reality and providential care of the world, has given way to a "secular age" in which faith in God has been restricted to a private sphere and thus policed out of public life. The predominant assumption is that the "natural" and "social" are no longer gifts and expressions of the creator's infinite love, which is received and returned in gratitude, but are rather a construction of autonomous human reason, emotion, and self-creativity.

This insightful account assists us in seeing how sustaining communities that made belief in God seem normal and natural have been lost, overcome by a pervasive, expressive individualism. The consequence of this, according to Taylor, is the projection and creation of what he describes as a "buffered self" resistant to social commitments and attachments. For Taylor, it is important to see just how the "buffered self," which is dependent on nothing other than the self and one's choices, limits dramatically the possibility of transformation by transcending the self in encountering a reality other than the self, a deeper reality that is indeed life-changing.[3] Here he makes an important turn to the Christian belief in the incarnation, "the Word made flesh": "At the heart of orthodox Christianity, seen in terms of communion, is the coming of God through Christ into a personal relation with disciples, and beyond them others, eventually ramifying through the Church to humanity as a whole. God establishes the new relationship with us by loving us, in a way we cannot unaided love each other."[4]

Taylor concludes the challenge of our time is recovering a sense of what the incarnation means for humanity, thus overcoming the hopeless condition of what he terms *"excarnation."* By excarnation he means an uneasiness with and aversion to being "in the flesh, dependent, vulnerable, and destined to die." In pointing to the significance of the incarnation for the meaning or purpose of being human, Taylor suggests a way forward may be discerned in the deep hunger of consumerist and technological cultures for communion with God through Christ, and in Christ, for communion with others.[5]

This seems to be an acknowledgment that for certain kinds of people, those who may still possess a religious predisposition or inclination, divine action may yet be encountered through the means of grace, such as the Word and sacramental life of the church. And divine action also may still penetrate the buffered self and change the heart and mind of a person. But Taylor also fears the ways this change may happen, for example, in worship, preaching, and the study of Scripture, and may end up as merely a matter of moving from the secular sphere to the religious sphere. This will occur when the aim is to use such activities for either reestablishing or preserving the church's cultural influence or attracting individuals to church as an option among many to support their self-made, self-sufficient projects in search of authentic self-expression.

In the case of preaching, I would think of this as an exercise in what could be described as "homiletical minimalism." By this I mean, rather than speaking of God in a way that invites others into a new humanity revealed and given in the word and reality of Jesus, people are instead invited to become religious, stay religious, or become more religious in loyalty to religious institutions that operate without a need for encountering God's present speech and action in the Word. This may be accomplished by emphasizing a need for more doctrine and biblical literacy, apologetic arguments for Christianity, moral exhortation to activism, or increased participation in church programs and activities. I also think it significant that Taylor sees our current culture wars as an expression of this strategy of recovering, protecting, or expanding religious influence and participation, an ecclesiastical turf battle over shrinking institutional and ideological commitments and affiliations.

Lastly, Taylor points to what he describes as the "immanent frame," by which he means a way of framing our lives without the possibility of religion, as a space of the modern or postmodern social imaginary that rules out any possibility of transcendent authority and wisdom.[6] Located within the immanent frame, preaching is oriented to and centered on the self. Religious beliefs and institutional affiliation are irrelevant, since attracting people to church or keeping people in church is no longer what matters. What matters is whatever may be personally useful, so that spirituality, or spiritual practices, may be of interest but need not point the "buffered self" to acknowledge anything or anyone beyond itself as plausible or believable.[7]

The well-known description provided by the work of Christian Smith captures this approach to ministry well: MTD—"Moralistic, Therapeutic, Deism"—which goes well with what I have named "homiletical minimalism" and the excarnate way of life it produces.[8] MTD refers to a self-managed program or rules to live by, a therapeutic orientation that seeks individual happiness as defined by the self, and a God who does not intrude on or interfere with the life plans of the sovereign self. However, our neither seeking to recover or preserve the church's social and political influence, nor constantly working to keep up with the newest and latest cultural trends through innovation and change, will lead the church to see the union of Jesus with the Word, and the Word, and hence Jesus, with God.[9] In John's Gospel it is Jesus, the Word, whose love evokes and nourishes faith, and who gives the Spirit to constitute the church in God's life of self-expending service, which he, as the Son, fulfills in obedience to the Father even unto suffering and death on a cross—which, in his exaltation and glory, is the fullness of human life in God.

I have taken the concluding paragraph of Marianne Meye Thomspon's *The God of the Gospel of John* as a welcome and clarifying prompt for the following reflections on preaching. My aim is to sketch a vision of preaching that is dependent on John's high Christology as an alternative to homiletical minimalism and excarnate living, which has both accompanied and contributed to a modern/postmodern social imaginary in the west.

> In the incarnation God has taken on human form and entered into the world of death and darkness, has taken on an embodied presence that reveals God's ultimate purposes for the world are life-giving, and that God persistently and faithfully works to that end. Salvation is construed primarily as knowing God, as participation in God's life, and as having fellowship with God through the one in whom God's presence became embodied in this world, for the salvation and life of the world.[10]

What follows is the fruit of many years of reflecting on preaching as a homiletical form of Christian speech. I gladly acknowledge that beginning with God, the Word, incarnate in Jesus, makes preaching more difficult in comparison with beginning with ourselves. At the same time, it also makes preaching much more glorious, compelling, and most importantly, life-giving: "And the Word became flesh and lived among us, and we have seen his glory, the glory as of a father's only son, full of grace and truth" (John 1:14).

Raising the Question of God in Preaching

I want to begin with the example of Dietrich Bonhoeffer's *Ethics*, written during the early years of World War II. In this work, completed posthumously by Eberhard Bethge, Bonhoeffer chose to include an important but often overlooked chapter, "On the Possibility of the Church's Message to the World."[11] My interest here is that Bonhoeffer begins with a question concerning God, the church, and preaching that may assist us in understanding better the challenges described by Taylor and offered by "homiletical minimalism" and "excarnation." Bonhoeffer asks of his readers,

> What is behind the desire, which is awakening in Christendom throughout the world, to hear a message from the church that offers solutions? It is essentially the following ideas: the social, economic, and political, etc., problems of the world are out of hand; the ideological and practical solutions of technical progress has thus reached its limit; the car is stuck in the mud, the wheels are turning at top speed but cannot pull the car out: the problems are so universally human, both in their scope and their nature, that some quite fundamental remedy has become necessary; with respect to social, economic, political, sexual,

and educational problems, the church has thus far failed; through its own fault it has given offense, which hinders people from believing its message.[12]

Bonhoeffer viewed this kind of preaching as a failure of the church since it was not sufficient for discerning and addressing the need of "concrete directive in the concrete situation."[13]

There was a popular view in Germany that assumed the church's key to strengthening its influence and increasing its numbers in a world that had outgrown the need for God was to offer solutions for the world's problems, answers for its social and political questions, and advice on how to put its life back in order. Bonhoeffer was convinced the church had much to say to the world about "worldly things." However, he was convinced the church does not have solutions and answers in advance that are waiting to be applied. The gospel exposes the arrogance of this view—Jesus did not solve the problems of the world; Jesus did not answer every question; nor did Jesus implement a program that would make the world a better place. The word of Jesus is the divine answer to the divine question posed to humankind. His word is not an answer or a solution but rather is the Word who brings redemption to unite human beings in the Son with the will of the Father. It is Jesus alone who brings the solution to all human problems—"all these things will be given"—though from a completely different and transcendent vantage point that is made visible in the world.[14]

Bonhoeffer judged preaching that begins with human problems and seeks useful solutions as "unbiblical." The way of Jesus Christ, and thus the way of all Christian thinking, speaking, and living is not the way from the world to God, but is the way from God to the world. "The message of the church can be none other than the word of God to the world. This word is Jesus Christ, and salvation in his name. It is in Jesus Christ that God's relationship to the world is determined. We do not know any other relationship of God to the world apart from Jesus Christ." The church's responsibility to the world, therefore, begins with hearing, believing, and embodying its message. This is the church's witness to the world, as offensive as it may be, that makes room for the gospel in the world.[15] Bonhoeffer summed up the church's message as follows: "The church's message to the world is the word about the coming of God in the flesh, about God's love for the world in the sending of God's Son, about God's judgment on unbelief. The church's message is the call to turn around, to believe in God's love in Christ, to prepare for the second coming of Christ, the kingdom of God. It is thus the word of redemption for all people."[16]

The church, then, does not have a double message, a double ethic, religious and nonreligious ways of living, a sacred and secular division of the world; God's word extends to wherever Christians find themselves. Because God became fully human in Christ, proclamation is both Christian and worldly. Everything created is for the sake of Christ and sustained in Christ (Col 1:15). For this reason, there is no room for Christian triumphalism in preaching. Proclamation requires patience and humility shaped by faith in the One whom it announces: the divine Word taking human form and expression in a shared life of concrete service and responsibility.[17]

For Bonhoeffer, God is determined to speak to the world in person through the human proclamation and life of the church. The church's specific mandate, then, is that "God wants a place at which, until the end of time, God's word is again and again spoken, pronounced, delivered, expounded and spread." The word of preaching is Jesus Christ who came from heaven, and who wants to come again in the form of human speaking and living. Significantly, the church's mandate is the divine Word and not itself, its life and mission, its needs, survival, or self-preservation.[18]

"God is determined to speak in person" is a concise summary of Bonhoeffer's mature homiletical theology. He believed the moment of the Word in preaching is the "advent" of Christ's presence. The sermon is determined by neither the preacher's choice nor the peoples' will, but rather "God's will and mercy descend on human beings from heaven, a word commanded and initiated by Jesus Christ." Only the presence and action of Christ in the Spirit's life can legitimize preaching as "Christian." As Bonhoeffer claims, "On the basis of Holy Scripture the preaching office proclaims Jesus Christ as the Lord and Savior of the world . . . so that any other message is just 'empty chatter.'"[19]

Bonhoeffer spoke from within the Lutheran tradition, which shared the conviction of the church in its history that preaching is a gift that takes place within the speech of the Father through the Son as a gift of the Holy Spirit. Preachers and listeners have believed themselves to be gathered by the Spirit in the presence of God, whose Word spoken in Jesus Christ through the witness of Scripture evokes trust, love, and fruitful obedience. Preaching is therefore situated within the church's central calling of worship as an offering of itself in the Spirit to the Father as an act of praise to Christ who speaks through Scripture, sermons, and the existence of the church, which is his body, for the life of the world.

Preachers as Exemplary Listeners
Conversing with the Word

Since God is the primary speaker and actor in the world, preachers are called to listen before speaking, following the leading of the Spirit to Christ, the living Word who communicates God's life.[20] Because the life of God's people is generated by the conversation of the Son and the Father in the Spirit, the language of preaching is not a human creation. The Holy Spirit awakens us to hear the voice of the living Word so that we ourselves are transformed into the words spoken with the authority and wisdom of Another.[21] Nicholas Lash comments, "Speech that has forgotten that the fundamental form of speech is conversation; forgotten that to be able to converse with others is to have been schooled in a culture of relationships; forgotten that all conversation and all culture are, ultimately, answerable not only to each other but to God—such speech would, in the long run, cease to be speech at all and, with this cessation, its utterers would be less than human."[22]

Many contemporary preaching books assert the primary task of preaching is producing "effective," "relevant," "authentic," and "innovative" communication, shaped by the self-defined needs, expectations, and expressiveness of a consumerist culture that assumes empirically derived knowledge and ways of knowing are comprehensive and complete.[23] However, if preaching has primarily to do with attending to the Word of the Father in the Spirit, its nature and purpose cannot be determined by terms less than those given by the triune God. As one theologian states the matter, "What does God's Word say?" and "What, in this utterance that finds flesh in Jesus, does God announce?" He continues: "Christianity does not provide magical solutions or satisfying explanations; offer us tranquilizers or quick fixes, furnish us with shortcuts past the endless, bewildering, and painful labor of making sense of things, of mending our confused and battered world. God's utterance announces nothing in particular: it announces—life! . . . As performative utterance, what the Word says is what it does. And what it does is bring all things to life, in God."[24]

As a gift of the Spirit and an act of faith, Christian preaching requires a particular kind of listening to the Word that is best understood as prayer. Although preachers are called to the ministry of speaking, they do so as members of a community of listeners who participate in a conversation with the Word initiated, sustained, and made life-giving and fruitful by the Spirit. And while I am sure most preachers would surely agree that listening is integral to the task of preparing to proclaim the Word, I doubt many would affirm their primary task as preachers is prayer, attentive listening to God as an act of trust, love, and openness to receive that which is spoken by God in Christ. And if faith is inseparable from Christ, preaching will be seen as a gift of the Spirit to the church that is taken up as a graced participant in the conversation of the triune God. As Robert Jenson comments: "As the church speaks and hears the gospel, and as the church responds in prayer and confession, the church's life is a great conversation, and this conversation is none other than our anticipatory participation in the converse of the Father and the Son in the Spirit; as the church is enlivened and empowered by this hearing and answer, the inspiration is none other than the Spirit who is the life between the Father and the Son."[25]

Ephraim Radner argues that much of conservative and liberal biblical criticism of the past two centuries has been driven by a lack of memory—the forgetfulness of God's providential activity given in the forms of Scripture by which the life of the church takes narrative shape within a diversity of expressions in time according to God's thinking, seeing, and moving with respect to creation. Within this providential story, the activity of a preacher and listening congregation is seen as more than an isolated event, but it is woven into the very fabric of the Word enfleshed in history for the renewal and re-creation of the world. Christian preaching speaks out of a particular past, present, and future lovingly spoken and upheld by the Word of the Father in the Spirit's gift of life.[26]

As women and men called by the Spirit and the church, we are not free to determine how we think and speak without reference to the church's scriptural memory, which recalls God's speech as the source and end of all that is. In our time, many who call into question the validity of preaching may have little acquaintance with, or interest in, a tradition generated by the initiative of God, which begins with the speaking of creation into being, extends through the calling of Israel and the life shaped by its Scriptures, finds its central focus in the history of the incarnate Word and creation of the church, has been sustained by the Spirit through time to the present, and will continue until the consummation of all things in God's reign. We speak because God has first spoken all things into being through the Word made flesh in Jesus Christ. Rowan Williams's comments on the gift of Christian speech are especially helpful:

> We speak because we are called, invited, and authorized to speak, we speak what we have been given, out of our new 'belonging', and this is a 'dependent' kind of utterance, a responsive speech. But it is not a dictated or determined utterance: revelation addresses not so much to a will called upon to submit as to an imagination called upon to 'open itself'. . . . The integrity of theological utterance [including preaching] . . . does not fall into line with an authoritative communication, but in the reality of its rootedness, its belonging in the new world constituted in the revelatory event or process. . . . God 'speaks' in the response as in the primary utterance: there is a dimension of 'givenness', generative power, and the discovered new world in the work of the imagination opening itself.[27]

Through the ministry of the incarnation, God has provided not so much a program, a set of beliefs or moral rules to follow, but rather the gift of divine Wisdom as a way of life, love reordered according to God's words and actions in the person of Christ as animated and directed by the Spirit.

The person and the work of a preacher is therefore created by, and continuous with, the self-communication of God in the Word who calls, gathers, and builds up the church to be a truthful witness both to and of the gospel in particular times, places, and circumstances. Our vocation as preachers is integral to our identity as human creatures, made and remade in God's image, in that we achieve genuine selfhood precisely as witnesses to Christ, living and speaking the truth about the union of God and humankind. "The Christian God is found in Israel and Jesus. God refuses to be known apart from our life in God, which means to be made part of God's speech lies at the heart of the Christian understanding of God."[28] Faith knows and loves the image of God in the Word made flesh, just as faith contemplates the Son of God in becoming like the One who is loved and adored. Christ, then, is the paradigm of homiletical wisdom. As the Wisdom of God incarnate, he speaks in and through human weakness, ignorance, neediness, suffering, and death. And Christ's gift of the Spirit illumines us to see ourselves and others united with him through the self-giving love of the Father.

Attending to God the Word

Arguably, the greatest need for cultivating homiletical wisdom in our time is the recovery of contemplation, prayerful attentiveness and faithful receptivity to the Word who creates and calls human creatures to participation in the life in God. Attending to God's self-communication in Christ, the transcendent mystery of divine love that draws us to realities beyond ourselves, this seeing unites theology *and* prayer, knowledge *and* love, being *and* doing: "Full knowledge of God, the contemplation of God, comes by shifting the center of moral gravity from oneself to God. One comes to know God by willing to be taught and led by God."[29] Prayer is neither a technique nor a means to other ends; prayer is making our selves available to be taken up by the Spirit into God's own life, as enlightened by the vision of God's grace and glory in the Word made flesh.

God, therefore, is the truthteller who sheds light on human darkness. To turn one's gaze, sight, or vision toward God is to be made alive within from outside oneself, to become a participant in loving conversation with the Word, the source of grace and truth as enabled by the Spirit he gives.[30] As Thompson notes, "However, precisely because Jesus embodies the Father in flesh, word, and deed, the revelation of God always remains hidden; and knowledge of God, mediated through the words and works of Jesus, is always indirect. Because in this world the Son makes the Father known, one may truly 'see' God, but always and only indirectly. It is the role of the Paraclete to enable such continued 'seeing' after the departure of Jesus in such a manner to re-present Jesus among them."[31]

Knowing God through faith in the Word of God's self-communication in Jesus fosters the gift of humility, a capacity to acknowledge that our truest and best speech lies beyond our feeble attempts to make things "work" or come out right. This is a matter of theological integrity; the language of the church becomes empty and even destructive of faith when it is isolated from a lively and converting worship and spirituality that is not afraid of silence and powerlessness. Preachers enjoy both the opportunity and responsibility to recover the mystery and generative power of the living Word through the words of Scripture that may have become familiar, detached from life, and dismissed as boring and dead.[32]

As Christian speech, preaching is congruent with the One of whom and with whom we speak. Preaching will be primarily a receptive activity: responsiveness to the Word as led by the Spirit of the risen Christ who breathes life into texts and contexts, speakers and listeners, assimilating hearts, minds, and bodies into the grace and truth he gives. Only the Holy Spirit can enliven gatherings of listeners into a body of people capable of hearing and being formed by seeing the Word incarnate in Jesus. It is therefore foolish to think that we can make a "preaching event" happen, create "meaningful" experiences for listeners, or "save" the church in a time of declining cultural influence, denominational loyalty, and church attendance.

Preaching, moreover, is an activity of humble confession, the surrender of self-possession and control of ourselves and our words to Christ, the mystery of God's Word spoken within and addressed to our common human life. A true sign of pastoral "effectiveness" is the enactment of the Word through faith, participation in Christ, the mediator who receives his life from God and who gives the faithful a share in that life.[33] Here Julian Hartt's description of the church's calling to be a living embodiment of the gospel, of which preaching serves as a prayerful, obedient, and exemplary witness is apt: "We have a great and desperate need for the gospel. The power of that word is not in utterance but in concrete life. The power of the word is that real, transcendently righteous, and creative love. That alone is the power which can place us in solid and productive relationship to the real world. Hence, while the church has an utterance to make, sermons to preach, hymns to sing, and prayers to offer; above all it has a life to share. This life is God's free sharing of himself in Jesus Christ."[34]

Sermons as Acts of Service to God and Church

The work of theologian Arthur McGill provides a challenge to familiar ways of imagining God and human life in a secular age. Following the wisdom of Scripture and the Creeds, McGill affirms that service, defined as the power of God, is a "shockingly impractical creed."[35] Discussing the character of life as given by Christ, he writes: "Self-expenditure is self-fulfillment. He who loses his life is thereby finding it. Loving is itself life, and not just a means to life. He who expends himself for his neighbor, even to death, truly lives. But he who lives for himself and avoids death truly dies: 'He who does not love remains in death.'"[36] McGill calls attention to the need for congruence between who we are, what we believe, and how we speak, since it is the gospel, spoken and enacted by Jesus Christ, that unites message and messenger. For example, if we aim to expand ourselves and our influence over others by our preaching, rather than expending ourselves in serving the Word in the form of Christ's self-emptying, we are dead. And no matter how popular or successful our method, style, or brand in speaking, our words will lack the truth and reality of God. For this reason, the spirit of Jesus's ministry, which was to serve by communicating himself to others, cannot be understood as a strategy that was chosen to gain mastery and control for his own success or survival.[37]

McGill notes that, for Jesus, self-expending was not a form he put on himself to see how well it would work. It was not a technique he was testing to see how nicely it would help him manage his career or improve his relations with people or God. He did not stand in the carpenter's shop in Nazareth surveying his human possibilities and perhaps consulting the local library until he came to the decision to adopt service as his style. He was solely because of what God is, for he was the presence of God dwelling among humanity. It is God's own love that stands forth in and as Jesus Christ and that informs loving self-expenditure for one another.[38]

In Jesus, the Word made flesh, divine power is vindicated in that it does not dominate, manipulate, or impose itself by force or violence, but instead serves by sharing itself completely. The distinctive mark of God's power that works in the weakness of human beings is service, "the self-giving love which dwells with the poor and not the rich, with the sinful and not the righteous, with the weak and not the strong, with the dying and not those full of life."[39]

McGill shows that while the early church distinguished, it did not divide knowledge of God's works and activity from knowledge of God's nature or inner life: *economia* and *theologia*. Following the logic of the Trinity and incarnation, McGill argues that a God who is absolute, self-enclosed and contained, one who is superior and transcendent, is not the mark of divinity revealed in Jesus; and that to admire and bow down to God because he is immune from all need and dependence is to worship him falsely: "For the true God exists eternally—in one of his modes—as the Son—that is the state of dependence."[40]

Commenting on the Prologue of the Gospel of John, McGill points to the fleshly, contingent nature of Jesus, that the union he shares with God is a loving gift of the Father to the Son whose glory is manifested as knowledge, power, and life. Thus, the being and life of the incarnate Son is nourished and established in God's order of reality, since he comes from the Father and is of the Father. And because he receives union with God at his center, because he constantly receives himself from God as within God's knowledge, life, and power, gratitude is his most fundamental attitude at the core of his existence: "The Father is in me, and I am in the Father."[41]

McGill sees the glory of the Son announced in the Prologue of John's Gospel as the glory Jesus also receives at his death. This is an expansion; a sharing of the glory Jesus receives from the Father to include his disciples. "This is the glory he wins by death. Through his death, he comes to his followers and his followers come to him, extending to them the relationship between himself and God. But this loving relationship is primarily and essentially God's doing. This glory is the gift made by Jesus to his followers by which they are found in union with one another and sharers in Jesus union with the Father."[42] Giving careful attention to the wisdom of Scripture and the fathers, McGill shows that in the place of self-sufficient autonomy, early Christian theologians saw the defining mark of divinity as the totality of self-giving and other-receiving love that proceeds between the Father and the Son. The Father gives all he has to the Son; the Son obeys the Father and offers all he has back to the Father. However, the Father and Son are not divine in terms of the richness of reality they possess and pass within themselves, since their existence is not closed within their own being. Instead, they are divine in terms of the richness of this reality they communicate to and share with the other.[43]

Drawing from the grammar of trinitarian faith, McGill's work helps to illumine our understanding of the nature of divine power and its effects on and within human life and speech. If force is no attribute of God, then God's divinity, as revealed in the humanity of Christ, does not consist in his ability to push things around, to impose the divine will and purpose from the security of detached, self-enclosed remoteness, or to sit in grandeur while the world carries out his demands. Far from being a neutral, impersonal force, distant and external to the world, God manifests his glory in the world through the form of weakness, slavery, humiliation, suffering, and death on a cross.[44]

Far from imposing, God draws near, invites, and embraces creatures in loving communion. Far from demanding service from others for enhancing his influence, God generously gives and expends his life in service to others for their enhancement. God acts toward the world in this way because, in himself, God is a perfect communion of the Spirit uniting the Father and the Son. Divine powerfulness is therefore exercised in self-giving, by how much God nourishes his creatures, and by how he fully communicates and shares his own life, reality, and goodness with them.[45]

McGill calls attention to a significant but much-overlooked theological and moral truth: "We are as the power that rules us."[46] Rather than asking what kind of style we should use, or what methods will be most effective, or how we can make Jesus or the church more innovative and creative, the more fitting question for a preacher to ask might be: *What kind of power, honor, and glory do we worship; and what kind of power, honor, and glory informs and shapes our life and animates our actions and speech?* Seen from this perspective, the conditions of human weakness that render us vulnerable before power that deprives, dispossesses, and impoverishes can easily conspire with violent and thus demonic power that kills by subordinating and subjugating those whose identity is established by others in defining their "needs."[47]

Thus, when preaching is reduced to producing predetermined effects and outcomes, rather than witnessing to the Word through which the Spirit communicates the divine gift of life, the means of its use will dominate rather than serve. Human weakness, deficiency, and need will be seen as flaws to be hidden, denied, or rejected, rather than signs of human dependence within a community that claims the source of its life is the Word who generously shares himself in the Spirit.

The truth of Jesus's words, the Word behind the words, calls us to a shift in the center of gravity in our self-understanding as spoken and embodied by him. The center of our being is not constituted by what we possess, preserve, extend, manage, or control.[48] In Jesus, the Word who fully shares himself and his glory, our being is constituted not by what we do but by what God does. And because of Jesus, the incarnate Son of the Father in whom our being is fully from God, we are free to give ourselves away in love that serves, which, when seen in the light of the cross, communicates the power of life instead of death.

The life and work of a preacher participates in the reality of God's saving action, submitting itself to be worked out in the history of weak and sinful people revealed in the historical contingencies of Israel and Jesus. As Nicholas Lash notes, "In the Fourth Gospel the truth which shall make us free is truth en-fleshed, enacted, made finite and particular, arrested, tried, and crucified; but it is not truth sought elsewhere." The truth that authorizes us to speak and live is received in the appropriation of vulnerability, the form of God's self-giving, the incarnate knowing and loving by which the world is renewed.[49]

Lash challenges dualistic assumptions of modern theology that divide by emphasizing the integral relation of the incarnate Word and the vulnerability of human life and speech. He argues that the capacity for speaking is to be answerable to and responsible for each other and to the mystery of God. Amid abstract, empty God-talk and idle chatter there must be a school of silence or attentiveness, since we are constituted "as 'hearers of the word' in every fiber of our being, turned towards, and attentive to, the voice that makes us and calls us home. . . . It is, after all, Jesus who is confessed to be God's Word made flesh; it is his life, and history, and destiny that speak to us, inviting our response."[50]

The Integrity of Preaching Is the Worship of God

The integrity, fullness, and beauty of preaching are defined and guided by the church's primary vocation of worship—giving glory to God by whom we have been called in our baptism to a lifelong pedagogy of union with Christ in his teaching, ministry, passion, and resurrection. This is a way of following and imitating Christ, through whom we return ourselves and our words to the Word spoken in and as Jesus, whose self-giving is the originating source of all that is. "Just as the Incarnate Word is fully God, yet not the entire fullness of God, and just as one sees the Father in the Son and yet does not see the Father in fullness, so too the life that the Word grants to human beings is fully the life of God, but not yet fullness of that life."[51] The gift of the Spirit schools us in the life of faith as glad recipients of, respondents to, and participants in the Father's creative and re-creative Word made flesh in Jesus Christ. Lash describes the integral relation between the incarnate Word and human authority: "The God whom we confess is a God whose self-expression as a man has convinced us, wooed us, compelled us to answering recognition, love, and trust. . . . [I]f we appeal too exclusively to external authority, then we shall be implicitly appealing to the authority of a God who is simply alien to our human experience, who simply contradicts it and stands over against it. Such a God is not the Father of our Lord Jesus Christ who has breathed his Spirit into our hearts."[52]

The high Christology of John's Gospel directs us to see the image of preacher as an exemplary listener, speaker, and witness to the Word incarnate in Jesus: "It is the nature of preaching to demand embodiment by the preacher, performance, and incarnation, in order that it evoke response, embodiment, and enactment among the hearers." Congregations need to believe their preachers either do or do not believe their own witness to the Word. Truthful embodiment of the gospel by the one who preaches is not without significance for congregational receptivity and responsibility to the reality of Christ and the Spirit speaking and dwelling among them. Scripture, by its very nature and purpose—words that demand concrete enactment and discipleship in following Jesus, God's self-communicative Word—demands a preacher who not only talks to a congregation but also walks with them in the Spirit given by Jesus as a truthful alternative to excarnation.[53]

Such conformation to the shape of God's self-communication is integral and not just optional to speaking and enacting the Word with and for the church in the contingent conditions into which we are called to share and serve. In a manner analogous to Jesus, the message and medium of preaching cannot be separated. Our life and speech are guided to maturity by learning the wisdom of Christ through sharing in the story of his life, death, and resurrection, and thus re-created into "holy performances" of the Word. Without such conformance, which is derivative and participatory of God's prior revelatory speech in Jesus, no amount of moral exhortation, therapeutic advice, or innovation and creativity can substitute for attending to the gift of divine life spoken in the Word becoming flesh, full of grace and truth.

CHAPTER SIXTEEN

The Book of Deeds and the Book of Life

On Being Held Accountable for the State of Our Humanity

Miroslav Volf

IN CHRISTIANITY, AND in monotheisms more broadly, human beings are accountable above all to God. We may be, and in fact almost always are, also accountable to many created entities—to ourselves, to our family, to various institutions, or to our nation. But if we are monotheists, our accountability to God trumps every other accountability. By definition. God is the source of all life and the original instantiation of all value. God is, therefore, also the final arbiter between all value and disvalue. Being able to give a satisfying account before God for whatever it is that we are accountable is, ultimately, the only thing that matters.

In this brief essay, I will explore what Christians can mean when they speak about accountability to God by examining the theology of judgment in the Gospel of John, the most extensive and sophisticated engagement with the theme of divine judgment anywhere in the Christian Bible. But first, I need to frame my theological reading of the Gospel with some general comments on accountability.

On Being Accountable to God

For What Are We Accountable?

For what is it that God holds us accountable? The answer is simple: "To obey God's commandments." We must do what God commands, and God holds us

---

This text was originally prepared as a lecture for the Baylor University conference on "Living Accountably" (October 28, 2021). I wrote it as I was completing a book on "the home of God," which is largely an interpretation of Exodus, John's Gospel, and the last part of Revelation (Miroslav Volf and Ryan McAnnally-Linz, *The Home of God: A Brief Story of Everything* [Grand Rapids: Brazos, 2022]). Writing this book, especially the sections on John's Gospel, I was in intense conversation with my friend since our days as students at Fuller Theological Seminary. These conversations were an essential help in understanding John's Gospel, whose theology of judgment is the centerpiece of the present essay. I have revised it after the conference, and I offer it here to honor my friend and theological conversation partner of almost half a century, a wonderful exegete and a very good theologian. I am grateful to Taylor Craig and Dr. Karin Fransen for editorial comments on and critical reading of an earlier version of this text.

accountable. Now, God's commandments are not mere behavioral rules designed to make cohabitation and collaboration possible, the traffic rules of social life. Even less are they arbitrary orders of some fickle and grumpy Master of the Universe, as I was tempted to think in my teenage years.[1] God's commandments are the key features of the kind of life God created human beings to live, expressed in the imperative mood.

"The whole law," wrote the apostle Paul, referring to God's law, "is summed up in a single commandment, 'You shall love your neighbor as yourself'" (Gal 5:14). That single, summary commandment rests on another commandment that is its ultimate foundation: "You shall love the Lord your God with all your heart, and with all your soul, and with all your mind" (Matt 22:37). Echoing the entire Jewish tradition, Jesus affirmed the commandment to love God to be "the greatest and first" (v. 38). But what does it mean to love God? If God *is* love, as the apostle John writes (1 John 4:16), Augustine brilliantly concluded that we love God "by loving love"[2]—by loving the very love that God is, the kind of loving that God does, and everything that God loves. This brings us back to where we started, to the commandment to love our neighbor as ourselves, in fact, to the duty to love all things God loves.

Love is the kind of life for which God created human beings: (1) to act out of love,[3] (2) to be surrounded and sustained by embodiments of love, and (3) to feel the joy of loving and of being loved.[4] And the life of such love is what God holds humans accountable for—whether that accountability is for us living our lives in such a way to the extent we have control or for helping others live such lives.

Two Books of Account

In the book of Revelation, John the seer expresses the idea of accountability to God using a simple but powerful image: two books of account, the Book of Deeds and the Book of Life. In the course of history, God is recording—both writing down and editing—all deeds, good or evil, in the Book of Deeds and the names in the Book of Life. At the end of history, all must appear before God's judgment seat. God will then open the books and judge people "according to their works, as recorded in the books" (Rev 20:12; cf. 2 Cor 5:10).

The image of the all-seeing God, scrupulously writing down our every deed and, at the end of our lives, as judge, looking into the open book and doling out rewards and (mostly?) punishments—that image has been a source of dread for many conscientious people. "But you, you are to be feared!" writes the psalmist. "Who can stand before you when once your anger is roused?" (Ps 76:7). Frail and fallible as we are, and unable either to hide or justify ourselves, the thought of God erasing us from the Book of Life has driven many into either anguished despair or proud rebellion.

For countless others, however, especially for the weak and downtrodden, the Judge of All the Earth has been the only source of consolation. The same psalmist continues:

From the heavens you uttered judgment;
the earth feared and was still,
when God arose to establish judgment,
to save all the humble of the earth. (Ps 76:8–9)

For a while, the righteous may suffer while the wicked, the oppressors of the righteous, prosper. But God is keeping a record. Vindication is therefore assured (see Isa 65:6a).[5] The idea is not just biblical and ancient. In the aftermath of the Holocaust, philosophers like Max Horkheimer found themselves rebelling not against God, as third-party observers and many first-party participants have done, instead, as objects of cruelty, they rebelled against the horrible idea of an utterly amoral world in which torturers everlastingly triumph over their victims. Consequently, they longed for God who alone can bring about justice to victims of history.[6]

Living Accountably

As we will see shortly, the way God holds humans to account is much more nuanced than the image of God as a conscientious bookkeeper and implacable judge suggests. In its starkness, however, the image helps identify key elements of accountability before God, the first two of which concern God, and the second two, humanity.

The first is *discernment*, which is tied to the Book of Deeds. To make an entry in the book, God must make an assessment about what is going on in human lives. What exactly merits entry into one column or the other, and on what grounds? Discernment is difficult because humans are complicated, so much so that it is best left in God's hands. The second element is *judgment*, which is tied primarily to the Book of Life. What goes into the decision about which names to keep and which to erase, whom to vindicate and whom to condemn?

The effect of God holding humans to account is that *humans have to hold themselves to account*. In some forms of piety, at the end of each day, in a quiet hour, a person would "anticipate" the judgment scene, taking account of the day past analogously to the way God is taking account of that day and will, at the end of history, seek it from each person (cf. Matt 25:30). Humans holding themselves accountable have also two elements, and both aim to ensure that God would write well of them in the books of account. The first element is the *effort to live rightly*, seeking to do good and shun evil, which requires *vigilance* before any act and *self-examination* after.[7] The second element is the *effort to make right what one has done wrongly*, which requires *repentance* and *restitution*. In these two ways, God's judgment at the end of time reaches into every moment of lived life and exerts pressure on every thought and every deed. The idea may be either unbearable or deeply comforting. It depends on how we imagine God and the way God holds us accountable. Is God a stern and hostile judge whose judgment we fear and resent? Or is God love itself, whose judgment we welcome as the path of our liberation, from captivity to sin into fullness?

In the remainder of this text, I will explore how God holds humans accountable. I will leave aside the effect of God's holding us accountable on how we hold ourselves accountable. My concern here is God's judgment, not our self-disciplining and self-purifying "anticipations" of that judgment in daily life. When it comes to accountability, the character of God's judgment—the way God holds us accountable—is the most important question. In one sense, it is also the most difficult one. For we cannot observe God at work in the heavenly chamber of God's recordkeeping. Nor can we access God's books of account, compare what is written with what has transpired in the lives of humans, and then draw inferences about how God's discerning and judging work. Fortunately, we do not have to do any of that. We have a report of God at the work of judging in the ministry of Jesus.

Judgment in John

No other text in the Bible has nearly as comprehensive and as nuanced an account of judgment as does the Gospel of John.[8] Since in John, Jesus is the incarnate Word, "the only begotten God" (1:14, 18),[9] the way Jesus does or does not go about judging is the way God is judging and holding humans accountable.

"I Have Not Come to Judge"

In John's Gospel, at each bookend of his public ministry, Jesus states that he did not come "to judge the world, but to save the world" (3:17; 12:47). As God's love for the world in action, Jesus does not merely identify what is opposite to him and then, in negation of negation, hold that "opposite in its opposition" to himself, as Hegel put it in "The Spirit of Christianity and Its Fate."[10] In fact, Jesus does not leave the opposite in its opposition even when that opposite is highly hostile to him, as is explicitly the case in John's Gospel. An essential part of his mission is to overcome hostility and opposition. His goal is salvation. But even so—rather, just because it is so—*judgment is one of the inevitable consequences of Jesus's coming*. What is the relation, on the one hand, between Jesus's coming to save, and, on the other, his effecting of judgment?

Note that the Jesus who says, "I do not judge anyone who hears my words and does not keep them" (12:47) is, according to John's Gospel, the Word "in whom was life," the source not just of vitality but of life's goodness (1:3). That good and true life, made manifest in Jesus's words, works, death, and resurrection, is the "light of all people" (1:4).[11] "Light" here is not what makes things visible, but "the brightness in which existence itself is illumined."[12] *As the light of the world, Jesus's life is a beam of the creation-preceding, creation-generating, and creation-restoring goodness through which people can come to know the truth of their lives.*[13] In that light, the true life becomes visible *as* true and the false life becomes visible *as* false. This is "judgment" (*krima*) in the most basic sense (9:39): the distinction between light and darkness drawn by God's life simply coming into the world and being manifest in it. Those who encounter him—and in one sense all humans do, since, even apart from incarnation, the Word enlightens everyone (1:4)—come to see their own life in the light of his life. Depending on the form of their life and their investment in continuing in that form of life, they either reject or embrace the kind of life that Jesus manifests.

Rejection of Jesus, which is rejection of his kind of life, results in condemnation. For, as the creator and the original source of life in its vitality and goodness, Jesus is the measure of the truth and falsity of life. As such, he is, as Hegel has put it, not so much the judge as he is "the criterion of judgment."[14] We can also say that, being the incarnate criterion of judgment, he is the judge *who does not judge.* Instead, as he puts it, "On the last day the word that I have spoken will serve as judge" (12:48). The "word" (*logos*) is here distinct from "words" (*rhemata*) that Jesus speaks and stands here for the entirety of his life.[15] The condemnation of those who reject Jesus is a self-condemnation: a decision not to trust in the source of life and not to live in sync with the intended character of their lives.

Complexities of Self-Condemnation

From one angle, as we have just seen, the distinction between the saved and the condemned is the *effect* on people of the coming of the light itself. "I have come into this world for judgment so that those who do not see may see, and those who do see may become blind," says Jesus (9:39). "Those who do not see" are those who, like the blind man whom Jesus healed (9:1–38), are aware of their blindness and therefore willing to receive the gift of sight. "Those who see" are those who *think* that they see but are in fact blind—"you say, 'We see'," Jesus says to them, implying that what they say is false (9:41)—and they therefore remain blind for refusing to receive the gift of sight. The blind who claim to see—who take their blindness to be sight—are accountable for their state and therefore culpable. They "have sin" (9:41).

Since people are held accountable for imagining their own blindness as sight, from another angle, the distinction between the saved and the condemned—between those whose names are in the Book of Life and those whose names are not—goes back to the agency of individuals. Jesus makes the point early in the Gospel when he explains that self-condemnation is tied to a person's basic love or desire. He says, "And this is the judgment, that the light has come into the world, and people loved darkness rather than light because their deeds were evil. For all who do evil hate the light and do not come to the light, so that their deeds may not be exposed. But those who do what is true come to the light, so that it may be clearly seen that their deeds have been done in God" (3:19–21). The decision to "come to the light," too, reflects a person's basic love. And people are accountable for their basic loves (for loving either light or darkness) as they are accountable for their deeds (either good or evil).

Cross-Pressured Lives

Still, the Gospel of John does not leave people's destiny simply in their own hands. What draws people to Jesus and his kind of life is their sensitivity to the Word's prior light that enlightens everyone, and that manifests itself both in individuals' love for true life and in doing "what is true," i.e., what befits the true life (3:20). The one whom Jesus calls the Father in the Gospel is drawing them to Jesus as well (6:44). At the same time, routinized patterns of life—a habit of doing "evil" (3:19–20)—push people away from Jesus as the true life. These patterns are in part the character-sediment of accumulated individual decisions made by satisfying misdirected desires. To a significant degree, however, an environment (a powerful form of "the world") dominated by the "ruler of this world" (12:31) elicits and reinforces love for false life and doing what is false.

According to the Fourth Gospel, each person is caught in a complex field of forces—individuals' wills and proclivities, God's light shining on them and God's lure pulling them, social attractions and pressures, and finally the agency of the mysterious ruler of this world. This complex field of forces goes a long way toward explaining a great diversity of stances to Jesus we find in the Gospel.[16] The decision to come to Jesus, whose life is the light of people's lives, is possible and free. But humans are heavily cross-pressured as they exercise that freedom.

The Judgment of the God Who Loves

Given that judgment is human self-condemnation, it would seem that the last judgment would be merely the ratification of the stances people have taken toward Jesus in the course of their lives. Jesus's statement about the matter seems to confirm the inference: at the end of the age, people will be raised from their graves, "those who have done good, to the resurrection of life, and those who have done evil, to the resurrection of condemnation (*kriseōs*)" (5:29). We get the same impression from the book of Revelation as well. Standing before "a great white throne," the dead are "judged according to their works" (Rev 20:12). The Book of Life, which contains the names of the saved, and the Book of Deeds, which contains the record of good and evil deeds, are aligned in that the Book of Deeds determines the contents of the Book of Life. The final judgment seems to ratify choices already made.

But that cannot be quite right. Both in John's Gospel and in the book of Revelation, God is not a neutral observer and evaluator of human decisions for or against life, an impartial judge. God *loves* human beings, all of them sinful and all heavily cross-pressured. And God loves them with eternal and unalterable love. God is opposed to their perishing. Much of the story of the entire Bible is a history of that divine love for humans and that divine opposition to their perishing. In both John's Gospel and the book of Revelation, Jesus does not simply place before people the choice: either act as you should or you are doomed. Instead, he takes on and defeats the forces that ensnare people and lead them into self-defeating self-condemnation.

The Judgment of This World

While in John's Gospel Jesus does not judge and condemn humans—his life "judges" and they condemn themselves—Jesus judges and condemns *the world and its ruler*. Shortly before his crucifixion, Jesus addresses God, the Father: "Father, glorify your name. . . . Now is the judgment of this world; now the ruler of this world will be driven out. And I, when I am lifted up from the earth, will draw all people to myself" (John 12:28, 31–32). "Now" is the hour toward which Jesus's entire mission was aiming, the hour of his dying as the witness to the truth of human life and as the Lamb who takes away the burden and the stain of sin. It is also the hour of his rising from the dead. Jesus's death and resurrection are the culmination of his entire life as the saving judgment of the world; it is *a cosmic exorcism* in which the ruler of the world—who is in fact the destroyer of the world—is banished and destroyed.

The "world" here is not created reality as such, but its present *self-alienated form*. As God's creation, the world is an object of God's presuppositionless and unconditional love (cf. 3:16). Condemnation of the world is thus the creation's liberation from its illegitimate "ruler" and its alien form, an indispensable aspect of the world's coming to be what I have come to think of as the home of God.[17] The positive obverse of this judgment against the "world" is Jesus's drawing to himself "all people" (as we read in 12:32), and even "all things," as the text reads in some manuscripts, which likely do not preserve the original text but are nonetheless theologically correct.[18] The "hour" of Jesus's death and resurrection is the pivot-point of world history, the eschatological "now" of the passing away of the old world and the creation of the new world taking place in the middle of history. *Everything* that happens unfolds within the household of the world whose fallen form Jesus condemned, which he liberated from its ruler and drew to himself, and whose members he reconciled to God and with one another. That astonishingly bold claim about the world's salvation corresponds to an equally bold claim about creation. From the dawn of creation, the light, which "shines in the darkness" and which "the darkness did not overcome" (1:5), enlightens all people (1:9).

In and through this judgment, which is the salvation of the world, the glory of the God who creates, loves, and desires to dwell in the world shines. No sheep are missing from the shepherd's fold. No names are missing from the Book of Life.

How Accountability Works

Jesus Christ, the judge who condemns and overcomes the world but who does not condemn humans, is the one who keeps records in the books of account throughout history. At the end of history, he is also the one who will sit on the "great white throne" and before whom "the dead, great and small" will stand as the books are opened. With this Johannine theology of judgment in mind, let us return to the problem of accountability.

Freedom and Risk of Accountability to God

To live is to be held to account, judged, and, if we fail to meet expectations, often to be condemned. Family and friends, employers and educators, acquaintances and strangers on social media—they all observe, judge, and impose punishments. Accountability to God unchains us from all earthly bonds and our ultimate accountability to them. In relation to God we, like Abraham, become free from all ties and free in all ties.

The obverse of the radical freedom that accountability to God gives is radical risk. Any moment, God may call us to leave "home or homeland" for some promised future, as God called Abraham. Any moment, we must be ready to take what may be dearest to us and start the frightening journey to Mount Moriah.

The wager of faith is that God, whose very being is love, gives generously rather than takes away. As love, God is the abiding source of all things. As love, God also mediates our relationship to ourselves and to the world.[19] Created to be with God at home in the world, we are truly ourselves and come into our fullness when we correspond to God's own character. *To be accountable to this God is to be held accountable for what we and the world in the deepest sense are.*

The Book of Deeds—The Book of Life

God, we are told, makes entries in the Book of Deeds; each one of our deeds, every word and every thought, they all count. Still, God does not hold us first of all accountable for aligning our deeds with God's moral code (for instance, for telling the truth or honoring everyone) or for accomplishing certain tasks (for instance, selling all we have and giving to the poor or proclaiming the good news) or for having certain emotions (for instance, empathy or joy). All these things matter, though not so much as discrete "things" but as part of the character of our life. Behind all entries into the Book of Deeds is one central question that has in view the new commandment that Jesus gave to his disciples: Do we love as Christ loved?

To be held accountable for living lives whose measure is the God incarnate is to be doomed to condemnation. If having lived as Christ did is the standard we need to pass for our names not to be erased from the Book of Life, God might as well not have written our names in it in the first place. One way to relieve the pressure of the impossible task would be to say that God holds us accountable, not for actually living as Christ did, but for *striving* to do so. The effort, rather than success, would then be what God would be mainly after. But the mere effort would be, in all cases, too little and, in some cases, too much.

Christian faith is most fundamentally neither about mastering the art of Christlike living nor about striving to do so. Instead, it is about Christ coming by the Spirit dwelling in us and living God's kind of life in and through us. When it comes to the Book of Life, *God holds us accountable for letting God bring us into the fullness of our humanity*—for letting God give us eyes that see the light of true life and the new birth, so we can start growing into it. That new life, like the joy that is one of its chief features, is *not strictly the same kind* of life and the *same kind* of joy that Jesus had but is in fact *his* life and *his* joy in us.[20]

God gives everything for what God holds us accountable. Not receiving what God gives is our self-condemnation, a tragic squandering of a life by not letting ourselves be loved and indwelled by God.

In Place of a Conclusion
Moses, God, and the Book of Life

In the Bible, the first time the Book of Life is mentioned is in Exodus. After the incident with the golden calf, Moses intercedes for the people before God and says: "Alas, this people has sinned a great sin; they have made for themselves gods of gold. But now, if you will only forgive their sin—if not, blot me out of the book that you have written" (Exod 32:31–32). We are at a critical moment in Israel's history. The very existence of Israel hangs in the balance. God had liberated them from slavery in Egypt and, at Mount Sinai, made a covenant with them to be their God and they God's people. After the covenant was ratified, Moses went to the mountain of God to receive the tablets of the law. He stayed longer than expected, and people felt abandoned in the wilderness. In fear, they insisted that Aaron make for them gods "who shall go before us" (Exod 32:1). Seeing the calf that Aaron made from the gold they had supplied, they exclaimed: "These are your gods, O Israel, who brought you out of the land of Egypt!" (v. 4).

Israel had broken the covenant, and the agreed upon punishment for apostasy and idolatry was death. God was determined to destroy Israel and told Moses that he, Moses, should be the progenitor of a nation that was to replace Israel. In response, Moses undertook what turns out to be the greatest diplomatic effort of the Bible. Moses first persuaded God to spare Israel by appealing to the unconditional character of God's covenant with Abraham. He then insisted that God fully forgive Israel. In trying to wrest forgiveness from God, he declared to God his willingness to have his name erased from the Book of Life, presumably to share in the destiny of the people. Negotiating with God, Moses chose death with the people over life and glory without them. This act of radical solidarity with the people was rightly one of the most celebrated moments of Moses's life.

For the history of salvation—and for the history of the world, in fact—even more important than Moses's solidarity with the people was the deep conviction that informed it. For that conviction became the key to the way God relates to humanity. Rejecting the offer to become progenitor of the new people of God, *Moses implied that if God decides to reject people who reject God*—if God decides to relate to people by writing or erasing their names from the Book of Life depending on their relation to God—God will in the end be left without people. For the progeny of Moses will likely do no better than the progeny of Jacob, and no better than all the rest of the progeny of Adam. For all humans, though crowned with glory and only a little lower than the angels, are mere flesh, all of them also fragile, all of them fallible, all of them, in fact, fallen.

The story of Israel's apostasy ends with God making the covenant on Mount Sinai into *an unconditional covenant,* as was God's original covenant with Abraham. Appearing to Moses in glory, God, who not long before was determined to destroy Israel in fierce judgment, says to Moses, in a moment of self-revelation:

> The Lord, the Lord,
> a God merciful and gracious,
> slow to anger,
> and abounding in steadfast love and faithfulness,
> keeping steadfast love for the thousandth generation,
> forgiving iniquity and transgression and sin,
> yet by no means clearing the guilty,

> but visiting the iniquity of the parents
> upon the children
> and the children's children,
> to the third and the fourth generation. (34:6–7)

God is the God of justice and truth, and God "by no means clears the guilty." But no iniquity and no transgression can alter God's will for Israel to live and thrive. God's love is unconditional, but Israel is still accountable. Indeed, Israel is accountable just because of God's unconditional love.

God's unconditional love both frames and grounds human accountability. This is the foundational conviction of the book of Exodus and of the Gospel of John. In the Christian Scripture, however, the circle of those whom God loves unconditionally expands to include the whole world and every person in it. It is this God of love to whom human beings are ultimately accountable to live lives worthy of being God's image bearers.

NOTES

MARIANNE MEYE THOMPSON

1. John Calvin, *Institutes of the Christian Religion*, 2 vols. (Louisville: Westminster John Knox, 1960), 1:69–70 (1.6.1; cf. 1.1.1–2).
2. The phrase comes from Karl Barth's draft preface to the first edition of his Romans commentary; it is exegeted in Richard Burnett's insightful study, *Karl Barth's Theological Exegesis: The Hermeneutical Principles of the* Römerbrief *Period* (Grand Rapids: Eerdmans, 2001), 125–220.
3. Marianne Meye Thompson, *John: A Commentary*, NTL (Louisville: Westminster John Knox, 2015), 187–94; see also the broader discussion on pp. 195–204.
4. Thompson, *John*, 196.
5. C. Kavin Rowe, "What If It Were True? Why Study the New Testament," *NTS* 68 (2022): 144–55.
6. Marianne Meye Thompson, *1–3 John*, IVP New Testament Commentary Series (Downers Grove, IL: InterVarsity Press, 1992), 24.
7. George Eldon Ladd, *The New Testament and Criticism* (Grand Rapids: Eerdmans, 1967).
8. Paul J. Achtemeier, Joel B. Green, and Marianne Meye Thompson, *Introducing the New Testament: Its Literature and Theology* (Grand Rapids: Eerdmans, 2001). A second edition is forthcoming from Eerdmans.
9. D. Moody Smith, *John among the Gospels: The Relationship in Twentieth-Century Research* (Minneapolis: Fortress, 1992).
10. See Marianne Meye Thompson, "The Humanity of Jesus in the Gospel of John," (PhD diss., Duke University, 1985); later published as *The Humanity of Jesus in the Fourth Gospel* (Philadelphia: Fortress, 1988; repr. *The Incarnate Word: Perspectives on Jesus in the Fourth Gospel* [Peabody, MA: Hendrickson, 1993]).

CHAPTER ONE

1. The term, used only here in the NT, can denote a member of a royal family or a person in the service of a king, but not necessarily military service. The "king" involved is most probably not the Roman emperor but Herod Antipas who was not officially a "king" though he was called king (cf. Mark 6:14, 22; Matt 14:9; Gos. Pet. 2).
2. Cf., e.g., the famous painting by Veronese (ca. 1571) in the Museo Nacional del Prado in Madrid: http://images.zeno.org/Kunstwerke/I/big/14k0050a.jpg.

3. A significant exception is found in the Bible manuscript Codex Aureus Escorialensis (El Escorial, Real Biblioteca de San Lorenzo, *Cod. Vitrinas* 17) from the eleventh century. .

4. R. Bultmann, *Das Evangelium des Johannes*, 21st ed., KEK 2 (Göttingen: Vandenhoeck & Ruprecht, 1986), 151–52.

5. Cf. M. M. Thompson, *John: A Commentary*, NTL (Louisville: Westminster John Knox, 2015), 112–15.

6. T. Nicklas, "Jesu zweites Zeichen (Joh 4,43–45.46–54): Abgründe einer Glaubensgeschichte," in *Miracles and Imagery in Luke and John, Festschrift Ulrich Busse*, ed. J. Verheyden, G. van Belle, and J. G. van der Watt, BETL 218 (Leuven: Peeters, 2008), 89–104.

7. Nicklas, "Zeichen," 103.

8. Thus, e.g., M. Theobald, *Das Evangelium nach Johannes: Kapitel 1–12*, RNT (Regensburg: Pustet, 2009), 347, who raises the suspicion that the hospitality of the Galileans (v. 45) was selfish and was performed only in hope of seeing miracles in their region.

9. Premodern interpreters reasoned why Jesus was willing to enter the centurion's house but not the royal man's house, or why he could praise the faith of the centurion but rebuke the petitioner here.

10. See F. C. Baur, *Kritische Untersuchungen über die kanonischen Evangelien* (Tübingen: Fues, 1847), 240–41; cf. also H. Windisch, *Johannes und die Synoptiker: Wollte der vierte Evangelist die älteren Evangelien ergänzen oder ersetzen?* UNT 12 (Leipzig: Hinrichs, 1926), 42–54.

11. On the history of the theory, see G. van Belle, *The Signs Source in the Fourth Gospel: Historical Survey and Critical Evaluation of the Semeia Hypothesis*, BETL 116 (Leuven: Peeters, 1994).

12. Thus, e.g., S. Landis, *Das Verhältnis des Johannesevangeliums zu den Synoptikern: Am Beispiel von Mt 8,5–13; Lk 7,1–10, Joh 4,46–54*, BZNW 74 (Berlin: de Gruyter, 1994); or A. Dauer, *Johannes und Lukas: Untersuchungen zu den johanneisch-lukanischen Parallelperikopen Joh 4,46–54/Lk 7,1–10; Joh 12,1–8/Lk 7,36–50, 10,38–42; Joh 20,19–29/Lk 24,36–39*, FB 50 (Würzburg: Echter, 1984). Cf., most recently, Theobald, *Evangelium*, 351–52.

13. Bultmann, *Evangelium*, 152: "V. 48, der in der Geschichte weder motiviert ist noch Konsequenzen für sie hat."

14. Bultmann, *Evangelium*, 152.

15. Bultmann, *Evangelium*, 150: "Höhepunkt."

16. Bultmann, *Evangelium*, 153.

17. Cf. R. T. Fortna, *The Gospel of Signs: A Reconstruction of the Narrative Source Underlying the Fourth Gospel*, SNTSMS 11 (Cambridge: Cambridge University Press, 1970); R. T. Fortna, *The Fourth Gospel and Its Predecessor* (Edinburgh: T&T Clark, 1988).

18. On the problems of Bultmann's image of the evangelist, see J. Frey, *Die johanneische Eschatologie 1: Ihre Probleme im Spiegel der Forschung seit Reimarus*, WUNT 96 (Tübingen: Mohr Siebeck, 1997), 129–50. On the sacraments, see J. Frey, "Die Taufe im Johannesevangelium: Forschungsgeschichtliche Perspektiven," in *Taufe*

und Heil im Johannesevangelium, ed. J. Frey and U. Poplutz, BThS 190 (Göttingen: Vandenhoeck & Ruprecht, 2022), 13–17.

19. Cf. W. Bauer, *Das Johannesevangelium*, 3rd ed., HNT 6 (Tübingen: Mohr Siebeck, 1933), 78: "die wundersüchtigen Juden"; W. Heitmüller, "Das Evangelium des Johannes," in *Die Schriften des Neuen Testaments*, vol. 4 (Göttingen: Vandenhoeck & Ruprecht, 1918), 86: "die wunderlüsternen Juden"; R. Schnackenburg, *Das Johannesevangelium*, vol. 1, 3rd ed., HThKNT 4.1 (Freiburg: Herder, 1972), 498: "Wundersucht" of the Galileans.

20. *In Evangelium secundum Iohannem Commentarius Pars Prior*, ed. H. Feld, Iohannes Calvini Opera Exegetica 11.1 (Geneva: Droz, 1997), 147, lines 3–4 and 16–17.

21. Among the commentaries, see especially F. J. Moloney, *Belief in the Word: Reading John 1–4* (Minneapolis: Fortress, 1993), and X. Léon-Dufour, *Lecture de l'évangile selon Jean*, vol. 1 (Paris: Cerf, 1988).

22. On the parallels, see Thompson, *John*, 114.

23. Cf. R. E. Brown, *The Gospel according to John (i–xii)*, AB 29 (Garden City, NY: Doubleday, 1966), 93; H.-J. Klauck, "Von Kana nach Kana (Joh 2–4): Die erste Missionsreise Jesu," in *Studien zum Korpus der johanneischen Schriften*, ed. H.-J. Klauck, WUNT 439 (Tübingen: Mohr Siebeck, 2020), 3–4.

24. On this double structure, see C. Welck, *Erzählte Zeichen: Die Wundergeschichten des Johannesevangeliums literarisch untersucht: Mit einem Ausblick auf Joh 21*, WUNT 2/69 (Tübingen: Mohr Siebeck, 1994), 141–45. See also J. Frey, "From the Sēmeia Narratives to the Gospel as a Significant Narrative: On 'Genre-Bending' in the Johannine 'Miracle Stories,'" in *Vom Ende zum Anfang: Studien zum Johannesevangelium: Kleine Schriften 4*, ed. R. A. Bühner, WUNT 492 (Tübingen: Mohr Siebeck, 2022), 363–85.

25. See especially the word of Jesus, ὁ υἱός σου ζῇ, in v. 50, which is repeated in indirect speech in v. 51 and then exactly in the father's memory in v. 53.

26. On this structure, see C. H. Giblin, "Suggestion, Negative Response, and Positive Action in St. John's Portrayal of Jesus (John 2,1–11; 4,46–54; 7,2–14)," *NTS* 26 (1979/1980): 197–211; A. Reinhartz, "Great Expectations: A Reader-Oriented Approach to Johannine Christology and Eschatology," *JLT* 3 (1989): 61–76; Frey, *Eschatologie*, 1:327–28; Moloney, *Belief*, 190–91.

27. See the recent research report about this figure in F. Tolmie, "The Characterisation of the Royal Official in the Fourth Gospel," in *Expressions of the Johannine Kerygma in John 2:23–5:18*, ed. R. A. Culpepper and J. Frey, WUNT 423 (Tübingen: Mohr Siebeck, 2019), 219–27. On the characterization of the figure, see C. A. Bennema, *Encountering Jesus: Character Studies in the Gospel of John*, 2nd ed. (Minneapolis: Fortress, 2014), 175–83; P. J. Judge, "The Royal Official: Not so Officious," in *Character Studies in the Fourth Gospel: Narrative Approaches to Seventy Figures in John*, ed. S. A. Hunt, D. F. Tolmie, and R. Zimmermann, WUNT 314 (Tübingen: Mohr Siebeck, 2013), 306–13.

28. Thus Judge, "Official," 308, and Bennema, *Encountering*, 180, in contrast with the "classical" view in R. A. Culpepper, *Anatomy of the Fourth Gospel: A Study in Literary Design* (Philadelphia: Fortress, 1983), 137.

29. Judge, "Official," 312.

30. Unlike Nicodemus in 3:4 or the Samaritan woman in 4:11–12. Cf. P. D. Duke, *Irony in the Fourth Gospel* (Atlanta: Society of Biblical Literature, 1985), 95–96.

31. On *anagnorisis*, see Aristotle, *Poet.* 1452a; on six methods of getting to *anagnorisis* see 1454b–1455a. Cf. T. Y. Lee, *Reading Johannine Dramatic Irony through Ancient Dramatic Devices* (Carlisle: Langham, 2021), 60, 135–36.

32. Cf. also the frequent statement "your faith has saved you" (Mark 5:34; 10:52; Luke 7:50).

33. A similar view is expressed by the sisters Mary and Martha in John 11:21 and 11:32 in their desperate saying, "Lord, if you had been here, my brother would not have died."

34. Thus, Martin Luther, in a sermon from October 16, 1524 (WA 15, 717); see *D. Martin Luthers Evangelien-Auslegung*, ed. E. Mülhaupt, vol. 4 (Göttingen: Vandenhoeck & Ruprecht, 1954), 197: "Der Königische hatte wirklich einen echten Glauben, wenn er aus Galiläa dem Herrn Christus entegenlief. . . . Wenn er nicht geglaubt hätte, Christus könne ihm helfen, . . . dann wäre er sicherlich nicht ihm entgegengegangen."

35. Thus, Martin Luther (see previous footnote): v. 48 "sagt der Herr nur deswegen, daß sein Glaube wachse."

36. Thus, John Chrysostom, *Hom. Jo.* 35.3.

37. Thus Bonaventure, *Comm. in Ioh* on 4:49, see M. S. Kamanzi, *Le second signe de Cana: Étude exégétique et théologique de Jn 4,46–54*, LD (Paris: Cerf, 2020), 60.

38. John Cassian, *Thirteenth Conference: On God's Protection 16,1–2* (SC 54: 176); cf. B. A. Stewart and M. A. Thomas, eds., *John: Interpreted by Early Christian and Medieval Commentators*, ChB (Grand Rapids: Eerdmans, 2018), 146.

39. Thus J. Zumstein, *Das Evangelium nach Johannes*, KEK 2 (Göttingen: Vandenhoeck & Ruprecht, 2016), 202.

40. Thus many English translations, e.g., RSV, NEB, NAB, and NIV. Cf. J. McHugh, *John 1–4: A Critical and Exegetical Commentary*, ICC (London: T&T Clark, 2009), 320: "your son is going to live," which is also too weak.

41. In a sermon from November 6, 1530 (WA 32, 138–39); see *Evangelien-Auslegung*, 203: "Da wird er von neuem geboren."

42. In a sermon from October 29, 1531 (WA 34/2, 355,6–15); see *Evangelien-Auslegung*, 203.

43. Such a technique can be observed elsewhere in the Fourth Gospel. The most striking parallel is the plot of the Lazarus episode. Not only are the figures of Lazarus and of Mary and Martha, who appear in different episodes in Luke, now connected in one family or episode. Even more interestingly, the contents of Luke 16:27–31, that even if Lazarus came back from the dead, they would not believe, is set on stage in John 11:1–12:19. Cf. J. Frey, *Theology and History in the Fourth Gospel: Tradition and Narration* (Waco, TX: Baylor University Press, 2018), 46–47.

44. On the temporal notes in John, see J. Frey, *Die johanneische Eschatologie*, vol. 2, *Das johanneische Zeitverständnis*, WUNT 110 (Tübingen: Mohr Siebeck, 1998), 173–202.

45. The absolute ἐπίστευσεν does not need an object here.

46. On this, see Frey, *Theology and History*, 27–41.

47. See n26 above.

48. See the still valuable discussion in Marianne Meye Thompson, *The Humanity of Jesus in the Fourth Gospel* (Philadelphia: Fortress, 1988).

49. On the hermeneutics of the Johannine passion narrative, see J. Frey, "'Seht, euer König!': Die Johannes-Passion als Sehschule des Glaubens," in *Vom Ende zum Anfang*, 489–509.

50. On the function of the Spirit with regard to the "Spiritual Gospel," see Frey, *Theology and History*, 144–203; J. Frey, "The Gospel of John as a Narrative Memory of Jesus," in *Vom Ende zum Anfang*, 53–76.

51. Cf. Welck, *Erzählte Zeichen*.

52. Sermon from October 5, 1516 (WA 1, 87); see *Evangelien-Auslegung*, 181–83. Subsequent quotes from there (translation mine).

53. Here, the mystical background of the early Luther is still clearly visible.

54. Sermon from November 9, 1522 (WA 10/3, 420–28); see *Evangelien-Auslegung*, 185–91, here 186: "Wenn einer auch nur das geringste Tröpflein oder Fünklein von der Liebe und Gnade hat, so wird er selig. Die Schrift (aber) lehrt, daß man zunehmen muß und fortfahren."

55. *Evangelien-Auslegung*, 187: "Also tut Gott mit allen, die er im Glauben stärkt. So bringt er ihn auf einen anderen und höheren Grad und Stand, daß er stark wird und nun auf eine andere Weise glaubt als zuvor."

CHAPTER TWO

1. See τὸ ἱερόν in John 2:14, 15; 5:14; 7:14, 28; 8:2, 20, 59; 10:23; 11:56; 18:20; ὁ ναός in John 2:19–21.

2. See Johanna Rahner, *"Er aber sprach vom Tempel seines Leibes": Jesus von Nazareth als Ort der Offenbarung Gottes im vierten Evangelium*, BBB 117 (Bodenheim: Philo, 1998); Johannes Frühwald-König, *Tempel und Kult: Ein Beitrag zur Christologie des Johannesevangeliums*, BU 27 (Regensburg: Pustet, 1998); Mary L. Coloe, *God Dwells with Us: Temple Symbolism in the Fourth Gospel* (Collegeville, MN: Liturgical Press, 2001); Alan R. Kerr, *The Temple of Jesus' Body: The Temple Theme in the Gospel of John*, JSNTSup 220 (Sheffield: Sheffield Academic, 2002); Paul M. Hoskins, *Jesus as the Fulfillment of the Temple in the Gospel of John* (Milton Keynes: Paternoster, 2006); Stephen T. Um, *The Theme of Temple Christology in John's Gospel*, LNTS 312 (London: T&T Clark, 2006).

3. Some of the studies mention "temple festivals" and therefore also the Festival of the Dedication (John 10:22); see Coloe, *God Dwells with Us*, 145–61; Kerr, *The Temple of Jesus' Body*, 205–17; none refers to John 10:1 or John 10:36 (see below).

4. See on this relation Marianne Meye Thompson, *The God of the Gospel of John* (Grand Rapids: Eerdmans, 2001); Ruben Zimmermann, "Jesus in the Image of God," in Ruben Zimmermann, *Breaking New Ground in John: Imagery, Parables, Characters, Christ-Poetics, and Ethics in the Fourth Gospel*, ed. Dieter T. Roth, WUNT (Tübingen: Mohr Siebeck, forthcoming).

5. Cf. Elizabeth Struthers Malbon, "Narrative Christology and the Son of Man: What the Markan Jesus Says Instead," *BibInt* 11 (2003): 373–85; C. Kavin Rowe, *Early Narrative Christology: The Lord in the Gospel of Luke* (Grand Rapids:

Eerdmans, 2009); M. Eugene Boring, "Matthew's Narrative Christology: Three Stories," *Int* 64 (2010): 356–67; Jan Rüggemeier, *Poetik der markinischen Christologie: Eine kognitiv-narratologische Exegese*, WUNT 2/458 (Tübingen: Mohr Siebeck, 2017); Ruben Zimmermann, *Christologie der Bilder im Johannesevangelium: Die Christopoetik des vierten Evangeliums unter besonderer Berücksichtigung von Joh 10*, WUNT 171 (Tübingen: Mohr Siebeck, 2004); Ruben Zimmermann, "Der erzählte Erzähler: Zum narrativen Christusbild der Parabeln," in *Das Christusbild in der Gegenwart: Eine Leerstelle auf dem Weg zu neuer Anschaulichkeit? Beobachtungen und Einsichten aus Theologie, Philosophie und Kunst*, ed. Thomas Erne, Malte Dominik Krüger, and Anna Niemeck (Darmstadt: Wissenschaftliche Buchgesellschaft, 2022), 425–36; Ruben Zimmermann, "From a Jewish Man to the Savior of the World: Narrative and Symbols Forming a Step by Step Christology in John 4:1–42," in Zimmermann, *Breaking New Ground in John*, forthcoming.

6. Cf. Zimmermann, *Christologie der Bilder*, 355–70 (some parts of this chapter are presented here in English translation).

7. Cf. Marianne Meye Thompson, *John: A Commentary*, NTL (Louisville: Westminster John Knox, 2015), 220–37.

8. Cf. Zimmermann, *Christologie der Bilder*, 241–50.

9. Cf. Klaus Scholtissek, *In ihm sein und bleiben: Die Sprache der Immanenz in den johanneischen Schriften*, HBS 21 (Freiburg: Herder, 2000), 322–24.

10. (τὰ πρόβατα) τὰ ἐμά (v. 27–v. 14); τῆς φωνῆς μου ἀκού(σ)ουσιν (v. 27–v. 16, cf. v. 3); γινώσκω (v. 27–v. 14).

11. See Zimmermann, *Christologie der Bilder*, 337–39.

12. These texts were read in the three-year cycle of synagogue readings; cf. Aileen Guilding, *The Fourth Gospel and Jewish Worship* (Oxford: Clarendon, 1960), 129–32.

13. So also James C. VanderKam, "John 10 and the Feast of the Dedication," in *Of Scribes and Scrolls: Studies on the Hebrew Bible, Intertestamental Judaism, and Christian Origins, Presented to John Strugnell on the Occasion of His Sixtieth Birthday*, ed. Harold W. Attridge, John J. Collins, and Thomas H. Tobin (Lanham, MD: University Press of America, 1990), 205–6.

14. Cf. Ludger Schenke, "Joh 7–10: Eine dramatische Szene," *ZNW* 80 (1989): 172–92.

15. Cf. also, for example, Acts 3:2, 10: The paralytic "was set daily at the door of the temple, which is called 'Beautiful' so that he might beg alms from those who went into the temple."

16. The "Second Temple" was fundamentally expanded and redesigned according to the construction type of the Kaisareion, beginning around 20 BCE under Herod the Great. This so-called Herodian temple was completed in 63 CE, i.e., only seven years before its final destruction by the Romans. On the Herodian temple, cf. Josephus, *Ant.* 9.237; 15.381–390, 396, 401; *J.W.* 6.281–287. On the archaeological excavations at the Temple Mount, see also Benjamin Mazar, "Die archäologischen Ausgrabungen in der Nähe des Tempelberges," *Ariel* 40 (1976): 59–72, and the various architectural reconstruction attempts of the Herodian temple

complex by Johann Maier, "The Architectural History of the Temple in Jerusalem in the Light of the Temple Scroll," in *Temple Scroll Studies: Papers Presented at the International Symposium on the Temple Scroll (Dec. 1987)*, ed. George J. Brooke (Sheffield: Sheffield Academic, 1989), 23–62; David M. Jacobson, "The Plan of Herod's Temple," *BAIAS* 10 (1990/1991): 36–66; and comprehensively, Jostein Ådna, *Jerusalemer Tempel und Tempelmarkt im 1. Jahrhundert n. Chr.*, ADPV 25 (Wiesbaden: Harrassowitz, 1999), 32–71.

17. Cf. Josephus, *Ant.* 20.9.7 §§220–222: "It was the work of King Solomon, who was the first to build the entire temple" (ἔργον Σολόμωνος τοῦ βασιλέως πρώτου δειμαμένου τὸ σύμπαν ἱερόν); similarly, Josephus, *J.W.* 5.5.1 §185. Ådna has pointed out that the eastern wall, along which the portico ran, could still date to a time before the Second Temple, for without this wall the whole temple plateau would have collapsed, which would have made rebuilding the temple at that time impossible; cf. Ådna, *Jerusalemer Tempel*, 12. The Solomonic portico, if located along the eastern wall, would at least not be identical with the magnificent three-aisled "royal portico" along the southern wall in the Herodian Kaisareion. On the porticoes in different phases of construction but especially in the Herodian temple, cf. Ådna, *Jerusalemer Tempel*, 51–66, 72–90.

18. Acts 3:11: "All the people ran together to them in the so-called hall of Solomon" (ἐπὶ τῇ στοᾷ τῇ καλουμένῃ Σολομῶντος); 5:12: "But many signs and wonders were done among the people by the hands of the apostles, and they were all of one accord in Solomon's portico" (ἅπαντες ἐν τῇ στοᾷ Σολομῶντος).

19. With Schenke, *Johannes*, 179–80.

20. The ἐγκαινία can also be spoken of in the LXX as the dedication of the altar of the tabernacle (Ezra 6:16–17) or of the Jerusalem wall (Neh 12:27). Furthermore, the synonyms ἐγκαινισμός (Num 7:10–11, 84 [altar]; 2 Chr 7:9; Ps 29:1 [temple]; 1 Macc 4:56, 59; 2 Macc 2:9, 19) or ἐγκαίνωσις (Num 7:88) are also used for acts of consecration of the altar or the temple. 1 Sam 11:14 as well as Dan 5:1 speak of a renewal of kingship; verbally (ἐγκαινίζω), an ordinary house may also be consecrated (Deut 20:5) or a spirit renewed (Ps 50:12).

21. Cf. M. D. Herr, "Hanukkah," *EncJud* 7:1282–83; G. Steins, "Tempelweihfest," *NBL* 3:814–15; generally, also Jerry R. Lancaster and R. Larry Overstreet, "Jesus' Celebration of Hanukkah in John 10," *BSac* 152 (1995): 318–23; comprehensively, Dorit Felsch, *Die Feste im Johannesevangelium: Jüdische Tradition und christologische Deutung*, WUNT 2/308 (Tübingen: Mohr Siebeck, 2011), 219–44.

22. According to 2 Macc 10:1–8 it is the 25th Kislev in the year 165 BCE; a decision between both dating options is not possible according to Steins, "Tempelweihfest," 3:814.

23. Cf. G. Baumbach, "Antiochus," *BHH* 1:99–101.

24. Martin Hengel, *Judentum und Hellenismus*, WUNT 10 (Tübingen: Mohr Siebeck, 1973), 537–38. On the other hand, the formerly more frequently held view that Antiochus IV had a statue of Zeus erected, which is based on a presumably unhistorical message of Porphyrios (cf. Jerome, *Expl. Dan.* 8.5 [PL 25, 536]), has to be rejected.

25. On these references, see VanderKam, "John 10," 211–13, as well as Maarten J. J. Menken, "Die jüdischen Feste im Johannesevangelium," in *Israel und seine*

Heilstraditionen im Johannesevangelium: Festgabe für Johannes Beutler SJ zum 70. Geburtstag, ed. Michael Labahn, Klaus Scholtissek, and Angelika Strotmann (Paderborn: Schöningh, 2004), 281–83; Kerr, *Temple of Jesus' Body*, 252–53, lists nine motif parallels in tabular form, which prove the close connection of John 10 to 1 Maccabees.

26. Efforts at self-deification are also evidenced by coins minted during the reign of Antiochus; cf. VanderKam, "John 10," 211–12.

27. 1 Macc 1:41: καὶ ἔγραψεν ὁ βασιλεὺς πάσῃ τῇ βασιλείᾳ αὐτοῦ εἶναι πάντας εἰς λαὸν ἕνα ("and it was written by the king to all his kingdom that all should become one [single] people"); on this, cf. Baumbach, "Antiochus," 1:100–101; further, Coloe, *God Dwells*, 148. Kerr, *Temple of Jesus' Body*, admittedly goes too far when he wants to find the shepherd motif from John 10 in 1 Maccabees: "One flock with Antiochus as shepherd (1 Macc. 1.41–53)" (253).

28. This possible parallel is pointed out by Menken, "Feste," 283.

29. See also 3 Macc 2:9, 16.

30. Raymond E. Brown, *The Gospel according to John*, AB 29 (New York: Doubleday, 1966), 404, 411, and VanderKam, "John 10," 206, have further associated the *terminus technicus* ἁγιάζειν ("sanctify") for Hanukkah with the torah reading for the temple dedication of Num 7 (cf. m. Meg. 3:6). Numbers 7:1 explicitly speaks of the sanctification and anointing of the tabernacle (καὶ ἔχρισεν αὐτὰ καὶ ἡγίασεν αὐτά); Menken, "Feste," 282, even sees a reference to the messiah conflict in John 10:24 through the keyword of "anointing."

31. 1 Macc 4:38: "There they saw the sanctuary (τὸ ἁγίασμα) desolate, the altar profaned, and the gates (τὰς θύρας) burned. In the courts (ἐν ταῖς αὐλαῖς), they saw bushes sprung up as in a thicket, or as on one of the mountains. They saw also the chambers of the priests in ruins" (NRSV).

32. For example, Kerr, *Temple of Jesus' Body*, 253: "The Jews . . . show themselves to be followers of Antiochus because they are ready to *desecrate* the true Temple of God (2.21) by taking up stones, not to build an altar as the Maccabean Jews did, but to stone Jesus (10.31)."

33. The Hebrew word אוּלָם (*'ûlām*) or אֵלָם (*'ēlām*), used in 2 Chr 29:7, denotes the front or forecourt of the temple (1 Kgs 6:3; 1 Chr 28:11; Ezek 40:7–9, etc.), but in the LXX it is usually translated nonspecifically as ναός (temple), so also in 2 Chr 29:7: τὰς θύρας τοῦ ναοῦ.

34. Cf. 2 Chr 29:5: ἐκβάλετε τὴν ἀκαθαρσίαν ἐκ τῶν ἁγίων; further 2 Chr 29:16: καὶ εἰσῆλθον οἱ ἱερεῖς ἔσω εἰς τὸν οἶκον ἁγνίσαι καὶ ἐξέβαλον πᾶσαν τὴν ἀκαθαρσίαν τὴν εὑρεθεῖσαν ἐν τῷ οἴκῳ κυρίου καὶ εἰς τὴν αὐλὴν οἴκου κυρίου καὶ ἐδέξαντο οἱ Λευῖται ἐκβαλεῖν εἰς τὸν χειμάρρουν Κερδων.

35. 2 Chr 29:5: καὶ εἶπεν αὐτοῖς ἀκούσατε οἱ Λευῖται νῦν ἁγνίσθητε καὶ ἁγνίσατε τὸν οἶκον κυρίου θεοῦ τῶν πατέρων ὑμῶν ("and he said to them, 'You, Levites, listen! Sanctify yourselves now and sanctify the house of the Lord God of your fathers'"); 2 Chr 29:17: καὶ ἤρξαντο τῇ ἡμέρᾳ τῇ πρώτῃ νουμηνίᾳ τοῦ μηνὸς τοῦ πρώτου ἁγνίσαι καὶ τῇ ὀγδόῃ τοῦ μηνὸς εἰσῆλθαν εἰς τὸν ναὸν κυρίου καὶ ἥγνισαν οἶκον κυρίου ἐν ἡμέραις ὀκτὼ καὶ τῇ ἡμέρᾳ τῇ ἐκκαιδεκάτῃ τοῦ μηνὸς τοῦ πρώτου ("But with the consecration they began on the first day of the first month, and on the eighth day of the month

they went into the porch of the Lord and consecrated the house of the Lord for eight days, and on the sixteenth day of the first month they completed the work").

36. Thus, also the concluding judgment of VanderKam, "John 10," 213: "In sum, it is evident that the reference to the Dedication in John 10:22 is not merely one of little importance meant only to indicate the passage of time."

37. 2 Chr 24:19–22 reports the stoning of Zechariah in the courtyard of the Lord's house, which parallels John 10. Cf. especially 2 Chr 24:21: καὶ ἐπέθεντο αὐτῷ καὶ ἐλιθοβόλησαν αὐτὸν δι᾽ ἐντολῆς Ιωας τοῦ βασιλέως ἐν αὐλῇ οἴκου κυρίου ("And they made a conspiracy against him and stoned him at the command of King Joash in the court of the house of the Lord").

38. On the court of the tabernacle, see Exod 37:7–18 (38:9–20 MT); on Solomon's temple, see 1 Kgs 6:36; 8:64; on the temple vision, see Ezek 40:16–42:14; 115 of 177 references within the LXX alone are about the temple court. Also, in Rev 11:12, part of the Corpus Johanneum, αὐλή is known as temple forecourt, i.e., court of the gentiles.

39. This is also true in other references, such as Acts 3:2, where θύρα denotes the "beautiful gate" of the temple.

40. Cf. 2 Chr 4:9 (ἐποίσεν … θύρας τῇ αὐλῇ, "he made gates for the outer court"). In the description of the tabernacle, the phrase θύρα τῆς σκηνῆς ("door/entrance of the tent") is encountered several times, while the "gate of the court" (πύλη τῆς αὐλῆς) is spoken of; cf. Exod 38:20; 39:20 (39:40 MT); 37:7–18 (38:9–20 MT); Ezek 40:16, 23, 27; 42:14. Tob 7:1 and 11:10 speak of the door to the outer court (θύρα τῆς αὐλῆς) of a private house.

41. A direct connection of κλέπτης and ἀναβαίνω is only given in Joel 2:9. However, even here it only speaks of "going in" and then of the "coming of the thieves": "They raid the city, run on the wall, climb into the houses (ἐπὶ τὰς οἰκίας ἀναβήσονται); they enter like the thief (εἰσελεύσονται ὡς κλέπται) through the windows."

42. Thus, for example, John 7:10 (Jesus's brothers); 11:55 (Jews); 12:20 (Greeks); even for Jesus (2:13; 5:1). Cf. also Frühwald-König, *Tempel und Kult*, 71–72; Charles Kingsley Barrett, *Das Evangelium nach Johannes*, trans. Hans Bald, KEK Sonderband (Göttingen: Vandenhoeck & Ruprecht, 1990), 219: "Cultic character is gained in connection with Jerusalem by the verb ἀναβαίνω insofar as it becomes the *terminus technicus* for the pilgrimage to the capital city."

43. For example, Walter Bauer and Barbara Aland, *Griechisch-deutsches Wörterbuch zu den Schriften des Neuen Testaments und der übrigen urchristlichen Literatur*, 6th ed. (Berlin: de Gruyter, 1988), 746.

44. Bauer and Aland, *Wörterbuch*, 746.

45. Cf. Otto Proksch, "ἅγιος κτλ.," *TWNT* 1:87–90, 101–16, 112–13; Horst Balz, "ἅγιος κτλ.," *EWNT* 1:38–48, 43–44.

46. See also Felsch, *Die Feste im Johannesevangelium*, 227–32.

47. Think here of key terms such as γινώσκειν, οἶδα, ζωή, ἀγάπη, ἔργα, or of striking verbs such as σκορπίζειν, which, besides John 10:12, occurs in 11:52; 16:32.

48. Frühwald-König, *Tempel und Kult*, 220.

49. There are two scholarly positions regarding the interpretation of Jesus's appearance in the forecourt of the temple: (1) It was a *political action* that was downplayed

by the evangelist but was actually the occasion for Jesus's execution; (2) It was a *prophetic symbolic action*. Ulrich Luz, *Das Evangelium nach Matthäus, Teilband 3, Mt 18,1–25,46*, EKK 1/3 (Neukirchen-Vluyn: Neukirchener Verlag, 1997), 184–96. Jostein Ådna, *Jesu Stellung zum Tempel: Die Tempelaktion und das Tempelwort als Ausdruck seiner messianischen Sendung*, WUNT 2/119 (Tübingen: Mohr Siebeck, 2000), 334–431, differentiates the various interpretive options into a (1) non-eschatological interpretation (335–52), (2) eschatological interpretation (353–75), and (3) messianic interpretation (376–91), himself taking the last position and interpreting "Jesus' temple action as a messianic symbolic act" (387), which points "to the replacement of the atonement cult by Jesus' atoning death" (424–35).

50. For a detailed analysis of the pericope in all forms of transmission, cf. Ådna, *Jesu Stellung*, 157–299. For a comparison between the synoptic accounts and the Johannine account, cf. Ådna, *Jesu Stellung*, 179–89. Ådna comes to the conclusion that none of the synoptic versions "served as a literary source for the Johannine version of the temple action" (*Jesu Stellung*, 189); also Frühwald-König, *Tempel und Kult*, 77–80. On the Johannine version, see Thompson, *John*, 68–75.

51. See Sandra Hübenthal, "Wie kommen Schafe und Rinder in den Tempel? Die Tempelaktion (Joh 2,13–22) in kanonisch-intertextueller Lektüre," *Intertextualität* (2007): 69–81.

52. According to Ådna, *Jerusalemer Tempel*, 123–25, there is not a single ancient record, other than John 2:14–15, that suggests a sale of large cattle in the temple precinct.

53. Frühwald-König, *Tempel und Kult*, 85.

54. A *TLG* search yielded only one record that mentions ἐκβάλλειν in connection with leading sheep: Aristotle, *Hist. an.*, 604a: ἐκβάλλουσιν ὥσπερ καὶ τὰ πρόβατα· ("they drive [them] out as well as the sheep"); in Alexander Aphrodisiensis, however, ἐκβάλλειν does not mark the driving of sheep but the changing of teeth (the object is not πρόβατα but τοῦς ὀδόντας), cf. Alex. Aphr., *Probl.* IV, 142.4: διὰ τί τὰ μὲν ἄλλα τετράποδα οἷον ἵπποι καὶ τὰ ὑποζύγια ἐκβάλλουσι τοὺς ὀδόντας καὶ κύων περὶ ἑπτάμηνον καὶ αἶγες καὶ πρόβατα καὶ ἄνθρωποι, ὗς δὲ οὐκ ἐκβάλλει; ("Why do the other quadrupeds like horses and draft animals and a dog drop out their teeth around the seventh month, also goats and sheep and humans, but a pig does not drop [them] out?").

55. On the Jesus-Lamb metaphor in the horizon of Jesus's death, see Ruben Zimmermann, "Lamb of God in John 1:29 and 1:36: Metaphorical Christology," in *Breaking New Ground in John*, forthcoming.

56. Possibly the exodus of the sheep from the gate of the court also corresponds to Jesus's exodus from the city of Jerusalem, because a gate of the city wall was known as the "sheep gate" (ἡ πύλη ἡ προβατική, cf. Neh 3:1, 32; 12:39). That John is familiar with this linguistic arrangement is evident from John 5:2, where the "sheep gate" is even spoken of in abbreviated form as ἡ προβατικός. This consideration gains plausibility when one considers that this sheep gate—like the associated porticoes—was explicitly known as the work of the high priest according to Jewish tradition (Neh 3:1) and thus was directly related to the temple. Within the Gospel

of John, the porticoes of the Pool of Bethesda (5:2) could represent an inclusion with the portico of the temple (10:23), as, e.g., Mark W. G. Stibbe, *John*, Readings: A New Biblical Commentary (Sheffield: Sheffield Academic, 1993), 117, assumes, and which Coloe, *God Dwells*, 145, takes up.

57. Cf. Ådna, *Jesu Stellung*, 25–153.

58. Thus, for example, Ådna, *Jesu Stellung*, 128, 151 (according to historical analysis). For Luz, Matthew already "no longer calls his version of Jesus' temple word a false testimony," but it stands in the context of Jesus's show of power (cf. Matt 12:6; 26:53). On this, see Ulrich Luz, *Das Evangelium nach Matthäus, Teilband 4, Mt 26–28*, EKK 1/4 (Zürich: Neukirchener Verlag, 2002), 175–76. In the announcement of the fall of the temple in Mark 13:2 par., Jesus is not named as the agent of destruction.

59. Thus, e.g., 4Q174 I, 1–5; MekhY Shirata X, as well as (without direct citation of Exod 15:17) 1 En. 90:29; 91:13; Jub. 1:17, 29; Tob 14:5. Cf. with many textual examples in Ådna, *Jesu Stellung*, 91–110.

60. Ådna, *Jesu Stellung*, 145.

61. Thus Ådna, *Jesu Stellung*, 151, as before Anna Maria Schwemer, "Irdischer und himmlischer König: Beobachtungen zur sogenannten David-Apokalypse in Hekhalot Rabbati §§122–126," in *Königsherrschaft Gottes und himmlischer Kult im Judentum, Urchristentum und in der hellenistischen Welt*, ed. Martin Hengel and Anna Maria Schwemer, WUNT 55 (Tübingen: Mohr Siebeck, 1991), 356: "The earthly temple was built by human hands, the eschatological one will be built by God's hands, and then the reign of God will dawn."

62. Cf. Johanna Rahner, "Mißverstehen, um zu verstehen: Zur Funktion der Mißverständnisse im JohEv," *BZ* 43 (1999): 212–19.

63. Since the rebuilding of the Herodian temple was not completed until 63 CE, but with a beginning of construction in 20 or 19 BCE that lasted forty-six years (i.e., completed ca. 27/28 CE), it can be assumed that John mistakenly assumed from the flashback that the construction had already been completed during Jesus's lifetime; so also Barrett, *Evangelium nach Johannes*, 222.

64. So also, Josef Blank, *Das Evangelium nach Johannes I–III*, GSLNT 4 (Düsseldorf: Patmos, 1979), 212: "Jesus in his person is the 'new temple,' the place of God's presence." Franz Mussner, "Jesus und 'das Haus des Vaters': Jesus als Tempel," in *Freude am Gottesdienst: Aspekte ursprünglicher Liturgie: Festschrift für Weihbischof Dr. Josef G. Plöger zum 60. Geburtstag*, ed. Josef Schreiner (Stuttgart: Katholisches Bibelwerk, 1983), 267–75; Ulrich Busse, "Die Tempelmetaphorik als ein Beispiel von implizitem Rekurs auf die biblische Tradition im Johannesevangelium," in *The Scriptures in the Gospels*, ed. Christopher M. Tuckett (Leuven: Peeters, 1996), 395; Felsch, *Die Feste im Johannesevangelium*, 227–32.

65. Busse, for whom the temple metaphor represents the "theological center" of Johannine imagery, reckons with allusions to the temple in John 1:14b, 19–23, 29, 36 (with 19:14, 36), 51; 2:13–22; 4:4–44; 6:45; 7:15, 37–39; 11:47–49; 14:2–3; 15:1–8; 16:33; 19:31–37; cf. Ulrich Busse, *Das Johannesevangelium: Bildlichkeit, Diskurs und Ritual: Mit einer Bibliographie über den Zeitraum 1986–1998*, BETL 162 (Leuven: Leuven University Press, 2002), 314–61. On the temple motif, see

the comprehensive work in Coloe, *God Dwells*, and Kerr, *Temple of Jesus' Body*, who, going beyond Busse, also assumes temple references in John 17.

66. Scholtissek, *In ihm sein*, 164.

67. Thus Frühwald-König, *Tempel und Kult*, 221 (more detailed on the atonement function, 166–67; on the source location, 200).

68. Jesus claims to be the true content and fulfillment of the Jewish feasts: on the Sabbath, see John 5:1–47; on the Passover, see 6:1–71; 19:14; on the Feast of Tabernacles, see 7:1–10, 21; on Hanukkah, see 10:22–42. Cf. also Francis J. Moloney, *Signs and Shadows: Reading John 5–12* (Minneapolis: Fortress, 1996), ix: "It suggests that John 5–10 presents *Jesus as the perfection of Jewish liturgy and theology*, and that John 11–12 points to a 'lifting up' that attracts all nations" (italics mine); also Frühwald-König, *Tempel und Kult*, 225: "Individual festival customs and rites of the Feast of Tabernacles and the Passover are transferred to Jesus and receive a new meaning in him." Most recently, Menken, "Feste," 285, differently speaks of a "typological fulfillment (that) remains mostly implicit in the text.... In this way, the salvation mediated in the feasts is surpassed by the Johannine Jesus." However, Frühwald-König, *Tempel und Kult*, 225 n1090, is rather skeptical with regard to a transfer of the Feast of the Dedication of the temple to Jesus. Similarly critical is Gale A. Yee, *Jewish Feasts and the Gospel of John* (Wilmington, DE: Glazier, 1989), 88.

69. Thus, first Brown, *Gospel according to John*, 401; then clearly Kerr, *Temple of Jesus' Body*, 253: "The reader knows that Jesus is the true Temple (2.21), and John wants him/her to see that the Festival of Dedication finds its fulfillment in the *consecration of* Jesus by the Father (10.36)."

70. Frühwald-König, *Tempel und Kult*, 89, for whom the "supposedly cult-critical statement is only a vehicle"; similarly, Jürgen Becker, *Das Evangelium nach Johannes*, 3rd ed., ÖTK 4/1 (Gütersloh: Mohn, 1991), 148–49. The differentiation between an implicitly cult-critical and explicitly cult-critical dimension of the temple metaphor, however, does not seem to me to be as clearly possible as Frühwald-König thinks.

71. Cf. Frühwald-König, *Tempel und Kult*, passim. This guideline is elaborated in many places of the monograph, including in the introduction: "Jesus' rejection of cult or temple [cannot] be spoken of sweepingly" (14); on 2:13–22 (89), on 5:1–18 (167: it is "again not about an abolition of the temple"). In summary he speaks of a "Christologization of cultic places" (221–24).

72. Frühwald-König, *Tempel und Kult*, 221, as well as on the following.

73. Frühwald-König, *Tempel und Kult*, 221.

74. A subtle reminiscence of the scene in John 1:36 is possibly already given with the rare term περιπατεῖν in 10:23.

75. See Ruben Zimmermann, "Lamb of God in John 1:29 and 1:36: Metaphorical Christology," in Zimmermann, *Breaking New Ground in John*, forthcoming.

76. 2 Sam 5:8: διὰ τοῦτο ἐροῦσιν τυφλοὶ καὶ χωλοὶ οὐκ εἰσελεύσονται εἰς οἶκον κυρίου. ("Therefore, they will say, 'the blind and the lame will not enter the house of the Lord'"); in the MT the proverb speaks unspecifically of the "house," which in context means David's mountain stronghold of Zion. Cf. further 11Q19 XLV,

12–13: "All blind people (13) must not come to it (i.e., city of the sanctuary) all their days, and shall not defile the city, since I dwell (14) in it, for I, YHWH, dwell in the midst of the sons of Israel forever and ever."

77. How much this aspect is evoked in the cleansing of the temple becomes clear in the version in Matthew, according to which the blind men demonstratively come to Jesus in the temple after the expulsion of the merchants in order to be healed; cf. Matt 21:14–16 and the comments by Luz, *Evangelium nach Matthäus*, 3:88–89.

78. A stone barrier, the *soreg*, separated the outer court of the gentiles from the inner courts accessible only to Jews. On the barrier were inscriptions forbidding gentiles to enter the inner temple precinct under penalty of death; cf. Josephus, *J.W.* 5.194; 6.124–126; *Ant.* 15.417; on archaeological finds concerning this wall, cf. Ådna, *Jerusalemer Tempel*, 30–31.

79. The reference made in John 1:51 to the Bethel narrative (Gen 28:10–22) is significant in our context insofar as Gen 28:17 is the only OT passage (besides Ps 78:23) that explicitly speaks of the "gate to heaven" (ἡ πύλη τοῦ οὐρανοῦ). On John 1:51 in the horizon of early Jewish Jacob traditions, cf. Michèle Morgen, "La promesse de Jésus à Nathanaël (John 1,51) éclairée par la hagaddah de Jacob-Israël," *RevScRel* 67 (1993): 3–21. In Tertullian, *Marc.* 3.24.9–10, a synthesis between Gen 28:10–22 and John 10:7–10 is probably accomplished.

80. With Kerr, *Temple of Jesus' Body*, 253, 255: "I believe the consecration of Jesus described in John 10.36 echoes the consecration of the Temple courts celebrated in the Feast of Dedication. . . . Jesus is here presented as the fulfillment and replacement of this Jewish festival." Cf. also VanderKam, "John 10," 213–14.

CHAPTER THREE

1. "Ma la frase ha un senso molto piú profondo, che, come sempre, nei modi simbolici, è quello letterale" (Carlo Levi, *Cristo si è fermato a Eboli* [Torino: Einaudi, 1945], 1). Levi continues, "Christ never came this far, . . . just as the Romans never came, content to garrison the highways without penetrating the mountains and forests, nor the Greeks, who flourished beside the Gulf of Taranto. . . . No one has come to this land except as an enemy, a conqueror, or a visitor devoid of understanding. . . . But to this shadowy land, that knows neither sin nor redemption from sin, where evil is not moral but is only the pain residing forever in earthly things, Christ did not come. Christ stopped at Eboli" (Carlo Levi, *Christ Stopped at Eboli: The Story of a Year*, trans. F. Frenaye [New York: Farrar, Straus & Giroux, 2006], 4).

2. The NT scholar Paula Fredriksen once listed it among her "five best books on sin." While reflecting on Levi's service as "a kind of cross-class penance," she did not note the irony of his self-portrayal in a quasi-sacrificial, redemptive humanist agency. See Fredriksen, "The Best Books on Sin," July 23, 2012, https://fivebooks. com/best-books/paula-fredriksen-on-sin/.

3. John 11:54 NIV.

4. Modern English translations prefer "town," while NIV even alters πόλις to "village." As we will see, John's nomenclature is likely correct.

5. Cf. John 6:15, 22–25; 7:1–14; 8:59; 10:39–40. The theme of a messiah in secret is attested by many other texts, starting arguably with 1:10–11, 26, 31–33; 2:24; 3:2.

6. Paul Katz argues that, everywhere else, John links Jesus's identified locations with named or known individuals, and that here too Jesus is therefore likely hosted by friends ("Wieso gerade nach Efrajim? (Erwägungen zu Jh 11,54)," *ZNW* 88 [1997]: 130–34).

7. Punctuated only by the visit to Bethany to raise Lazarus, the three or four months between Jesus's December pilgrimage to the temple for Hanukkah (10:22) and his arrival at Bethany six days before Passover (12:1; late March or April, if not specifically just before April 3, 33) are marked by extended stays (ἔμεινεν), first near the Jordan (10:40; Aenon?) and then at Ephraim (11:54).

8. For the denial, see most famously Percival Gardner-Smith, *Saint John and the Synoptic Gospels* (Cambridge: Cambridge University Press, 1938); for the affirmation of "certainty" about dependence, see, e.g., Troels Engberg-Pedersen, "The Messianic Secret in the Fourth Gospel: On the Fundamental Importance of Mark for John's Rewriting of the Story of Jesus," in *Rewriting and Reception in and of the Bible*, ed. Jesper Høgenhaven, Jesper Tang Nielsen, and Heike Omerzu, WUNT 396 (Tübingen: Mohr Siebeck, 2018), 109 and passim; Eve-Marie Becker, Helen K. Bond, and Catrin H. Williams, eds., *John's Transformation of Mark* (London: T&T Clark, 2021).

9. Mark 1:23–25, 34; 3:11–12; 5:7; cf. 9:20.

10. Mark 1:43–45; 5:43; 7:36; 8:26.

11. E.g., Mark 8:30; 9:9.

12. E.g., Mark 4:10–13, 40–41; 6:51–52; 7:18; 8:17–21, 33; 9:5–12, 19, 32; 10:24–33; 13:3–4, 21, 35–37; 14:41; and possibly 16:6, 8.

13. William Wrede, *Das Messiasgeheimnis in den Evangelien* (Göttingen: Vandenhoeck & Ruprecht, 1901); ET: William Wrede, *The Messianic Secret*, trans. J. C. G. Greig (Cambridge: James Clarke, 1971).

14. So, e.g., Hans Rollmann and Werner Zager, "Unveröffentlichte Briefe William Wredes zur Problematisierung des messianischen Selbstverständnisses Jesu," *JHMTh* 8 (2001): 277.

15. William Baird, *From Jonathan Edwards to Rudolf Bultmann,* vol. 2 of *History of New Testament Research* (Minneapolis: Fortress, 2003), 148–20. Cf., e.g., James D. G. Dunn, *Jesus Remembered*, vol. 1 of *Christianity in the Making* (Grand Rapids: Eerdmans, 2003), 625; Walter Schmithals, "Das Messiasgeheimnis und die Spruchquelle," *HvTSt* 64 (2008): 355.

16. Wrede, *Messiasgeheimnis*, vi.

17. In Rollmann and Zager, "Briefe," 317: "Ich bin geneigter als früher zu glauben, daß Jesus selbst sich als zum Messias ausersehen betrachtet hat."

18. Jesus made no claim to divine sonship and to assert otherwise is to add to his gospel: "Der Satz: 'Ich bin der Sohn Gottes', ist von Jesus selbst nicht in sein Evangelium eingerückt worden, und wer ihn als einen Satz neben anderen dort einstellt, fügt dem Evangelium etwas hinzu" (Adolf von Harnack, *Das Wesen des Christentums: Sechzehn Vorlesungen*, 5th ed. [Leipzig: Hinrichs, 1901], 92; cf. 91).

19. "Daß Jesus 'Sohn Gottes' in dem von Ihnen angedeuteten spezifischen Sinne gewesen sie [*sic*: read sei], bezweifle ich allerdings meinerseits. . . . kann ich [Paulus] nicht als Interpreten und Fortsetzer Jesu in dem Sinne anerkennen, wie man diese Prädikate sonst in der Geschichte zu gebrauchen pflegt" (Wrede in Rollmann and Zager, "Briefe," 317).

20. Wrede, *Messiasgeheimnis*, 145.

21. Wrede, *Messiasgeheimnis*, 179–206, especially 181–83.

22. Engberg-Pedersen, "Secret," following an unreconstructed account of Wrede.

23. Patrick Chatelion Counet, "Het messiasgeheim in Johannes: Analyse van het impliciete gebod tot zwijgen," *TvT* 41 (2001): e.g., 279 (citing in support John Ashton, *Understanding the Fourth Gospel* [Oxford: Clarendon, 1991], 459; Wayne A. Meeks, "The Man from Heaven in Johannine Sectarianism," *JBL* 91 [1972]: 46): "Dit 'medium' bestaat uit zowel het leven van Jezus, het paradigma van zijn gedrag, als uit *het Johannesevangelie zelf*. . . . 'Ho logos ho sos aletheia estin' (17, 17): *Uw boek* is waarheid" (ital. mine).

24. ἁρπάζειν αὐτὸν ἵνα ποιήσωσιν βασιλέα . . . ἀνεχώρησεν πάλιν εἰς τὸ ὄρος αὐτὸς μόνος.

25. The misgivings of NA²⁸ notwithstanding, ὡς is far better supported across the full range of manuscripts. Its secondary omission in ℵ D 1424 and a handful of versions could express scribal intent (e.g., to prevent any impression of Jesus merely pretending secrecy) at least as plausibly as its insertion supposedly "to soften the force of the expression ἐν κρυπτῷ" (Bruce M. Metzger, *A Textual Commentary on the Greek New Testament*, 2nd ed. [New York: American Bible Society, 1994], 185).

26. John 12:37–41, quoting Isa 6:10; cf. Mark 4:12; Matt 13:13, 15.

27. Arguably more "neutral" queries might include 1:45–46; 4:25–26, 29; 7:26–27, 31, 41; 10:24–25; 12:34.

28. This debated suggestion ostensibly rides on the supposed substitution of Thaddeus for "Judas son of James" in the Lukan list of the Twelve (Luke 6:16 and Acts 1:13; cf. Matt 10:3 // Mark 3:18). New Testament scholars continue to contradict each other on this point with merry abandon but with little evidence, some declaring it "likely" (Thomas D. Lea and David Alan Black, *The New Testament: Its Background and Message*, 2nd ed. [Nashville: Broadman & Holman, 2003], 197) or "probable" (Grant Osborne, "The Gospel of John," in *Cornerstone Biblical Commentary*, ed. Philip W. Comfort, 20 vols. [Carol Stream, IL: Tyndale House, 2007], 13:216) without further ado. John P. Meier, meanwhile, finds "no basis in reality" (*A Marginal Jew: Rethinking the Historical Jesus*, 5 vols. [New York: Doubleday, 1991–2016], 3:200), substituting for this conflation a new one with its basis in the imagination: a Jude might theoretically have left the Twelve and been replaced by a Thaddeus during the pre-Easter ministry (Meier, *Marginal Jew*, 3:198 and n1). Judas-not-Iscariot's identification with Thaddeus dates back at least to the third-century Abgar Legend and associated texts, reflected in apocryphal Acts (e.g., Thaddeus; Simon and Jude) and traditions from Edessa and later from Armenia.

29. Marianne Meye Thompson, *John: A Commentary*, NTL (Louisville: Westminster John Knox, 2015), 168.

30. Thompson, *John*, 369.

31. Epicurus, frag. 551.

32. Morna D. Hooker, "The Johannine Prologue and the Messianic Secret," *NTS* 21 (1974): 50.

33. So also Engberg-Pedersen, "Secret," 119.

34. E.g., Engberg-Pedersen, who sharpens this point: "In John, the Markan motif of the Messianic secret became the motif of the hiddenness of the only Son of God.... Mark has *invented* and developed this motif. . . ." The idea that it might in some form be traditional, let alone historically realistic, is dismissed as "quite empty" and patently untrue because of the apathy with which it is treated by Matthew and Luke (Engberg-Pedersen, "Secret," 121 [italics mine]; cf. 115; contrast Wrede, *Messiasgeheimnis*, 145, for the fierce denial, even in 1901, that Mark had invented the Messianic Secret).

35. Elements of "messianic secrecy" in eighteenth-century Hasidic groups are analyzed by Mor Altshuler, *The Messianic Secret of Hasidism*, BSJS 39 (Leiden: Brill, 2006). Hiddenness and secrecy about the messiah's identity are indeed par for the course and continue to the present day. One might compare the controversies around R. Yitzhak Kaduri's (1898–2006) widely reported sealed note about the name of the messiah (e.g., Yosef, "הפתק של הרב כדורי—המשיח: יהושוע" *News1*, January 23, 2007, http://www.news1.co.il/Archive/001-D-121332-00.html).

36. That Bethel and Ephraim were neighboring towns is also the view of Epiphanius, *Pan.* 30.9.4 (GCS 1:344), who recounts his journey with a Jewish Jesus-believer "in the wilderness of Bethel and Ephraim" (ἐν τῇ ἐρήμῳ τῆς Βαιθὴλ καὶ Ἐφραΐμ) on his way up from Jericho to the Judean hills.

37. 1 Macc 11:34; Josephus, *Ant.* 13.127.

38. ἀφαίρεμα denotes a separation, tribute, or reserved portion. Jonathan A. Goldstein, *I Maccabees: A New Translation, with Introduction and Commentary*, AB 41 (New Haven: Yale University Press, 2008), 432, suggests a deliberate play on words.

39. Eusebius *Onomasticon*: καὶ νῦν ἐστι κώμη Αἰφραίμ τῆς Βηθὴλ ἀπὸ σημείων εʹ πρὸς ἀνατολάς (28.4); καὶ ἔστι νῦν κώμη Ἐφραΐμ μεγίστη περὶ τὰ βόρεια Αἰλίας ὡς ἀπὸ σημείων κʹ (86.1); Ἐφραΐμ ἐγγὺς τῆς ἐρήμου, ἔνθα ἦλθεν ὁ Χριστὸς μετὰ τῶν μαθητῶν. κεῖται καὶ ἀνωτέρω Ἐφρών (90.18; GCS 11.1: 90). For the proximity of (this) Ephron to Bethel see also 2 Chr 13:19.

40. Epiphanius, *On Weights and Measures* 67 (MS Brit. Mus. Or. Add. 17148, 74a–b; James E. Dean, ed., *Epiphanius' Treatise on Weights and Measures: The Syriac Version* [Chicago: University of Chicago Press, 1935], Syriac 114, English 72–73); cf. *Panarion* 29.2.5. As noted above (n36), he makes one additional reference to "the wilderness of Bethel and Ephraim" in passing at *Panarion* 30.9.4.

41. "Ephron or Ephraim: the Lord went there" (Εφρων ἢ Εφραιμ ἔνθα ἦλθεν ὁ Κ[ύριο]ς). In addition to neighboring "Luza which is also Bethel," the map also includes Gophna to the west—as well as "Akrabim, which is now Akrabittin," apparently about 30 km due north near Neapolis (Nablus) and Mount Ebal.

42. Note, e.g., Maria C. Khoury, "Taybeh's Plea for the Last Christians of the Holy Land," *Road to Emmaus* 11.4 (2010): 3–43.

43. Among recent verdicts see, e.g., Jerome Murphy-O'Connor, "Place-Names in the Fourth Gospel: 2. Bethany (Jn 1:28; 11:18) and Ephraim (Jn 11:54)," *RB* 120

(2013): 98: Taybeh "remains the prime candidate for the Ephraim of Jn 11:54" (similarly Jerry A. Pattengale, "Aphairema (Place)," *ABD* 1:275; Pierre Médebielle, *Ephrem-Taybeh et son histoire chrétienne* [Jerusalem: Latin Patriarchate, 1993]; Yoel Elitzur, *Ancient Place Names in the Holy Land: Preservation and History* [Jerusalem: Magnes, 2004], 268–72; Robert D. Miller, *Baal, St. George, and Khidr: A Study of the Historical Geography of the Levant*, HACL 8 [University Park: Pennsylvania State University Press, 2019], 63; and many others).

44. Cf. Murphy-O'Connor, "Place-Names," 98.

45. See e.g., Richard Hartmann, "Zum Ortsnamen aṭ-Ṭajjiba," *ZDMG* 65 (1911): 536–38, noting the possible original Taybet el-Ism طيبة الاسم, "the good name"; also Gustaf Dalman, *Orte und Wege Jesu*, 3rd ed. (Gütersloh: Bertelsmann, 1924), 231. An "inn of Tibtah/Tayibtah" (פונדקא דטיבתא) marks the Caesarean rabbis' halakic boundary for doubtful tithe in y. Demai 2:1, 22c, and in the Rehob Inscription (ופנדקה דטביתה), but this concerns a different Taybeh, ten kilometers from the coast between Nablus and Netanya. Cf. Michael Avi-Yonah, "Gazetteer of Roman Palestine," *Qedem* 5 (1976): 101; Efraim Orni, "Ṭayyiba, Al-," *EncJud* 19:562.

46. W. F. Albright, "The Ephraim of the Old and New Testaments," *JPOS* 3 (1923): 36–40; W. F. Albright, "Ophrah and Ephraim," *AASOR* 4 (1922): 124–33. Murphy-O'Connor, "Place-Names," 96, dismisses Albright's view as "entirely sentimental" because he thought Khirbet Samiyeh/Khirbet Marjameh a more plausible place to spend the cold months before Passover. Support for Samiyeh came from Avi-Yonah, "Gazetteer," 29, 56, 101, who identified Ephraim as the closely adjacent "Khirbet el-Bayadir." Similarly, Henry O. Thompson, "Ephraim (Place)," *ABD* 2:556, and, emphatically, Ehud Keinan et al., "Where Was the City of Ephraim?" *PEQ* 147 (2015): 223–24.

47. The center of the site is located at 31.9151° N, 35.2500° E (What3Words, w3w.co/never.breakaway.proton; Palestine Grid MR 173780 146930). Giv'at Asaf is an unauthorized "outpost" (מאחז) rather than an authorized settlement, i.e., illegal under Israeli as well as international law (although successive right-wing governments have encouraged retroactive legalization).

48. Cf., e.g., Scott Stripling et al., "A Scarab of Psametik I from Kh. el-Maqatir," *PEQ* 149 (2017): 193–94.

49. A reconstruction by the site architect is offered at https://www.ritmeyer.com/product/image-library/buildings/towers/ephraim-tower/.

50. Scott Stripling, "חירבת אל־מקטיר בגבול בנימין־אפרים," *Qad* 150 (2015): 82.

51. Hezki Baruch, "Victims of Great Revolt Brought to Rest in Ofra," *Israel National News*, September 1, 2017, https://www.israelnationalnews.com/news/234892.

52. Stripling, "אל־מקטיר," 81. Suetonius, *Vesp.* 6.3 confirms the new emperor's troops in Palestine swore allegiance to him *apud ipsum*, i.e., in person, on July 11, 69 (a week earlier according to Tacitus, *Hist.* 2.79), before his departure for Alexandria and eventually Rome, where he arrived in mid-70.

53. On Khirbet el-Maqatir see further Stripling, "אל־מקטיר"; early *IEJ* excavation reports include Bryant G. Wood, "Khirbet el-Maqatir, 1995–1998," *IEJ* 50 (2000): 123–30; Bryant G. Wood, "Khirbet el-Maqatir, 1999," *IEJ* 50 (2000): 249–54;

Bryant G. Wood, "Khirbet el-Maqatir, 2000," *IEJ* 51 (2001): 246–52; also Urban C. von Wahlde, "The Gospel of John and Archaeology," in *The Oxford Handbook of Johannine Studies*, ed. Judith M. Lieu and Martinus C. de Boer (Oxford: Oxford University Press, 2017), 108.

54. Stripling, "אל־מקטיר," 81.

55. Because of its property in preserving the religious purity of food and liquids, stoneware was in first-century Judea and Galilee typically favored by halakhically observant Jews—a function it probably also serves in John 2:6; cf. m. Beṣah 2:3. See Roland Deines, *Jüdische Steingefäße und pharisäische Frömmigkeit: Ein archäologisch-historischer Beitrag zum Verständnis von Joh 2,6 und der jüdischen Reinheitshalacha zur Zeit Jesu*, WUNT 2/52 (Tübingen: Mohr Siebeck, 1993), 166–236.

56. E.g., Cyprian, *Laps.* 10.196: *et docuit et fecit* (*De Lapsis; De Ecclesiae Catholicae Unitate*, ed. Maurice Bévenot, *Cyprianus: Opera* 1 [Turnhout: Brepols, 1972]); Athanasius, *Fug.* 12 (*Athanase: Deux apologies*, ed. Jan M. Szymusiak, rev. ed., *Sources chrétiennes* 56 [Paris: Cerf, 1987]). See further Elias J. Bickermann, "Utilitas crucis: Observations sur les récits du procès de Jésus dans les Évangiles canoniques," *RHR* 112 (1935): 213–16.

57. Origen, *Comm. Jo.* 28.198–99 (from Ronald E. Heine, trans. and ed., *Origen: Commentary on the Gospel according to John*, 2 vols., FC 80 and 89 [Washington, DC: Catholic University of America Press, 1989], 2:333; GCS 10:417–18).

58. Origen, *Comm. Jo.* 28.192 (trans. Heine, *Origen*, 2:332): ἀναγεγράφθαι νομίζω βουλομένου τοῦ λόγου ἐπιστρέφειν ἡμᾶς ἀπὸ τοῦ θερμότερον καὶ ἀλογιστότερον ἐπιπηδᾶν τῷ ἕως θανάτου ἀγωνίζεσθαι περὶ τῆς ἀληθείας καὶ μαρτυρεῖν.

59. David Maxwell, ed. and trans., *Cyril of Alexandria: Commentary on John*, 2 vols. (Downers Grove, IL: InterVarsity Press, 2013–2015), 2:97 (Edward Bouverie Pusey, ed., *Sancti Patris Nostri Cyrilli Archiepiscopi Alexandrini In D. Joannis Evangelium*, 3 vols. [Oxford: Clarendon, 1872], 2:296: διδάσκει δὲ καὶ ἡμᾶς ὑπείκειν ταῖς τῶν ὀργιζομένων ἀκμαῖς, καὶ μὴ ἐπιρρίπτειν ἑαυτοὺς τοῖς κινδύνοις, μηδ' ἂν ὑπὲρ τῆς ἀληθείας ὦσιν· ἀλλὰ καταλαμβανομένους μὲν ἵστασθαι, μέλλοντας δὲ ἀναδύεσθαι, διὰ τὸ τῆς ἐκβάσεως ἄδηλον).

60. τοιοῦτόν ἐστιν καὶ τὸ ἐν τῷ κατὰ Ματθαῖον γεγραμμένον (Origen, *Comm. Jo.* 28.202 [trans. Heine, *Origen*, 2:334]).

61. Origen, *Comm. Jo.* 28.202 (trans. Heine, *Origen*, 2:334); *Cels.* 2.9 (κρυπτόμενος μὲν καὶ διαδιδράσκων ἐπονειδιστότατα ἑάλω), 10.

62. καὶ οὐκ ἔστιν θεοῦ λόγος ἐν Ἰουδαίοις, καὶ ἀπελθὼν ἐκεῖθεν—λέγω δὲ ἀπὸ τῶν Ἰουδαίων (Origen, *Comm. Jo.* 28.211 [trans. Heine, *Origen*, 2:336]).

63. See, e.g., *Homilies on Joshua*, ed. Thomas P. Halton and Cynthia White, trans. Barbara J. Bruce, FC 105 (Washington, DC: Catholic University of America Press, 2002), 186–87; *Homilies on Jeremiah and 1 Kings 28*, ed. Thomas P. Halton, trans. John Clark Smith, FC 97 (Washington, DC: Catholic University of America Press, 1998), 308–9; *Homilies on the Psalms: Codex Monacensis Graecus 314*, trans. Joseph W. Trigg, FC 141 (Washington, DC: Catholic University of America Press, 2020), 315, 406.

64. Origen, *Comm. Jo.* 28.213–214, 221–222 (trans. Heine, *Origen*, 2:336–37). The etymology here rides on the commonplace that the name אפרים ("Ephraim") derives from the word פרי ("fruit"), an idea inherited from Philo (*Prelim. Studies*

40; *Alleg. Interp.* 3.93–94; *Sobriety* 28; *Migration* 205) and anticipated in Gen 41:52 (cf. Hos 9:16; 14:8).

65. Ephrem, *Hymns on Virginity* 20:6–8; 21:3, 6, 8–9 (Ignatius Ephraem II Rahmani, ed., *S. Ephraemi Hymni de Virginitate: Ephrem's Hymns on Virginity*, SStL 143 [Piscataway, NJ: Gorgias Press/G&C Kiraz, 2006 (1906)], 55–61; trans. Kathleen E. McVey, *Ephrem the Syrian: Hymns* [New York: Paulist, 1989], 345–53). The *gematria* at 21:8 evidently makes "Ephraim" (ܐܦܪܝܡ: 1+80+200+10+40=331) the sum of "cross" (ܨܠܝܒܐ: 90+30+10+2+1=133) and "crucified" (ܙܩܝܦܐ: 7+100+10+80+1=198).

66. The name of the Israeli settlement of Ma'aleh Ephraim reflects no ancient settlement of that name, and is located fifteen kilometers northeast of Taybeh, well outside the area envisaged by the ancient sources here in view.

67. Cf. also the medieval midrash Num. Rab. 14:1. My brief summary here is indebted to Jonathan Kaplan, "Ephraim: II.B. Rabbinic Judaism," in *Dress—Essene Gate*, vol. 7 of *Encyclopaedia of the Bible and Its Reception* (Berlin: de Gruyter, 2013); Martha Himmelfarb, "The Messiah Son of Joseph in Ancient Judaism," in vol. 2 of *Envisioning Judaism: Studies in Honor of Peter Schäfer on the Occasion of His Seventieth Birthday*, ed. Ra'anan S. Boustan and Alex Ramos, 2 vols. (Tübingen: Mohr Siebeck, 2013), 771–90; David Campbell Mitchell, "Messiah bar Ephraim in the Targums," *AS* 4 (2006): 221–41; David Campbell Mitchell, "Messiah Ben Joseph: A Sacrifice of Atonement for Israel," *RRJ* 10 (2007): 77–94.

68. E.g., Tg. Ps.-J. Exod 40:11b (through Joshua's descendant Messiah ben Ephraim, Israel will defeat Gog); cf. Tg. Jon. Isa 53; also Deut 33:17.

69. E.g., Tg. Song 4:5: תרין פריקיך דעתידין למפרקיך משיח בר דויד ומשיח בר אפרים; similarly, 7:4.

70. So David Campbell Mitchell, "A Dying and Rising Josephite Messiah in 4Q372," *JSP* 18 (2009): 181–205; David Campbell Mitchell, "Firstborn Shor and Rem: A Sacrificial Josephite Messiah in 1 Enoch 90.37–38 and Deuteronomy 33.17," *JSP* 15 (2006): 211–28; Mitchell, "Messiah Ben Joseph"; cf. somewhat differently the controversial arguments of Israel Knohl, *The Messiah before Jesus: The Suffering Servant of the Dead Sea Scrolls* (Berkeley: University of California Press, 2000).

71. Joseph Heinemann, "The Messiah of Ephraim and the Premature Exodus of the Tribe of Ephraim," *HTR* 68 (1975): 1–15; cf. David Berger, "Three Typological Themes in Early Jewish Messianism: Messiah Son of Joseph, Rabbinic Calculations, and the Figure of Armilus," *AJSR* 10 (1985): 143–48; previously, Joseph Klausner, *The Messianic Idea in Israel, from Its Beginning to the Completion of the Mishnah* (New York: Macmillan, 1955), 492–501.

72. See Pesikta Rabbati 37.1–2; cf. 36.1; 34.2. Cf. further Rivka Ulmer, "The Contours of the Messiah in *Pesiqta Rabbati*," *HTR* 106 (2013): 142–43 and passim.

73. Rudolf Bultmann, *The Gospel of John: A Commentary* (Oxford: Blackwell, 1971), 412 n3.

74. This frequently noted theme of the impending passion also impressed itself on Charles de Foucauld's imagination during his 1898 retreat in the village (*Meditations of a Hermit: The Spiritual Writings of Charles de Foucauld* [London: Oates & Washbourne, 1930], 94–129).

CHAPTER FOUR

1. Marianne Meye Thompson discusses the question in *John: A Commentary*, NTL (Louisville: Westminster John Knox, 2015), 37–39.
2. All translations are my own, but many of the expressions in inverted commas are paraphrases rather than quotations.
3. Thompson, *John*, 34.
4. See Thompson, *John*, 392, and elsewhere.
5. Marianne Meye Thompson, *The God of the Gospel of John* (Grand Rapids: Eerdmans, 2001), 11.
6. Thompson, *John*, 220.
7. Thompson discusses the use of the word *theos* of human beings in *The God of the Gospel of John*, 17–48.
8. The word "father" interestingly recurs in a number of these confrontations. See Marianne Meye Thompson, *The Promise of the Father: Jesus and God in the New Testament* (Louisville: Westminster John Knox, 2000).

CHAPTER FIVE

1. For a summary of this scholarship, see Andrew Chester, "High Christology—Whence, When, and Why?," *EC* 2 (2011): 22–50, here 45–50. See also Brittany E. Wilson, *The Embodied God: Seeing the Divine in Luke-Acts and the Early Church* (New York: Oxford University Press, 2021), esp. 162–64.
2. For iconic examples of such visions and theophanic encounters, see, e.g., Gen 3:8–21; 18:1–33; 32:22–32; Exod 24:9–18; 33:17–23; Isa 6:1–13; Ezek 1:1–28; Dan 7:9–14; 1 En. 14:20–21; 2 En. 22:1–6; 39:3–6 [A]. For examples from the NT, see below.
3. See especially Carey C. Newman, *Paul's Glory-Christology: Tradition and Rhetoric*, NovTSup 69 (Leiden: Brill, 1992). On the *kavod* as God's visible presence in Jewish scriptural texts, see, e.g., Exod 13:21–22; 14:24; 16:10; 24:9–18; 33:17–34:8; 40:34–38; Num 12:8; 1 Kgs 8:10–11; Isa 6:1–4; Ezek 1:26, 28; Dan 7:9–13; Sir 17:13.
4. Wilson, *The Embodied God*, 176–81.
5. All translations are based on the NRSV, although I have sometimes adapted the translation to reflect the Greek more closely. I also refer to the implied author as "John," regardless of whether the Fourth Gospel is composed from different sources.
6. Note, though, that God also says that Moses cannot see God's face and live (Exod 33:20–23), even though Moses elsewhere speaks to God face to face (e.g., Exod 33:11; Num 12:8; Deut 34:10). On the allusions to Sinai in John 1:14–18; 5:37–47, see below.
7. For John's rejection (and/or reworking) of heavenly ascent traditions, see, e.g., Jey J. Kanagaraj, *"Mysticism" in the Gospel of John: An Inquiry into Its Background*, JSNTSup 158 (Sheffield: Sheffield Academic, 1998), esp. 194–206; April D. DeConick, *Voices of the Mystics: Early Christian Discourse in the Gospels of John and Thomas and Other Ancient Christian Literature*, JSNTSup 157 (Sheffield: Sheffield Academic, 2001), esp. 68–85.

8. In the Synoptic Gospels, God becomes visibly manifest at Jesus's birth (Luke 2:9), baptism (Matt 3:16 // Mark 1:10 // Luke 3:21–22 [cf. John 1:32–34 and discussion below]), and transfiguration (Matt 17:5 // Mark 9:7 // Luke 9:34–35). Although some may counter that only God's Spirit—and not God—becomes visibly manifest during Jesus's baptism, the Spirit is clearly a part of God, while also being distinct. For a fuller account of these visual manifestations, as well as God's visual manifestations in Acts, see Wilson, *The Embodied God*, 77–94. For a discussion of the literary and reception-historical relationship between the Gospel of John and Revelation, especially with respect to apocalyptic themes, see Benjamin E. Reynolds, *John among the Apocalypses: Jewish Apocalyptic Tradition and the "Apocalyptic" Gospel* (Oxford: Oxford University Press, 2020), 167–200.

9. The popularity of reading John against the Middle Platonic backdrop of Philo (who views God as an invisible, immaterial being) largely stems from C. H. Dodd, *The Interpretation of the Fourth Gospel* (Cambridge: Cambridge University Press, 1953). The assumption that God is invisible in John is widespread and often relies on John 1:18 and 5:37 to support this claim. For a recent, more specific argument that God is invisible in John, see Jutta Leonhardt-Balzer, "Divine Manifestations in the Gospel of John," in *Epiphanies of the Divine in the Septuagint and the New Testament*, ed. Roland Deines and Mark Wreford, WUNT (Tübingen: Mohr Siebeck, forthcoming).

10. For Philo's depiction of God in these terms, see, e.g., *Names* 1–9; *Creation* passim; *Posterity* 13–16, 167–169.

11. See also Rom 1:20; 1 Tim 6:16; 3 John 11. For a discussion of these verses, and how Col 1:15, 1 Tim 1:17, and Heb 11:27 in particular, may speak to God being "unseen" rather than ontologically "invisible," see Andrew Malone, "The Invisibility of God: A Survey of a Misunderstood Phenomenon," *EvQ* 79 (2007): 311–29; Wilson, *The Embodied God*, 72–77.

12. For a discussion of how the early church fathers reconciled their belief in God's invisibility with scriptural theophanies, see Robin M. Jensen, *Face to Face: Picturing the Divine in Early Christianity* (Minneapolis: Fortress, 2005), 69–99.

13. Marianne Meye Thompson has written on this topic at length. See the following works in particular: *The God of the Gospel of John* (Grand Rapids: Eerdmans, 2001), esp. 110–17; "Jesus: 'The One Who Sees God,'" in *Israel's God and Rebecca's Children: Christology and Community in Early Judaism and Christianity: Essays in Honor of Larry W. Hurtado and Alan F. Segal*, ed. David B. Capes, April D. DeConick, Helen K. Bond, and Troy Miller (Waco, TX: Baylor University Press, 2017), 215–26. On this same topic, see especially the following: Catrin H. Williams, "Seeing the Glory: The Reception of Isaiah's Call-Vision in Jn 12.41," in *Judaism, Jewish Identities and the Gospel Tradition: Essays in Honour of Maurice Casey*, ed. James G. Crossley (London: Routledge, 2014), 186–206; Catrin H. Williams, "(Not) Seeing God in the Prologue and Body of John's Gospel," in *The Prologue of the Gospel of John: Its Literary, Theological, and Philosophical Contexts: Papers Read at the Colloquium Ioanneum 2013*, ed. J. G. van der Watt, R. Alan Culpepper, and Udo Schnelle, WUNT 359 (Tübingen: Mohr Siebeck, 2016), 79–98; Jakob Ole Filtvedt, "Seeing and Hearing God: On the Relationship

between John 5:37 and Deut 4:12," *DTT* 5 (2016): 308–23; Jakob Ole Filtvedt, "The Transcendence and Visibility of the Father in the Gospel of John," *ZNW* 108 (2017): 90–118; Luke Irwin, "Jesus and the Visibility of God: Sight and Belief in the Fourth Gospel" (PhD diss., Durham University, 2022). This focus on the theme of "seeing God" in John also intersects with the renewed interest in how apocalyptic and "mystical" traditions inform John. See, e.g., John Ashton, *Understanding the Fourth Gospel*, 2nd ed. (New York: Oxford University Press, 2007), 240–76 (1st ed. 1991; cf. John Ashton, "The Johannine Son of Man: A New Proposal," *NTS* 57 [2011]: 508–29); Kanagaraj, *"Mysticism" in the Gospel of John*; Catrin H. Williams and Christopher Rowland, eds., *John's Gospel and Intimations of Apocalyptic* (London: Bloomsbury T&T Clark, 2013); Reynolds, *John among the Apocalypses*; Nadine Ueberschaer, "Joh 20,1–18 als intra- und intertextuelle Leseanleitung zum ‚Sehen' Gottes im Sohn," in *Johannes Lesen und Verstehen: Im Gespräch mit Jean Zumstein*, ed. Jörg Frey and Nadine Ueberschaer (Göttingen: Vandenhoeck & Ruprecht, 2021), 129–51.

14. For Platonic understandings of God, see George Boy-Stones, *Platonist Philosophy 80 BC to AD 250: An Introduction and Collection of Sources in Translation* (Cambridge: Cambridge University Press, 2018), esp. 147–83.

15. Irwin makes this point ("Jesus and the Visibility of God," esp. 71–72).

16. As Thompson rightly observes, "The biblical point of view is not that God is invisible but that God is hidden from human sight" ("Jesus: 'The One Who Sees God,'" 221). (To Thompson's point, however, I would add that in many scriptural texts, God only remains hidden until God reveals God's self.) On the distinction between "invisible" and "unseen," see Malone, "The Invisibility of God," 311–29; Wilson, *The Embodied God*, 72–77; Irwin, "Jesus and the Visibility of God," 68–74.

17. On this point concerning God's "form," see Brittany E. Wilson, "God's 'Form' in John's Gospel and Paul's Letter to the Philippians," forthcoming. On how both of Jesus's statements in 5:37 can be heard as polemical (i.e., that Jesus critiques his interlocuter's inability to see God's form *and* hear God's voice [not just the latter]), see Filtvedt, "Seeing and Hearing God."

18. On the numerous parallels between John 1:14–18 and Exod 33–34, see Craig A. Evans, *Word and Glory: On the Exegetical and Theological Background of John's Prologue*, JSNTSup 89 (Sheffield: Sheffield Academic, 1993), 79–83.

19. Notice, though, that Moses's witnessing to Jesus is strictly verbal—i.e., through his writing of the law. Others, such as Abraham and Isaiah, are visual witnesses to Jesus. See discussion below.

20. See Irwin, "Jesus and the Visibility of God," 74–77. As Williams notes, however, John may still have viewed Moses's vision of God as a competing claim to Jesus's own ("(Not) Seeing God," 87–90, 97–98).

21. For this audition terminology, see John B. F. Miller, *Convinced that God Had Called Us: Dreams, Visions, and the Perception of God's Will in Luke-Acts*, BibInt 85 (Leiden: Brill, 2007), 11–14.

22. Irwin also makes this point ("Jesus and the Visibility of God," 71). On how Jesus's words render God accessible in the somatic realm, see Deborah Forger, "Jesus as

God's Word(s): Aurality, Epistemology and Embodiment in the Gospel of John," *JSNT* 42 (2020): 274–302.

23. The Spirit's connection to God in John's Gospel is even more striking than in the Synoptics since Jesus says that "God *is* spirit/Spirit" (John 4:24, emphasis added).

24. Note also how Jesus says that "you hear" (ἀκούεις) "the sound" (τὴν φωνήν) of the wind, or Spirit (πνεῦμα), even if you do not know where it comes from or where it goes (John 3:8). I thank Alicia Myers for this observation.

25. On this theme, see Kasper Bro Larsen, *Recognizing the Stranger: Recognition Scenes in the Gospel of John*, BibInt 93 (Leiden: Brill, 2008).

26. Leonhardt-Balzer makes this point ("Divine Manifestations in the Gospel of John"), even though we differ on the interpretation of this Sinai connection.

27. Hence the title of Thompson's essay: "Jesus: 'The One Who Sees God.'"

28. On the use of ὁράω to depict physical sight (on at least one level) elsewhere in John, see, e.g., 1:34, 39, 47, 48, 51, 4:45; 6:14, 22, 24, 26, 36; 9:1, 37; 14:9; 15:24; 16:22; 20:18, 25, 29, cited and discussed in Irwin, "Jesus and the Visibility of God," 203–10. On the use of βλέπω, θεάομαι, and θεωρέω to depict physical sight in John (again, on at least one level), see, e.g., 1:29, 32, 36, 38; 4:35; 6:2, 5, 19; 7:3; 9:7, 8, 15, 19, 21, 25; 11:9, 45; 13:22; 20:1, 5, 6, 14; 21:9, 20.

29. On the dual sense of ὁράω in John (with respect to physical and noetic sight), see esp. Irwin, "Jesus and the Visibility of God," 180–212. See also Thompson, who writes: "The double-layered significance of 'seeing' should not be construed so as to deny its primary simple sense of (physical) seeing" ("Jesus: 'The One Who Sees God,'" 218).

30. See esp. Thompson, "Jesus: 'The One Who Sees God.'"

31. Thompson, for example, makes this point by emphasizing the indirect nature of scriptural theophanies (esp. "Jesus: 'The One Who Sees God'").

32. Some, however, argue that John deliberately subverts or undermines Jewish Scripture in 1:18 (e.g., A. J. Droge, "'No One Has Ever Seen God': Revisionary Criticism in the Fourth Gospel," in *From Prophecy to Testament: The Function of the Old Testament in the New*, ed. Craig A. Evans [Peabody, MA: Hendrickson, 2004], 169–84).

33. See Irwin, "Jesus and the Visibility of God," 81–84.

34. On how John 1:14 points to Jesus's humanity (and not that the Word only enters into the guise of human flesh, per Ernst Käsemann, *The Testament of Jesus: A Study of the Gospel of John in the Light of Chapter 17*, trans. Gerhard Krodel, 2nd ed. [Philadelphia: Fortress, 1968]), see in particular Marianne Meye Thompson, *The Humanity of Jesus in the Fourth Gospel* (Philadelphia: Fortress, 1988), esp. 33–52; Marianne Meye Thompson, "The Human Jesus in the Gospel of John: The Word Made Flesh," in *Portraits of Jesus in the Gospel of John: A Christological Spectrum*, ed. Craig R. Koester, LNTS 589 (London: T&T Clark, 2019), 17–30.

35. Interpreters often argue that Jesus's vision of God is noetic or "spiritual" and transcends physical sight. For a classic example of this argument, see the discussion of John's "hierarchy" of seeing verbs in G. L. Phillips, "Faith and Vision in the Fourth Gospel," in *Studies in the Fourth Gospel*, ed. F. L. Cross (London: A. R. Mowbray,

1957), 83–96. Even Thompson, however, indicates that God's visibility in Jesus is ultimately indirect when she concludes that "the vision of the Father in the Son remains a mediated vision" ("Jesus: 'The One Who Sees God,'" 226). On this point, therefore, I diverge from our esteemed honoree and instead follow Ole Jakob Filtvedt and Luke Irwin, who maintain that God's "mediation" in Jesus does not somehow dispel the directness of God's visibility (Filtvedt, "The Transcendence and Visibility of the Father," esp. 109–10, 116–18; Irwin, "Jesus and the Visibility of God," esp. 15, 79–80).

36. Although there is some ambiguity as to whether 1 John 3:1–2 refers to the future sight of God or Jesus, Thompson makes a good case for reading the referent as God (*The God of the Gospel of John*, 116–17). On how John's hearers can presently "see" Jesus through John's incorporation of the rhetorical technique of ekphrasis, see Kasper Bro Larsen, "Rhetorical Vividness in John 20: Making Jesus Present before the Eye," in *Come and Read: Interpretive Approaches to the Gospel of John*, ed. Alicia D. Myers and Lindsey S. Jodrey (Lanham, MD: Lexington/Fortress Academic, 2020), 185–99.

37. John, however, does include the theophanic tradition in a manner akin to the Synoptics when he includes episodes that depict people experiencing Jesus along the lines of an epiphany or a theophany. In John, this particularly occurs when Jesus walks on the water (John 6:16–21; cf. Matt 14:22–33; Mark 6:45–52) and when Jesus appears to his followers in his resurrected state (John 20:11–29; cf. Luke 24:13–43).

38. Again, on this coupling of "flesh" with "Glory," see Thompson, *The Humanity of Jesus in the Fourth Gospel*, 33–52; Thompson, "The Human Jesus in the Gospel of John," 17–30.

39. Again, on the prologue's allusions to Exod 33–34, see Evans, *Word and Glory*, 79–83.

40. Other places where John arguably interprets scriptural theophanies as "Christophanies" include his reference to Abraham seeing Jesus's "day" (John 8:56–59; cf. Gen 18:1–33) and his comment that "they will look on the one whom they have pierced" during the scene of Jesus's crucifixion (John 19:37; cf. Zech 12:10 MT). On the former, see the discussion below. On the latter, see William Randolph Bynum, "Quotations of Zechariah in the Fourth Gospel," in *Abiding Words: The Use of Scripture in the Gospel of John*, ed. Alicia D. Myers and Bruce G. Schuchard (Atlanta: SBL Press, 2015), 47–74, esp. 65–74.

41. On the role of Isaiah, and especially Isa 6, in John 12, see Daniel J. Brendsel, *"Isaiah Saw His Glory": The Use of Isaiah 52–53 in John 12*, BZNW 208 (Berlin: de Gruyter, 2014), esp. 67–97, 123–34; Williams, "Seeing the Glory"; Williams, "(Not) Seeing God," 91–97.

42. Note that the LXX arguably softens the anthropomorphic language of Isaiah's vision since it states that "the house was full of his Glory" rather than saying that "the hem of his robe filled the temple" (Isa 6:1 MT). It may be the case, though, that John also draws from the Hebrew of Isa 6 (e.g., John 12:40 [cf. Isa 6:10 MT], 41 [cf. Isa 6:3 MT]) (see Brendsel, *"Isaiah Saw His Glory"*, 83–88). Regardless, the LXX still retains the anthropomorphic character of the vision since it portrays

"the Lord," whom Isaiah sees directly ("I saw *the Lord*" [εἶδον τὸν κύριον]), sitting on a throne. Moreover, Williams helpfully points out that John 12:41 intersects with a broad canvas of traditions in which God's Glory has a human appearance or human-like form, as when Ezekiel sees an enthroned figure "like the appearance of a human" (Ezek 1:26) and calls this appearance "the Glory of the Lord" (1:28) (Williams, "Seeing the Glory," 195–96). See also Williams on the foundational role of Isa 6:1–5 in Jewish apocalyptic and mystical traditions ("Seeing the Glory," 190–94).

43. See Williams, "Seeing the Glory," 187–90; Williams, "(Not) Seeing God," 91–97. As Williams explains, Jesus may also be included as a referent of the title "Lord" in John 12:38 (cf. Isa 53:1) ("Seeing the Glory," 187; cf. Brendsel, *"Isaiah Saw His Glory"*, 110–11). John refers to Jesus as κύριος at least 44 times, and he refers to God as κύριος at least once (see 12:13). There are also two occasions when the title could apply to either God or Jesus (or perhaps to both) (see 1:23; 12:38); Brendsel, *"Isaiah Saw His Glory"*, 111.

44. Williams, "Seeing the Glory," 189; Williams, "(Not) Seeing God," 91.

45. See, e.g., Rudolf Schnackenburg, "Joh 12,39–41: Zur christologischen Schriftauslegung des vierten Evangelisten," in *Neues Testament und Geschichte: Historisches Geschehen und Deutung im Neuen Testament: FS Oscar Cullmann zum 70*, ed. H. Baltensweiler and B. Reicke (Zürich: Theologischer, 1972), 167–77, here 175–76; Droge, "'No One Has Ever Seen God,'" 182.

46. See, e.g., Justin Martyr, *1 Apol.* 62–63; *Dial.* 56–60, 126–29; Jensen, *Face to Face*, 69–99; Jaeda C. Calaway, *The Christian Moses: Vision, Authority, and the Limits of Humanity in the New Testament and Early Christianity*, Studies in Christianity and Judaism 2 (Montreal: McGill-Queen's University Press, 2019), esp. 86–104.

47. See Williams, "Seeing the Glory," 196–200; Williams, "(Not) Seeing God," 93–97. See also Brendsel, *"Isaiah Saw His Glory"*, 125–34. This is not to deny, however, that John 12:41 participates in the wider tradition of reading "the Word" as the subject of "Old Testament" theophanies.

48. Note that some scholars stress that Isaiah specifically saw Jesus's *crucified* glory, or the paradoxical moment when Jesus's glory is most fully on display through his shameful death on the cross (e.g., Jonathan Lett, "The Divine Identity of Jesus as the Reason for Israel's Unbelief in John 12:36–43," *JBL* [2016]: 159–73, here 169–73; Filtvedt, "The Transcendence and Visibility of the Father," 111–16). On this point, see also Brendsel, *"Isaiah Saw His Glory"*, 125–34, 137–60.

49. For a more in-depth discussion of Abraham's vision, see Ruth Sheridan, *The Figure of Abraham in John 8: Text and Intertext*, LNTS 619 (London: Bloomsbury, 2020), 315–63.

50. Note too that in John's recontextualization, Isaiah "foretells" Jesus's rejection "because" (ὅτι) or "when" (ὅτε) he saw "his Glory," thus further linking Isaiah's vision with Jesus's earthly ministry (John 12:41). On this point and the others discussed in this paragraph, see Williams, "Seeing the Glory," esp. 196–200; Williams, "(Not) Seeing God," 93–97.

51. Furthermore, note that some manuscripts, such as Codex Bezae and Koridethi, specify that Isaiah saw the glory "of God" (τοῦ θεοῦ) (John 12:41).

52. Irwin, "Jesus and the Visibility of God," 79, 80. See also Filtvedt, "The Transcendence and Visibility of the Father," esp. 109–10, 116–18.
53. Williams, "Seeing the Glory," 198. See also Filtvedt, "The Transcendence and Visibility of the Father," 97–99. For an argument that Jesus himself is a visionary seer, see Ashton, "The Johannine Son of Man."
54. Benjamin D. Sommer's watershed book, *The Bodies of God and the World of Ancient Israel* (Cambridge: Cambridge University Press, 2009), is largely responsible for this renewed interest in divine embodiment and its relationship with theophanies. For an application of Sommer's argument to Second Temple Judaism and the NT, particularly Luke-Acts, see Wilson, *The Embodied God*.

CHAPTER SIX

1. I use the first-person plural throughout this essay almost as if it is a character in the Fourth Gospel's narrative, as it is a convenient way to refer to *us as the Fourth Gospel would have us human beings be,* but I do not assume that all readers of this essay will identify with the first-person plural and I do not mean to collapse the hermeneutical distance between the text and its readers.
2. Ernst Käsemann, *The Testament of Jesus: A Study of the Gospel of John in the Light of Chapter 17,* trans. Gerhard Krodel, JMS 6 (Eugene, OR: Wipf & Stock, 2017 [1967]), 26.
3. Käsemann, *Testament of Jesus,* 9. Marianne Meye Thompson adds: "What sort of human being . . . changes water to wine, feeds five thousand people with five loaves and two fishes, heals the sick, and raises the dead?" See *The Humanity of Jesus in the Fourth Gospel* (Philadelphia: Fortress, 1988), 53.
4. Käsemann, *Testament of Jesus,* 15–21.
5. Käsemann, *Testament of Jesus,* 10.
6. Thompson is here explaining the offense of the bread of life discourse, especially Jesus's words about his flesh (*Humanity of Jesus,* 52; see John 6:51–58).
7. Thompson, *Humanity of Jesus,* 122. For a recent articulation of how the juxtaposition of Jesus's "true, uncontested humanity" with his divine identity is "the strongest theological challenge of the Fourth Gospel," see Jörg Frey, *Theology and History in the Fourth Gospel: Tradition and Narration* (Waco, TX: Baylor University Press, 2018), 13–58, here 19–20.
8. Thompson, *Humanity of Jesus,* 128.
9. Richard Sorabji, *Self: Ancient and Modern Insights about Individuality, Life, and Death* (Chicago: University of Chicago Press, 2008), 43.
10. For example, Sorabji outlines sixteen ancient views of Self, not all of which focus on the same conceptual issues (*Self,* 32–47).
11. Sorabji, *Self,* 17.
12. According to James Phelan, "deficient narration" happens when the flesh-and-blood audience does not go along with the author, narrator, and implied reader, whether because of "discrepancies between the representation of extratextuality in nonfiction and that reality itself" or because of "some inconsistency or other

flaw in the overall design of the narration"; see *Somebody Telling Somebody Else: A Rhetorical Poetics of Narrative*, Theory and Interpretation of Narrative (Columbus: Ohio State University Press, 2017), 235–36. My claim pertains only to the latter sense.

13. Grant Macaskill, *The New Testament and Intellectual Humility* (Oxford: Oxford University Press, 2018), 92.

14. Karl Barth, *The Word of God and the Word of Man*, trans. Douglas Horton (New York: Harper & Row, 1959), 195.

15. Because the signs of Jesus are written down and narrated with a rhetorical purpose (John 20:30–31), Thompson regards the purpose of the signs as the evocation of faith; see her discussion in *Humanity of Jesus*, 63–81.

16. On the limitations (and possibilities) of an imitative ethic with respect to the signs, see Lindsey Trozzo, *Exploring Johannine Ethics: A Rhetorical Approach to Moral Efficacy in the Fourth Gospel Narrative*, WUNT 2/449 (Tübingen: Mohr Siebeck, 2017), 88–96.

17. Unless otherwise noted, translations of Scripture are taken from the NRSV.

18. Where trust based on signs is judged as inadequate is where the signs have not (yet) been interpreted christologically through a discourse by Jesus (2:23–25; 4:48; 6:14, 30).

19. For an argument about the incommensurability of these interpretations, see Fernando F. Segovia, "John 13:1–20: The Footwashing in the Johannine Tradition," *ZNW* 73.1–2 (1982): 36.

20. For a reading of the footwashing as an act of love, see Jan G. van der Watt, "The Meaning of Jesus Washing the Feet of His Disciples (John 13)," *Neot* 51.1 (2017): 25–39. For a reading that emphasizes the social ramifications of Jesus's lowly act, see Richard Bauckham, *The Testimony of the Beloved Disciple: Narrative, History, and Theology in the Gospel of John* (Grand Rapids: Baker Academic, 2007), 205–6.

21. It is possible to find continuity between the christological and ethical interpretations given by Jesus, on which see Marianne Meye Thompson, "'His Own Received Him Not': Jesus Washes the Feet of His Disciples," in *The Art of Reading Scripture*, ed. Ellen F. Davis and Richard B. Hays (Grand Rapids: Eerdmans, 2003), 258–73, here 259.

22. James L. Resseguie identifies this as the Fourth Gospel's "ideological perspective" in his essay "Point of View," in *How John Works: Storytelling in the Fourth Gospel*, ed. Douglas Estes and Ruth Sheridan, RBS 86 (Atlanta: SBL Press, 2016), 93.

23. The essay that classically represents what I called the old consensus is Wayne A. Meeks, "The Ethics of the Fourth Evangelist," in *Exploring the Gospel of John: In Honor of D. Moody Smith*, ed. R. Alan Culpepper and C. Clifton Black (Louisville: Westminster John Knox, 1996), 317–26. On this emerging new consensus and for further bibliography, see Christopher W. Skinner, "Ethics and the Gospel of John: Toward an Emerging New Consensus?," *CurBR* 18.3 (2020): 280–304.

24. Lindsey Trozzo has helped me in seeing that Jesus is most imitable in his unity with God. Her argument is compelling especially for its rhetorical approach to ancient *bioi* and its demonstration that the narrator applies the same topics from

rhetorical handbooks for praising character to both Jesus and his disciples; see *Exploring Johannine Ethics*, 33–129.

25. I took this phrase from Rowan Williams, *Christ the Heart of Creation* (London: Bloomsbury, 2018), 51.

26. Jan G. van der Watt, "The Gospel of John's Perception of Ethical Behavior," *IDS* 45.2–3 (2011): 432–36.

27. John Behr subsumes anthropology to Christology, drawing from John's Gospel, Ignatius of Antioch, Irenaeus of Lyons, and Gregory of Nyssa; see "Humanity," in *The New Cambridge Companion to Christian Doctrine*, ed. Michael Allen (Cambridge: Cambridge University Press, 2022), 37–52.

28. On divine identity, see Richard Bauckham, *God Crucified: Monotheism and Christology in the New Testament* (Grand Rapids: Eerdmans, 1998); though she does not use the term, Marianne Meye Thompson arrives at a synonymous concept in her work on John's theology (proper); see *The God of the Gospel of John* (Grand Rapids: Eerdmans, 2001).

29. John 5–10 can be understood as a coherent literary unit because of a sequence of Jewish feasts beginning with an unnamed feast (5:1) and ending with the Feast of Dedication (10:22) and also because of an escalating conflict between Jesus and the *Ioudaioi* about his oneness with God; on which, see Christopher Blumhofer, *The Gospel of John and the Future of Israel*, SNTSMS 177 (Cambridge: Cambridge University Press, 2020), 103–75.

30. For further examples from Jewish and Greco-Roman literature, see Marianne Meye Thompson, *John: A Commentary*, NTL (Louisville: Westminster John Knox, 2015), 123–25. For a historical-critical approach to the rhetoric of Jesus's "self-deification," see M. David Litwa, *Desiring Divinity: Self-Deification in Early Jewish and Christian Mythmaking* (Oxford: Oxford University Press, 2016), 67–90.

31. So argues Anthony A. Long, "Ancient Philosophy's Hardest Question: What to Make of Oneself?," *Representations* 74.1 (2001): 19–20, 25–26.

32. Long, "Ancient Philosophy's Hardest Question," 21–26.

33. Christopher Gill, *The Structured Self in Hellenistic and Roman Thought* (Oxford: Oxford University Press, 2006), 1–126.

34. On contemplation as godlike activity, the characteristics of godlikeness, and the qualified manner that humans could become godlike in Plato and Aristotle, see David Sedley, "Becoming Godlike," in *The Cambridge Companion to Ancient Ethics*, ed. Christopher Bobonich, Cambridge Companions to Philosophy (Cambridge: Cambridge University Press, 2017), 322–28.

35. Translations of Epictetus are taken from Epictetus, *Discourses, Fragments, Handbook*, trans. Robin Hard, OWS (Oxford: Oxford University Press, 2014).

36. See Maren Niehoff, *Philo of Alexandria: An Intellectual Biography*, AYBRL (New Haven: Yale University Press, 2018), 195–200.

37. Niehoff, *Philo of Alexandria*, 215. Cf. Philo, *Migration* 134–38; *Flight* 91–92.

38. So argues Mira Balberg, *Purity, Body, and Self in Early Rabbinic Literature*, S. Mark Taper Foundation Imprint in Jewish Studies (Berkeley: University of California Press, 2014), 1–47, 148–79, here 149.

39. So argues Sorabji, *Self*, 32–53, 115–53.

40. In this paragraph I am indebted to Sorabji's reading of Cicero's *On Duties* and its significance for individual differentiation (*Self*, 157–71). Christopher Gill emphasizes the difference between Cicero's concern for Cato's action and modern subjective individualism by showing that individual moral action cohered with a larger ethical and social framework, but this observation does not preclude an emergent concern for each person's peculiarity. See the exchange between Sorabji and Gill in Pauliina Remes and Juha Sihvola, eds., *Ancient Philosophy of the Self*, SYNL 64 (Dordrecht: Springer, 2008).

41. On the modern European concept of Self as buffered and disembedded, see Charles Taylor, *A Secular Age* (Cambridge: Harvard University Press, 2007), 90–158. For an articulation of how emerging ancient views of differentiated individuality were developed with reference to humanity as a species, see M. J. O. Verheij, "Selves in Conflict: Gill vs. Sorabji on the Conception of Selfhood in Antiquity: A Reconciliatory Review," *CW* 107.2 (2014): 169–97.

42. Interestingly, the works Jesus does are not works that are associated with the messiah in extant early Jewish writings (Thompson, *John*, 232).

43. Litwa, *Desiring Divinity*, 84.

44. Though it is a live question among contemporary scholars about just whom God addresses—whether a council of deities, human judges, or divine kings—ancient Jewish and early Christian interpreters understood the addressees as human beings. On the former, see James M. Trotter, "Death of the אלהים in Psalm 82," *JBL* 131.2 (2012): 221–39. On the latter, see Carl Mosser, "The Earliest Patristic Interpretations of Psalm 82, Jewish Antecedents, and the Origin of Christian Deification," *JTS* 56.1 (2005): 30–74.

45. Raymond E. Brown suggests that viewing Jesus's words as an *a fortiori* argument lessens the sense that his response is a "deceptive fallacy"; see *The Gospel according to John*, 2 vols., AB 29–29A (Garden City, NY: Doubleday, 1966), 1:409–10. Jo-Ann A. Brant calls Jesus's question to the Jews a "rhetorical trap," in that it cannot be answered in its own terms without the Jews implying that Scripture is annulled; see *John*, PaidCNT (Grand Rapids: Baker Academic, 2011), 163.

46. Thompson, *John*, 234.

47. Among the commentaries that make this connection, see especially J. Ramsey Michaels, *The Gospel of John*, NICNT (Grand Rapids: Eerdmans, 2010), 602–3. On rabbinic interpretations of Ps 82:6–7 and Jewish theology, see the insightful essay by Joel S. Kaminsky, "Paradise Regained: Rabbinic Reflections on Israel at Sinai," in *Jews, Christians, and the Theology of the Hebrew Scriptures*, ed. Alice Ogden Bellis and Joel S. Kaminsky, SymS 8 (Atlanta: Society of Biblical Literature, 2000), 18–21, 35–37.

48. This manner of thinking is not unlike what one finds in Ben Sira's reflection on wisdom, where it turns out the knowledge and understanding given humanity in creation is that which is written in the law (Sir 24:1–23).

49. The interpretive path I take in this paragraph was suggested to me by Behr's interesting reading of John's use of Ps 82 ("Humanity," 40–41).

50. Translations of the Septuagint are from Albert Pietersma and Benjamin G. Wright, eds., *A New English Translation of the Septuagint* (New York: Oxford University Press, 2007).

51. Richard Bauckham, "The Holiness of Jesus and His Disciples in the Gospel of John," in *Holiness and Ecclesiology in the New Testament*, ed. Kent E. Brower and Andy Johnson (Grand Rapids: Eerdmans, 2007), 95–113.

52. Williams reflects, "The conceptual and imaginative challenge of Jesus' suffering and death continues to unsettle the language of Jesus as straightforwardly the manifestation of a heavenly power or personage" (*Christ the Heart of Creation*, 52).

CHAPTER SEVEN

1. E.g., Marianne Meye Thompson, *The Incarnate Word: Perspectives on Jesus in the Fourth Gospel* (Peabody, MA: Hendrickson, 1993); Marianne Meye Thompson, *The God of the Gospel of John* (Grand Rapids: Eerdmans, 2001); Marianne Meye Thompson, *John: A Commentary*, NTL (Louisville: Westminster John Knox, 2015).

2. Marianne Meye Thompson, "The Human Jesus in the Gospel of John: The Word Made Flesh," in *Portraits of Jesus in the Gospel of John*, ed. Craig R. Koester, LNTS 589 (London: T&T Clark, 2019), 17; emphasis original (see also pp. 24–27).

3. Thompson, "Human Jesus," 29–30.

4. John's Gospel often blends Jesus's works with his words as he cures, heals, and raises people, not by touching them, but by speaking (4:50–53; 5:8; 11:40–44). In this way, the Gospel shows not only that Jesus "has the words of eternal life" (6:69b), but that he is and gives this life (1:14; 11:25). For Thompson, Jesus's not touching ritually impure people is a part of the Gospel's distinctive view of purification that occurs through Jesus's word and the giving of the Holy Spirit (Marianne Meye Thompson, "Baptism with Water and with Holy Spirit: Purification in the Gospel of John," in *The Opening of John's Narrative (John 1:19–2:22)*, ed. R. Alan Culpepper and Jörg Frey, WUNT 385 [Tübingen: Mohr Siebeck, 2017], 60, 77–78).

5. Thompson, *John*, 364; Raymond E. Brown, *The Gospel according to St. John*, AB 29–29A (Garden City, NY: Doubleday, 1966–1970), 2:764, 811; D. Francois Tolmie, "Elected and a Devil? The Characterization of Judas Iscariot in the Fourth Gospel," in *Signs and Discourses in John 5 and 6*, ed. Jörg Frey and Craig R. Koester, WUNT 463 (Tübingen: Mohr Siebeck, 2021), 307. Hartwig Thyen also ties Jesus's not losing any disciples to the Lord's protection on the day of judgement in Isa 34:16 (*Das Johannesevangelium*, 2nd ed. [Tübingen: Mohr Siebeck, 2015], 707).

6. The term "apotropaism" emphasizes the conflict between Jesus, as God's representative, and evil throughout the Gospel. Apotropaism certainly includes protection, but it highlights the intensity of the conflict and employs a mode of thought and practice common in the first-century Mediterranean world. See below.

7. Cf. Jörg Frey, *The Glory of the Crucified One: Christology and Theology in the Gospel of John*, trans. Wayne Coppins and Christoph Heilig, BMSEC (Waco, TX: Baylor University Press, 2018), 280; Craig R. Koester, "Portraits of Jesus in the Gospel of

John: A Spectrum of Roles," in *Portraits of Jesus in the Gospel of John: A Christological Spectrum*, ed. Craig R. Koester, LNTS 589 (London: T&T Clark, 2019), 10.

8. Mary L. Coloe, *God Dwells with Us: Temple Symbolism in the Fourth Gospel* (Collegeville, MN: Liturgical Press, 2001); cf. Alan Kerr, *The Temple of Jesus' Body: The Temple Theme in the Gospel of John*, JSNTSup 220 (London: T&T Clark, 2002).

9. Mary Douglas, *Leviticus as Literature* (Oxford: Oxford University Press, 2000), 149–50; Jacob Milgrom, *Leviticus: A Book of Ritual and Ethic*, Continental Commentary (Minneapolis: Fortress, 2004), 8–16, 64.

10. Matthew Thiessen calls these signs of mortality "forces of death," which are indicators of ritual and moral impurity (*Jesus and the Forces of Death: The Gospels' Portrayal of Ritual Impurity with First-Century Judaism* [Grand Rapids: Baker Academic, 2020], 14–17). While purity/impurity are distinct from holiness and its corollary (profane or common), these categories are related insofar as one needed to be pure to approach God's holiness safely. For more on the important distinctions between ritual and moral impurities, see Jonathan Klawans, *Impurity and Sin in Ancient Judaism* (Oxford: Oxford University Press, 2000), 23–31; cf. Thompson, "Baptism with Water," 69–70.

11. Robert Parker, *Miasma: Pollution and Purification in Early Greek Religion* (Oxford: Clarendon, 1983), 160–63. Thompson cites Hippocrates, *De morbo sacro* 1, which reads: "We mark out the boundaries of the temples and the groves of the gods, so that no one may pass them unless he be pure, and when we encounter them we are sprinkled with holy water, not as being polluted, but as laying aside any pollution which we formerly had" ("Baptism with Water," 72).

12. Brian Neil Peterson, *John's Use of Ezekiel: Understanding the Unique Perspective of the Fourth Gospel* (Minneapolis: Fortress, 2015), 109–20; Josiah B. Hall, "'The World Will See Me No Longer': Themes of Divine Presence and Absence in the Fourth Gospel" (PhD diss., Baylor University, 2022), 91–110.

13. Wally V. Cirafesi, *John within Judaism: Religion, Ethnicity, and the Shaping of Jesus-Oriented Jewishness in the Fourth Gospel*, AJEC 112 (Leiden: Brill, 2022), 248. For a more thorough exploration of this passage see Alicia D. Myers, "Revelation through Violence? Jesus in the Temple in John 2:13–22," *RevExp* 120 (2023): 46–59.

14. Hall, "The World," 91. Hall also helpfully compares this departure to the Roman practice of *exvocatio*, which called out deities from their temples and cities prior to their conquest (64–68).

15. Hall, "The World," 42.

16. Hall, "The World," 252–56.

17. Following the reading πάντα from P[66] and ℵ[*].

18. As Thompson ("Baptism with Water," 69 n31) notes, ἁγιάζω ("consecrate" or "sanctify") indicates someone or something set aside for "a specific task." In the LXX certain days, people, animals, and objects are sanctified to mark them as specifically connected to God (e.g., Gen 2:3; Exod 13:1, 12; 19:14–22; 29). Leviticus 20:8 emphasizes that Yahweh is the one who "sanctifies" (ὁ ἁγιάζων) the people through the covenant.

19. Judith L. Kovacs, "'Now Shall the Ruler of This World Be Driven Out': Jesus' Death as Cosmic Battle in John 12:20–36," *JBL* 114.2 (1995): 227–47.

20. Kovacs, "Now Shall the Ruler of This World Be Driven Out," 246.

21. Jutta Leonhardt-Balzer, "The Ruler of the World, Antichrists, and Pseudo-Prophets: Johannine Variations on an Apocalyptic Motif," in *John's Gospel and Intimations of Apocalyptic*, ed. Catrin H. Williams and Christopher Rowland (London: Bloomsbury, 2013), 180–99. In addition to Leonhardt-Balzer's work, see, for example, John A. Dennis, "The 'Lifting Up of the Son of Man' and the Dethroning of the 'Ruler of This World': Jesus' Death as the Defeat of the Devil in John 12,31–32," in *The Death of Jesus in the Fourth Gospel*, ed. Gilbert van Belle, BETL 200 (Leuven: Leuven University Press, 2007), 677–92; Sigve K. Tonstad, "'The Father of Lies,' 'the Mother of Lies,' and the Death of Jesus (John 12:20–33)," in *The Gospel of John and Christian Theology*, ed. Richard Bauckham and Carl Mosser (Grand Rapids: Eerdmans, 2008), 193–208; André van Oudtshoorn, "Where Have All the Demons Gone? The Role and Place of the Devil in the Gospel of John," *Neot* 51.1 (2017): 65–82; Mary L. Coloe, *John 11–21*, Wisdom Commentary Series 44B (Collegeville, MN: Liturgical Press, 2021), 344–46.

22. Leonhardt-Balzer, "The Ruler of This World," 186–87.

23. On Spirit possession in John in light of ancient Mediterranean understandings, see Pamela E. Kinlaw, *The Christ Is Jesus: Metamorphosis, Possession, and Johannine Christology*, AcBib 18 (Atlanta: SBL Press, 2005). An-Ting Yi applies Kinlaw's theory to a reading of John's contrasting the opponents of Jesus as being possessed by the devil or Satan, with Jesus and the disciples' possession by the Holy Spirit, suggesting that this language functions to create boundaries between insiders and outsiders ("'You Have a Demon!': An Anthropological Reading of the Notion of Possession in the Gospel of John," *BTB* 46.3 [2016]: 115–22).

24. Thiessen, *Jesus*, 127–39; Graham H. Twelftree, "Jesus the Exorcist and Ancient Magic," in *A Kind of Magic: Understanding Magic in the New Testament and Its Religious Environment*, ed. Michael Labahn and Bert Jan Lietaert Peerbolte (London: T&T Clark, 2007), 57–75; Clint Wahlen, *Jesus and the Impurity of the Spirits in the Synoptic Gospels*, WUNT 2/185 (Tübingen: Mohr Siebeck, 2004), 24–68; Noga Ayali-Darshan, "The Origin and Meaning of the Crimson Thread in the Second Temple Period Scapegoat Ritual in Light of an Ancient Syro-Anatolian Custom," *JSJ* 44 (2013): 530–52.

25. Peter Artz-Grabner and Kristin De Troyer, "Ancient Jewish and Christian Amulets: How Magical They Are," *BN* 176 (2018): 7. The belief in amber's protective qualities for infants continues today with amber teething bracelets and necklaces, though the protective qualities have been medicalized as homeopathic (e.g., Genevieve Howland, "The Natural Mama's Guide to Amber Teething Necklaces," Mama Natural, https://www.mamanatural.com/amber-teething-necklaces/).

26. Wahlen, *Jesus and the Impurity of Spirits*, 18.

27. Wahlen, *Jesus and the Impurity of Spirits*, 170; citing Gen 18:23–32; Exod 32:11–13; Num 14:13–19.

28. Twelftree, "Jesus the Exorcist," 85.

29. Loren T. Stuckenbruck ("Evil in Johannine and Apocalyptic Perspective: Petition for Protection in John 17," in Williams and Rowland, *John's Gospel*, 212–27) compares Jesus's prayer in John 17 with various prayers for protection at Qumran (1QS II, 19; 4Q444; 4Q510; 4Q511; 11Q5 XIX, 15–16; 4Q213a) and Jubilees (1:19–20; 10:3–6; 12:19–20; 15:30–32; 19:28).

30. Michael J. Morris, *Warding off Evil: Apotropaic Tradition in the Dead Sea Scrolls and Synoptic Gospels*, WUNT 2/451 (Tübingen: Mohr Siebeck, 2017), 261–62. Morris notes the semantic overlap between Matt 6:13 and John 17:15.

31. The emphasis on human control of the divine is usually associated with definitions of "magic" as opposed to "religion." In the past apotropaism has often been associated with magic, and thus, separated from Jesus's work. Nevertheless, the distinction between magic and religion is fraught since "magic" is often a pejorative term and modern notions of religion vary significantly from ancient ones. For my purposes, I am emphasizing that in John, Jesus's prayer is apotropaic even as it acknowledges that God alone decides whether or not to act. For more on this issue see Jan N. Bremmer and Jan R. Veenstra, eds., *The Metamorphosis of Magic from Late Antiquity to the Early Modern Period* (Leuven: Peeters, 2002).

32. Kovacs, "Now Shall the Ruler of This World Be Cast Out," 233–34; cf. Tolmie, "Elected and a Devil," 293.

33. Gail R. O'Day, "'I Have Overcome the World' (John 16:33): Narrative Time in John 13–17," *Semeia* 53 (1991): 156.

34. Brown, *Gospel*, 2:766.

35. Thompson, *John*, 320–21.

CHAPTER EIGHT

1. Particularly, Marianne Meye Thompson, *The God of the Gospel of John* (Grand Rapids: Eerdmans, 2001); Marianne Meye Thompson, *John: A Commentary*, NTL (Louisville: Westminster John Knox, 2015); Marianne Meye Thompson, *The Promise of the Father: Jesus and God in the New Testament* (Louisville: Westminster John Knox, 2000); Marianne Meye Thompson, *The Humanity of Jesus in the Fourth Gospel* (Philadelphia: Fortress, 1988); and Marianne Meye Thompson, "God," *DJG* 315–28.

2. Her commentary on Colossians and Philemon in the Two Horizons series is an exemplar of theological thinking rooted in, and in conversation with, careful historical and literary analysis. See Marianne Meye Thompson, *Colossians and Philemon*, THNTC (Grand Rapids: Eerdmans, 2005).

3. Thompson, *The God of the Gospel of John*, 76.

4. All translations, unless otherwise noted, are taken from the New International Version (2011).

5. Thompson highlights the connection between the divine identity and the divine gifts: "as the eternally existent, living God, God alone is the source of all life" (*The God of the Gospel of John*, 76).

6. For a careful review of OT and Second Temple Jewish traditions highlighting God as the living God, see Thompson, *The God of the Gospel of John*, 73–76.

7. A phrase Thompson refers to as "a recasting of the common biblical phrase 'the living God'" ("God," 326).

8. Thompson highlights that "Father" (πατήρ) occurs about 120 times in John alone ("God," 326).

9. Thompson, *The God of the Gospel of John*, 76. For Thompson's thorough review of "Father" language for Yahweh in the OT and Second Temple Judaism, see *The God of the Gospel of John*, 58–72. For an example of language that ties "father" closely to creation and the origin of humanity, see Jer 2:27.

10. Thompson, *The God of the Gospel of John*, 71. See also her conclusion: "God's identity as 'Father' expresses itself first in the specific and distinctive relationship to Jesus, the Son. That God is 'Father' is not some 'ontological' predication in and of itself that can be separated from speaking of the Father's relationship to the Son, in whom the Father's life is embodied" (*The God of the Gospel of John*, 98). Amy Peeler observes that "the New Testament assertion of divine paternity is extremely particular, even exclusive. In that exclusivity, the fatherhood of God is defined and accessed through the sonship of the Jewish Messiah" (*Women and the Gender of God* [Grand Rapids: Eerdmans, 2022], 199).

11. Thompson, *The God of the Gospel of John*, 77. We discuss this aspect of John's Christology more fully below.

12. Jeannine K. Brown, "Creation's Renewal in the Gospel of John," *CBQ* 72.2 (2010): 275–90.

13. Schaser identifies intertextual terminology connecting John 19–20 even into Genesis 3; e.g., linking Jesus's crown of "thorns" (ἀκανθῶν; John 19:2) to the "agricultural curse" of Genesis 3, resulting in the land producing "thorns [ἀκάνθας] and thistles" (3:18 LXX). Nicholas J. Schaser, "Inverting Eden: The Reversal of Genesis 1–3 in John's Passion," *WW* 40.3 (2020): 263–70, here 266.

14. Jan A. Du Rand, "The Creation Motif in the Fourth Gospel: Perspectives on Its Narratological Function within a Judaistic Background," in *Theology and Christology in the Fourth Gospel: Essays by the Members of the SNTS Johannine Writings Seminar*, ed. G. Van Belle, J. G. Van der Watt, and P. Martiz, BETL 184 (Leuven: Leuven University Press, 2005), 21–46, here 43.

15. On the correlation of light and life in John 1 with the motif of (new) creation, see George R. Beasley-Murray, *John*, 2nd ed., WBC 36 (Nashville: Nelson, 1999), 11.

16. Brown, "Creation's Renewal," 277; Karen H. Jobes, *John through Old Testament Eyes* (Grand Rapids: Kregel), 32–33. As Craig R. Koester explains, "The Greek term *logos* resonates with Jewish traditions about the power and wisdom of God as well as with philosophical teachings concerning the energy that shapes the universe" (*The Word of Life: A Theology of John's Gospel* [Grand Rapids: Eerdmans, 2008], 26). For the suggestion of a common literary pattern between John 1 and Genesis 1, see Mary Coloe, "The Structure of the Johannine Prologue and Genesis 1," *ABR* 45 (1997): 40–55, here 53.

17. Gail R. O'Day and Susan E. Hylen, *John*, Westminster Bible Companion (Louisville: Westminster John Knox, 2006), 23; Calum M. Carmichael, *The Story of Creation: Its Origin and Its Interpretation in Philo and the Fourth Gospel* (Ithaca, NY: Cornell University Press, 1996).

18. Du Rand, "Creation Motif," 39.

19. For a partial listing of such commentators, see Brown, "Creation's Renewal," 282 n33.

20. Du Rand ("Creation Motif," 45 n72) raises the possibility that the evangelist may have been accessing Genesis in a form of a text that included πνεῦμα ζωῆς, aligning John even more closely with Genesis (cf. πνεύμα ζωῆς for Gen 2:7 in Philo, *Worse* 22.80).

21. See 1 Kgs 17:21 LXX; Job 4:21 LXX; Ezek 21:36 LXX; 37:9 LXX; Nah 2:2 LXX; Tob 6:9 (א); 11:11 (א); Wis 15:11.

22. John Suggit, "Jesus the Gardener: The Atonement in the Fourth Gospel as Re-Creation," *Neot* 33 (1999): 161–68, here 163.

23. Du Rand ("Creation Motif," 44) understands John 20:22 to be the second "pivotal moment" of the Gospel's emphasis on new creation.

24. The evangelist also employs a temporal motif (a "first day" designation) to evoke creational themes. Language in 20:1 (τῇ δὲ μιᾷ τῶν σαββάτων), reiterated and expanded in 20:19 (τῇ ἡμέρᾳ ἐκείνη τῇ μιᾷ σαββάτων), signals to the reader the arrival of a new *first day*. "The 'first day' of creation's renewal has begun on resurrection morning" (Brown, "Creation's Renewal," 284). See also Mary L. Coloe, "The Garden as a New Creation in John," *TBT* 53.3 (2015): 159–64, here 162; Sandra M. Schneider, "The Raising of the New Temple: John 20.19–23 and Johannine Ecclesiology," *NTS* 52 (2006): 337–55, here 345.

25. These and other allusions and echoes discussed in what follows have been both strongly affirmed by some and hotly contested by others. For key examples of the latter, see Raymond E. Brown, *The Gospel according to John*, I–XII, AB 29 (New York: Doubleday, 1966), 806; Carlos Raúl Sosa Siliezar, *Creation Imagery in the Gospel of John*, LNTS (London: Bloomsbury T&T Clark, 2015). We propose that the clear allusions to Genesis 1–2 in John 1:1–5 and 20:22 support the likelihood of additional echoes in 18:1; 19:5, 28, 30; and 20:15, based on Hays's methodological category of "recurrence" for arbitrating intertextual echoes (Brown, "Creation's Renewal," 288–90; esp. 288 n64; Richard B. Hays, *Echoes of Scripture in the Letters of Paul* [New Haven: Yale University Press, 1989], 30).

26. Anthony M. Moore argues that the generality of κῆπος applied to two different locations (18:1; 19:41) suggests its use at a "theological level" (*Signs of Salvation: The Theme of Creation in John's Gospel* [Cambridge: Clarke, 2013], 62).

27. See Brown ("Creation's Renewal," 280) for a discussion of the synonymous relationship between John's term, κῆπος, and its Genesis counterpart, παράδεισος (Gen 2:8 LXX). For a complete list of Septuagint uses of both κῆπος and παράδεισος to translate the Hebrew גן (*gan*, "garden"; Gen 2:8) across the OT, see Moore, *Signs*, 68–70. As Suggit ("Jesus the Gardener," 166) proposes, John likely chooses κῆπος since παράδεισος refers to the final state in the NT (e.g., Luke 23:43; Rev 2:7) and so would not be appropriate for the inauguration of creation's renewal prior to final and full restoration. For an extended argument against seeing κῆπος as echoing the garden of Genesis 1–3, see Siliezar, *Creation Imagery*, 174–90.

28. Edwyn C. Hoskyns, "Genesis I–III and St John's Gospel," *JTS* 21 (1920): 210–18, here 214.

29. In narrative criticism, the story level involves the characters, plot, and setting, with the discourse level focused on the often-implicit communication between the implied author and the implied reader. While a character might have a specific point of view, the narrator can employ that point of view for purposes beyond what a character can "see." See Jeannine K. Brown, *The Gospels as Stories: A Narrative Approach to Matthew, Mark, Luke, and John* (Grand Rapids: Baker Academic, 2020), 11–14, 73–75.

30. Jamie Clark-Soles, *Reading John for Dear Life: A Spiritual Walk with the Fourth Gospel* (Louisville: Westminster John Knox, 2016), 137.

31. Thompson notes how the early encounters of Jesus in John (Nicodemus, the Samaritan woman) "are characterized by questioning [and] misunderstanding" (*John*, 40).

32. R. H. Lightfoot, *St. John's Gospel: A Commentary* (Oxford: Clarendon, 1956), 322.

33. Coloe, "Garden as a New Creation," 162.

34. E.g., Lightfoot, *St John's Gospel*, 322; Suggit, "Jesus the Gardener," 167; Fabien Blanquart, *Le premier jour: Étude sur Jean 20*, LD 146 (Paris: Cerf, 1991), 64. This is also the focus in Brown, "Creation's Renewal," 281.

35. As Thompson suggests, "In every encounter in the Gospel, those who hear, see, follow, or challenge Jesus are in fact coming face-to-face with the agent of their creation" (*John*, 14).

36. See Gen 1:26, 27; 2:5, 7, 8, 15, 18 LXX, where the Hebrew אָדָם [*adam*] is rendered as ἄνθρωπος. See also Gen 3:22, where the Septuagint reads, "Behold, Adam!" (Ἰδοὺ Αδαμ). Litwa proposes that this divine proclamation is a direct echo of Gen 3:22, where, after Adam has eaten from the tree of the knowledge of good and evil, God pronounces, "Behold, Adam (Ἰδοὺ Αδαμ) has become as one of us, in that he knows good and evil" (LXX; AT). See M. David Litwa, "Behold Adam: A Reading of John 19:5," *HBT* 32 (2010): 129–43.

37. E.g., John Suggit, "John 19:5: 'Behold the Man,'" *ExpTim* 94 (1982–1983): 333–34, here 334; Thomas Barrosse, "The Seven Days of the New Creation in St. John's Gospel," *CBQ* 21 (1959): 507–16, here 516; N. T. Wright, *John for Everyone*, 2 vols. (Louisville: Westminster John Knox, 2004), 2:146.

38. This idea is bolstered by John's emphasis on the Sabbath's arrival immediately following Jesus's death; see Paolo Ricca, *Die Eschatologie des vierten Evangeliums* (Zurich: Gotthelf, 1966), 69. After Jesus declares "It is finished" and gives up his spirit (19:30), John specifies, "Now it was the day of Preparation, and the next day was to be a special Sabbath. Because the Jewish leaders did not want the bodies left on the crosses during the Sabbath, they asked Pilate to have the legs broken and the bodies taken down" (19:31). The death of the Messiah brings to completion God's original and ongoing creative work, ushering in God's eschatological Sabbath (Brown, "Creation's Renewal," 286).

39. Thompson, *The Humanity of Jesus*, 113.

40. For additional proposed allusions and echoes to Gen 1–2 (and Gen 3) in John 18–20, see Schaser ("Inverting Eden"). Coloe ("Garden as a New Creation," 159–60) offers a number of echoes—e.g., the suggestion that the placement of Jesus's cross "in the middle" (μέσος), that is, with two others on either side (John

19:18), echoes the location of the tree of life in the middle (μέσος) of the garden (Gen 2:9 LXX).

41. Adam Kubiś, "The Creation Theme in the Gospel of John," *ColT* 90.5 (2020): 375–414, here 407.

42. As Koester notes, "'Life' is a central theme for John, though the concept is never fully defined. Instead, the characteristics of 'life' are suggested by the Gospel's imagery" (*The Word of Life*, 56).

43. Koester, *The Word of Life*, 98–99.

44. Koester, *The Word of Life*, 100.

45. Brown, *John*, 217.

46. Thompson, *The God of the Gospel of John*, 77. She goes on to highlight the "remarkable status of the Son" in this regard, "one which is not made of any other mediator figure, either in John or in the literature [of Judaism she has surveyed]. The Son 'has life in himself'" (78).

47. John's affirmation of Jesus's unique life-giving prerogative resonates with Paul's distinction between "the first man Adam bec[oming] a living being" and Jesus, "the last Adam, [as] a life-giving spirit" (1 Cor 15:45).

48. Leon Morris, *The Gospel according to John*, NICNT (Grand Rapids: Eerdmans, 1971), 99, 857. Brown reads "life in his name" as indicating that "unless Jesus is the true Son of God, Jesus has no divine life to give. Unless he bears God's name, he cannot fulfill toward [humanity] the divine function of giving life" (*John*, 1061).

49. We can also hear associations with life in other "I am" affirmations, including Jesus as the light of the world who gives "the light of life" (8:12); Jesus as the good shepherd (10:2, 11) "who brings abundant life" (Koester, *The Word of Life*, 99; see 10:10–11); Jesus as "the way the truth and the life" (14:6); and Jesus as the true vine whose life provides the possibility of fruit-bearing for the branches that remain in him (15:1).

50. Thompson, commenting on these verses, clarifies the difference between believers and the Son: though believers receive life from Jesus, "they do not become the source of life for others," as is Jesus (*John*, 155–56).

51. Thompson refers to this declaration as "the heart and pivot of the narrative" of John 11 (*John*, 245).

52. Thompson, *John*, 246. Koester notes that these actions further display Jesus's unity with God, as "it was understood that [only] God could give life to the dead" (5:21). See Craig R. Koester, *Symbolism in the Fourth Gospel: Meaning, Mystery, Community*, 2nd ed. (Minneapolis: Fortress, 2003), 121.

53. Thompson, *John*, 90.

CHAPTER NINE

1. On the ocular drama of Glory as visible, movable, divine presence, see Carey C. Newman, *Paul's Glory-Christology: Tradition and Rhetoric*, NovTSup 69 (Leiden: Brill, 1992).

2. Luke 2:14.

3. Luke 9:31–32; 2 Pet 1:17. While neither fully theophany or throne vision, the transfiguration, by its liminal suspension of Jesus between heaven and earth, presents transfigured Glory as transcendent prolepsis of a kingdom Glory to come. John has no use for such transfigured Glory precisely because Glory for John is not the intrusion of future Glory in the resurrection. John prefers a disfigured Glory—not a transfigured one. John anchors Glory, by distinction, in a distant past that finds its *telos* on a cross and not in a cloud.

4. Acts 7:55.

5. Rev 15:8; 21:11, 23.

6. Heb 2:10.

7. Jude 24; cf. 11QH XII, 29–30; Rom 3:23; Pr Man 5.

8. 1 Pet 5:4; cf. 1 Cor 9:25; 2 Tim 2:4; Jas 1:12.

9. Acts 7:2; 1 Clem. 17.2; Herm. Vis. 1.3.3.

10. Rom 9:3.

11. Heb 1:3; 2 Cor 4:6.

12. Phil 2:11: ἐξομολογήσηται ὅτι κύριος Ἰησοῦς Χριστός cryptically masks two confessions: Jesus is the Christ (i.e., Israel's Messiah), and Jesus, Israel's Messiah, is the Lord (i.e., Yahweh). As Nils Dahl, *Jesus the Christ: The Historical Origins of Christological Doctrine*, ed. Donald H. Juel (Minneapolis: Fortress, 1991), 15–25, notes, the fact that "Christ," early on, became a cognomen for Jesus does not mean that at an even earlier stage Χριστός was a title. Further, and again an emphasis of Dahl, just as a particular deed of Jesus (his crucifixion) defined his vocation of the Messiah—there was no preexisting resume for a messiah to which Jesus conformed; Jesus himself filled out what constitutes a messiah—so too a particular deed (resurrection) of Jesus defined the identity of Jesus as "Lord." The transcendent (always and only) arises from the particular. This is as true for John as it is for other early expressions of Christ devotion. The genesis of christological belief is to be traced back to the singularity of Jesus's crucifixion as Messiah and to the outlandish claim he was resurrected as Lord. "Messiah" links Jesus's death with Israel's troubled history while "Lord" links Jesus's resurrection with a troubled cosmos. Messiah covenantal, Lord apocalyptic. The all too popular moves of either outright ignoring κύριος language (thus sidestepping the profound sociological implications in the claim "Jesus is Lord") or, more cleverly, collapsing all κύριος language into Χριστός (thus making the followers of Jesus just another flavor of Judaism) is to claim that the early followers of Jesus originated (and make sense as a movement) apart from resurrection or, even more unintelligible and unlikely, that early followers of Jesus were as foggy as can be and thus confused crucifixion with resurrection. The way Χριστός comes to be defined by Jesus and his cross in early Christianity proves instructive for the way δόξα comes to be defined by cross in John.

13. On the praxis of Christ devotion see, above all, Larry W. Hurtado, *Lord Jesus Christ: Christ Devotion in Earliest Christianity* (Grand Rapids: Eerdmans, 2003). While Hurtado rightly makes the practice of reverencing Christ as the true litmus test for how the earliest followers of Jesus valued their risen Lord, the act of confession (to take but one of the many ways Jesus was reverenced as Lord) was not

unrelated to the content of that confession. Devotional praxis and christological formulations were not wasted on each other.

14. There was a time when Christians were Jews, true enough. But (1) there came a moment when those who gave allegiance to Jesus as both Christ and Lord could no longer remain (with)in the community of their ancestral faith; (2) the line in the sand between the fledgling Christian communities and their former communal identity was drawn early—and not late; and (3) this line was drawn by the praxis of Christ devotion (and all that such devotion implied, both christologically and theologically). The parting of the ways cannot be recast as merely rhetoric, internal disagreements about law observance, despite all the expended effort to style it as such. For my own take on why the earliest followers of Jesus were destined to part ways with the co-religionists, see Carey C. Newman, "God and Glory and Paul, Again: Divine Identity and Community Formation in the Early Jesus Movement," in *Monotheism and Christology in Greco-Roman Antiquity*, ed. Matthew V. Novenson, NovTSup 180 (Leiden: Brill, 2020), 99–138.

15. The way the earliest followers of Jesus refigured Glory as resurrection spoke volumes about how they used the scriptural tradition they inherited to craft a new communal identity. For how Glory was used to mark the communal boundaries with their former co-religionists and with pagan culture, see Carey C. Newman, "Resurrection as Glory: Divine Presence and Christian Origins," in *The Resurrection: An Interdisciplinary Symposium on the Resurrection of Jesus*, ed. Gerald O'Collins, Stephen T. Davis, and Daniel Kendall (Oxford: Oxford University Press, 1997), 59–89.

16. The noun δόξα appears nineteen times in John, while there are twenty-three occurrences of the verb δοξάζω. The relative parity between noun and verb marks John as unique among early Christian authors. While John's use of the noun rivals that of δόξα in Romans and 2 Corinthians, in neither of those two letters does Paul use the verb with the frequency (and semantic force) of John. That John stands alone in the use of both noun and verb equally, and in abundance, cues to the mystery of Glory in John: in John the verb surpasses the noun in its semiotic Glory—and not the other way round. Among the many virtues—and there are many—of G. B. Caird's "The Glory of God in the Fourth Gospel: An Exercise in Biblical Semantics," *NTS* 15 (1968): 265–77, is the fact that he recognizes the distinctive importance of the verb in John. The uniqueness of δοξάζω in John sharpens when it is observed that in the LXX, the Greek pseudepigrapha, the NT, and in early Christian literature the overwhelming percentage (my informal, but educated, guess is north of 95%) of occurrences of the verb δοξάζω features a human subject and a deity as the direct object—"x glorified (i.e., praised/worshiped/venerated) God." But in what can only be called a true syntactic curiosity, John reverses the subject-object relationship by placing God (either expressly so or by implication in the use of the passive voice) as the subject and, astonishingly, Jesus as the object. The formulation of a deity Glorying a human is rare, especially when the Glorying depicts human (spiritual) transformation in biomorphic/physiomorphic terms (Exod 34:29, 30, 35 LXX; 1 Esd 9:52 LXX; Pss 14:4 LXX; 90:15 LXX; T. Iss. 5:7; T. Jos. 10:3; Acts 3:13; Rom 8:28; Barn. 6.16)—and yet it is the most frequent and important in both

Isaiah (Isa 4:2; 43:3; 44:23; 49:3, 5; 52:13; 55:5) and John (e.g., John 7:39; 8:54; 11:4; 12:16, 23, 28, 31, 32; 16:14; 17:1, 5, 10). It is hard to resist the conclusion that John learned his distinctive Glory grammar in the schoolroom of Isaiah.

17. John 21:19 forms an (intentional, editorial) *inclusio* to 1:14, placing the whole of John's narration under a sign of Glory. This means that John joins Ezekiel and Romans as canonical works whose literary architecture finds structure via Glory. One might argue that Glory in the mountain, tabernacle, and wilderness narratives of Exodus, Leviticus, and Numbers, as well as the prophecy of Isaiah, are also candidates. While the exploration of Jesper Tang Nielsen, "The Narrative Structures of Glory and Glorification in the Fourth Gospel," *NTS* 56 (2010): 343–66, of the relationship between Glory and John's storytelling proves an unconvincing use of Aristotle's theory of narrative, Nielsen does make a persuasive case that all of John's Glory talk turns on "recognition" (rightly emphasizing the inner noetic rather than the visual and dramatic). Thus, for Nielsen (363 n63), 21:19 is "atypical" precisely because it does not fit his conjured plot structure. However, 21:19 underscores the episodic character of John's narrative: God's Glorying of Peter is a mimetic repetition of God's Glorying of Jesus in death and, thus, in the incarnation of 1:14.

18. Inexplicably, John employs all the language of theophany without any of its visual drama. John attests Glory can be seen (θεάομαι, ὁράω) and manifested (φανερόω). Yet, there is not a single text in John that characterizes the appearance of Yahweh's Glory. Glory is present, but never seen.

19. Cf. Marianne Meye Thompson, *The God of the Gospel of John* (Grand Rapids: Eerdmans, 2001), 121–26, and Richard Bauckham, *Gospel of Glory: Major Themes in Johannine Theology* (Grand Rapids: Baker Academic, 2015), 43–62, who both use the theophanic-call narrative-throne vision trajectory to frame their analyses of Glory in John (although Bauckham occasionally adds a concurrent doxological reading), which, in turn, allows them to pivot and read Glory in John as an expression of Yahweh's covenant with Israel established through Moses at Sinai. Both Thompson and Bauckham struggle to makes sense of the ocular dimension of this Glory trajectory (Glory is Yahweh's visible presence) in their readings, resorting to "splendor" as a mushy semantic substitute. Both Thompson and Bauckham, it can be suspected, were unduly influenced by John 1:17: "The law came through Moses, but grace and truth came through Jesus Christ." However, to equate the Glory of Jesus in John with Yahweh's Glory at Sinai (and thus standing in a long series of Yahweh's Gloryophanies) cuts against the grain of John's Glory talk. John, unlike Paul in 2 Cor 3, is not comparing and contrasting theophanic Glory with christophanic Glory; John is attempting something more ambitious. He obsesses over just one Glory, Jesus's Glory, and he claims that this Jesus Glory is a preexistent Glory. Thus, while having argued that this theophanic-call narrative-throne vision tradition best informs the Son of Man sayings in the Synoptic Gospels, Paul's Christology, Hebrews, and the Petrine tradition, I resist that reading for John. Paul's Glory language is rooted in his Christophany, his experience of Jesus's resurrection, while John's Glory language hangs on a cross, the experience of Jesus's death.

20. Jacque Lacan's retracing of the letter's curious path in "Seminar on 'The Purloined Letter,'" *YFS* 48 (1972): 38–72, proves instructive for how Glory behaves as a signifier in John. Like the unread letter in Poe's tale, the possession (or nonpossession) of (the right kind of) Glory determines the subject positions and relations of all the main characters in John's diegesis—just how John "glances" at God and Jesus, Jesus and the Holy Spirit, Jesus and the disciples, Jesus and the Jews. The tale John tells reveals Glory's valence as an, if not the, intersubjective sign, and a semiotic reading of Glory in John allows John's reassignment of Glory to be retraced.

21. Hebrew could negate כבוד, as in אִי־כָבוֹד, "Where Glory?" or, better, "No Glory!" (1 Sam 4:21). Applying an alpha privative to δόξα was not an available option, so the LXX's translators freely rendered the grief of Glory's departure with Οὐαὶ βαρχαβωθ.

22. That John's Glory language is discontinuous with the theophany of Yahweh's Glory as visible, movable presence is but one anomaly. It signals that the focus of Glory in John is primarily christological, not theological. That is, unlike Paul and other early Christian authors, Glory is used almost exclusively by John to say something about the (ultimate) significance of Jesus, not Yahweh. Glory in John is also largely discontinuous with doxological Glory—i.e., "glory (as praise) to God," the most numerically prevalent use of Glory among the earliest followers of Jesus (see Newman, "Glory and God and Paul, Again," 103–7; Carey C. Newman, "Glory," *DLNT* 394–400 (esp. 395–96). A third anomaly is John's (apparent) adoption of honor/shame social networks, as Jerome H. Neyrey argues in *The Gospel of John*, NCBC (Cambridge: Cambridge University Press, 2007), 216–18. But John's Glory language cannot be reduced to honor/shame without remainder, as if all Christology is just sociology. John's Glory Christology is both metaphysical and phenomenological and thus stands on its own theological legs, as is demonstrated by Jörg Frey in *The Glory of the Crucified One: Christology and Theology in the Gospel of John*, BMSEC (Waco, TX: Baylor University Press, 2018), 237–58.

23. Clifford Geertz's thick description of social structure in "Deep Play: Notes on the Balinese Cockfight," *Daedalus* 134 (2005): 56–86, throws fresh light onto how John's consistent depiction of the "game at the side" (the Glory exchanged between humans), into which Jesus's opponents wish to draw (even trick) Jesus, contrasts with "the game at the middle" (Glory exchanged between God and Jesus).

24. Nicole Chibici-Revneanu, *Die Herrlichkeit des Verherrlichten: Das Verständnis der Doxa im Johannesevangelium*, WUNT 2/273 (Tübingen: Mohr Siebeck, 2007), deploys a range of Glory compounds (e.g., Exodus Glory, royal Glory, temple Glory, cultic Gory, eschatological Glory, justice Glory, luminous Glory) in her attempt to wrestle to ground the unwieldy way Glory signs in John. These many compounds do not prevent Chibici-Revneanu from discovering a unity (*Einheit*) to John's diverse Glory language.

25. οἱ Ἰουδαῖοι and Φαρισαῖοι are much discussed terms in John, and the consultation of the secondary literature about them repays the effort, richly so. This is especially true of Thompson's careful observations (*John*, 199–205). What needs saying here, as Thompson's comments rightly insinuate, is that Jesus's othering of "the Jews" was not because of their ethnicity.

26. Thompson, *John*, 132, renders λαμβάνω passively as "welcomes" in her translation but then in her comments cannot resist the active "seeks" (*John*, 135). Thompson can be forgiven, as it is hard to believe that the active-passive ambiguity inherent to λαμβάνω is not both present and intentional here and in v. 44. Unless otherwise noted, all translations are my own.

27. Thompson, *John*, 135–36, understands the Glory pun at work—human Glory (as honor given and exchanged) and divine Glory (as that which is exclusive and inextricable to the one God).

28. John 9:24a: δὸς δόξαν τῷ θεῷ. Thompson, *John*, 217, notes their command for the one just healed to make this confession indicates social allegiance—not authentic devotion to Yahweh.

29. John 9:16a, 24b.

30. John 9:22: ἀποσυνάγωγος γένηται. Notwithstanding Thompson's judicious caution about this troublesome hapax, it is likely that John betrays a historical context where such sanction had, and still was, occurring (*John*, 217–18).

31. Thompson, *John*, 276, again correctly points to the way John puns Glory.

32. The eschatological/apocalyptic role of ἡ ὥρα in John (2:4; 4:21, 23; 5:25, 28; 7:30; 8:20; 12:23, 27; 13:1; 16:2, 4, 21, 25, 32; 17:1) not only depends on, but demands, an intertextual referent. In this case, the text to be supplied is the LXX of Daniel, with its distinctive, eschatological use of ὥρα (Dan 4:26; 8:17, 19; 9:21; 11:35, 40, 45; 12:1, 13), on which see Stefanos Mihalios, *The Danielic Eschatological Hour in the Johannine Literature*, LNTS 436 (London: Bloomsbury, 2011). John's intertextual conversation with Daniel over "the hour" places the events of Jesus's life squarely in the middle of Israel's story with Yahweh and as the decisive turning point for an apocalyptic/cosmic story—Yahweh's war with the Powers. But cf. Thompson, *John*, 61, who does not see any eschatological significance to "my hour has not yet come" (it is just Jesus asserting independent judgment), even if she does sense (61 n68) the links of the hour here to the hour of Jesus's death (which is clearly an eschatological event for John).

33. John 2:4a: τί ἐμοὶ καὶ σοί, γύναι; Thompson, *John*, 61, downplays any potential affront in the response by Jesus to his mother.

34. John 2:10. That every element of the wedding unfolds as riddle requiring abduction underscores that hermeneutics is nothing other than a debate over a signifier's signified. In this case, only Mary and Jesus (and, later, the editor and the editor's community) were able to decode the events.

35. John 2:11: δόξαν αὐτοῦ. It can hardly be a mistake that the first two Glory texts in John, 1:14 and 2:11 (and then 12:41!), make it clear that the Glory in question, and at stake, in John is Jesus's (and not Yahweh's). This point cannot be overstated, as the history of interpretation of Glory in John gradually, almost inevitably, overwrites Jesus's Glory with Yahweh's, (re)placing Yahweh's Glory in the subject position. This is especially true in the way that Yahweh's Glory in Isa 6 comes to displace Jesus's Glory of John 12:41.

36. John 2:11: καὶ ἐφανέρωσεν τὴν δόξαν αὐτοῦ. Jesus manifested his own Glory. The construction begs theophany—and yet there is no theophany, no call narrative, no throne vision. Further, theophanies of Glory traditionally employ the passive

voice̯ (e.g., ὤφθη), not the active. By contrast, John's Jesus presents as a powerful agent who redefines what Glory is and how it is made known.

37. Thompson, *John*, 249–50, perceives the many questions that wrap themselves tightly around Lazarus, not the least of which are: what does it mean to "see" and just what constitutes "the Glory of God"? Because Glory is epiphanic, and not theophanic, seeing lands as the noetic perception rather than ocular drama. As Thompson notes, Martha is asked to see "in" Jesus's deed, i.e., to understand it, to make sense of it.

38. Lazarus's death is not Jesus's, but the two are connected and connected by Glory. Lazarus's death shows how Jesus's death as Glory influences all of John's Glory talk. In fact, the Glorying of Jesus in death shapes the Glory of/to God—and not the other way round, of/as in Paul. Glory in John is mercurial, a semiotic wonder. John knows the theophanic tradition, but recasts, redefines, plays, toys, and puns. Seeing the Glory of God occurs by looking squarely at the disfigured face of Jesus.

39. On the phenomenon of retrospective exegesis for christological formulation in the Gospels, see Richard B. Hays, *Echoes of Scripture in the Gospels* (Waco, TX: Baylor University Press, 2016), and on John 12:16, in particular, Hays, *Echoes*, 312, 325.

40. Thompson, *John*, 268–69, identifies the Greeks as Greek-speaking Jews from the diaspora present for the feast. Their request to see Jesus ties to the fears that "the world has gone after him" and the mission to the Greeks after his death. However, it is not so clear how the desire of Jews to see Jesus, even Greek-speaking ones, presages a full-on mission to the Greeks (non-Jews) after Jesus's death. It is best to read the Greeks here as non-Jews.

41. If John can be fairly accused of knowingly resisting the theophanic Glory tradition informing Paul, then, here, John can also be accused of avoiding the Son of Man coming in Glory of the Synoptics. Glory in the Synoptics is not something that happens to Jesus, as in John. Glory in the Synoptics characterizes Jesus at his eschatological advent—Jesus comes "in" or "with" Glory: ἐν τῇ δόξῃ τοῦ πατρὸς αὐτοῦ (Matt 16:27 // Mark 8:38 // Luke 9: 26), μετὰ δυνάμεως καὶ δόξης πολλῆς (Matt 24:30 // Mark 13:26 // Luke 21:27), or ἐν τῇ δόξῃ αὐτοῦ (Matt 25:31).

42. John 1:32–34, 50–51 sets the expectation for mystical experience—but no such experiences are recorded in the Gospel, save for the voice from heaven. Jesus's resurrection appearances in John 20 and 21 are notable for their lack of theophanic, call narrative, throne visionary language. Even though John acknowledges how the mystical mediates knowledge (e.g., 3:13), it is hard to resist the temptation that John intends to replace the ocular dramatics of theophany with the cognitive perception of the epiphanic.

43. John here (re)traces the semiotics inherent to Jesus's death. The manner of Jesus's death, the cross, itself is a speaking sign: σημαίνων ποίῳ θανάτῳ ἤμελλεν ἀποθνήσκειν.

44. Daniel J. Brendsel, *"Isaiah Saw His Glory": The Use of Isaiah 52–53 in John 12*, BZAW 208 (Berlin: de Gruyter, 2014), traces the way Isaiah's vision of Yahweh in Isa 6 and Isaiah's figuration of the servant in Isa 52–53 drove the Christology of John, especially John 12, as does Jonathan Lett, "The Divine Identity of Jesus as the Reason for Israel's Unbelief in John 12:36–43," *JBL* 135 (2016): 159–73.

45. A host of ancient witnesses read ὅτε for ὅτι here. But, as Raymond Brown observes in *The Gospel according to John I–XII*, AB 29 (Garden City, NY: Doubleday, 1966), 484, the rhetorical effects of the two net the same.

46. The LXX exchanges the MT's "robe for Glory" for πλήρης ὁ οἶκος τῆς δόξης αὐτοῦ while the Targums exchange it for Shekinah. John's ταῦτα εἶπεν Ἡσαΐας ὅτι εἶδεν τὴν δόξαν αὐτοῦ, καὶ ἐλάλησεν περὶ αὐτοῦ can be read in one of several ways: (1) John interpreted Isaiah's temple vision of God's Glory (Isa 6) as a revelation of the Glory of the pre-incarnate, preexistent Jesus, and he then spoke about him, Jesus, in his prophecy (Isa 49, 52, 60); (2) John interpreted Isaiah's temple vision of God's Glory (Isa 6) as a throne vision, in which Isaiah peered into the heavens to see the pre-incarnate, preexistent Jesus as a human shaped figure of Glory (like that of Dan 7 or 1 En. 69 and akin to the extended throne vision of Ascension of Isaiah) and, then, spoke about him (Isa 49, 52, 60); (3) John interpreted Isaiah as having looked into the future to see the Glory of the incarnated Jesus as realized in his earthly signs that culminated in Jesus's death (i.e., as recounted in John's Gospel) and spoke about it (Isa 49, 52, 60); or (4) John interpreted Isaiah as having (fore) seen the Glory of Jesus (Isa 49, 52, 60) and spoke about him (Isa 49, 52, 60). The last option is to be preferred. Rather than making Isaiah say he saw something he did not (Isa 6 says the prophet saw Yahweh's Glory, not Jesus's), or transforming the setting of the experience from the temple to the heavens, or having Isaiah prophesy about the specifics of the life of Jesus, option (4) depends only on John interpreting Isaiah's servant as Jesus. The connection between suffering/death and Glory is already present in Isaiah. On the reception history of John 12:41, which understands Isaiah's temple vision of God as a throne vision of Jesus, see Bogdan Gabriel Bucur, *Scripture Re-envisioned: Christophanic Exegesis and the Making of a Christian Bible*, BAC 13 (Leiden: Brill, 2018), 157–90.

47. Brevard S. Childs, *Isaiah: A Commentary*, OTL (Louisville: Westminster John Knox, 2001), 412, points to the way Isa 52:13 interweaves Isa 49, 60, and 6.

48. Cf. Gal 4:4: ὅτε δὲ ἦλθεν τὸ πλήρωμα τοῦ χρόνου, ἐξαπέστειλεν ὁ θεὸς τὸν υἱὸν αὐτοῦ.

49. Cf. Rev 13:8: τοῦ ἀρνίου τοῦ ἐσφαγμένου ἀπὸ καταβολῆς κόσμου.

50. The temptation to read John as Paul ever crouches at the door. Whereas Paul assigned eschatological significance to Glory—Glory was a standin for resurrection—John assigns protological significance.

51. John does not say: "In the beginning was the Glory. The Glory was with God. And the Glory was God. And the Glory became Flesh, and we beheld Wordishness, the Wordishness of Glory was full of Grace and Truth," though Glory is often read as ontological predication.

52. For John's theology of incarnation in the context of the Bible, see Reinhard Feldmeier and Hermann Spieckermann, *God Becoming Human: Incarnation in the Christian Bible* (Waco, TX: Baylor University Press, 2021), 311–36.

53. Luke 2:14; Acts 7:2; Rom 1:23; 3:23; 9:4; 2 Cor 3:7; Eph 1:17; 2 Thess 1:9; Heb 9:5; 2 Pet 1:3; Rev 15:8; 21:11.

54. Acts 7:52; Rev 18:1.

55. Matt 16:26; 19:28; 24:30; Mark 8:38; 10:37; 13:26; Luke 21:27; Rom 8:18; Col 1:27; 3:4; Tit 2:13; 1 Pet 4:13; 5:1, 4; Herm. Vis. 3.2.1.

56. Luke 9:31–32; 2 Pet 1:17.

57. Luke 24:26; Acts 3:13; Rom 5:2; 6:4; 8:21, 30; 1 Cor 2:7; 15:43; 2 Cor 3:8–11; 4:17; Phil 3:21; 2 Thess 2:14; 1 Tim 3:16; 2 Tim 2:10; Heb 2:7, 9; 1 Pet 1:11, 21; Jude 24; Pol. 2.1.

58. 1 Cor 2:8; 2 Cor 4:4, 6; Heb 1:3; Jas 2:1; Barn. 21.9.

59. Christopher Southgate, *Theology in a Suffering World: Glory and Longing* (Cambridge: Cambridge University Press, 2018) captures the semitic wonders of a Christian theology of Glory. In many ways, Southgate's book is John's Glory (and not Paul's) writ large.

CHAPTER TEN

1. D. Moody Smith, *The Theology of the Gospel of John*, NTT (Cambridge: Cambridge University Press, 1995), 86–87, 125. So also Rudolf Schnackenburg, *The Gospel according to St. John*, trans. Cecily Hastings et al., vol. 2, HTCNT (New York: Seabury, 1980), 158: John "has no desire to establish the legitimacy of his Christ by the criteria of Jewish messianic expectation"; Raymond E. Brown, *An Introduction to the Gospel of John*, ed. Francis J. Moloney (New York: Doubleday, 2003), 135, refers to "the prevailing view that the fourth evangelist disassociates Jesus from David."

2. Emil Schürer, "Messianism," in *The History of the Jewish People in the Age of Jesus Christ*, rev. and ed. Geza Vermes, Fergus Millar, and Matthew Black, vol. 2 (Edinburgh: T&T Clark, 1979), 550–54; John J. Collins, "'He Shall Not Judge by What His Eyes See': Messianic Authority in the Dead Sea Scrolls Author(s)," *DSD* 2.2 (1995): 146.

3. Andrew Chester, *Messiah and Exaltation: Jewish Kingship and Visionary Traditions and New Testament Christology*, WUNT 207 (Tübingen: Mohr Siebeck, 2007), 205–30, summarizing Kenneth E. Pomykala, *The Davidic Dynasty Tradition in Early Judaism: Its History and Significance for Messianism*, EJL 7 (Atlanta: Scholars Press, 1995); Antti Laato, *A Star Is Rising: The Historical Development of the Old Testament Royal Ideology and the Rise of the Jewish Messianic Expectations*, ISFCJ 5 (Atlanta: Scholars Press, 1997); William Horbury, *Jewish Messianism and the Cult of Christ* (London: SCM, 1998), esp. 63.

4. Pomykala, *The Davidic Dynasty Tradition*, 67; disputed by Laato, *A Star Is Rising*, 240–42.

5. Pomykala, *The Davidic Dynasty Tradition*, 68.

6. Pomykala, *The Davidic Dynasty Tradition*, 68.

7. Johannes Tromp, "The Davidic Messiah in Jewish Eschatology of the First Century BCE," in *Restoration: Old Testament, Jewish, and Christian Perspectives*, ed. James M. Scott, JSJSup 72 (Leiden: Brill, 2001), 200–201.

8. Howard Clark Kee, *OTP*, 1:778.

9. Kee, *OTP*, 1:801; cf. Num 24:17; Mal 4:2; Ps 45:4 LXX; Isa 11:1 LXX; 53:9; CD VII, 11–20; T. Levi 18:3; Nicholas G. Piotrowski, *Matthew's New David at the End of Exile: A Socio-Rhetorical Study of Scriptural Quotations*, NovTSup 170 (Leiden: Brill, 2016), 111.

10. See Pomykala, *The Davidic Dynasty Tradition*, 157; Jonathan A. Goldstein, *I Maccabees*, AB 41 (New York: Doubleday, 1976), 507–8; Laato, *A Star Is Rising*, 275–79.

11. Pomykala, *The Davidic Dynasty Tradition*, 173.

12. Florentino García Martínez, *The Dead Sea Scrolls Translated: The Qumran Scrolls in English*, trans. Wilfred G. E. Watson (Leiden: Brill, 1994).

13. Pomykala, *The Davidic Dynasty Tradition*, 198.

14. Pomykala, *The Davidic Dynasty Tradition*, 202; Serge Ruzer, *Early Jewish Messianism in the New Testament: Reflections in the Dim Mirror*, JCPS 36 (Leiden: Brill, 2020), 46–47.

15. Piotrowski, *Matthew's New David*, 111; cf. Beth M. Stovell, "Son of God as Anointed One? Johannine Davidic Christology and Second Temple Messianism," in *Reading the Gospel of John's Christology as Jewish Messianism: Royal, Prophetic, and Divine Messiahs*, ed. Benjamin E. Reynolds and Gabriele Boccaccini, AJEC 106 (Leiden: Brill, 2018), 158.

16. Pomykala, *The Davidic Dynasty Tradition*, 192.

17. Adela Yarbro Collins and John J. Collins, *King and Messiah as Son of God: Divine, Human, and Angelic Messianic Figures in Biblical and Related Literature* (Grand Rapids: Eerdmans, 2008), 64. Cf. Craig A Evans, "Are the 'Son' Texts at Qumran Messianic? Reflections on 4Q369 and Related Scrolls," in *Qumran-Messianism: Studies on the Messianic Expectations in the Dead Sea Scrolls*, ed. James H. Charlesworth et al. (Tübingen: Mohr Siebeck, 1998), 141; Stovell, "Son of God as Anointed One," 158, 169.

18. Yarbro Collins and Collins, *King and Messiah as Son of God*, 67.

19. John J. Collins, "The *Son of God* Text from Qumran," in *From Jesus to John: Essays on Jesus and New Testament Christology in Honour of Marinus de Jonge*, ed. Martinus C. de Boer (Sheffield: JSOT Press, 1993), 64–81; Yarbro Collins and Collins, *King and Messiah as Son of God*, 65–74; Gerbern S. Oegema, *The Anointed and His People: Messianic Expectations from the Maccabees to Bar Kochba*, JSPSup 27 (Sheffield: Sheffield Academic, 1998), 122–27; Tucker S. Ferda, "Naming the Messiah: A Contribution to the 4Q246 'Son of God' Debate," *DSD* 21.2 (2014): 150–75; John J. Collins, "The Background of the 'Son of God' Text," *BBR* 7 (1997): 51–62; E. M. Cook, "4Q246," *BBR* 5 (1995): 43–66.

20. Yarbro Collins and Collins, *King and Messiah as Son of God*, 73.

21. Chester, *Messiah and Exaltation*, 232; so also Evans, "Are the 'Son' Texts at Qumran Messianic?" 142–43; Johannes Zimmermann, "Observations on 4Q246: The 'Son of God,'" in *Qumran-Messianism: Studies on the Messianic Expectations in the Dead Sea Scrolls*, ed. James H. Charlesworth et al. (Tübingen: Mohr Siebeck, 1998), 187–88.

22. Gerbern S. Oegema, "Tradition-Historical Studies on 4Q252," in *Qumran-Messianism: Studies on the Messianic Expectations in the Dead Sea Scrolls*, ed. James H. Charlesworth et al. (Tübingen: Mohr Siebeck, 1998), 171–72; cf. Pomykala, *The Davidic Dynasty Tradition*, 191, 188; Craig A. Evans, "A Note on the 'First-Born Son' of 4Q369," *DSD* 2.2 (1995): 188–89; Laato, *A Star Is Rising*, 285, 297.

23. Craig A. Evans, "The Messiah in the Dead Sea Scrolls," in *Israel's Messiah in the Bible and the Dead Sea Scrolls*, ed. Richard S. Hess and M. Daniel Carroll R. (Grand Rapids: Baker Academic, 2003), 98; based on M. O. Wise, M. G. Abegg Jr., and E. M. Cook, *The Dead Sea Scrolls: A New Translation* (San Francisco: HarperCollins, 1996).

24. Pomykala, *The Davidic Dynasty Tradition*, 212.

25. See John J. Collins, *The Apocalyptic Imagination*, 3rd ed. (Grand Rapids: Eerdmans, 2016), 166–67.

26. See Pomykala, *The Davidic Dynasty Tradition*, 205.

27. Laato, *A Star Is Rising*, 286–87.

28. Chester, *Messiah and Exaltation*, 235.

29. Laato, *A Star Is Rising*, 294.

30. Chester, *Messiah and Exaltation*, 237. The designation of the fragment as 1.1 in Chester should read 1.2.

31. Evans, "A Note on the 'First-Born Son,'" 198; Evans, "Are the 'Son' Texts at Qumran Messianic?," 152–53; Chester, *Messiah and Exaltation*, 237–38.

32. Evans, "A Note on the 'First-Born Son,'" 200.

33. James Kugel, "4Q369 'Prayer of Enosh' and Ancient Biblical Translation," *DSD* 5.2 (1998): 119–48.

34. Benjamin Wold, "Is the 'Firstborn Son' in 4Q369 a Messiah? The Evidence from 4QInstruction," *RevQ* 29 (2017): 18.

35. Chester, *Messiah and Exaltation*, 240.

36. Chester, *Messiah and Exaltation*, 241.

37. Laato, *A Star Is Rising*, 289; cf. Chester, *Messiah and Exaltation*, 271–72, 286–87. See further: 4Q534 (Chester, *Messiah and Exaltation*, 254–56); 4Q504 1–2 IV, 5–8 (Stovell, "Son of God as Anointed One," 159, 161).

38. Chester, *Messiah and Exaltation*, 272.

39. Chester, *Messiah and Exaltation*, 282.

40. Chester, *Messiah and Exaltation*, 266.

41. Chester, *Messiah and Exaltation*, 267–68.

42. Tromp, "The Davidic Messiah," 190. Kenneth Atkinson, "Understanding the History, Theology, and Community of the Psalms of Solomon in Light of the Dead Sea Scrolls," in *The Psalms of Solomon: Texts, Contexts, and Intertexts*, ed. Patrick Pouchelle et al., EJL 54 (Atlanta: SBL Press, 2021), 80, concludes: "Rather than attempting to connect them with the Qumran sect, the Psalms of Solomon should be viewed as another witness to Jewish frustrations of the Second Temple period that their prayers had yet to be answered."

43. R. B. Wright, "Psalms of Solomon," *OTP*, 2: 640–41; Kenneth Atkinson, *I Cried to the Lord: A Study of the Psalms of Solomon's Historical Background and Social Setting*, JSJSup 84 (Leiden: Brill, 2004), 15–87; Stovell, "Son of God as Anointed One," 164. Pomykala, *The Davidic Dynasty Tradition*, 159, dates Pss. Sol. 17 between 61 and 57 BCE.

44. Kenneth Atkinson, "On the Herodian Origin of Militant Davidic Messianism at Qumran: New Light from Psalm of Solomon 17," *JBL* 118 (1999): 435–60. Johannes Tromp, "The Sinners and the Lawless in Psalm of Solomon 17," *NovT* 35 (1993): 344–61, agrees the setting is Roman but denies a more precise dating.

45. John J. Collins, "Messianism in the Maccabean Period," in *Judaisms and Their Messiahs at the Turn of the Christian Era*, ed. Jacob Neusner et al. (Cambridge: Cambridge University Press, 1987), 104–5; Piotrowski, *Matthew's New David*, 112; Laato, *A Star Is Rising*, 280.

46. Dennis C. Duling, "The Therapeutic Son of David: An Element of Matthew's Christological Apologetic," *NTS* 24 (1978): 407; Pomykala, *The Davidic Dynasty Tradition*, 162.

47. M. A. Knibb, "Messianism in the Pseudepigrapha in the Light of the Dead Sea Scrolls," *DSD* 2 (1995): 169.

48. Schürer, "Messianism," 504; James H. Charlesworth, "The Concept of the Messiah in the Pseudepigrapha," *ANRW* 2.19.1 (Berlin: de Gruyter, 1979), 198–99; Pomykala, *The Davidic Dynasty Tradition*, 162; Tromp, "The Davidic Messiah," 191.

49. Pomykala, *The Davidic Dynasty Tradition*, 215.

50. Joel Willitts, "Matthew and *Psalms of Solomon*'s Messianism: A Comparative Study in First-Century Messianology," *BBR* 22 (2012): 27–50, argues that the parallels between these two documents have not been fully appreciated; cf. also Joel Willitts, *Matthew's Messianic Shepherd-King: In Search of "the Lost Sheep of the House of Israel"* (Berlin: de Gruyter, 2007), 79–85; Wayne Baxter, *Israel's Only Shepherd: Matthew's Shepherd Motif and His Social Setting*, LNTS 457 (London: T&T Clark, 2012), 74–76.

51. Stovell, "Son of God as Anointed One," 167.

52. Stovell, "Son of God as Anointed One," 159, 161; cf. Pomykala, *The Davidic Dynasty Tradition*, 176, 179.

53. Chester, *Messiah and Exaltation*, 250.

54. Pomykala, *The Davidic Dynasty Tradition*, 271.

55. See R. Alan Culpepper, *Matthew*, NTL (Louisville: Westminster John Knox, 2021), 31–35. Second Baruch 53–74 divides world history into fourteen periods, from Adam to the messiah.

56. Culpepper, *Matthew*, 190–91.

57. Duling, "The Therapeutic Son of David," 410; cf. Dennis C. Duling, "Solomon, Exorcism, and the Son of David," *HTR* 68 (1975): 235–52; Christoph Burger, *Jesus als Davidssohn: Eine traditionsgeschichtliche Untersuchung*, FRLANT 98 (Göttingen: Vandenhoeck & Ruprecht, 1970), 87–91.

58. Culpepper, *Matthew*, 434–37.

59. Lidjia Novakovic, "Matthew's 'Messianization' of Mark," in *"A Temple Not Made with Hands": Essays in Honor of Naymond H. Keathley*, ed. Mikeal C. Parsons and Richard Walsh (Eugene, OR: Pickwick, 2018), 19. Cf. Lidjia Novakovic, *Messiah, the Healer of the Sick: A Study of Jesus as the Son of David in the Gospel of Matthew*, WUNT 2/170 (Tübingen: Mohr Siebeck, 2003).

60. William R. G. Loader, "Son of David, Blindness, Possession, and Duality in Matthew," *CBQ* 44 (1982): 570–85.

61. Wayne Baxter, "Healing and the 'Son of David': Matthew's Warrant," *NovT* 48 (2006): 36–50, esp. 42–43.

62. Duling, "The Therapeutic Son of David," 404, observes that Matthew interprets the "Coming One" in Ps 118:25–26 as the Son of David, so he interprets Mark's Hosanna acclamation as "Hosanna to the Son of David."

63. Chester, *Messiah and Exaltation*, 505.

64. Culpepper, *Matthew*, 191.

65. Ruzer, *Early Jewish Messianism*, 122, argues that "The basic Matthean claim [is] that Jesus' interpretation of the Torah in the *SM* [Sermon on the Mount] is derived from his messianic anointment of the Spirit."

66. Piotrowski, *Matthew's New David*, 113.

67. See Marianne Meye Thompson, *John*, NTL (Louisville: Westminster John Knox, 2015), 177.

68. Margaret Daly-Denton, *David in the Fourth Gospel: The Johannine Reception of the Psalms*, AGJU 47 (Leiden: Brill, 2000), 7.

69. Daly-Denton, *David in the Fourth Gospel*, 55.

70. Daly-Denton, *David in the Fourth Gospel*, 108.

71. Daly-Denton, *David in the Fourth Gospel*, 319.

72. Daly-Denton, *David in the Fourth Gospel*, 258.

73. Daly-Denton, *David in the Fourth Gospel*, 259–60.

74. Kirsten Nielsen, "Old Testament Imagery in John," in *New Readings in John: Literary and Theological Perspectives: Essays from the Scandanavian Conference on the Fourth Gospel in Århus 1997*, ed. Johannes Nissen and Sigfred Pedersen, JSNTSup 182 (Sheffield: Sheffield Academic, 1999), 79.

75. Daly-Denton, *David in the Fourth Gospel*, 309.

76. Daly-Denton, *David in the Fourth Gospel*, 315.

77. Stovell, "Son of God as Anointed One," 161; cf. Beth M. Stovell, *Mapping Metaphorical Discourse in the Fourth Gospel: John's Eternal King*, LBS 5 (Leiden: Brill, 2012).

78. Stovell, "Son of God as Anointed One," 173–74.

79. Joel Willitts, "David's Sublation of Moses: A Davidic Explanation for the Mosaic Christology of the Fourth Gospel," in *Reading the Gospel of John's Christology as Jewish Messianism: Royal, Prophetic, and Divine Messiahs*, ed. Benjamin E. Reynolds and Gabriele Boccaccini, AJEC 106 (Leiden: Brill, 2018), 204–5. Cf. John Wesley Wright, "The Founding Father: The Structure of the Chronicler's David Narrative," *JBL* 117 (1998): 45–59; Daly-Denton, *David in the Fourth Gospel*, 98–102.

80. Willitts, "David's Sublation of Moses," 218, 219.

81. Marida Nicolaci, "Divine Kingship and Jesus's Identity in Johannine Messianism," in *Reading the Gospel of John's Christology as Jewish Messianism: Royal, Prophetic, and Divine Messiahs*, ed. Benjamin E. Reynolds and Gabriele Boccaccini, AJEC 106 (Leiden: Brill, 2018), 198.

82. John Lierman, "The Mosaic Pattern of John's Christology," in *Challenging Perspectives on the Gospel of John*, ed. John Lierman, WUNT 219 (Tübingen: Mohr Siebeck, 2006), 233. So also Paul N. Anderson, *The Christology of the Fourth Gospel*, WUNT 78 (Tübingen: Mohr Siebeck, 1996), 229: "It is entirely conspicuous that John is nearly devoid of Davidic messianic motifs."

83. Thompson, *John*, 384. See also pages 7, 50, 94 n169, 172, 232, and 237.

84. Thompson, *John*, 72.

85. Thompson, *John*, 177; cf. 214.

86. Thompson, *John*, 225–26.

87. Thompson, *John*, 237.

88. Thompson, *John*, 265 n359.

89. Thompson, *John*, 272.

90. Thompson, *John*, 260.

91. Thompson, *John*, 380.

92. Thompson, *John*, 393.

93. Ruzer, *Early Jewish Messianism*, 227.

CHAPTER ELEVEN

1. All translations are mine. I thank Chris Blumhofer for his suggestions on the translations of patristic texts.

2. For R. T. France, it is "a christological high point in the gospel," a "saying which has understandably been declared more in keeping with the language of the Fourth Gospel than with the rest of Matthew or Luke." See *The Gospel of Matthew*, NICNT (Grand Rapids: Eerdmans, 2007), 442. Similarly, noting the parallels with John, Donald A. Hagner claims, "The present passage constitutes without question one of the highest points of Synoptic Christology." See *Matthew 1–13*, WBC 33A (Waco, TX: Word, 1993), 317–18. Douglas Hare avers that "the reciprocal knowledge of the Father and the Son is clearly a theme more characteristic of John than of the Synoptic Gospels. It is not impossible that this saying, which belonged to a collection on which both Matthew and Luke have drawn, was known to John and served, in part at least, as a point of departure for his distinctive theology." See *Matthew*, IBC (Louisville: Westminster John Knox, 2009), 128. Robert H. Gundry is especially blunt: "Even though we were to accept a mere illustration [of sonship and fatherhood], its application to Jesus and God requires a Johannine Christology of Jesus as the Father's unique Son"; he goes on to speak of "the high Christology in these sayings." See *Matthew: A Commentary on His Literary and Theological Art* (Grand Rapids: Eerdmans, 1982), 217–18.

3. Karl von Hase was apparently the first to describe Matt 11:27 in these terms, calling it "ein Aerolith aus dem johanneischen Himmel." See *Geschichte Jesu, nach akademischen Vorlesungen* (Leipzig: Breitkopf & Härtel, 1876), 422 [527 in 2nd ed. of 1891].

4. Mark Goodacre, "Johannine Thunderbolt or Synoptic Seed? Matt 11:27 // Luke 10:22 in Christological Context" (paper presented at the Annual Meeting of the SBL, San Antonio, TX, 16 November 2016).

5. Goodacre, "Johannine Thunderbolt," 14.

6. Goodacre, "Johannine Thunderbolt," 14. Here Goodacre seems to echo W. D. Davies and D. C. Allison Jr.: "Mt. 11:25–7 par. was probably one of the vital seeds from which Johannine theology sprouted." See *A Critical and Exegetical Commentary on the Gospel according to Saint Matthew*, ICC 2 (Edinburgh: T&T Clark, 1988–1997), 282 n218.

7. Illustrative of this sort of exegesis is that of Ulrich Luz, *Matthew 8–20: A Commentary on the Gospel of Matthew*, trans. James E. Crouch, Hermeneia (Minneapolis: Fortress, 2007), 169. More on this below.

8. Rudolf Bultmann lists Matt 11:27 among the select passages whereby Matthew "raises the stature of Jesus *into the divine*" (*The History of the Synoptic Tradition*,

trans. John Marsh, rev. ed. [New York: Harper & Row], 358, emphasis original). Consider the Düsseldorfer Erklärung der Bekenntnisbewegung »Kein anderes Evangelium« of 1967: "Jesus Christus spricht: »Wer mich sieht, der sieht den Vater « (aus Joh 14,9). Jesus Christus spricht: »Niemand kennt den Vater denn nur der Sohn und wem es der Sohn will offenbaren« (aus Mt 11,27). Wir bekennen das Evangelium, daß der ewige Sohn Gottes in dem geschichtlichen Jesus von Nazareth Mensch wurde und zugleich Gott blieb ... *Es muß daher die falsche Lehre verworfen werden, Jesus sei nur bloßer Mensch...*" (emphasis mine). See *Kirchen- und Theologiegeschichte in Quellen*, IV/2, *Neuzeit*, ed. Hans-Walter Krumwiede et al. (Neukirchen-Vluyn: Neukirchener Verlag, 1980), 210.

9. Goodacre ably shows that the "Johannine ring" of "the absolute use of 'the father' and 'the son' rather than 'my father' and 'my son'" is "an accident of context" rather than something identifiably Johannine in Matthew ("Johannine Thunderbolt," 10–11).

10. Consider, for example, the exegetical judgment of Ulrich Luz: "The tendency of v. 27 justifies the later trinitarian interpretation. . . . The Son belongs substantially, and not only accidentally, on the side of the Father. Without Jesus, God's Godness is unthinkable" (*Matthew*, 169). Similarly, v. 27 "in principle places Jesus on the side of the Father *in contrast to all humanity* (Hagner, *Matthew*, 320, emphasis mine). Likewise, for F. Dale Bruner, v. 27 confirms that Jesus "does indeed seem to give things that we ordinarily expect *only deity* to deliver." See *Matthew: A Commentary*, vol. 1, *The Christ Book: Matthew 1–12* (Grand Rapids: Eerdmans, 2004), 533, emphasis mine.

11. Luz summarizes the modern departure that begins with Grotius this way: "Instead of the second person of the trinity one has a human being to whom is granted special *knowledge* or *experience* of God. And that is what our text says, especially for the critical Protestant exegetes of the nineteenth century" (Luz, *Matthew*, 160, emphasis his).

12. For this line of criticism, I am indebted to many, most consciously to Dietrich Bonhoeffer in his fine lectures, *Christ the Center*, trans. Edwin H. Robertson (New York: Harper & Row, 1960, 1966, 1978).

13. Goodacre, "Johannine Thunderbolt," 13. Note, too, that Goodacre judiciously, if perhaps also misleadingly, avoids explicitly considering the claim that Jesus is divine and instead speaks of Jesus's "divine authority" (14).

14. It is beyond the scope of this essay to address the question of how ecumenical Christian creeds are in fact related to Gospel testimony. I, myself, hold that they do not express the force of such testimony per se without significant qualification, certainly not positivistically. Instead, they enunciate conceptual limits and outlines according to which the church catholic has variously interpreted the force of such testimony. And we should be mindful of how, at such levels of abstraction—which are appropriate for certain, sound purposes—creedal statements can carry power associations that are opposed to Gospel testimony.

15. It also appears in the LXX of Isa 42:1–4, from which Matthew quotes in 12:18–21. In Isa 42:1–4, the prophet speaks of a world ruler as a servant who speaks lowly.

16. For helpful precedents for Jesus's words in Matt 11:27 in Jewish tradition, scriptural and non-scriptural, especially related to divine Wisdom and Moses, see Davies and Allison, *Matthew*, 271–87.

17. Cf. Bonhoeffer, *Christ the Center*, 110.

18. I mean the town where he has settled in Matthew, Capernaum. But the same is true of his hometown of Nazareth (13:54–58).

19. Lest the reader wrongly infer that Jesus, according to Matthew, offers some unique, "Christian" critique of other Jewish authorities of his day, note that a consensus of Jewish sages delivered a similar critique in the wake of the judgment of Jesus's generation that Jesus prophesied. See Shaye J. D. Cohen, "The Significance of Yavneh: Pharisees, Rabbis, and the End of Jewish Sectarianism," *HUCA* 55 (1984): 27–53.

20. Lars Koen appears to have coined the term "partitive exegesis" in "Partitive Exegesis in Cyril of Alexandria's Commentary on the Gospel according to St. John," *StPatr* 25 (1993): 115–21. "Partitive exegesis implies a separation or partition of the interpretation of certain Scriptural statements vis-à-vis the human and divine natures of Christ" (116). "Athanasius is not the originator of this exegetical device. . . . It is definitely a feature common in Alexandrian theology and exegesis" (117). See also John Behr, *The Nicene Faith, Part I*, vol. 2 of *Formation of Christian Theology* (Crestwood, NY: St. Vladimir's Seminary Press, 2004), 208–15.

21. *Ar.* 3.34. Here Athanasius uses 1 Pet 4:1, "Since, therefore, Messiah suffered in flesh," as his hermeneutical key for understanding testimony to apparently not-divine manifestation of passibility in Jesus in the Gospels and elsewhere in the NT.

22. Cyr., *Thes.* 22; PG 75,368. Cyril goes on to say, "If, then, before the humanization of the Divine Logos it is found somewhere that he said something lowly of himself, one might attack his deity and point against his own words."

23. *Or.* 29.18. But note how for Gregory of Nazianzus here, Jesus is implicitly a communication between the divine nature and the human, communication that is itself pedagogical. As such he is the transformation of the rest of the human as people grow in their perception of him and thus of God and themselves, even of God in themselves, i.e., their deification.

24. For a compelling defense of this patristic theological sensibility, see David Bentley Hart, "No Shadow of Turning: On Divine Impassibility," *ProEccl* 11.2 (2002): 184–206. Key to this sensibility, in my view, even if it is not always well expressed, is that the divine nature and human nature are not intrinsically, mutually competitive; the latter is created for transformative participation in the former. Cf. Bonhoeffer's comment: "The mistake [in early Christian thought was that] the nature of God and the nature of man were spoken of in a theoretical and objectifying way. . . . The two natures were treated like two distinguishable entities, separated from each other until they came together in Jesus Christ. The relationship between God and man cannot be thought of as a relationship between two objects, but only between persons" (*Christ the Center*, 101).

25. "Since any passage of Scripture might refer to Christ in view of either nature or both, partitive exegesis asks, 'Which dimension of Christ's existence is the author talking about?'" See R. B. Jamieson and Tyler R. Wittman, *Biblical Reasoning: Christological and Trinitarian Rules for Exegesis* (Grand Rapids: Baker Academic, 2022), 163. Jamieson and Wittman offer a recent defense of what I am arguing is

problematic about partitive exegesis. They also take partitive exegesis, wrongly in my view, to provide the force of scriptural teaching: "Partitive exegesis depends on the prior distinction between theology and economy. It clarifies *the target and amplitude* of scriptural statements *that refer to* each" (166, emphasis mine).

26. See Hart, "No Shadow of Turning," 203–5, for a discussion of the *communicatio idiomatum* in the enfleshed Word and of how "the impassible suffered," as espoused by Gregory of Nyssa, Cyril of Alexandria, and Gregory of Nazianzus.

27. Goodacre, "Johannine Thunderbolt," 13. But contrary to Goodacre's implication, this quality is not an incompleteness to be completed by the reader or other writers. It is itself the revealed way of knowledge. As such it is as characteristic of John as it is of the Synoptics.

28. *Hom. Matt.* 11:27. Elsewhere Athanasius treats the sonship in view as divine in relation to the Father. But my point here is that the text poses for Athanasius a problem for "high" Christology, not an unequivocal expression of it.

29. Part of the problem among modern exegetes is the treatment of Gospel words as bearing meaning according to underlying sources and thus independently of their Gospel narrative contexts. Patristic writers often did something similar, not per source or redaction criticism but per the pressures of politically significant doctrinal debates among them and the assumption of the stable meaning of textual fragments effectively divorced from their narrative contexts.

30. It is worth noting here that a number of patristic writers held to human souls' preexisting their embodiment, such that preexistence was not itself indicative of divinity. See Philip Schaff, *History of the Christian Church: AD 311–600*, vol. 3 (New York: Scribner, 1867), 831.

31. This is not to deny that "the Son of God" of John can be the second person of the Trinity. It is to insist that, whoever the second person of the Trinity might be, he must be the Son of God of John, and descriptions of him as the second person of the Trinity should serve rather than obscure his presentation in John or other scriptural testimony. Widespread descriptions of Jesus as the second person of the Trinity do not do so.

32. Marianne Meye Thompson, *John: A Commentary*, NTL (Louisville: Westminster John Knox, 2015), 248, emphasis mine.

33. Thompson, *John*, 249.

34. Cf. John 1:51. Note that conceiving of the subject of the Gospels as the ultimate communication between the nature of God and human nature can go only so far in Gospel interpretation, since these abstractions should be subject to the concreteness attested by the narratives.

CHAPTER TWELVE

1. Scholars who recognize "divine Christology" in Mark include M. Eugene Boring, "Markan Christology: God-Language for Jesus?," *NTS* 45 (1999): 451–71; Simon J. Gathercole, *The Pre-Existent Son: Recovering the Christologies of Matthew, Mark, and Luke* (Grand Rapids: Eerdmans, 2006), 46–79; Timothy J. Geddert, "The

Implied YHWH Christology of Mark's Gospel: Mark's Challenge to the Reader to 'Connect the Dots,'" *BBR* 25 (2015): 325–40; Richard B. Hays, *Echoes of Scripture in the Gospels* (Waco, TX: Baylor University Press, 2016), 15, 61–87; Daniel Johansson, "Kyrios in the Gospel of Mark," *JSNT* 33 (2010): 101–24; John J. R. Lee, *Christological Rereading of the Shema (Deut 6.4) in Mark's Gospel*, WUNT 2/533 (Tübingen: Mohr Siebeck, 2020). For a critical assessment, see Michael Kok, "Making a Difference: The Gospel of Mark and the 'Early High Christology' Paradigm," *JJMJS* 3 (2016): 102–24. There is a good historical survey of views in Daniel Johansson, "The Identity of Jesus in the Gospel of Mark: Past and Present Proposals," *CurBR* 9 (2010): 364–93.

2. On this I am in broad agreement with Geddert, "The Implied YHWH Christology."

3. Jesus's questions to the disciples in 8:27–29 do not belong to the series: they receive straightforward answers at once.

4. See especially Lee, *Christological Rereading*.

5. Richard Bauckham, *Jesus and the God of Israel: "God Crucified" and Other Studies on the New Testament's Christology of Divine Identity* (Grand Rapids: Eerdmans, 2008), 21–23, 41–45, 152–81.

6. Hebrew ‎ם‎י refers to any large body of water.

7. Many, if not all, such passages reflect the mythic picture of YHWH overcoming the opposition of the Sea in the course of creating the world. But we should be cautious of assuming that they were read in that way in the late Second Temple period. Readers in that period may have thought simply of the ocean as an unruly part of creation that God needed to keep under control.

8. Translations from the Old Greek in this essay are taken from *The Bible*, trans. Nicholas King (Buxhall, Suffolk: Kevin Mayhew, 2013).

9. Howard Clark Kee, "The Terminology of Mark's Exorcism Stories," *NTS* 14 (1968): 232–46.

10. Gordon J. Hamilton, "A New Hebrew-Aramaic Incantation Text from Galilee: 'Rebuking the Sea,'" *JSS* 41 (1996): 215–49. This text dates from ca. 500 CE.

11. See J. R. Daniel Kirk, *A Man Attested by God: The Human Jesus of the Synoptic Gospels* (Grand Rapids: Eerdmans, 2016).

12. J. R. Daniel Kirk and Stephen L. Young, "'I Will Set His Hand on the Sea': Psalm 88:26 LXX and Christology in Mark," *JBL* 133 (2014): 333–40.

13. Kirk and Young, "I Will Set," 336 n13.

14. Kirk and Young, "I Will Set," 335.

15. Robert Alter, *The Book of Psalms* (New York: Norton, 2007), 314.

16. John Goldingay, *Psalms,* vol. 2, *Psalms 42–89*, BCOTWP (Grand Rapids: Baker, 2007), 678, thinks the terms "sea" and "rivers" refer to "the wide extent of an empire upon which the king will put his hand," and can be taken either in a literal geographical sense (the Mediterranean and the Euphrates-Tigris) or in a more metaphorical way, referring to "the sea and rivers that mark the edge of the earth's land mass." Arnold A. Anderson, *The Book of Psalms,* vol. 2, *Psalms 73–150*, NCB (London: Marshall, Morgan & Scott, 1972), 641, thinks similarly that the terms refer either to the literal geographical limits of the empire, or

signify universal dominion, as in Ps 24:1–2. "It is unlikely," he judges, "that David is . . . described as victor over the Chaos waters." Marvin E. Tate, *Psalms 51–100*, WBC 20 (Dallas: Word, 1990), 423–24, thinks that there may be both a "sociographic" meaning, referring to the literal extent of David's empire, as well as a "mythic" meaning. In the latter sense, the cosmic power of YHWH (89:10–13) has its counterpart in the Davidic ruler's subjugation of his human enemies, represented as the mythological figures of Sea and Rivers. Even on this view, the psalm does not represent the king as literally ruling over waters.

17. Cf. also Ps 2:8, where the Davidic ruler's God-given empire extends to "the ends of the earth."

18. Translation from David M. Stec, *The Targum of Psalms*, ArBib 16 (Collegeville, MN: Liturgical Press, 2004), 169.

19. There are two useful monographs on this pericope (in Matthew, Mark, and John): John Paul Heil, *Jesus Walking on the Sea: Meaning and Gospel Functions of Matt 14:22–43, Mark 6:45–52, and John 6:15b–21*, AnBib 67 (Rome: Biblical Institute Press, 1981); Patrick J. Madden, *Jesus' Walking on the Sea*, BZNW 81 (Berlin: de Gruyter, 1997). The latter includes a detailed history of exegesis (1–41).

20. For the genre of the story as an epiphany, see Madden, *Jesus' Walking*, 86–88, arguing against Heil's proposal of a "sea-rescue epiphany."

21. Richard T. France, *The Gospel of Mark*, NIGTC (Grand Rapids: Eerdmans, 2002), 271–72.

22. This is the view of Joel Marcus, *Mark 1–8*, AB 27 (New York: Doubleday, 2000), 432–33.

23. Another text to which reference is often made in the commentaries is Job 9:11, but, despite its proximity to 9:8, which may well be relevant to Mark's story, 9:11 is not really apposite. Job says that God passes by and he does *not* see him, whereas of course the disciples do see Jesus.

24. Wendy Cotter, *Miracles in Greco-Roman Antiquity: A Sourcebook for the Study of New Testament Miracle Stories* (London: Routledge, 1999), 151–52, 153, 155–62.

25. Another text often mentioned is Hab 3:15, which describes God riding over the sea in his chariot, as Poseidon also does in Greek literature.

26. I have added the word "alone" to King's translation, which fails to translate the Greek μόνος.

27. Mark adds the definite article τῆς before θαλάσσης, but this is a necessary stylistic adjustment.

28. Job 9:8 goes unmentioned in Kirk's rather cursory discussion of this story: *A Man*, 446–50.

29. See Joel Marcus, *The Way of the Lord: Christological Exegesis of the Old Testament in the Gospel of Mark* (Louisville: Westminster John Knox, 1992); Rikki E. Watts, *Isaiah's New Exodus in Mark* (Grand Rapids: Baker Academic, 1997).

30. In Rev 1:17–18, the risen Jesus identifies himself to John with the words, "Do not be afraid; I am the first and the last and the living one."

31. For details see Catrin H. Williams, *I Am He: Interpretation of 'Anî Hû' in Jewish and Early Christian Literature*, WUNT 2/113 (Tübingen: Mohr Siebeck, 2000), 55–62.

32. Williams, *I Am He*.

33. Timothy Dwyer, *The Motif of Wonder in the Gospel of Mark*, JSNTSup 128 (Sheffield: Sheffeld Academic, 1996), 18, counts thirty-two instances of "wonder" in Mark, but he is casting the net more widely than I have done here.

34. Watts, *Isaiah's New Exodus*, 233.

35. Marcus, *Mark 1–8*, 421.

36. France, *The Gospel*, 265.

37. See Lee, *Christological Rereading*, chapters 4–5.

38. See especially Dale C. Allison, "Psalm 23 in Early Christianity: A Suggestion," *IBS* 5 (1983): 132–37.

39. King translates κατέσκηνωσεν as "he has pitched my tent." But this is too literal. It is not what shepherds do for sheep. κατασκηνόω can mean "to dwell" or "to rest."

40. King translates ἐπί here as "on," which could suggest that the water is what the shepherd feeds to the sheep. That is not the meaning of the Greek. ἐπί here means "beside" or "by."

41. This is widely recognized, but the two stages are usually understood to be what the disciples have understood hitherto in the narrative and what will be disclosed to them in the second half of the Gospel, i.e., Jesus's understanding of messiahship as entailing suffering and death.

42. Richard Bauckham, "John for Readers of Mark," in *The Gospels for All Christians: Rethinking the Gospel Audiences*, ed. Richard Bauckham (Grand Rapids: Eerdmans; Edinburgh: T&T Clark, 1997), 147–71.

43. J. Ramsey Michaels, *The Gospel of John*, NICNT (Grand Rapids: Eerdmans, 2010), 355, infers that "we are presumed to be familiar with the basic elements of the story, whether from oral tradition or another Gospel account."

44. E.g., Michaels, *The Gospel*, 357–58; Charles Kingsley Barrett, *The Gospel according to St John*. 2nd ed. (London: SPCK, 1978), 281.

45. For further discussion of the "I am" sayings, see Richard Bauckham, *The Testimony of the Beloved Disciple: Narrative, History, and Theology in the Gospel of John* (Grand Rapids: Baker Academic, 2007), 243–50; Williams, *I Am He*, 255–303; Marianne Meye Thompson, *John: A Commentary*, NTL (Louisville: Westminster John Knox, 2015), 156–60.

46. For John's dependence on Mark in this narrative, see Richard Bauckham, "The Gospel of John and the Synoptic Problem," in *New Studies in the Synoptic Problem: Oxford Conference, April 2008: Essays in Honour of Christopher M. Tuckett*, ed. Paul Foster et al., BETL 239 (Leuven: Peeters, 2011), 657–88.

47. Bauckham, *The Testimony*, 221–23.

CHAPTER THIRTEEN

1. For a summary, see Craig R. Koester, *Revelation*, AYB 38A (New Haven: Yale University Press, 2014), 80–83.

2. On this framing of the issue see Larry W. Hurtado, *Lord Jesus Christ: Devotion to Jesus in Earliest Christianity* (Grand Rapids: Eerdmans, 2003), 27–78; Richard

Bauckham, *God Crucified: Monotheism and Christology in the New Testament* (Grand Rapids: Eerdmans, 1998); Jörg Frey, *The Glory of the Crucified One: Theology and Christology in the Gospel of John* (Waco, TX: Baylor University Press, 2018), 285–344.

3. To be "in the Spirit" is not only a spiritual state but presupposes the activity of God's Spirit (Koester, *Revelation*, 243).

4. Marianne Meye Thompson, *The God of the Gospel of John* (Grand Rapids: Eerdmans, 2001), 52–54.

5. Koester, *Revelation*, 99–101.

6. Marianne, Meye Thompson, *John: A Commentary*, NTL (Louisville: Westminster John Knox, 2015), 90–91.

7. Marianne Meye Thompson, *The Humanity of Jesus in the Fourth Gospel* (Philadelphia: Fortress, 1988), 33–52.

8. Raymond E. Brown, *The Gospel according to John*, 2 vols., AB 29–29A (Garden City, NY: Doubleday, 1966–1970), 1:520–23.

9. Cf. Pss. Sol. 17:24; 4Q161 8–10 III, 15–19; 1 En. 62:2.

10. Cf. Pss. Sol 17:23–24, 35; 1QSb V, 24–26.

11. Apollodorus, *Library* 2.4.9; Suetonius, *Aug.* 79.2. Fiery eyes could also suggest angelic status (Dan 10:6; 1 En. 106:5–6).

12. On the blood as Christ's own blood, not the blood of his adversaries, see Koester, *Revelation*, 755–56.

13. Benjamin E. Reynolds, *The Apocalyptic Son of Man in the Gospel of John*, WUNT 2/249 (Tübingen: Mohr Siebeck, 2008), 27–64.

14. Thompson, *John*, 84; Reynolds, *The Apocalyptic Son of Man*, 104–17; Benjamin E. Reynolds, "Jesus the Son of Man: Apocalyptic Interpretations and Johannine Christology," in *Portraits of Jesus in the Gospel of John: A Christological Spectrum*, ed. Craig R. Koester, LNTS 589 (London: T&T Clark, 2019), 125–39.

15. "Lifted up" (ὑψωθῆναι) depicts Jesus's physical elevation on the cross as his "exaltation," underscoring that the exaltation occurs in the crucifixion itself. See Francis J. Moloney, *The Johannine Son of Man*, BSRel 14, 2nd ed. (Rome: Libreria Ateneo Salesiano, 1978), 59–65. I disagree with those who argue that "lifted up" includes crucifixion, resurrection, and return to the Father—e.g., Reynolds, *The Apocalyptic Son of Man*, 122–27.

16. 1 En. 48:5; 51:3; 62:2–5; 69:27–29; cf. 2 Bar. 30:1; Matt 25:31; Reynolds, *The Apocalyptic Son of Man*, 191–96.

17. Thompson, *John*, 269; Craig R. Koester, *The Word of Life: A Theology of John's Gospel* (Grand Rapids: Eerdmans, 2008), 120–22.

18. The role of the Son of Man is also redefined as the future judgment is brought into the present. Paradoxically, Jesus was sent to save and not to judge the world (3:17; 12:47), yet judgment occurs as people judge themselves by their negative or positive responses to him, so that the future judgment at the resurrection confirms the judgments people have already made in response to Jesus. See R. Alan Culpepper, "Jesus the Judge (John 5:21–30): The Theme of Judgment in the Gospel of John," in *Designs for the Church in the Gospel of John: Collected Essays 1980–2020*, WUNT 465 (Tübingen: Mohr Siebeck, 2021), 656–83.

19. E.g., Exod 4:22; 1 Sam 2:27; 7:7–8; Isa 1:24; 7:7; Jer 2:2, 5; Ezek 2:4; 3:11; Amos 1:6, 9, 11, 13; Mic 2:3; Hag 1:2; Zech 1:3–4.

20. The title "Son of God" is sometimes used alongside "Son of Man" (John 3:13–14, 18; 5:25, 27), but it has its own connotations.

21. Cf. 4Q174 I, 10–13; 4Q246 II, 1–9.

22. John J. Collins, *The Scepter and the Star: Messianism in Light of the Dead Sea Scrolls*, 2nd ed. (Grand Rapids: Eerdmans, 1995), 171–90.

23. 2 Macc 1:24; 7:28; Jos. Asen. 8:4.

24. Deut 5:26; Josh 3:10; 1 Sam 17:26, 36; 2 Kgs 19:4, 16; Pss 42:2; 84:2; Jer 10:10; 23:36; Hos 1:10; 4Q504 1–2 V, 9. See Thompson, *The God of the Gospel of John*, 73–77.

25. Deut 32:40; Dan 12:7; Tob 13:1; Sir 18:1; Bel 5; 1 En. 5:1; 4Q504 8 I, 2.

26. Thompson, *The God of the Gospel of John*, 78–79.

27. Thompson, *The God of the Gospel of John*, 53. Also see Alicia D. Myers, "Jesus the Son of God in John's Gospel: The Life-Making Logos," in Koester, *Portraits of Jesus*, 141–55.

28. Thompson, *John*, 234.

29. For quotations and allusions to Ps 110:1, see Matt 22:44; 26:64; Mark 12:36; 14:62; Luke 20:42; 22:69; Acts 2:34; Rom 8:34; 1 Cor 15:25; Eph 1:20; Heb 1:3, 13; 10:12; 12:2.

30. On the motif of the shared throne see David E. Aune, *Revelation*, 3 vols., WBC 52ABC (Waco, TX: Word, 1997–1998), 1:261–63.

31. Richard Bauckham, *The Theology of the Book of Revelation*, NTT (Cambridge: Cambridge University Press, 1993), 60–61.

32. Catrin H. Williams, *I Am He: The Interpretation of 'Anî Hû' in Jewish and Early Christian Literature*, WUNT 2/113 (Tübingen: Mohr Siebeck, 2000).

33. Williams, *I Am He*, 255–303.

34. Craig R. Koester, *Symbolism in the Fourth Gospel: Meaning, Mystery, Community*, 2nd ed. (Minneapolis: Fortress, 2003), 112–16, 152–59.

35. Bauckham, *The Theology of the Book of Revelation*, 27.

36. Bauckham, *The Theology of the Book of Revelation*, 56.

37. Bauckham, *The Theology of the Book of Revelation*, 63–64.

38. Thompson, *John*, 104–5.

39. Koester, *Symbolism in the Fourth Gospel*, 86–89.

40. Martijn Steegen, "To Worship the Johannine 'Son of Man': John 9,38 as Refocusing on the Father," *Bib* 91 (2010): 534–54; Thompson, *The God of the Gospel of John*, 223–26.

41. Pss 40:3; 96:1; 98:1; 144:9; 149:1.

42. Richard Bauckham, "The Worship of Jesus," in *Climax of Prophecy: Studies on the Book of Revelation* (Edinburgh: T&T Clark, 1991), 118–49; Hurtado, *Lord Jesus Christ*, 590–95; Craig R. Koester, "Heavenly Prayer and Christian Identity in the Book of Revelation," in *Early Christian Prayer and Identity Formation*, ed. Reidar Hvalvik and Karl Olav Sandnes, WUNT 336 (Tübingen: Mohr Siebeck, 2014), 183–207.

CHAPTER FOURTEEN

1. Edith L. Blumhofer and Mark A. Noll, eds., *Singing the Lord's Song in a Strange Land: Hymnody in the History of North American Protestantism* (Tuscaloosa: University of Alabama Press, 2004); Edith L. Blumhofer and Mark A. Noll, eds., *Sing Them Over Again to Me: Hymns and Hymnbooks in America* (Tuscaloosa: University of Alabama Press, 2006); Christopher N. Phillips, *The Hymnal: A Reading History* (Baltimore: Johns Hopkins University Press, 2018).

2. On the relationship between hymns and poetry, see Phillips, *The Hymnal*, 161–83.

3. Metaphors of kingship could be added to this list, including the question of Jesus's messianic identity and the language of God's kingdom (John 1:19–28, 41, 49; 3:3, 5, 28); see Beth M. Stovell, *Mapping Metaphorical Discourse in the Fourth Gospel: John's Eternal King*, LBS 5 (Leiden: Brill, 2012).

4. These examples are drawn from the listing of the most frequently published hymns in modern hymnals at https://hymnary.org/browse/popular/texts.

5. That is not to say that the image is entirely unknown. Drawing on John 10, for example, Philip Doddridge's "Awake, Our Souls, and Bless His Name" (1755) identifies Jesus as "the door": "Enter, my soul, with cheerful haste // For Jesus is the door." More common, however, is language that associates Jesus with opening the gate(s) of heaven, as in the classic hymn "Jesus Loves Me" (1859) by Anna Bartlett Warner: "Jesus loves me, he who died // heaven's gate to open wide."

6. Unless otherwise indicated, all translations in this essay are my own.

7. In this essay, I am working with the assumption that, while the Gospel of John was known and used in the second century (see the definitive study of Charles E. Hill, *The Johannine Corpus in the Early Church* [Oxford: Oxford University Press, 2004]; cf. Tuomas Rasimus, ed., *The Legacy of John: Second-Century Reception of the Fourth Gospel*, NovTSup 132 [Leiden: Brill, 2010]); there is no clear evidence for use of the Gospel of John among the writings or authors considered in this essay. There are no convincing parallels between 1 Clement and the Gospel of John (see Andrew F. Gregory, "*1 Clement* and the Writings that Later Formed the New Testament," in *The Reception of the New Testament in the Apostolic Fathers*, vol. 1 of *The New Testament and the Apostolic Fathers*, ed. Andrew F. Gregory and Christopher Tuckett [Oxford: Oxford University Press, 2005], 129–57 [139–40]). Similarly, in spite of some thematic overlaps, the case for Ignatius's use of the Gospel of John is not strong (see Paul Foster, "The Epistles of Ignatius of Antioch and the Writings That Later Formed the New Testament," in *The Reception of the New Testament in the Apostolic Fathers*, vol. 1 of *The New Testament and the Apostolic Fathers*, ed. Andrew F. Gregory and Christopher Tuckett [Oxford: Oxford University Press, 2005], 159–86 [183–84]). The question of possible Johannine influence on the Shepherd of Hermas is more complex and admits a variety of opinions (see Joseph Verheyden, "The *Shepherd of Hermas* and the Writings That Later Formed the New Testament" in *The Reception of the New Testament in the Apostolic Fathers*, vol. 1 of *The New Testament and the Apostolic Fathers*, ed. Andrew F. Gregory and Christopher Tuckett [Oxford: Oxford University Press, 2005], 293–329). I am not persuaded that the author of the Shepherd of Hermas cites or

alludes to the Fourth Gospel, although some scholars have suggested evocations of the exclusivist soteriology in John 10:1–10 in Hermas's explanation of the tower and the virgins (89.1–93.7; so Hill, *The Johannine Corpus in the Early Church*, 374–80; Édouard Massaux, *Influence de l'Évangile de saint Matthieu sur la littérature chrétienne avant saint Irénée* [Leuven: Peeters, 1986], 290). Finally, although it is likely that Hegesippus knew the Gospel of John and traditions about its apostolic authorship (see Eusebius, *Hist. eccl.* 3.18.1; 3.20.9; Hill, *The Johannine Corpus in the Early Church*, 88–90), there are no citations of or allusions to the Gospel of John in Hegesippus's account of James's death. In addition to my skepticism regarding Johannine influence on the second-century writings considered in this essay, I also assume that there are no relationships of literary dependence between 1 Clement, the letters of Ignatius, the Shepherd of Hermas, and Hegesippus's *Hypomnemata*. (I do not consider the reference to a "Clement" in Herm. 8.3 to be evidence of knowledge of 1 Clement.)

8. In English, the main difference between a gate and a door would seem to be that a gate allows and prevents access to the perimeter of a space (e.g., a gate allows access through a fence or some other barrier) or provides security for an interior space (e.g., a baby-gate prevents access to stairs for young children), whereas a door allows and prevents access to the interior of a building or to a room. In Koine Greek, there is significant semantic overlap between θύρα and πύλη, as is evidenced by the fact that both nouns are regularly used to translate שַׁעַר in the LXX. For example, in Ezek 46:12 LXX the two occurrences of the noun שַׁעַר, which have the same referent, are translated with πύλη in the first instance and θύρα in the second (see Andrew Brunson, *Psalm 118 in the Gospel of John: An Intertextual Study of the New Exodus Pattern in the Theology of John*, WUNT 2/158 [Tübingen: Mohr Siebeck, 2003], 328); cf. the phrase καθήμενοι ἐν τῷ εὐρυχώρῳ θύρας πύλης Σαμαρείας ("[they were] sitting at the open place of the entrance of the gate of Samaria") in 2 Chr 18:9 as a rendering of פֶּתַח שַׁעַר שֹׁמְרוֹן. A higher degree of semantic overlap between θύρα and πύλη in Koine Greek than between "door" and "gate" in modern English may be due to the fact that modern English allows for a greater distinction between internal/domestic space, on the one hand, and external space, on the other, than one would expect in Mediterranean antiquity. The NRSV rightly renders θύρα as "gate" in John 10 because it provides access to an αὐλή, an open-air space that could be used for holding sheep.

9. On the Johannine "I am" statements more broadly, still helpful is Catrin H. Williams, *I Am He: The Interpretation of 'Anî Hû' in Jewish and Early Christian Literature*, WUNT 2/113 (Tübingen: Mohr Siebeck, 2000).

10. The LXX version of the psalm is numbered 117. For the sake of convenience, this essay will refer to the psalm as 118, even when citing the Greek text, which is the version with which most early Christian authors would have been familiar. It is, of course, possible that the author of the Gospel of John cites Hebrew scriptural traditions (see Wm. Randolph Bynum, *The Fourth Gospel and the Scriptures: Illuminating the Form and Meaning of Scriptural Citation in John 19:37*, NovTSup 144 [Leiden: Brill, 2012]). Also, in the case of Hegesippus, it is possible that he engaged a Hebrew or Syriac version of the Psalms, even though his history is written in Greek. Eusebius

reports that Hegesippus quotes from The Gospel of the Hebrews in Hebrew and Syriac (*Hist. eccl.* 4.22.7), and the psalms were likely translated into Syriac by the middle of the second century CE; see Harry F. Van Rooy, "The Psalms in Early Syriac Tradition," in *The Book of Psalms: Composition and Reception*, ed. Patrick D. Miller and Peter W. Flint, VTSup 99 (Leiden: Brill, 2005), 537–50. Hegesippus's knowledge of Hebrew and/or Aramaic is debated, however; see John-Christian Eurell, "The Hypomnemata of Hegesippus," *SJT* 75 (2022): 148–57.

11. Marianne Meye Thompson, *John: A Commentary*, NTL (Louisville: Westminster John Knox, 2015), 223.

12. Brunson (*Psalm 118 in the Gospel of John*) presents a maximalist case, arguing for allusions to Ps 118:24 in John 8:56, Ps 118:18–19 in John 10:7, 9, and Ps 118:5, 21, 28 in John 11:41–42. On the use of Ps 118:26 in the Johannine account of Jesus's triumphal entry, see Marianne Meye Thompson, "'They Bear Witness to Me': The Psalms in the Passion Narrative of the Gospel of John," in *The Word Leaps the Gap: Essays on Scripture and Theology in Honor of Richard B. Hays*, ed. J. R. Wagner, C. K. Rowe, and A. K. Grieb (Grand Rapids: Eerdmans, 2008), 267–83.

13. As Thompson perceptively notes in a comment on John 14:6, "The assertion that Jesus is 'the way to the Father' (14:6) is the result of, and gives expression to, Johannine Christology" (*John*, 309).

14. Cf. R. Alan Culpepper, "Inclusivism and Exclusivism in the Fourth Gospel," in *Designs for the Church in the Gospel of John: Collected Essays, 1980–2020*, WUNT 465 (Tübingen: Mohr Siebeck, 2021), 62–83; Jörg Frey, "'Die Juden' im Johannesevangelium und die Frage nach der 'Trennung der Weg' zwischen der johanneischen Gemeinde und der Synagoge," in *Die Herrlichkeit des Gekreuzigten: Studien zu den Johanneischen Schriften I*, ed. Juliane Schlegel, WUNT 307 (Tübingen: Mohr Siebeck, 2013), 339–80; Miroslav Volf, "Johannine Dualism and Contemporary Pluralism," *ModTh* 21 (2005): 189–217; Sajan George Perepparambil, *Jesus as the Way to the Father in the Gospel of John: A Study of the Way Motif and John 14,6 in Its Context*, WUNT 2/584 (Tübingen: Mohr Siebeck, 2023), 328–33. Perepparambil writes, "[Jesus's] claim to be the gate underscores the exclusiveness of salvation offered by him because the sheepfold has only one gate" (336).

15. Thompson, *John*, 223–24.

16. The term "exclusivist soteriology" is adopted from E. P. Sanders, *Paul, the Law, and the Jewish People* (Philadelphia: Fortress, 1983), 17.

17. The specific phrase "the name of the Lord" is found only in 1 Clem. 47.7, although the concept of God's "name" features elsewhere in the letter (e.g., 43.6 ["the name of the true and only God"]; 45.7; 58.1; 59.2–3; 60.4; 64.1). Given the ensuing citation of Ps 118:19–20, one wonders if the notion that the Corinthians are blaspheming the name of the Lord is implicitly contrasted with the blessedness of the one who comes "in the name of the Lord" in Ps 118:26.

18. On the theme of love for others in 1 Clement, see David J. Downs, "'Many Have Sold Themselves into Slavery': Voluntary Imprisonment and Slavery, Survival Strategies among Associations, and the Reception of 1 Corinthians in *1 Clement* 55," in *Greco-Roman Associations, Deities, and Early Christianity*, ed. Bruce W. Longenecker (Waco, TX: Baylor University Press, 2022), 397–415.

19. The text of Ps 118:19–20 in 1 Clem. 48.2 in Holmes's edition (which follows the Latin, Syriac, and Coptic manuscripts) agrees with the Göttingen text of Ps 117 LXX, aside from the addition of ἵνα in 1 Clement and the consequent change of the verb ἐξομολογήσομαι into the subjunctive. Both Alexandrinus and Hierosolymitanus lack the ἵνα, however. See Michael W. Holmes, *The Apostolic Fathers: Greek Texts and English Translations*, 3rd ed. (Grand Rapids: Baker Academic, 2007).

20. For examples of christological exegesis in 1 Clement, see 12.7; 16.1–17; 22.1–8; and 36.3–6; on scriptural interpretation more broadly in 1 Clement, see Katja Kujanpää, "Scriptural Authority and Scriptural Argumentation in 1 Clement," *NTS* 66 (2020): 125–43; Donald A. Hagner, *The Use of the Old and New Testaments in Clement of Rome*, NovTSup 34 (Leiden: Brill, 1973). Some scholars contend that Christ himself is the gate of righteousness in 1 Clem. 48.2–4 (e.g., Odd Magne Bakke, *"Concord and Peace": A Rhetorical Analysis of the First Letter of Clement with an Emphasis on the Language of Unity and Sedition*, WUNT 2/143 [Tübingen: Mohr Siebeck, 2001], 338).

21. Brunson (*Psalm 118 in the Gospel of John*, 102–37) reflects on the role of Ps 118 in the Synoptic Gospels. On the interpretation of Ps 118 by the author of Luke-Acts, see J. Ross Wagner, "Psalm 118 in Luke-Acts: Tracing a Narrative Thread," in *Early Christian Interpretation of the Scriptures of Israel: Investigations and Proposals*, ed. Craig A. Evans and James Sanders (Sheffield: Sheffield Academic, 1997), 154–78.

22. I am assuming the authenticity of the middle recension of the Ignatian letters; for a recent discussion see Jonathon Lookadoo, "The Date and Authenticity of the Ignatian Letters: An Outline of Recent Discussions," *CurBR* 19 (2020): 88–114.

23. On this point, see the excellent treatment in Jonathon Lookadoo, "Ignatius of Antioch and Scripture," *ZAC* 23 (2019): 201–27; cf. Olavi Tarvainen, *Glaube und Liebe bei Ignatius von Antiochen*, SLAG 14 (Helsinki: Luther-Agricola-Gesellschaft, 1967).

24. Lookadoo, "Ignatius of Antioch and Scripture," 207.

25. Translation from Holmes, *The Apostolic Fathers*, 244–45.

26. The phrase θύρα τοῦ πατρός might be better translated "door *to* the Father"; see Jonathan Lookadoo, *The High Priest and the Temple: Metaphorical Depictions of Jesus in the Letters of Ignatius of Antioch*, WUNT 2/473 (Tübingen: Mohr Siebeck, 2018), 86–90.

27. On Hegesippus and his context, see Eurell, "The Hypomnemata of Hegesippus," 148–57.

28. Richard Bauckham, "For What Offence Was James Put to Death?," in *James the Just and Christian Origins*, ed. Bruce Chilton and Craig A. Evans, NovTSup 98 (Leiden: Brill, 1999), 199–232. Bauckham highlights numerous points of connection between Ps 118 and Hegesippus's narrative of James's death (212–15).

29. Bauckham, "For What Offence Was James Put to Death?," 232.

30. James H. Charlesworth, "The Gospel of John: Exclusivism Caused by a Social Setting Different from That of Jesus (John 11:54 and 14:6)," in *Anti-Judaism and the Fourth Gospel: Papers of the Leuven Colloquium 2000*, ed. Reimund Bieringer,

Frederique Vandecasteele-Vanneuville, and Didier Pollefeyt, JCH 1 (Leiden: Brill, 2001), 479–513.

31. Charlesworth, "The Gospel of John," 493.

32. Charlesworth, "The Gospel of John," 481.

33. Charlesworth raises but then quickly dismisses the issue of christological exclusivist soteriology associated with the gate imagery in John 10: "I do not think that John 14:6b is similar to 10:9 in which Jesus depicts himself as 'the gate (or door).' John 14:6b is blatantly exclusivistic, but in 10:9 we do not find a claim that one can reach God only through Jesus, or that Jesus is the only door" ("The Gospel of John," 504).

34. D. Moody Smith, *John*, ANTC (Nashville: Abingdon, 1999), 269. Thoughtful and critical comments on this historicizing interpretative strategy may be found in R. W. L. Moberly, "Johannine Christology and Jewish-Christian Dialogue," in *Scripture's Doctrine and Theology's Bible*, ed. Markus Bockmuehl and Alan J. Torrance (Grand Rapids: Baker Academic, 2008), 45–58; see also the helpful Forschungsberichte on modern interpretation of John 14:6 in Perepparambil, *Jesus as the Way to the Father*, 1–30.

35. See, e.g., Adele Reinhartz, *Cast Out of the Covenant: Jews and Anti-Judaism in the Gospel of John* (Lanham: Lexington/Fortress Academic, 2018); Edward W. Klink III, *The Sheep of the Fold: The Audience and Origin of the Gospel of John*, SNTSMS 141 (Cambridge: Cambridge University Press, 2010); Andrew J. Byers, *Ecclesiology and Theosis in the Gospel of John*, SNTSMS 166 (Cambridge: Cambridge University Press, 2017), 3–24; Andrew J. Byers, *John and the Others: Jewish Relations, Christian Origins, and the Sectarian Hermeneutic* (Waco, TX: Baylor University Press, 2021).

CHAPTER FIFTEEN

1. Charles Morerod, "John Paul II's Ecclesiology and St. Thomas Aquinas," *NV* 3.3 (2005): 477.

2. Charles Taylor, *A Secular Age* (Cambridge: Harvard University Press, 2007). I have benefited here from the discussion of Taylor's work by Robert P. Imbelli, *Rekindling the Christic Imagination: Theological Meditations for the New Evangelization* (Collegeville, MN: Liturgical Press, 2014); Stanley Hauerwas, *Working with Words: On Learning to Speak Christian* (Eugene, OR: Cascade, 2011); Andrew Root, *Faith Formation in a Secular Age: Responding to the Church's Obsession with Youthfulness* (Grand Rapids: Baker Academic, 2017).

3. Taylor, *A Secular Age*, 170–82.

4. Taylor, *A Secular Age*, 282.

5. Taylor, *A Secular Age*, 288, 730–51.

6. Taylor, *A Secular Age*, 513.

7. For an excellent primer on the challenges of pastoral ministry in an age that demands constant innovation and change to keep up with cultural trends and demands to accommodate ministry to the immanent frame, see Andrew Root,

The Pastor in a Secular Age: Ministry to People Who No Longer Need God (Grand Rapids: Baker Academic, 2019).

8. On MTD, see Christian Smith, *Soul Searching: The Spiritual and Religious Lives of American Teenagers* (New York: Oxford University Press, 2005).

9. See here the excellent assessment of and alternative to mainline preaching that seeks to recover cultural establishment in Ronald P. Byars, *Preaching and Praying as Though God Matters: In the Post-establishment Church* (Eugene OR: Cascade, 2022).

10. Marianne Meye Thompson, *The God of the Gospel of John* (Grand Rapids: Eerdmans, 2001), 240.

11. Dietrich Bonhoeffer, *Ethics,* vol. 6 of *Dietrich Bonhoeffer Works,* ed. Clifford J. Green, trans. Reinhard Krauss, Charles C. West, and Douglas W. Stott (Minneapolis: Fortress, 2000).

12. Bonhoeffer, *Ethics,* 352–53.

13. Bonhoeffer, *Ethics,* 356.

14. Bonhoeffer, *Ethics,* 352–54; See here the discussion in Richard Lischer, *The End of Words: The Language of Reconciliation in a Culture of Violence* (Grand Rapids: Eerdmans, 2005).

15. Bonhoeffer, *Ethics,* 356–57.

16. Bonhoeffer, *Ethics,* 356.

17. Bonhoeffer, *Ethics,* 358–59. See the discussion on the need of the church for patience in Alan Kreider, *The Patient Ferment of the Early Church: The Improbable Rise of Christianity in the Roman Empire* (Grand Rapids: Baker Academic, 2016), 1–132.

18. Bonhoeffer, *Ethics,* 396.

19. Bonhoeffer, *Ethics,* 397–99.

20. See the excellent discussion in David S. Yeago, "The Bible," in *Knowing the Triune God: The Work of the Spirit in the Practices of the Church,* ed. James J. Buckley and David S. Yeago (Grand Rapids: Eerdmans, 2001), 49–94.

21. Here I am indebted to Oliver Davies, *A Theology of Compassion: Metaphysics of Difference and the Renewal of Tradition* (Grand Rapids: Eerdmans, 2001), 189–209.

22. Nicholas Lash, *Holiness, Speech, and Silence: Reflections on the Question of God* (Aldershot: Ashgate, 2004), 60.

23. See the insightful discussion in Andrew Root, *The Church after Innovation: Questioning Our Obsession with Work, Creativity, and Entrepreneurship* (Grand Rapids: Baker Academic, 2022).

24. Nicholas Lash, *Believing Three Ways in God: A Reading of the Apostles' Creed* (Notre Dame: University of Notre Dame Press, 1993), 72–73.

25. Robert W. Jenson, *Systematic Theology,* vol. 1, *The Triune God* (Oxford: Oxford University Press, 1997), 228.

26. Ephraim Radner, *Hope among the Fragments: The Broken Church and Its Engagement of Scripture* (Grand Rapids: Brazos, 2004), 16–19, 172–75.

27. Rowan Williams, *On Christian Theology* (Oxford: Blackwell, 2000), 146–47.

28. Stanley Hauerwas, *Performing the Faith: Bonhoeffer and the Practice of Nonviolence* (Grand Rapids: Brazos, 2004), 77. See also the discussion in Kevin Vanhoozer,

"Human Being, Individual and Social," in *The Cambridge Companion to Christian Doctrine*, ed. Colin E. Gunton (Cambridge: Cambridge University Press, 1997), 158–88.

29. Eric O. Springsted, *The Act of Faith: Christian Faith and the Moral Self* (Grand Rapids: Eerdmans, 2002), 124.

30. Paul J. Griffiths, *Lying: An Augustinian Theology of Duplicity* (Grand Rapids: Brazos, 2004), 73–80.

31. Thompson, *The God of the Gospel of John*, 239.

32. Williams, *On Christian Theology*, 40.

33. Springsted, *The Act of Faith*, 94.

34. Julian N. Hartt, *Toward a Theology of Evangelism* (repr., Eugene, OR: Wipf & Stock, 2006), 117.

35. Arthur C. McGill, *Suffering: A Test of Theological Method* (Philadelphia: Westminster, 1982), 55.

36. McGill, *Suffering*, 57.

37. McGill, *Suffering*, 57.

38. McGill, *Suffering*, 59.

39. McGill, *Suffering*, 62.

40. McGill, *Suffering*, 74.

41. Arthur C. McGill, *Dying unto Life: On New God, New Death, New Life*, ed. David Cain, Theological Fascinations 2 (Eugene, OR: Cascade, 2013), 134.

42. McGill, *Dying unto Life*, 135.

43. McGill, *Suffering*, 76–77.

44. McGill, *Suffering*, 82.

45. McGill, *Suffering*, 82.

46. McGill, *Suffering*, 90.

47. McGill, *Suffering*, 91.

48. McGill, *Dying unto Life*, 137.

49. Nicholas Lash, *The Beginning and the End of "Religion"* (Cambridge: Cambridge University Press, 1996), 247–48.

50. Lash, *Holiness, Speech, and Silence*, 92; see pp. 69–90.

51. Thompson, *The God of the Gospel of John*, 87.

52. Nicholas Lash, *Voices of Authority* (repr., Eugene, OR: Wipf & Stock, 2005), 11–12.

53. William H. Willimon, *Pastor: The Theology and Practice of Ordained Ministry* (Nashville: Abingdon, 2002), 157–58.

CHAPTER SIXTEEN

1. Some think that God demands exclusive allegiance and claims the right to hold us accountable for it because, being almighty, God can demand anything. Those with an image of a less authoritarian and more beneficent God sometimes think that God can demand exclusive allegiance and claim the right to hold us accountable because God has given us all that we have and are, and that such a total gift creates total obligation in return. Jon Levenson grounds obligations to God in the gifts received from God (see Jon Levenson, *The Love of God: Divine Gift, Human*

Gratitude, and Mutual Faithfulness in Judaism [Princeton: Princeton University Press, 2015], 52: by the favors received a person has "incurred moral debt to his benefactor"). As I see it, in the first case, God would be a bit like the Supreme Narcissist; in the second case, God would be a bit like the Patron-in-Chief or even Merchant-in-Chief.

2. Augustine, *Homilies on the First Epistle to John*, 9.10, WSA III/14 (Hyde Park, NY: New City, 2008), 143.

3. Acting out of love can involve both more and less than bestowing maximum benefits to the maximum number of people. Max Scheler makes this important point in his distinction between "love" and "benevolence" (see *The Nature of Sympathy*, trans. Peter Heath [New Brunswick, NJ: Transaction, 2009], 140–43; and Max Scheler, *Ressentiment*, trans. Lewis B. Coser and William W. Holdheim [Milwaukee, WI: Marquette University Press, 1998], 70–71), though the political implications he draws from it seem problematic to me.

4. These three categories cover three distinct but interdependent dimensions of a flourishing life. See Miroslav Volf, Matthew Croasmun, and Ryan McAnnally-Linz, "Meanings and Dimensions of Flourishing: A Programmatic Sketch," in *Religion and Human Flourishing*, ed. Adam Cohen (Waco, TX: Baylor University Press, 2020), 7–17. See also Miroslav Volf and Matthew Croasmun, *For the Life of the World: Theology That Makes a Difference* (Grand Rapids: Brazos, 2019), 11–34, 149–85.

5. See Paul D. Hanson, *Isaiah 40–66*, IBC (Louisville: Westminster John Knox, 1995), 243–44.

6. Max Horkheimer, *Die Sehnsucht nach dem ganz Anderen: Ein Interview mit Kommentar von Helmut Gumnior* (Berlin: de Gruyter, 1970).

7. The terms come from the great Muslim thinker Al-Ghazali. They are part of the title of Book XXXVII of his *Revival of the Religious Sciences*. See *Al-Ghazali on Vigilance and Self-Examination*, trans. Anthony F. Shaker (Cambridge: Islamic Texts Society, 2015). See Rowan Williams, *The Way of St. Benedict* (London: Bloomsbury, 2020).

8. This section largely takes up arguments developed in Volf and McAnnally-Linz, *The Home of God.*

9. I follow here Jörg Frey, *The Glory of the Crucified: Christology and Theology in the Gospel of John*, trans. Wayne Coppins and Christoph Heilig (Waco, TX: Baylor University Press, 2018). The honoree of this volume is uncomfortable calling Jesus, in a straightforward way, "God." After many email exchanges, neither of us has managed to persuade the other, though I have certainly learned a great deal.

10. Georg W. F. Hegel, "The Spirit of Christianity and Its Fate," in Georg W. F. Hegel, *On Christianity: Early Theological Writings*, trans. T. M. Knox (Gloucester: Peter Smith, 1970), 262.

11. As I see it, light is not so much the "consciousness that is equivalent to life" (Hegel, "The Spirit," 258), but the *manifestation* of life, its actual living before the eyes of the world. I have used "apprehension" of life and light for what Hegel describes as "consciousness" of it.

12. Rudolf Bultmann, *The Gospel of John: A Commentary*, trans. G. R. Beasley-Murray (Philadelphia: Westminster, 1971), 342.

13. For a somewhat similar analogy between the sun as the source of light and sight on the one hand, and the good as the source of knowledge and truth on the other, see Plato, *Rep.* 508d–509a (*Plato: Complete Works*, ed. John M. Cooper [Indianapolis: Hackett, 1997], 1129).

14. Hegel, "The Spirit," 263.

15. So Hartwig Thyen, *Das Johannesevangelium*, 2nd ed. (Tübingen: Mohr Siebeck, 2015), 578.

16. See Miroslav Volf, *Captive to the Word of God: Engaging Scriptures for Contemporary Theological Reflection* (Grand Rapids: Eerdmans, 2010), 115–26.

17. See Volf and McAnnally-Linz, *The Home of God.*

18. Many interpreters, including the honoree of this volume of essays, take the statement that Jesus will draw "all people" to refer to "all the world's peoples" (Marianne Meye Thompson, *John*, NTL [Louisville: Westminster John Knox, 2015], 272; cf. Richard Bauckham, *Gospel of Glory: Major Themes in Johannine Theology* [Grand Rapids: Baker, 2015], 31). That may be right, given the statements about condemnation and dying in sins (3:18; 5:29; 8:24), but the scope of Jesus's work— God loved the *world* (3:16) and Jesus gave his life "for the life of the *world*" (6:51)— is all-encompassing, and therefore, in a significant sense, he *has* drawn to himself all people and not just some individuals from all the world's peoples.

19. On God mediating Abraham's relation to the world, see Hegel, "The Spirit," 185–89 (though, given his predilection against God's transcendence and for casting Judaism as a foil for his own pan(en)theistic account of the God-world relation, Hegel misconstrues how God mediates the world to Abraham).

20. So Bultmann, rightly, on joy (*John*, 507).

INDEX OF BIBLICAL AND OTHER ANCIENT TEXTS

Old Testament and Deuterocanonical Books

Genesis
1–3   249
1–2   89–90, 92, 94, 249–250
1   48, 89, 248
1:1–3   160
1:1 LXX   89
1:3 LXX   89
1:6 LXX   89
1:9 LXX   89
1:11 LXX   89
1:14 LXX   89
1:20 LXX   89
1:24 LXX   89
1:26 LXX   89, 250
1:27 LXX   250
1:29 LXX   89
2   90, 92
2:2 LXX   92
2:3 LXX   245
2:5 LXX   250
2:7 LXX   90, 249–250
2:8 LXX   91, 249–250
2:9 LXX   91, 251
2:15 LXX   250
2:18 LXX   250
3   248, 250
3:8–21   234
3:8   91
3:18 LXX   248
3:22 LXX   250
18:1–33   234, 238
18:23–32   246
24:27   43
28:10–22   227
28:17   29, 227
32:10 (32:11 MT)   43

32:22–32   234
32:30   58
41:52   233
48:13–20   40
48:15   174
49:10–12   119
49:10   116
49:24   174

Exodus
3:5–6   154
3:14 LXX   167, 169
3:14 MT   149
4:22   118, 272
12:17–20   94
13:1 LXX   245
13:12 LXX   245
13:21–22   234
14–15   148
14:24   234
15:17–18   116
15:17b   26
15:20   117
16   151
16:10   234
19   48
19:14–22 LXX   245
19:19   57
19:21–23   77
20:2–3   47
20:2   167
24:9–18   234
24:12–34:35   54
28:38   171
29 LXX   245
32–33   43
32   48
32:1   212
32:4   212

32:11–13   246
32:31–32   211
33–34   54
33:11   58, 234
33:17–34:8   234
33:17–23   234
33:19   147
33:20–23   234
33:22   147
34:6–7   212–213
34:6   43, 48, 147, 170
34:7   48
34:29 LXX   253
34:30 LXX   253
34:35 LXX   253
37:7–18 (38:9–20 MT)   223
38:20   223
39:20 (39:40 MT) 223
40:11b   233
40:34–38   170, 234

Leviticus
19   48
19:2   47
20:8 LXX   245
26   49

Numbers
7   222
7:1–11   74
7:1   222
7:10–11   221
7:88   221
12:8   58, 234
12:12   146
14:13–19   246
21:4–8   163
24:17   119, 259
27:17   122, 151, 174

Deuteronomy
4:12 LXX   54, 56
5:26   272
6:4–5   47
10:17   162
20:5   221
28–29   49
32:39   149, 167
32:40   272
34:10   58, 234

Joshua
3:10   272
15:9   37
18:23   37

Judges
21:23   117

1 Samuel
2:27   272
4:21   255
7:7–8   272
11:14   221
16:12   124
17:26   272
17:36   272

2 Samuel
2:6   43
5:2   122, 174
5:8   29, 226
7   116, 120
7:7   174
7:11–16   113
7:12–14   115–116, 119
7:14   165
15:20   43
22:16   144
24:17   125

1 Kings
2:4   116
3:6   43
6:3   222
6:36   223
8   21, 28
8:10–11   234
8:63–64   74
8:64   223
10:11   146
10:22   146
17:21 LXX   249
17:24 LXX   11
19:11   147
22:17 (3 Kgdms 22:17 OG)   122,
                  151, 174

2 Kings
18:1–6   22
19:4   272
19:16   272

Josephus

Philo

13:29	65
13:31–32	100, 106, 163
13:31	44
13:34–35	175
13:34	48
13:36	48
13:37	82
14:1–7	83
14:2–3	225
14:3	49
14:4–8	34
14:6	27, 29, 44, 155, 168, 174–175, 182, 251, 275, 277
14:6b	182, 277
14:7–9	67
14:7	59
14:8–9	51
14:9	44, 59, 237, 265
14:11	59
14:12–14	67
14:13	100
14:15	48
14:16	83
14:17	83, 170
14:18	49
14:20	66
14:21	48
14:22	35
14:23	48
14:24	48
14:25–26	14
14:26–27	83
14:26	49, 83, 159
14:27	49, 175
14:31	76, 83, 163
15:1–14	84
15:1–8	67, 225
15:1	155, 168, 174, 251
15:4	49
15:5	67
15:7	48
15:9	44, 66
15:10	48
15:11	175
15:12	48
15:13	175
15:14	48
15:17	48
15:18–16:4	84
15:18–25	76
15:24	237
15:26	83, 170
16:2–11	78
16:2	76, 256
16:4	256
16:7–11	83
16:7	83
16:11	76, 79, 83
16:13–15	14, 159
16:13–14	102
16:13	83, 101, 170
16:14	101, 164, 254
16:21	256
16:22	237
16:24	49, 175
16:25	35, 256
16:29	35
16:30–31	51
16:31	49
16:32	48, 223, 256
16:33	14, 75, 175, 225
17	76, 83, 247
17:1–5	66
17:1	100, 107, 254, 256
17:3	67, 73, 83, 175–176
17:4	107
17:5	61, 107, 164, 254
17:6–8	83
17:8	57, 83
17:9	28
17:10	101, 254
17:11–19	80, 82
17:11	83
17:11b–13	81
17:12	81–82
17:13	175
17:14–19	81
17:14	83
17:15	79, 81–83, 247
17:17–19	74
17:17	44, 83
17:18–19	83
17:19	82, 84, 154
17:20–26	85, 175
17:20	85
17:22	66, 101, 108
17:24	33, 67, 108, 164

INDEX OF AUTHORS